ROYAL LAW

This book argues that prerogative powers encompass all the non-statutory powers of the Crown. Hence the Crown has no 'third source' powers, common law powers or 'Ram doctrine' style freedoms.

Royal Law builds on Dicey's definition of the prerogative, arguing that it comprises all residual non-statutory rights, powers, duties, and immunities historically ascribed to the Crown. However, it contends that Blackstone's alternative definition, that prerogative powers are only those powers exclusive to the Crown, is also correct. The book explains how Dicey and Blackstone can be reconciled.

The prerogative of justice is suggested as the original source of legal authority and legitimacy of common law judicial decisions. Common law is, or was, royal law. Defined as a putative non-statutory, non-prerogative third source of judicial legitimacy, authority or jurisdiction, 'common law' does not exist. There are only two ultimate sources of jurisdictional authority: statute and prerogative.

The book further argues that Wade was mistaken to contend that the Crown has 'common law powers'. It also has no 'third source freedoms', as suggested by Harris, or in the 'Ram Doctrine'. The book therefore reframes the relevant case law as examples of judicial regulation of prerogative powers, crucially including the largely-forgotten prerogative power to administer the realm. Hence the book concludes that legal powers such as a minister's power to enter contracts or make *ex gratia* payments of public money, are directly or indirectly grounded in prerogative power.

Royal Law

Prerogative Foundations

Robert Craig

• HART •
OXFORD • LONDON • NEW YORK • NEW DELHI • SYDNEY

HART PUBLISHING

Bloomsbury Publishing Plc

Kemp House, Chawley Park, Cumnor Hill, Oxford, OX2 9PH, UK

1385 Broadway, New York, NY 10018, USA

Bloomsbury Publishing Ireland Limited, 29 Earlsfort Terrace, Dublin 2, D02 AY28, Ireland

HART PUBLISHING, the Hart/Stag logo, BLOOMSBURY and the Diana logo are trademarks of Bloomsbury Publishing Plc

First published in Great Britain 2025

A catalogue record for this book is available from the British Library.

A catalogue record for this book is available from the Library of Congress.

Library of Congress Control Number: 2025930365

ISBN: HB: 978-1-50996-595-3
ePDF: 978-1-50996-597-7
ePub: 978-1-50996-596-0

Typeset by Compuscript Ltd, Shannon
Printed and bound in Great Britain

For product safety related questions contact productsafety@bloomsbury.com

To find out more about our authors and books visit www.hartpublishing.co.uk. Here you will find extracts, author information, details of forthcoming events and the option to sign up for our newsletters.

ACKNOWLEDGEMENTS

Writing this book has been an immensely enjoyable experience. The original research was done during a PhD which gave me the space and freedom to think carefully about some serious legal questions. I would like to thank the attendees and organisers of a series of events at Oxford, Cambridge, Liverpool, Durham, Glasgow, LSE, UCL and Bristol where I discussed the core ideas of the book, usually presenting a chapter each time. Richard Ekins, Shona Wilson Stark, Mike Gordon, Adam Tomkins (a major influence on my thinking and former administrative law tutor), Tom Poole and Colm O'Cinneide were the very helpful organisers of those events. I also had especially useful feedback from Adam Perry, which eventually resulted in a major rewrite of chapter 9 discussing his work.

No less useful were insightful comments from Paul Craig (no relation!), Robert Thomas, John Finnis (who beautifully channelled HLA Hart with a penetrating point about 'Rex I' and 'Rex II'), Michael Foran, Pat Capps, Paul Scott, Stefan Thiel, Nick Barber, Aileen McHarg, Timothy Endicott, Trevor Allan (sparking a lengthy email debate), Adam Tucker, David Kershaw, David Feldman, Tom Hickman and Daniella Lock. A single nod from the Regius Professor of Public Law in the audience at a conference in Dublin also lives long in the memory. Apologies to those I have missed. Martin Loughlin was the external examiner of the original PhD and his lively defence of his definition of the Crown during my viva forced me to confront the fact that, for once, I disagreed with him about something important in the UK constitution. Finally, I am exceptionally grateful to Julian Rivers at Bristol who not only read the PhD as the internal examiner but, unbelievably, also kindly agreed to read the final draft – providing the most precise and careful feedback and analysis. I would also to thank the Arts and Humanities Research Council for their financial support.

The person to whom I owe the greatest professional debt is of course Gavin Phillipson. Not only did he convince me that it was essential to do a PhD in the first place, but he is also probably the only person with the patience, maturity and experience necessary to handle the fact that I came to this project with nearly a quarter of a century of previous experience in teaching and thinking about constitutional law. Furthermore, the fact that we disagree on just about every aspect of the subject served to enhance, rather than damage, the progress of the project. Indeed, his rigorous and frequently strongly-felt disagreements with most of my views both professionally and personally has done nothing other than strengthen the eventual arguments. He never lets anything go and that is the standard I wish to meet. Any argument that I can get past Gavin has been tested in fire and there are many arguments that I have dropped due to his objections that I have been later relieved to have abandoned. His commitment, professionalism and ability to recall obscure arguments that he has not discussed for months at a moment's notice is astonishing.

You can thank Gavin, dear reader, for the fact that the book has been delayed by at least 18 months from its original planned publication date. It was his idea for me to do the pre-publication tour because, as he correctly pointed out, it would be better to get a round of feedback *before* publication rather than afterwards when it would be too late. The final version has been significantly improved, in my view, but of course full publication is the ultimate test. Looming large, no doubt, is the realisation of further errors of commission and omission, responsibility for which – of course – rests entirely with me.

I have moved between three institutions at various points during the process of writing, starting my PhD at Durham, but I must particularly thank the former Head of LSE Law School, Niamh Moloney, and before her Jeremy Horder, Emily Jackson and Martin Loughlin for their generosity over the years in allowing me to occupy a random desk space in their Law School with all my books, research materials and kit even at times of the year when I was not teaching part time at LSE. I would also like to pay tribute to the academic and professional staff at Bristol Law School who have been nothing but welcoming, friendly and professional throughout my time there, not least by granting me my first ever study leave to complete the project.

CONTENTS

PART II
THE CROWN

PART III
THIRD SOURCE

TABLE OF CASES

TABLE OF LEGISLATION

1

Introduction

English law starts with the Crown. Despite centuries of organic, and sometimes radical, changes in the constitutional law of this country, the Crown still plays an important contemporary role. As Martin Loughlin puts it, 'since 1688, the British constitution has evolved around the pivot of the Crown'.[1] The Crown is constituted by a set of important legal powers, known as 'royal prerogative' powers. It is the main claim of this book that all residual non-statutory institutional legal powers, duties and immunities of the government are grounded in royal prerogative. If this book can be summarised in one idea, it would be the seemingly controversial, but simple, central argument that the terms 'non-statutory legal powers of the Crown' and 'royal prerogative' are synonymous.[2] Furthermore, and relatedly, the Crown is best defined today as the legal bearer of the remaining prerogative powers.[3] This book draws no distinction between 'royal prerogative' and 'prerogative' – the two terms are used interchangeably. Both usages can mean the *set* of prerogative powers in the way commonly understood by the word 'statute' in other contexts.[4]

A great deal of damaging confusion has been caused in the literature and case law by three erroneous notions: first, that there are some legal powers of the Crown that are not royal prerogative powers but some other kind of legal power; second, that some important powers of the Crown are not actually prerogative powers because they are not legal powers at all; and third, that the Crown acts sometimes without using any kind of legal or *non*-legal power, but instead exercises some kind of 'freedom' rooted in some putative 'third source'. This book seeks to show that all three of these claims are wrong. This book, then, places the royal prerogative into its proper historical context and suggests that an accurate perspective is best achieved by understanding the genealogy, development and history of the concept. Whilst the claim that *all* non-statutory institutional legal

[1] M Loughlin, 'The Case of Prorogation' (Policy Exchange, 2019), policyexchange.org.uk/wp-content/uploads/2019/10/The-Case-of-Prorogation.pdf, 6–7.

[2] This book draws no distinction between 'royal prerogative' and 'prerogative' – the two terms are used interchangeably.

[3] *R (Miller) v Secretary of State for Exiting the European Union* [2017] UKSC 5, [2018] AC 61, [2017] 2 WLR 583, [47] ('*Miller I*').

[4] The phrase 'prerogative powers' will also be used analogously to the way 'statutory powers' is frequently deployed.

powers are prerogative powers may seem to some readers to be simple, even banal, it is conventionally believed that the Crown has other legal powers beyond statutory and prerogative legal powers. Much of the argument in this book involves developing and explaining why it is mistaken to think that the Crown has any 'common law' or 'third source' powers and why correcting this error, which is the purpose of chapter nine, is important and significant.[5]

A topic as large as the prerogative cannot be comprehensively addressed, even in a book-length analysis, so this chapter also explains how the issues considered by this book have been narrowed down to the core questions of constitutional taxonomy and conceptual definition of royal prerogative. The focus on the taxonomy of the prerogative within the United Kingdom's constitutional architecture is aimed at reconciling available competing analyses of the concept into a single useful synthesised definition in chapters two and three, the implications of which are then explored in later chapters. It further defines and explains the symbiotic relationship of prerogatives and the Crown in chapter six and maps out the implications of that claim for the relationship between the Crown and ministers in chapters seven and eight. It does this in large part by tracing the legal implications of defining the Crown as no more or less than the *bearer* of prerogative powers. This has further implications for the role and capacity of ministers in relation to the common law.

This book does not deal with judicial review of the exercise of royal prerogative powers, including the *Miller II* case.[6] Instead, in chapters ten and eleven it deals only with judicial review of a sub-category of cases previously thought to raise issues with so-called 'third source powers'. It draws on work I have done elsewhere to recategorise those cases in large part within the framework of two doctrines called the frustration and abeyance principles.[7] I first drew a distinction in 2016 between two principles that had not hitherto been clearly distinguished in the case law.[8] The first principle is known as the abeyance principle and comes from the *De Keyser's Hotel* case.[9] It states that where a statute overlaps with a prerogative, the prerogative goes into abeyance and the executive must use the statutory power. The second principle is the frustration principle, and it comes from *Laker Airways* and the *Fire Brigades*

[5] B Harris, 'The "Third Source" of Authority for Government Action' (1992) 108 *Law Quarterly Review* 626.

[6] *R (Miller) v Prime Minister; Cherry v Advocate General for Scotland* [2019] UKSC 41, [2020] AC 373, [2019] 3 WLR 589, [2019] 4 All ER 299 ('*Miller II*').

[7] Explained further in R Craig, 'A Simple Application of the Frustration Principle: Prerogative, Statute and Miller' (2017) *Public Law (Brexit Special Issue)* 25.

[8] See further R Craig, 'Casting Aside Clanking Medieval Chains: Prerogative, Statute and Article 50 after the EU Referendum' (2016) 79 *Modern Law Review* 1041, 1045–46. Both principles relate to the situation where a prerogative intersects with a statute as opposed to where a prerogative is exercised on its own and there is no relevant statute. The latter scenario is dealt with by the *GCHQ* line of case law: *GCHQ* (n 15 below).

[9] *Att Gen v De Keyser's Hotel* [1920] AC 508, 575.

Union case.[10] It states that the executive cannot exercise any prerogative if by doing so they would frustrate the intention of parliament in any Act. Both are rooted in Article I, Bill of Rights 1689.[11]

Methodology

This book does not engage in a normative defence of the current structure of the constitution. The book does not claim that a system designed 'rationally' from scratch would contain a set of legacy legal powers derived from a hereditary monarch and now in effect exercised by the democratically elected government. Nonetheless, the factual existence of two different sources of executive legal powers, only one of which is granted directly by parliament, is a legacy feature rather than a rational design feature and the analysis undertaken in this book should be understood in that light.

The methodological underpinnings of the book look to the history, development and genealogy of the relevant legal concepts, whose very familiarity and historical roots form a large part of their appeal and justification.[12] This book therefore does not defend the royal prerogative *per se*; rather it seeks solely to provide a more accurate analysis of the prerogative and its functions in the modern constitution when considered in its overall historical and constitutional context. A perspective that purports to take seriously the importance of the history, customs and traditions that underpin the modern constitutional framework is at risk of being accused of insufficiently delving into the historical texts and contemporaneous attitudes of past generations of office-holders over the centuries. But this is not a work of legal history. On the contrary, it seeks to understand the *contemporary* constitution in the light of an unavoidably selective account of how the current constitution developed. Methodologically, it is hard to improve on Janet McLean's, and indirectly FW Maitland's, approach. She claims that her book is 'not intended *primarily* as a work of history. Rather it adopts Maitland's historical method in order to glean what we can from the past that may be helpful to the present'.[13] AV Dicey said that his goal was 'not to know what the law of England was yesterday, still what it was centuries ago', but instead

[10] *R v Secretary of State for Home Department, ex parte Fire Brigades Union* [1995] 2 AC 513; *Laker Airways v Department of Trade* [1977] QB 643, 726.

[11] Article I, Bill of Rights 1689: That the pretended power of suspending the laws or the execution of laws by regal authority without consent of Parliament is illegal. That the pretended power of dispensing with laws or the execution of laws by regal authority, as it hath been assumed and exercised of late, is illegal.

[12] M Oakeshott, *Rationalism in Politics and Other Essays* (Liberty Fund 1991) ch 1; E Burke, *Reflections on the Revolution in France*, November 1790 in I Kramnick (ed), *The Portable Edmund Burke* (Penguin, 1999) 425–28.

[13] J McLean, *Searching for the State in British Legal Thought* (Cambridge University Press, 2012) 12.

to 'state what are the principles of law which actually and at the present day exist in England'.[14]

The next section explains the continuing importance of the prerogative in the modern constitution. The following section lays the groundwork for the rest of the chapter by considering some of the history and developments in the relationship between Crown, government and parliament before analysing perhaps the most important prerogative historically which is the prerogative of justice. It then considers the four potential meanings of common law before turning to the relationship between the Crown and the courts. It addresses how the fact that judicial power originates in the Crown still has ripple effects today. It ends with a chapter outline, picking out some of the key claims made in the book.

The Continuing Importance of Prerogative in the Modern Constitution

The ongoing relevance of the royal prerogative in the modern constitution can be illustrated by the number of occasions in recent years where actions taken under prerogative have been the focus of intense political and constitutional controversy. This is before mentioning the numerous cases in recent decades that have considered the meaning, relevance and effect of prerogatives without necessarily erupting into public controversy. The seminal case of *GCHQ*, for example, unleashed a series of subsequent judicial review proceedings against exercises of royal prerogative power even though the orthodox view for centuries had been that they were 'never reviewable'.[15] The apotheosis of the steady encroachment of judicial supervision over previously immune prerogative powers was the seminal *Miller II* case which addressed the decision to prorogue parliament in 2019.[16]

No less controversial was the previous *Miller I* decision in the Supreme Court.[17] This famously also considered the use of a prerogative power, in this case the prerogative power of conducting foreign affairs and, in particular, an offshoot

[14] AV Dicey, *Introduction to the Study of the Law of the Constitution*, 8th edn (Macmillan, 1927) 14.

[15] *Council for the Civil Service Unions v Minister for the Civil Service (GCHQ)* [1985] AC 374, 416 per Lord Roskill: 'Mr. Alexander for the respondent understandably did not press the argument that no action taken under the prerogative could ever be the subject of judicial review. But, helpfully, he thought it right to make available to your Lordships a selection from the classic pronouncements of many famous writers in this field from Locke through Blackstone and Chitty to Dicey and from the writings of distinguished modern authorities including de Smith, Wade, Hood Phillips and Heuston designed to show first the historic view that acts done under the prerogative were *never reviewable* and secondly the extent to which that classic doctrine may at least in this century be said to have been diluted' (emphasis added).

[16] *Miller II* (n 6).

[17] *Miller I* (n 3).

of this power which is the power to make, alter, amend or withdraw from treaties. The prerogative power of dissolving parliament has also played a prominent role in recent political debate, with the Fixed-term Parliaments Act 2011 temporarily putting that prerogative into abeyance before being eventually repealed by the Dissolution and Calling of Parliaments Act 2023.[18] It appears to be generally accepted that the latter Act successfully revived the prerogative and restored the *status quo ante*.[19]

What is the Prerogative?

Dicey's definition of prerogative is reasonably straightforward.

> Every act the executive government can lawfully do without the authority of the Act of Parliament is done in virtue of this prerogative.[20]

Sir William Blackstone's definition is supposedly narrower.

> By the word prerogative we usually understand that special pre-eminence, which the king has, over and above all other persons, and out of the ordinary course of the common law.[21]

Stephen Sedley points to this 'doctrinal dispute about what prerogative is'.[22] He asks whether it is 'purely the great functions of state which no private individual could perform' or is it 'what can be called the broad prerogative'.[23] The former paraphrases Blackstone's conception of royal prerogative.[24] The latter view, that prerogative encompasses everything that government can legally do that is not a function of statute, refers to Dicey's broader definition.[25] This doctrinal dispute has quietly rumbled on for decades, indeed ever since Dicey's time. The major purpose of part I of this book is to reconcile these two apparently conflicting definitions. The rest of the book works through the implications of that suggested reconciliation and the significant ripple effects of having a single definition that is consistent with both Dicey and Blackstone.

[18] See further R Craig, 'The Fixed-term Parliaments Act 2011: Out, Out Brief Candle' in R Johnson and Yuan Yi Zhu (eds), *Sceptical Perspectives on the Changing Constitution of the United Kingdom* (Hart Publishing, 2023).

[19] See, for example, A Young, 'The Constitutional Role of the Monarch' in the Constitution Unit and UK in a Changing Europe, *The British Monarchy* (25 April 2023).

[20] Dicey (n 14) 421.

[21] W Blackstone, *Commentaries on the Laws of England* (1765–69), reprinted in in G Jones, *The Sovereignty of the Law* (Macmillan Press, 1973), text to note 92.

[22] S Sedley, *Lions under the Throne: Essays on the History of English Public Law* (Cambridge University Press, 2015) 135.

[23] ibid.

[24] D Lemmings and W Prest (ed), *The Oxford Edition of Blackstone: Commentaries on the Laws of England, Vol 1: Of the Rights of Persons* (Oxford University Press, 2016) 232.

[25] Dicey (n 14).

Although Sir William Anson rather waspishly described Blackstone's definition as 'obviously too vague to be of practical value',[26] Blackstone was right to say that prerogative powers are those that are exclusive to the Crown – in contrast with ordinary people. It is also true that government ministers and departments enter into contracts like ordinary people, and making contracts is certainly not the exercise of statutory powers. How then are these two apparently conflicting claims to be reconciled? The answer is that we need to *disaggregate* the Crown and the ministers or departments who are entering or breaching contracts, which is the focus of part II. Dicey was clear that ministers are personally liable for the contracts they enter.[27] Ministers hold their position as a function of prerogative. If the distinction argued for in chapter seven between government ministers and Crown is kept in mind, then there is no tension between the claim that ministers enter contracts, and the Crown authorises those ministers to act using prerogative powers.

What is the Crown?

If it is mistaken to conflate the government and the Crown, then clarifying the distinction between the Crown and government is essential. This necessarily raises the question of the nature and definition of the Crown itself. Three definitions have been historically popular: Crown equated with state, government or king. All three are wrong. The king in his private capacity was once synonymous with the Crown but the long centuries of legal trouble generated by failing to differentiate the monarch in public and private capacities have put paid to equating king and Crown in the modern era. The state is a far thicker concept than the Crown, encompassing devolved institutions, local government and the like. It makes no sense to equate the Crown and the state. The government is too thin a concept to be equated to the Crown and, as we have already seen, must be distinguished from the Crown in any event precisely because the Crown does not, and never did, enter contracts itself.

The Crown remains outside the jurisdiction of the courts to this day, as clearly laid down in *M v Home Office*, discussed further below.[28] The government most certainly is not outside the jurisdiction of the courts, as also established in that seminal case. Furthermore, it is now clear that governmental exercise of prerogative powers is in principle judicially reviewable.[29] If the Crown is outside the jurisdiction of the courts, how can prerogative powers be judicially reviewed? The answer is that we must differentiate the legislative and executive aspects of

[26] WR Anson, *The Law and Custom of the Constitution*, 2nd edn (Clarendon Press, 1896) 3.
[27] Dicey (n 14) 189.
[28] *M v Home Office* [1994] 1 AC 377.
[29] *GCHQ* (n 15).

prerogative. It is commonly thought that ministers give 'advice' on the exercise of prerogative and, by convention, that advice must be followed. If the convention *encompasses* the advice, then the fact that conventions are agreed to be non-legal in nature makes judicial review of the advice nonsensical in a world where such advice can be reviewed as a matter of law. If advice is distinct from the convention, the legal status of the 'advice' is currently unclear.

Instead, it would be preferable to treat justiciable executive prerogative powers similarly to statutory powers. Parliament confers statutory executive powers but is immune from judicial review. Similarly, the Crown confers prerogative executive powers but is immune from judicial review. It follows that much judicial and academic agonising over whether the Crown is properly to be considered as a corporation sole or corporation aggregate or otherwise is something of a red herring because the Crown remains outside the jurisdiction of the courts. It is rather like asking what kind of corporation parliament is.

This opens the way to understanding a novel definition of the Crown. Parliament is the repository, or bearer, of the legislative power to make Acts of Parliament. Those statutes confer power on the executive to undertake legal actions. By analogy, therefore, the Crown is the repository, or bearer, of the legislative aspect of royal prerogative powers. The Crown also confers power on the executive to undertake legal actions. Those powers are not 'advice' and it makes no sense to describe them as such. Ministers are appointed by the prime minister using the executive power to do so conferred by the Crown. Ministers enter into contracts significantly constrained by the public nature of their role.

What are Third Source Powers?

Reconciling the definitions of prerogative set out by Dicey and Blackstone undermines claims that a third source of power is available to government that is rooted in neither prerogative nor statute. Sedley rightly describes this notion as the 'jurisprudential version of the emperor's new clothes'.[30] The alleged gap created by a narrow definition of prerogative extends not just to making contracts but also to the ordinary tasks of government such as setting policies, making lists and writing memos. As part III will argue, the exercise of these powers exercised by ministers can be swept up into a long overlooked prerogative, although mentioned by Joseph Chitty, which I label the 'administration prerogative'.[31] It underpins these actions and significantly undermines the claim made by some that the government has the freedom possessed by a natural person to do anything that is not prohibited.

[30] Sedley (n 22) 135.
[31] J Chitty, *A Treatise on the Law of the Prerogatives of the Crown: And the Relative Duties and Rights of the Subject* (Butterworth, 1820) 2, 3–4 and 7.

The revival of this long hidden aspect of prerogative power – the power to administer the realm – means that a series of recent cases considering the meaningless idea of third source powers must be reframed, a task undertaken in chapters ten and eleven.[32] Also in need of reconsideration is the original case of *Malone* which arguably first set the hares running on the claim that the government can do anything that an ordinary person can do.[33] Those cases can be reframed as obscured examples of the exercise of the prerogative of administration or, in the case of *Malone*, as testing the boundaries of the prerogative of keeping the King's peace.

The issues in this subsection, as well as the history and treatment of the prerogative of justice are the core themes of this monograph and explored in turn in the three parts of the book. The law relating to royal prerogative remains foundational to the constitution of the United Kingdom.

Groundwork: Crown, Prerogative and Parliament

The focus of this book is not on the king but on the Crown, not just because the latter is now the bearer of the vast majority of prerogative powers, but also because it is far more important in the modern British constitution than the monarch acting in his or her personal capacity.[34] Whilst there are prerogative powers that are still exercised by the monarch such as the power to counsel, encourage and warn the Prime Minister, the importance of these remaining powers is dwarfed by those exercised by the Crown through its ministers. English law began with kings and queens. Now it starts with the Crown.

That is why it is better and more accurate nowadays to refer to parliament as Crown-in-Parliament, as Lord Bingham did in *Jackson*, rather than the older formulation of King-in-Parliament.[35] The monarch is an individual. The Crown's powers are exercised by the duly elected government which has secured a direct democratic mandate for the policies in its manifesto by winning a general election.[36] When the Crown's ministers succeed in securing the support of the

[32] *R v Secretary of State for Health ex parte C* [2000] HRLR 400; *R (Hooper) v Secretary of State for Work and Pensions* [2005] UKHL 29, [2005] 1 WLR 1681, [2006] 1 All ER 487; *R (New London College Ltd) v Secretary of State for the Home Department)* [2013] UKSC 51, [2013] 1 WLR 2358, [2013] 4 All ER 195; *Shrewsbury & Atcham Borough Council, Congleton Borough Council v The Secretary of State for Communities and Local Government* [2008] EWCA Civ 148.

[33] *Malone v Metropolitan Police Commissioner* [1979] Ch 344, 357.

[34] This book focuses on English and Welsh law, recognising, however, that on issues of royal prerogative there may be some differences with Scottish law on occasion. See further A Tomkins, 'The Crown in Scots Law' in A McHarg and T Mullen (eds), *Public Law in Scotland* (Avizandum Publishing 2006).

[35] *R (Jackson) v Attorney General* [2005] UKHL 56, [2006] 1 AC 262, [2005] 3 WLR 733, [2005] 4 All ER 1253, [9]. Dicey (n 14) 37.

[36] See further R Craig (n 18) 125–50. The vagaries of what happens in a hung Parliament are outside the scope of this book.

two Houses for a legislative proposal in the form of a Bill, then the highest form of law known to our constitution – an Act of Parliament – is the result.[37] Strictly speaking, the proper full description is an Act of *Crown-in*-Parliament. Loughlin argues for an even more particular definition.

> The Crown-in-Council expresses governmental authority, the Crown-in-Council-in-Parliament signifies ultimate legislative authority …[38]

Similarly, Charles McIlwain explains how parliament has its origins in his 'curia' which means Council or court. He explains the history of the 'Curia, or central assembly' and how the 'House of Lords … springs out of it'.[39] This Curia, or Council, 'was court of law, advisory council and exchequer all in one', and all these institutions were originally rooted in the Crown.[40] McIlwain refers to the 'King's Council in his Parliaments' and also refers to 'The King's Court in his Council in His Parliaments' which is similar to Loughlin, save for the modern substitution of Crown for King.[41] So *all* English law started with the Crown, once upon a time.

The Prerogative of Justice

The Crown was not just the source of the power to legislate historically. The Crown also adjudicated on disputes. Arguably the most important prerogative power of the Crown historically was the prerogative of justice – expressed historically by the phrase 'the king is the fountain of justice'.[42] The monarch, and therefore eventually the Crown, was the original source of jurisdictional authority for all the ancient courts and all historic judicial decisions. Anson states baldly that 'all jurisdiction emanates from the Crown'.[43] Dicey argues that the 'whole judicial system may historically be treated as the transference to parts of the King's Council of judicial powers originally exercised by the King in Council'.[44]

[37] Private members bills are only successful with the tacit support of, and *de facto* adoption by, the government – outside the most extreme and controversial circumstances. The alternative Parliament Act procedure must also be mentioned.

[38] Loughlin (n 1); E Kantorowicz, *The King's Two Bodies A Study in Mediaeval Political Theology* (Princeton University Press 1957) 364.

[39] CH McIlwain, *The High Court of Parliament and its Supremacy* (Oxford University Press, 1910) 8–9.

[40] ibid 16.

[41] ibid 198–99.

[42] Per Lord Jones in *Ship Money (R v Hampden)* (1637) State Trials 825, at 1184 and submissions of Sir John Banks at 1024. See also Blackstone (n 21), Book 7, text to note 89. Chitty (n 31) 339. Lord Burnett, 'What's in a Name? The High Court and its Divisions' *(Pilgrim Fathers Lecture 2019, Plymouth* (14 November 2019), judiciary.uk/wp-content/uploads/2019/11/20191114-FINAL-Plymouth-lecture-Nov2019-For-publication-1.pdf at [2], quoting Lord Devlin in *Re K* [1965] AC 201 at 237, 'all justice flows from the prerogative'.

[43] Anson (n 26) 472.

[44] Dicey (n 14) 371.

It is difficult to argue that any other prerogative has had any broader reach or been of greater legal significance. The roots of this prerogative are in the role and function of the monarch as the 'feudal chief of the country' and is inextricably bound up with land.[45] Maitland comments that it 'may seem strange' that it is necessary to begin with land in a 'survey of public law', claiming

> even now it is impossible for us fully to understand our modern public law unless we know something of our law of property ...[46]

The administration of the land and the realm were indistinguishable, and this included administering justice as the monarch saw fit. It is for this reason that the prerogative of justice originated in the general prerogative of administration and why it was of such critical importance originally. The word 'court' is a legacy of history. The judges started as the King's judges, acting directly on his behalf. Circuit judges travelled the country administering the King's will and were administrators for centuries before they became adjudicators.[47] As Paul Halliday succinctly puts it, 'the jurisdiction of King's Bench rested on prerogative'.[48] Maitland and Sir Frederick Pollock put it well:

> Closely connected with its uniformity is another distinctive trait: in England the law for the great men has become the law for all men, because the law of the king's court has become the common law.[49]

The view, not shared by this author, that the jurisdiction of the courts is *still* rooted in the prerogative of justice has some modern judicial support. Lord Devlin held that 'all justice flows from prerogative' and that 'the jurisdiction parens patriae' is one aspect of 'the administration of justice as a whole' and this means that the judge in that case 'could do as he thought fit except in so far as he was controlled by statute'.[50] This can also be seen in the recent case of *Re X*. In discussing the inherent jurisdiction of the court to act in the interests of a child outside the jurisdiction of the relevant statutory scheme (in this case England/Scotland), the court referred to:

> the well-known and long-established principle that the exercise of the prerogative – and the inherent jurisdiction is an exercise of the prerogative, albeit the prerogative vested in the judges rather than in Ministers ...[51]

[45] Anson (n 26) 4.
[46] FW Maitland, *The Constitutional History of England* (Cambridge University Press 1919) 23.
[47] WS McKechnie, *Magna Carta* (James Maclehose and Sons 1914) 86.
[48] PD Halliday, *Habeas Corpus: From England to Empire* (Harvard University Press 2010) 12.
[49] FW Maitland and F Pollock, *The History of English Law before the Time of Edward I*, 2nd edn (Cambridge University Press, 1898–1899) 203.
[50] *Re K* (n 42) 237.
[51] *Re X (A Child), Re Y (A Child)* [2016] EWHC 2271 (Fam), [2016] 3 WLR 1718, [2017] 2 FLR 1717, [2017] 1 FCR 584 at [37], per Sir James Munby, former President of the Family Division and Court of Appeal judge.

A second example of the umbilical relationship between the Crown and the judiciary was pointed out by Lord Phillips in *R v Chaytor*, discussing the inappropriateness of the courts interfering in parliamentary proceedings.

> [Article IX ensures the] freedom for Parliament to conduct its legislative and deliberative business without interference from the Crown *or the Crown's judges*.[52] (Emphasis added)

English law, then, started with the prerogative of justice. As the great English legal historian, Sir William Holdsworth points out:

> If we return to the beginning of the thirteenth century, and take our stand in 1215, we can see that the Great Charter has made it clear that the future of English law is with royal justice, and that therefore there will be a law common to the whole of England.[53]

'Common' law replaced the multiplicity of local laws and customs across the land in the ancient manorial courts and hundreds.[54] As John Baker notes, the 'common law applied by the king's justices, and transmitted throughout the realm by a burgeoning legal profession, rapidly displaced local customs'.[55] This happened under Henry II, whose reign 'is the starting point of the history of modern English law, as well as of the modern English constitution'.[56] He laid down his law through his royal judges and thus made his royal law 'common' to the realm. Common law is, or was, therefore better labelled as originally *royal* law.

> [I]f we date the organisation of our judicial system from the accession of Henry II, we might say that a great legal revolution was carried through in not much more than a century.[57]

Before Henry II imposed royal law as a common set of legal norms across his kingdom enforced by his royal courts, there existed a whole set of local courts whose local, customary law was eventually superseded.

> Twelfth-century England was well supplied with courts of law. There were the courts of vill and the manor, hundred courts and shire courts, borough court, honorial courts and the ecclesiastical courts ... and of course there was the court of the lord king ... [but] competing and overlapping jurisdictions were a source of serious trouble in the twelfth century.[58]

Royal law, implemented uniformly across the realm, is therefore best understood as a top-down imposition on to the public by the elite rather than any mythical idea of it being drawn from the people from the bottom up. Democratic it was not,

[52] *R v Chaytor* [2011] 1 AC 684 at [61].
[53] WS Holdsworth, *A History of English Law*, 2nd edn (Methuen, 1938) vol 1, 63.
[54] McKechnie (n 47) 11–12.
[55] J Baker, *An Introduction to English Legal History*, 5th edn (Oxford University Press, 2019) 31.
[56] K Digby, *An Introduction to the History of the Law of Real Property* (Clarendon, 1875) 54.
[57] Dicey (n 14) 379.
[58] WL Warren, *Henry II* (Eyre Methuen, 1873) 317, 319.

however positive a development it might have been for stability and commerce. The story of one example of the top-down imposition of royal law and jurisdiction, this time on Ireland, is well told by William Johnston:

> And so the common law came to Ireland. It came as an essential part of the accoutrement of King Henry II and his knights and clerics when they set out with jingling spur and clanking armour on their march from Waterford to Dublin in November 1171 ... In the course of time, it displaced the older and less complex code that hitherto had sufficed.[59]

As Brian Simpson says, 'the king [was] the fount of all justice'.[60] This is the appropriate starting point for a proper understanding of English law, the Crown and royal prerogative. Simpson endorses Toby Milsom's claim that 'what had started as a mere system of royal judicial review by degrees became a take over'.[61] Common law therefore started as *royal* law. English *common* law starts with the Crown.

The Transition to Parliament as the Supreme Legal Authority

To modern eyes, the overwhelming importance and power of the doctrine of parliamentary sovereignty has understandably tended to obscure the crucial importance of the Crown. Adam Tomkins persuasively argues that an Act of Parliament is where the two 'sovereign authorities of England come together and agree'.[62] The Crown was the original source of all legal power; this has been whittled down to mostly executive functions.[63] The Houses of Commons and Lords have a mostly legislative function. When *both* branches agree then an Act is created.[64] This is the essence of the fused constitution where executive and legislature are not sharply delineated, so the executive has a legislative role in passing laws. This can be seen from the fact that ministers are also MPs and the fact that the legislature has an executive role because the Cabinet is a committee of Parliament drawn from the ranks of MPs, and sometimes peers. The historical roots of the

[59] WJ Johnston, 'First Adventure of the Common Law' (1920) 36 *Law Quarterly Review* 9, 30.

[60] AWB Simpson, *A History of Land Law*, 2nd edn (Clarendon Press, 1986) 26.

[61] ibid 36. At the early stages the royal courts had a difficult relationship with the original local courts. Sometimes royal courts claimed the power to judicially review those courts but it was patchy and unclear. Over time, the royal courts imposed their decisions universally.

[62] A Tomkins, *Public Law* (Oxford University Press, 2003) 48.

[63] The status of the plenary legislative powers available to the Crown outside the United Kingdom was considered in *R (Bancoult) v Secretary of State for Foreign & Commonwealth Affairs* [2008] UKHL 61, [2009] AC 453. See also Dicey (n 14) 51, footnote 2. See further ch 4, pp 81–84 and ch 6, pp 120–122.

[64] This leaves to one side the Parliament Acts procedure.

Cabinet lie in the Privy Council, but Walter Bagehot explains the constitutional reality:

> By [cabinet] … we mean a committee of the legislative body selected to be the executive body. The legislature has many committees, but this is its greatest. It chooses for this, its main committee, the men in whom it has most confidence. It does not, it is true, choose them directly; but it is nearly omnipotent in choosing them indirectly.[65]

What is sometimes overlooked, however, is that it is Ministers of the Crown who control (or on rare occasions acquiesce in) the process of *proposing* legislation in the first place. Thus, even today, nearly all English *statute* law starts, chronologically, with the Crown.

An Act of Parliament, therefore, represents the highest form of law and is in one sense the manifestation of the policy of the Crown's ministers expressed in law, having secured the approval of MPs and peers in parliament. Once clothed with that authority, there is no law that can compete with, or withstand, the force of an Act.[66] Hence the *Crown*-in-Parliament is sovereign. On one view, this sovereignty is a mere extension of the historical reality that the monarch was the original source not just of what became judicial precedent, but also what became statute. The difference between the two was that statutes were given the imprimatur of the two Houses as well. Crucially, the Glorious Revolution in the seventeenth century severed the root of final legislative authority previously possessed by the Crown, and the Crown-in-Parliament became the final authority.[67] Crown-in-Parliament became supreme over the Crown.

Four Usages of Common Law

Crucial to understanding the place of royal prerogative in the modern constitution is the relationship between prerogative and judicial common law. It has already been suggested that even the label 'Royal Courts of Justice' reveals the original roots of the common law in the royal prerogative of justice. Historically, 'justice flows from the King, as its fountain'.[68] Hence the source of the legal authority and jurisdiction of common law decisions of the *King's* Bench was ultimately the monarch. Whilst these claims are historically grounded, it is important to address one significant source of confusion in this area which is the fact that the phrase 'common law' is itself used in multiple different ways.

Four possible usages of the phrase 'common law' can be isolated. It is the conflation of these different usages that has caused, and continues to cause,

[65] W Bagehot, *The English Constitution* (1867) 11.

[66] This book leaves to one side internecine disputes *between* statutes and the emerging concept of 'constitutional statutes', for example the important, but now repealed, European Communities Act 1972.

[67] HLA Hart, *The Concept of Law* (Oxford University Press, 1961) 106.

[68] Chitty (n 31) 243.

problems in this area of law. Hence it is important to be clear about how this book will deal with 'common law' and the precise terminology it will use. The first usage refers to common law *systems* by contrast with civil law systems, such as France.[69] This usage need not concern us. A second definition of common law is 'all non-statutory law'; the phrase 'non-statutory' common law will be used where necessary in this book to denote this meaning of the phrase.[70] Third, common law can refer to all judicial precedents handed down by any court.[71] This book will use the term 'judicial common law' where necessary to denote this third meaning. Finally, common law can refer to the particular subset of judicial precedent handed down by the courts of King's Bench, (including the outcomes of appeals to the higher courts) by contrast with, say, judicial decisions in the courts of Chancery.[72] This fourth usage of the phrase 'common law', it is submitted, is the usage that is most consistent with the history and context of English law as well as arguably the most accurate use of the phrase 'common law'.

Once these four usages are properly disaggregated, the difficult issue of the relationship of the royal prerogative and the 'common law' can be considered. It can immediately be seen that the widely held view that the prerogative is 'part of the common law' is either an empty tautology or wholly wrong, depending on which definition of common law is selected. The first option, that prerogative is part of the common law in the narrow sense of judicial precedent, is obviously wrong. If common law is defined in the sense of judicial decisions handed down by the King's Bench it is clearly mistaken to claim that prerogative powers are somehow sourced in those decisions.

The historical reality is in fact the other way round. Court decisions handed down by the King's Bench were originally authorised because the jurisdictional roots of the court were in the prerogative of justice. Indeed, it was a polite fiction that the King continued to sit in his court even if he was not physically present.[73] The idea, then, that prerogative is part of the common law in the narrowest, and proper, sense of the phrase is the inverse of the historical legal reality. Common law originated as part of the prerogative, not the other way round.

Even if the meaning of 'common law' is broadened out to include *all* judicial precedent, it still makes no sense to claim that prerogative is part of common law for the same reasons. Decisions made under the equitable jurisdiction of the courts of chancery were no less originally rooted in the prerogative of justice or possibly administration prior to justice, than were the common law decisions of the court of King's Bench. It is therefore no less misleading to assert that the prerogative is part of common law in the wider sense of all judicial decisions.

[69] Digby (n 56) 55, fn 1.

[70] To avoid the use of 'non-statutory' and 'judicial' meanings of common law becoming excessive and distracting for the reader, the simple phrase 'common law' will sometimes be used where a more precise definition is not necessary for that stage of the argument.

[71] Digby (n 56) 55, fn 1.

[72] ibid.

[73] Chitty (n 31) 244.

The second option is that prerogative is 'part of common law' in the sense of 'all non-statutory law'. This claim is an empty tautology. It is of course a banal truism to claim that prerogative is part of common law if 'common law' is defined as 'all non-statutory law'. As a matter of definition, however, describing prerogative as part of common law in our second, 'non-statutory law' sense, whilst accurate, explains nothing. It is a just a semantic relabelling. It is also circular. One could just as well describe all non-statutory law as 'prerogative law', or at a minimum historically traceable to, originally rooted in, or ultimately coopted by, prerogative.

There is thus no doubt that prerogative is 'non-statutory'. Whether that tells you much about the meaning of 'common law' or what is or is not contained within 'common law' (or indeed what is contained within 'prerogative') is considerably more doubtful. Thus, the claim that the prerogative is part of 'common law' in the narrow sense is meaningless and wrong, while the second option, that prerogative is part of 'non-statutory law', is an empty tautology.

A further point to make is that breaking down what 'non-statutory law' means is itself quite revealing. We have already established that legal norms that are not based on statute include all judicial precedent and court decisions ('common law' in the narrow, judicial sense) which were originally rooted in the prerogative of justice. Another group of legal norms that are not based on statute are other prerogatives such as proroguing parliament, signing treaties and making *ex gratia* payments. Plainly, the prerogative of justice and these other prerogatives are properly labelled as prerogatives, not common law.

Once you put aside the prerogative of justice and other types of prerogative, it is in fact quite difficult to identify any other non-statutory legal norms. The non-statutory, non-prerogative cupboard looks rather bare. Some have argued for a 'third source' of powers, or freedoms. This book argues there are no such powers and that is addressed in chapter nine. It is possible that there may be some legal norms as part of ecclesiastical law, but that is outside the scope of this book. In any event, the relationship between ecclesiastical law and prerogative is itself fraught, to put it mildly.[74] The same could be said about the University Visitorial jurisdiction which is itself conducted by the University Visitor on behalf of the Crown so is hardly a truly distinct set of legal norms unrelated to prerogative. It is also of marginal importance.

It would therefore appear that the vast majority, if not all, 'non-statutory law' is of two types. First, the set of prerogatives still possessed by the Crown; second, law made by judges that was originally rooted in the prerogative of justice, itself a prerogative power. It would seem, then, that to describe the prerogative as part of non-statutory law would be in effect to say that the prerogative is part of the prerogative. Indeed, it might be more accurate to say that all non-statutory law was originally rooted in prerogative and that the better historic label for

[74] WE Hearn, *The Government of England* (Longmans, Green, Reader, and Dyer, 1867) 132.

all non-statutory law would not be 'common law' but 'Royal Law' – hence the title of this book.

Indeed as McIlwain points out, even statute law started out as a special kind of royal judicial decision, although 'there was no clear distinction between "legislative" and "judicial"'.[75] It was slowly realised that statutes were novel because they generated legal norms that had no precedent and therefore, uniquely, *altered* the existing law by laying down 'a new rule'.[76] Indeed, parliament 'until the time of the Tudors, was hardly thought of primarily … as a legislature', rather 'Parliament still seemed primarily a law-declaring machine'.[77] In that sense *all* law originally derived from the prerogative of justice until the Glorious Revolution removed Crown's power to legislate without the approval of the Commons and Lords. The power to legislate moved to parliament. That was the revolutionary change as a matter of law.

It is important to note that whilst the original source of the legal authority and legitimacy of judicial precedent was the prerogative of justice, that changed as a result of the Judicature Act 1873, discussed further in chapter five. After 1873 the legal validity of judicial decision-making was derived from statute. On this view, the class of legal norms rooted in prerogative was substantially, even dramatically, reduced after 1873. Indeed, given that this book rejects the notion of a separate 'third source', its argument is that the only remaining prerogatives post-1873 are those prerogatives remaining in the possession of the Crown such as conducting foreign affairs and the like.

The Crown and the Courts

An important aspect of the slow evolution of how the relationship between the Crown and ministers is perceived and understood is the case of *M v Home Office*.[78] In that case, the Secretary of State refused to obey a court order on the basis of legal advice that the court had no jurisdiction over the Crown. The House of Lords held that the monarch and the Crown remain immune from suit but that injunctions could be granted against a minister of the Crown, as distinct from the Crown itself. This immunity of the Crown is a legacy of the historic immunity of the monarch in their courts. The difficulty and confusion inherent in addressing the relationship between Crown and ministers in *M v Home Office*, however, provides startling evidence of how the Crown's tentacles still extend throughout the legal system. The serious problems caused to the judiciary in dealing with this case reflect the historic roots of the judiciary in the Crown and are a powerful reminder

[75] McIlwain (n 39) [30].
[76] ibid 120.
[77] ibid [109]–[110].
[78] *M v Home Office* [1994] 1 AC 377.

of our ancient legal past. As Tomkins, and indeed the former Lord Chief Justice, have pointed out, the label '*Royal* Courts of Justice' is not an accident.[79]

This book claims not only that all Crown powers are prerogative powers, but furthermore that the royal prerogative of justice historically underpinned the legitimacy and authority of the courts. If the argument as to the roots of common law made earlier is correct, then to say that the authority of the courts is derived from 'common law' is a constitutional solecism akin to arguing that the sovereignty of parliament is derived from the Bill of Rights 1689. This issue is explored further in chapter five. One practical constitutional effect of these historical facts is that the relationship between the courts and the Crown is fundamentally conditioned by the historical roots of the courts in Crown prerogative. The tentacles of Crown prerogative stretch all the way to the present.

This legacy can be seen in the modern era where the courts have had enormous difficulties when confronted with governmental actions that appear to be covered by the blanket immunity of the Crown from suit because of the prerogative of immunity. This prerogative originally prevented the monarch from being sued in his or her own courts but for governmental actions that are ostensibly done under the authority of the Crown, the historic immunity appeared to create a *lacuna* in legal accountability for the government in the courts.

One infamous legacy of the fact that judicial common law originated as royal law was that the courts were thought to have no power to grant injunctions against Ministers of the Crown and central government. This problem crystallised in *M v Home Office*, one of the most important cases in English constitutional history, where the legacy of the deep roots of the courts in Crown prerogative directly impacted on the reasoning. This subsection begins the process of exploring how the historical legacy of judicial common law being royal law makes the relationship between the Crown and the courts so difficult to this day, and presages part II of this book, which considers the status of alleged (judicial) 'common law' powers of the Crown in the modern era.

In *M v Home Office*, the courts struggled with the legal status of the Crown and whether they had any jurisdiction to grant a binding injunction against ministers of the Crown.[80] The reason this was even in issue was because the Crown is immune from suit and ministers claimed that immunity also covered their own actions in some circumstances, based on that ancient immunity. Thus, the history and genealogy of the courts rooted in the royal prerogative of justice had a direct and dramatic potential effect in a real-world dispute, with enormous constitutional implications, about the extent of executive power and the ability of the courts to insist that binding injunctions handed down by the courts were obeyed by the executive. If it was generally accepted that the courts gain their jurisdictional

[79] A Tomkins, *Our Republican Constitution* (Hart Publishing, 2005) 120. Lord Burnett (n 42) at [2].

[80] *M v Home Office* (n 78). See also the *Factortame* litigation, including most famously *R v Secretary of State for Transport, ex parte Factortame* [1990] 2 AC 85 and *R v Secretary of State for Transport, ex parte Factortame (No 2)* [1990] 3 WLR 818 [1991] 1 AC 603.

authority from 'common law', it is difficult to see why the case caused such legal mayhem.

The facts are well known but, in short, a binding undertaking was given by counsel to the Crown, which in effect amounted to an injunction not to deport Mr M. On legal advice, the Home Secretary disregarded that injunction because he did not believe that the court had jurisdiction to grant injunctions against the Crown or ministers of the Crown, given the ancient immunity of the monarch from being sued in his or her own courts. This immunity was a function of the historic plenary prerogative powers possessed by the Crown. Indeed, the facts and issues in this case supply some of the strongest evidence in support of the core themes of this book.

M v Home Office is a striking illustration of just how entangled even very recent cases can still be with centuries-old legacy implications of the deep roots of the common law in the prerogative of justice and therefore the Crown itself. Lord Atkin's clanking medieval chains still rattle from time to time.[81] In one sense, it is simply extraordinary that there could be doubt about the status of the executive in legal proceedings, and the ability of the courts to issue binding injunctions against the government, as late as 1994. Yet it was abundantly clear during that litigation that whether the court had jurisdiction to grant an injunction against the minister was a very live and difficult point.

If considered through a historic prism, the uncertainty is not that surprising.[82] Once it is accepted that the legal basis for the entirety of the courts' jurisdiction was originally the prerogative of justice, the legacy impact of that historical fact could easily explain the tortuous difficulties faced by counsel and the court in determining whether an injunction could be granted against a minister of the Crown. How could an applicant secure a remedy from the royal courts against the Crown when technically the roots of such a remedy used to lie in the *Crown* applying that remedy at the behest of the claimant? Can the Crown apply a remedy against itself?

Furthermore, the word 'jurisdiction' denotes that the court has the authority to make binding legal decisions. As noted above, the history of English law is that applications to the court were originally requests to the King's judges to provide a *remedy* against the defendant. English law traditionally focused on remedies not rights. Authority to do so came from the King. Lord Dunedin put the point well in a letter to the Times on 20 April 1928:

> The fundamental difference between the Common Law of England and that of Scotland lies in this: that in England you have to find the remedy in order to discover the right, whereas in Scotland you have to find the right in order to discover the remedy.[83]

[81] *United Australia Ltd v Barclays Bank Ltd* [1941] AC 1, 29.

[82] It is important to note that the Judicature Acts did not alter the privileges and immunities of the Crown, even though it substituted parliamentary legal authority for Crown legal authority.

[83] JW Gordon, 'The Crown as Litigant' (1929) 45 *Law Quarterly Review* 186, 194 – quoted in J Jacob, *The Republican Crown* (Dartmouth, 1996) 237.

An injunction is a type of remedy, originally granted by judges on behalf of the Crown. Even if all remedies, as the ultimate expression of jurisdiction, were placed on to a statutory footing in 1873, it is still somewhat strange for what used to be the Crown's judges to grant even a *statutory* remedy against the Crown's ministers.

The ingenious solution laid down by the House of Lords was to formally separate the Crown from its ministers and their departments as a matter of law. This meant that an injunction could be granted against a minister, and their department, so they could technically be in contempt of court for breaching an injunction. The Crown itself, however, was untouched and unaffected. This neat three-way split between first the Crown, second departments, and third ministers in their personal capacity, was key to the case. As is well known, the minister was held not to be personally liable because the minister had acted at all times on legal advice.[84]

Crucially, however, the court made clear that the Crown itself remained outside the jurisdiction of the courts.[85] This can only be explained by looking at the legacy and history of the legal system. *M v Home Office* unmistakeably demonstrates that the historical roots of the courts lay in the Crown and that it is a serious mistake to claim there is any alternative non-statutory or non-prerogative basis for the jurisdiction of the courts. Prior to 1873, the jurisdiction of the courts was rooted in prerogative. Since 1873, the courts' jurisdictional authority is rooted in statute.

Those who would defend the idea that the jurisdiction of the courts is instead rooted in some 'higher' legal source which they label (non-statutory) 'common law' face some serious difficulties in dealing with *M v Home Office*. The first problem is that if the jurisdiction of the courts is rooted in some non-statutory, non-prerogative third source, why did the courts struggle so much with *M*? If the courts have their own separate source of jurisdiction, why couldn't they simply grant an injunction against the Crown? Indeed, it is arguable that the only reason they were able to find a way past the obstacle is because, like *GCHQ*, their now independent statutory underpinning provided the justification for enforcing their authority *against* ministers of the Crown. Since this was clearly a significant novel development in the law, the claim that the authority for the change was rooted in existing 'common law' is self-refuting.

The reason the court struggled, of course, is that the judges were severely hampered, hobbled in fact, by the history, origin and legacy effects of the fact that the courts' original jurisdiction was sourced in the prerogative of justice not some mythical, higher, non-statutory 'common law'. The very fact that the decision contained such convoluted, tortured and difficult reasoning is strong evidence

[84] *M v Home Office* (n 78) 396 and 427.

[85] ibid 409–10 and 415–16.

against the common law narrative. Indeed, in this author's view, the case *fatally* undermines any purported 'common law' basis of judicial jurisdiction either historically or today. Judicial authority previously derived from prerogative. Now it derives from statute.

Rather, *M v Home Office* powerfully evidences one of the main claims in this book which is that the original source of judicial jurisdiction was for centuries royal prerogative. This was the sole and proximate reason for the enormous difficulties in the *M v Home Office* litigation. The historic roots of the courts in prerogative are explored further in chapters two and five. The implications of the fact that the Crown itself remains outside the jurisdiction of the courts is considered in part II.

The Structure of this Book

Following this introductory chapter, this monograph is structured in three parts. The final chapter of the book suggests, in outline only, that the arguments in this monograph may have contemporary implications for those who defend the idea that the courts should be able to challenge provisions in Acts of Parliament *in extremis*. Part I considers the definition and limits of royal prerogative. In particular, it addresses the core claim made in the Introduction, which is that all non-statutory Crown legal powers are prerogative powers and that the two terms are synonymous. It develops the argument by considering the two primary definitions of prerogative that have been taught to students for decades: Dicey's and Blackstone's, considered above.

Blackstone's definition has long been interpreted to mean that any so-called (judicial) 'common law' powers exercised by the Crown are not part of the prerogative such that the Crown has both prerogative powers and common law powers. Chapters two and three argue that these two definitions are reconcilable if it is accepted that the Crown does *not* exercise any (judicial) common law powers. Fleshing out this claim involves examining the roots of common law itself and in particular a consideration of the prerogative of justice which originally underpinned both judicial decisions from the King's Bench (common law) as well as chancery decisions (Equity).

The third chapter of part I argues that Sir William Wade's interpretation of Blackstone's argument is fundamentally flawed. Wade suggested a two-part definition of prerogatives:

> The two tests for a genuine prerogative power seem to me to be:
>
> (a) Does it produce legal effects at common law, and
> (b) Is it unique to the Crown and not shared with other persons?[86]

[86] HWR Wade, 'Procedure and Prerogative in Public Law' (1985) 101 *Law Quarterly Review* 180.

The first limb of Wade's definition is challenged in chapter four and the other limb is addressed in chapter seven. Chapter four considers why Wade decided to invent a requirement – he cites no authority for it – that prerogative power must have legal effects at judicial common law, particularly in light of the fact that case law appears to establish fairly conclusively that prerogative *cannot* be used 'to change statute or common law'.[87] The chapter suggests that prerogative can indeed affect rights, just not at judicial common law. It postulates two domains – prerogative and judicial common law – and argues that legal actions in the prerogative domain are treated separately by the judiciary. The final chapter of part I considers the place of the prerogative of justice, arguably the most important domestic prerogative, in the constitutional architecture. The chapter argues that whilst prerogative was the original source of the legal authority of the courts, a radical change occurred in the 1870s when the modern courts were created. The ordinary courts were constituted as creatures of statute and now gain their authority and legitimacy from parliament.

Part II of the book considers the Crown, centred around a new definition of the concept. This novel claim is that the Crown can be defined as the legal bearer of the remaining prerogative powers. In other words, there is a *definitional* relationship between Crown and prerogative. Chapter six considers the difficulties that others have experienced in attempting to define the Crown before explaining the novel definition in detail. Chapter seven addresses the Blackstonian claim, approved by Wade and others, that prerogative must necessarily be exclusive to the Crown and not shared with others. This requires consideration of the contentious issue of whether the Crown does actually share prerogatives with ordinary citizens. The central claim of this book is that legal powers of the Crown are all prerogative powers. Were the Crown to share legal powers with others, then the definitional relationship between Crown and prerogative that is argued for in this book would be wrong.

The chapter therefore seeks to refute Wade's claim that the Crown possesses judicial common law powers that are 'shared with' ordinary legal persons. The example of *ex gratia* payments is used to illustrate that the funding of governmental compensation schemes with public money and subject to a panoply of public law duties has little or no resemblance to the making of gifts or establishment of trusts by private persons. Instead, the two legal scenarios must be sharply distinguished. The argument is developed by unpicking a commonly glossed-over issue, which is who exactly exercises legal powers in the government. Dicey makes clear that ministers who enter contracts on behalf of the government are personally liable.[88] After all, Entick sued the King's Messenger, Mr Carrington, *personally* – the Crown was certainly not the defendant.[89] It seems, then, that

[87] *Miller I* (n 3) [51], citing Lord Hoffmann in *Bancoult* (n 63) [44].
[88] Dicey (n 14).
[89] *Entick v Carrington* (1765) 19 St Tr 1030. See further, A Tomkins and P Scott (eds), *Entick v Carrington: 250 Years of the Rule of Law* (Hart Publishing, 2015).

the Crown is neither the defendant nor claimant in judicial common law legal actions, leaving aside the unique issues raised by criminal law.[90]

It might be thought that the Crown Proceedings Act 1947 changed the legal status of the Crown and constituted it as a legal entity at judicial common law. Chapter eight challenges that interpretation, arguing that, interpreted in the light of the seminal decision of *M v Home Office*, the Act simply replaces the archaic 'Petition of Right' procedure with a right to sue Crown *servants* directly. If this is accepted, then it is the government that is subject to the judicial common law, not the Crown. Thus, the Crown does not itself exercise any common law legal powers.

This still leaves open the question of the nature of the relationship between the Crown and the minister. Chapter eight argues that contracts entered into by ministers, not the Crown, are valid only as long as they are underpinned by a valid exercise of *prerogative* power. This underpinning resembles the *statutory* underpinning of local councils when *they* make binding contracts which must be *intra vires* to be valid. The argument of the book – that the Crown is not within the jurisdiction of the judicial common law courts in the first place – has the beneficial side effect of rendering relatively unimportant, save for some minor exceptions, the vexed and long-standing question of whether the Crown should be treated as a natural person, a corporation sole or a corporation aggregate.[91]

Part III considers what is described as the 'myth' of third source powers. This concept was first suggested by Bruce Harris and is sometimes also referred to as the 'Ram doctrine'.[92] Chapter nine considers these supposedly common law powers or freedoms held by the Crown, which are neither statutory nor prerogative.[93] The chapter argues that, since it is virtually impossible to find a prerogative that satisfies Harris' definition, under his approach, *all* Crown powers would be third source powers/freedoms possessed at common law. It is suggested that there already exists a better and more accurate label for the set of all Crown legal powers and, rather than 'third source' powers or common law powers, the better label would be 'prerogative powers' because that would be more consistent with the history, genealogy and development of the constitutional law of this country.

Chapter nine then goes on to consider another important contribution to the debate over Crown legal powers by Adam Perry, who claims that the Crown has *non*-legal powers which he suggests includes such powers as issuing apologies

[90] JW Gordon, 'The Crown as Litigant' (1929) 45 *Law Quarterly Review* 186: 'the whole administration of criminal justice is carried on in the King's name'.

[91] The issue of judicial review of ministerial advice on the exercise of prerogative power is a separate matter dealt with earlier in this chapter.

[92] 'Report on Privacy and Data Sharing', issued by the Performance and Innovation Unit of the Cabinet Office: ntouk.files.wordpress.com/2015/06/privacy-and-data-sharing-the-way-forward-for-public-services-2002.pdf, para 3.46.

[93] B Harris, 'The "Third Source" of Authority for Government Action' (1992) 108 *Law Quarterly Review* 626.

and making promises. It is suggested, *contra* Perry, that such actions can be included within the exercise of what could usefully be labelled the 'administration prerogative'. The chapter discusses this somewhat neglected prerogative power, which is limited to administering the realm and which sweeps up many of the orphan powers such as re-arranging government, consulting officials and other administrative matters that Harris described as freedoms and Perry described as non-legal powers.

The wholesale repudiation by this book of the concept of third source powers inevitably requires a close consideration of the case law that has considered such powers. Some of the third source powers cases are reframed in chapter ten as examples of the exercise of the administration prerogative rather than of judicial common law or third source powers. One case in particular, *ex parte C*, is reframed as falling beyond the historical limits of the prerogative of administration.[94] The chapter then considers arguably the most important 'third source power' case – *Malone* – and argues that it can also be explained in terms of an exercise of prerogative power rather than as an action by the government that was lawful because it was not prohibited.[95] This unfortunately led to potentially unjustifiable, and certainly unjustified, extensions in executive power that might have been avoided if the issues had been considered through the prism of prerogative.

Since many of the relevant cases also involve statutes, it is essential to address the relationship between statute and prerogative. Chapter eleven applies the two categories delineated by the frustration and abeyance principles, laid out earlier, to the third source power case law. In relation to the Supreme Court *New College* case, this chapter suggests that the frustration principle should have been applied and, in effect, *was* applied.[96] The chapter then considers the *Hooper* case and argues that it falls on the borderline between the frustration principle and the abeyance principle and is a valuable prism through which to consider the details of the two concepts. Finally, the *Shrewsbury* case is re-analysed as a valuable example of the abeyance principle.[97] The book then concludes in chapter twelve by drawing together the core arguments before addressing some interesting potential codicils generated by the arguments in this book.

[94] *R v Secretary of State for Health, ex parte C* [2000] HRLR 400.

[95] *Malone v Metropolitan Police Commissioner* [1979] Ch 344.

[96] *New London College Ltd* (n 32).

[97] *Shrewsbury & Atcham Borough Council, Congleton Borough Council v The Secretary of State for Communities and Local Government* [2008] EWCA Civ 148.

PART I

Royal Law

2

Prerogative Foundations

Introduction

There have ultimately only ever been two original sources of institutional legal authority in English law: Crown and Crown-in-Parliament. Royal prerogatives were originally all the legal powers, duties and immunities possessed by the monarch. The law of England was originally derived entirely from royal prerogative, and 'even among our Saxon ancestors, the King was regarded as the authority by whom the judges were supported and upheld'.[1] The king was the fountain of justice, granting remedies through his judges to supplicants to his court, although there 'can be little doubt that the King once exercised in person his judicial will'.[2] William Hearn says that 'even at the close of the thirteenth century … his right to take part in the proceedings seems undisputed'.[3]

The set of prerogative powers was plenary in nature such that before the Glorious Revolution the Crown was the one and only source of valid institutional legal authority. The king was responsible for keeping the peace, delivering justice and administering his realm through his ministers, his judges and his parliament, who all operated downstream of his supreme legal authority.

> In our political system, the Crown always has been and still is the sun … ever since England was a nation, the Crown enacts laws; the Crown administers justice; the Crown makes peace and war, and conducts all the affairs of state at home and abroad …[4]

Historically, then, 'it is … from the Crown that all jurisdictions in the kingdom emanate' and therefore all legal power flowed from the monarch.[5] The Glorious Revolution was revolutionary precisely because it saw the creation of a new, original and superior source of legal norms authorised by the new 'Convention

[1] WE Hearn, *The Government of England* (Longmans, Green, Reader and Dyer, 1867) 66.
[2] ibid 68.
[3] ibid. Although Hearn later (at 70) appears to qualify that claim slightly by drawing a distinction between decisions of an 'executive' and 'judicial' nature, even though such a distinction would have been close to meaningless at the time.
[4] Hearn (n 1) 17.
[5] ibid 65.

Parliament'.[6] This was a completely novel body in constitutional terms, and it supplanted the Crown as the supreme authority. It is now accurately labelled as Crown-in-Parliament.[7] The Revolution meant that the new class of legal norms laid down by that parliament is supreme and therefore prevails over all other legal norms.

The history and development of royal prerogative underpins Dicey's definition:

> The residue of discretionary or arbitrary authority, which at any given time is legally left in the hands of the Crown.[8]

This general definitional claim is not controversial from a genealogical perspective. If all legal powers originated with the king, it is hardly surprising that all non-statutory legal norms can trace their original roots back to royal prerogative.

Stanley De Smith and Rodney Brazier suggest that Dicey's definition is 'incomplete because it is restricted to powers', but if we take a broad view of powers to include duties, immunities and privileges then Dicey's definition of prerogative is a sound starting point.[9] Anson describes prerogative as a 'complex and difficult term' and adds the concepts of 'rights, privileges and attributes' to the basic notion of powers.[10] It is also important to heed Lord Reid's warning in *De Keyser's Hotel* in relation to prerogative:

> I think we should beware of looking at older authorities through modern spectacles. We ought not to ignore the many changes in Constitutional law and theory which culminated in the Revolution Settlement of 1688–1689 and there is practically no authority between that date and 1915.[11]

The phrases 'prerogative' and 'prerogative powers' should be taken to include the broader concepts of duties and immunities of the Crown throughout this book. Basil Markesinis provided helpful support for Dicey's more comprehensive definition:

> the prerogative is the residue of executive powers, immunities or other attributes which the government possesses without the authority of an Act of Parliament ...[12]

[6] FW Maitland, *The Constitutional History of England* (Cambridge University Press, 1919) 282; D Kershaw, 'Revolutionary Amnesia and the Nature of Prerogative Power' (2022) 20(3) *International Journal of Constitutional Law* 1071, 1075.

[7] *R (Jackson) v Attorney General* [2005] UKHL 56, [2006] 1 AC 262, [2005] 3 WLR 733, [2005] 4 All ER 1253, [9], per Lord Bingham.

[8] AV Dicey, *Introduction to the Study of the Law of the Constitution*, 8th edn (Macmillan, 1927) 420.

[9] BS Markesinis, *The Theory and Practice of Dissolution of Parliament* (Cambridge University Press, 1972) 54; S De Smith and R Brazier, *Constitutional and Administrative Law*, 6th edn (Penguin, 1990) 129.

[10] WR Anson, *The Law and Custom of the Constitution*, 2nd edn (Clarendon Press, 1896) 3.

[11] *Burmah Oil Company (Burma Trading) Ltd v Lord Advocate* [1965] AC 75, 99.

[12] BS Markesinis, 'The Royal Prerogative Re-visited' (1973) 32 *Cambridge Law Journal* 287, 309.

Markesinis further explains, and this was confirmed in the first *Miller* case, that these powers were once sovereign, plenary powers, although McIlwain is right to urge caution to avoid imposing modern understandings of such concepts on to ancient societies with alien values.[13]

Prerogative powers have been steadily whittled down over centuries, but some extraordinarily important powers remain, including the power to declare war, dissolution of parliament and the appointment of the prime minister. This demonstrates that prerogative powers of the Crown remain an extremely important part of the constitutional framework of the United Kingdom. It is therefore important to establish an accurate definition of the concept at the outset.

Dicey, Blackstone, Locke and Wade

Modern literature has traditionally focused on two principal, competing definitions of royal prerogative given by Dicey and Blackstone, but as Sebastian Payne has pointed out, 'there is no single accepted definition of the royal prerogative. The various definitions appear to conflict with each other'.[14] As we have seen, the more recent, ostensibly broader definition was given by Dicey. In contrast, Blackstone proposed an apparently much narrower definition, claiming that prerogatives are only those legal powers that are exclusive to the Crown – that is, where there is no analogue legal power possessed by ordinary citizens.[15]

Famously, Wade argued that Blackstone's narrow definition was the better one and he gave his own particular gloss on that version. Wade was in no doubt that the Diceyan and Blackstonian definitions were in conflict.[16] For Wade, a prerogative could only properly be described as a prerogative if it is 'unique to the Crown'.[17] This led him to draw a sharp distinction between the 'unique' powers of the Crown and powers that he argued it 'shares equally with its subjects because of its legal personality, such as the power to make contracts, employ servants and convey land'.[18] Wade claimed that what he described as the 'loose usage' of the broader definition by the courts 'may derive from Dicey'.[19] Wade's neo-Blackstonian definition is addressed in depth in chapters four and seven.

[13] ibid 308; *R (Miller) v Secretary of State for Exiting the European Union* [2018] AC 61, [2017] UKSC 5, [2017] 2 WLR 583 ('*Miller I*'), [41]; CH McIlwain, *The High Court of Parliament and its Supremacy* (Oxford University Press, 1910) 21.

[14] S Payne, 'The Royal Prerogative' in M Sunkin and S Payne, *The Nature of the Crown* (Oxford University Press, 1999) 78.

[15] W Blackstone, *Commentaries on the Laws of England* (1753) Book 1, ch 7, 239.

[16] HWR Wade, 'Procedure and Prerogative in Public Law' (1985) 101 *Law Quarterly Review* 180, 191.

[17] W Wade, 'The Crown, Ministers and Officials: Legal Status and Liability' in M Sunkin and S Payne, *The Nature of the Crown: A Legal and Political Analysis* (Oxford University Press, 1999) 24, 30.

[18] W Wade, C Forsyth and J Ghosh, *Wade & Forsyth's Administrative Law*, 12th edn (Oxford University Press, 2022) 42.

[19] ibid at fn 30. See also Wade (n 16).

Despite the fact that the courts have mostly seemed to adopt the Diceyan definition, the Blackstone definition is critically important in the definitional debate. For decades, if not longer, academic textbooks have set out both Dicey's and Blackstone's definitions in their introduction to the meaning of royal prerogative. A good example is Mark Elliott and Robert Thomas, who happen to favour Blackstone.[20] Ian Loveland favours Dicey's definition.[21] Noel Cox says Dicey is the 'standard' definition but notes that 'the two views are of course divergent, if not inconsistent'.[22] In addition, recent years have seen the courts toy with a recognisably Blackstonian definition. Indeed, Wade and Forsyth are quick to point to some relatively recent cases that have appeared to give substantial credence to the non-Diceyan approach endorsed by Wade.[23] These cases are discussed in detail in part III, along with an important recent Court of Appeal case that makes some use of a third, slightly less well known, analysis of prerogative by John Locke. Locke's definition is addressed in the next chapter.

As the last chapter illustrated, the two *Miller* cases, the Fixed-term Parliaments Act saga and other high profile examples demonstrate that royal prerogative has been a significant element in public debate in recent years.[24] It is therefore highly unsatisfactory for there to continue to be such doubt as to the meaning and definition of the concept in the first place. While the uncertainty around the definition of the prerogative has not materially affected consideration of those prerogatives that came to public attention in the two *Miller* cases, this has been a function of luck rather than judgement. Clarity of definition may help to prevent future confusion. It is quite surprising that the definition of such a core constitutional concept has been clouded in confusion for so long.

It is therefore a matter of no small importance whether and how the various definitions of the prerogative can be distilled. That is the purpose of this chapter and part I generally. As we shall see, an accurate definition has real world implications in the context of the case law on third source powers which will be discussed in chapter nine. The point goes deeper, however, because if the prerogative is defined too narrowly, a selection of the powers actually exercised by the

[20] M Elliott and R Thomas, *Public Law*, 4th edn (Oxford University Press, 2020) 173. See also H Fenwick, G Phillipson and A Williams, *Text, Cases and Materials on Public Law and Human Rights*, 4th edn (Routledge, 2017) 474; De Smith and Brazier (n 9) 127; A Bradley, K Ewing and C Knight, *Constitutional and Administrative Law*, 17th edn (Pearson, 2018) 256; A Le Sueur, M Sunkin and J Murkens, *Public Law: Text, Cases and Materials* (Oxford University Press, 2010) 379–80; E Barendt, *An Introduction to Constitutional Law* (Oxford University Press, 1998) 111–12.

[21] I Loveland, *Constitutional Law, Administrative Law and Human Rights: A Critical Introduction*, 5th edn (Oxford University Press, 2009) 92.

[22] N Cox, *The Royal Prerogative and Constitutional Law: A Search for the Quintessence of Executive Power* (Routledge, 2021) 4.

[23] Wade and Forsyth (n 18) at 179 cites *R v Secretary of State for Health, ex parte C* [2000] 1 FLR 27 and *Shrewsbury and Atcham Borough Council v Secretary of State for Communities and Local Government* [2008] EWCA Civ 148, both discussed further in part III.

[24] See further ch 1, pp 4–5. *Miller I* (n 13); *R (Miller) v Prime Minister; Cherry v Advocate General for Scotland* [2019] UKSC 41, [2020] AC 373, [2019] 3 WLR 589, [2019] 4 All ER 299 ('*Miller II*').

executive suddenly appear to be of doubtful origin. The defenders of common law incrementalism have long been eager to expand the reach of common law so as to underpin those other powers. So, for example, the originator of the concept of so-called 'third source' powers or freedoms, Harris, has even suggested that 'common law powers' was an alternative label he had considered.[25] Thus, common lawyers think that there are at most *three* sources of institutional legal authority in the modern constitution: statute, prerogative and common law.

By contrast, this book claims that it is possible to *reconcile* the two classic definitions given by Dicey and Blackstone. Core to this distilled definition is that prerogative continues to play a very substantial role in the modern constitution. Indeed, prerogative provided the original source for, and legal authorisation of, judicial common law of the King's Bench in the first place, through the intertwined prerogatives of administration, peace and justice, but particularly justice.[26]

Structure of Part I

Part I therefore analyses the definitions of the prerogative suggested by Dicey and Blackstone in depth, before also considering Locke's analysis and Wade's alternative and conflicting viewpoint. A view of the prerogative is defended that sees it as an intertwined and connected set of powers originally rooted in the king's role as the feudal lord of the kingdom. The functions of the king included administering his realm, delivering his justice and keeping his peace and these duties particularly included, and naturally extended to, adjudicating on disputes amongst his tenants. The steady expansion, specialisation and derivation of further legal powers necessarily encompassed in good administration constitutes the grounding of all the original prerogatives possessed by the monarch and those remaining prerogative powers now possessed by the Crown, which is defined by that possession.

The remainder of this chapter addresses Dicey's definition in detail before exploring and detailing the early development of prerogative as a function of the monarch's administrative and legal powers necessarily inherent in running the country. From that starting point, it considers whether the legal structure of royal prerogative as analogous to land could lead us to the view that there are different 'estates' of prerogative. Although eventually rejecting this approach, analysing prerogative in terms of different 'estates' opens the way to understanding

[25] B Harris, 'The "Third Source" of Authority for Government Action' (1992) 108 *Law Quarterly Review* 626, fn 5. In a footnote, Harris says he could have labelled them 'common law' powers instead but that would be 'insufficiently precise' because that would include prerogative powers 'in the narrow sense'): ibid at fn 6. The claim that prerogatives are part of the common law is difficult to follow, as argued in ch 1.

[26] See ch 5, pp 92–97.

prerogative power in terms of distinct legislative and executive aspects, both derived from the same legal source.

Chapter three then considers arguably the other classic definition of prerogative that was suggested by Blackstone. It then sets out to demonstrate how Blackstone's and Dicey's definitions may be reconciled. The chapter also highlights some areas where Blackstone's arguments did not fully match the sources he cited in support of his position. When those are considered, it will be suggested that Blackstone was in fact defending a particular common law agenda which has perhaps obscured more than it has illuminated. The chapter then considers the importance and implications of Locke's views on royal prerogative.

Chapter four explores the limits of prerogative power, in particular in relation to the common law, and considers Wade's arguments as to whether prerogative can affect common law. The chapter then explores one area where Dicey went too far in his critique of Blackstone's arguments, arguing instead that Blackstone was correct to say that the power to set up courts was a prerogative power possessed by the Crown, and could be exercised on the advice of the government in the usual way – at least until statutory intervention put that power into abeyance. This leads to chapter five, the last chapter of part I, which considers the modern source of judicial legal authority, arguing that the prerogative of justice has gone into abeyance and the modern courts are now wholly statutory bodies.

Dicey's Definition of Royal Prerogative

Dicey's definition of the royal prerogative is:

> The residue of discretionary or arbitrary authority, which at any given time is legally left in the hands of the Crown.[27]

This definition is arguably the best starting point in considering the concept of royal prerogative as a set of legal powers that are 'legally left in the hands of the Crown'.[28] It has been endorsed at the highest level. In *Miller I*, the UK Supreme Court defined the prerogative in very similar terms:

> The Royal prerogative encompasses the residue of powers which remain vested in the Crown.[29]

Dicey refers in this definition to 'discretionary or arbitrary authority'. Sebastian Payne has pointed out that some prerogatives impose a *duty* on the Crown, such as defence of the realm, and are therefore not 'discretionary or arbitrary' exercises of power.[30] He cites in support of his argument Viscount Radcliffe in *Burmah*

[27] Dicey (n 8) 420.
[28] ibid.
[29] *Miller I* (n 13) [47].
[30] S Payne, 'The Royal Prerogative' in M Sunkin and S Payne, *The Nature of the Crown* (Oxford University Press, 1999) 91.

Oil, who held that 'executive acts of the Crown under the war prerogative ... are conspicuously not discretionary or arbitrary in any typical sense'.[31]

Viscount Radcliffe's implicit critique of Dicey's definition is perhaps a little unfair. As is well known, Dicey had a specific meaning in mind when he used words like 'discretionary' and 'arbitrary'. Dicey is famous for his definition of the rule of law as being connected to the (judicial) common law such that everybody came to the same court and the common law protected rights and prevented arbitrary power. For Dicey, therefore, the attribution of the adjectives 'discretionary or arbitrary' simply referred to the fact that prerogatives were non-justiciable in the courts. It did not mean that the *exercise* of all prerogative power was done in a discretionary or arbitrary manner in a semantic sense. It meant that the exercise of such power was judicially unsupervised and therefore 'discretionary' and arbitrary' in a rule of law sense, not in a despotic way.

This reality undermines Viscount Radcliffe's claim that 'in Dicey's terminology, every executive action not cognisable in a court of law tended to be categorised as arbitrary or irresponsible'.[32] Dicey simply meant by these phrases that the prerogative was not *justiciable*, not that those prerogatives that were non-discretionary (such as those governed by necessity) were not actually prerogatives, as Radcliffe appears, wrongly, to suggest. For Dicey prerogative underpinned all non-statutory legal powers.

It should also be pointed out that Dicey elsewhere defined the prerogative without reference to arbitrary or discretionary authority:

> The prerogative is the name for the remaining portion of the Crown's original authority ... Every act the executive government can lawfully do without the authority of the Act of Parliament is done in virtue of this prerogative.[33]

In many ways this restatement of the Diceyan definition is more satisfactory. It is conceptually clear and simple. It hints at the fact that the 'original authority' of the prerogative power of the Crown was a plenary power when, as Dicey put it, 'the Crown possessed in reality many of the attributes of sovereignty'.[34] This view was also endorsed by the majority in *Miller I*, when they said that 'originally, sovereignty was concentrated in the Crown'.[35] It is therefore no surprise that the original source of legitimate authority of the judiciary, and the source of the validity of court decisions, was that very sovereign power.

Prerogative power is indistinct, overlapping and organic, which reflects the fact that it was originally plenary and sovereign, in the sense of historically possessing something akin to supreme and final legal authority. As Dicey made clear, the pre-Revolution Crown possessed 'many of the attributes of sovereignty' without perhaps being directly comparable or equivalent to the pure and

[31] *Burmah Oil Company (Burma Trading) Ltd v Lord Advocate* [1965] AC 75, 117.
[32] ibid.
[33] Dicey (n 8) 421.
[34] ibid.
[35] *Miller I* (n 13) [41].

untrammelled legal authority possessed by the Crown-in-Parliament in more recent centuries. The sheer importance of prerogative as a formerly plenary power is shown by the extent to which it underpins the development of not only the administrative structures but also the judicial structures of previous times, recalling that the two functions were not sharply distinguished historically.

The Prerogatives of Administration, Peace and Justice

The diffuse yet intertwined nature of the royal prerogative can be usefully illustrated by considering the relationship between the ostensibly distinct prerogatives of administration, peace and justice. In one sense the prerogative power to administer the kingdom is the fundamental prerogative from which all others are derived. It spans executive, judicial and legislative powers. After all, the prerogative power to administer her realm is central to the monarch's 'position as feudal overlord'.[36] From the starting point that the monarch has the prerogative power, in a general sense, to administer the realm, the power to adjudicate on disputes is an inevitable corollary. Michael Foley claims that while the 'formal role' of judges was 'to preserve the integrity of the law, … they were also royal officers engaged in administering the King's justice'.[37]

The prerogative of administering the realm arguably also encompasses not only the prerogative of justice but also the prerogative of keeping the peace because without peace, as Thomas Hobbes famously argues, there is 'no culture … no arts, no letters, no society and … continual fear and danger'.[38] The prerogative of keeping the peace was expressly linked to the extension of the king's jurisdiction by Pollock:

> the King's Peace was enlarged … tending to become the general peace of the kingdom … It was for the king's manifest advantage to widen the bounds of his jurisdiction … the averment of trespass … against the King's Peace … was necessary to give the Superior Court jurisdiction.

The prerogative power of administration of the country through appointing officials to do the actual work on the monarch's behalf was well summarised by Blackstone:

> [T]he king, having the sole administration of the government in his hands, is the best and the only judge, in what capacities, with what qualified to serve, and to act under what distinctions, his people are the best qualified to serve, and to act under him.[39]

The administration of the country, over time, came to be delegated to representatives of the monarch who travelled around the country to do so, eventually

[36] T Poole, *Reason of State: Law, Prerogative, and Empire* (Cambridge University Press, 2015) 22.
[37] M Foley, *The Silence of Constitutions* (Routledge, 2011) 18.
[38] T Hobbes, *Leviathan* [1660], edited by R Tuck (Cambridge University Press, 1991) ch XIII; Poole (n 36) 41.
[39] Blackstone (n 15) Book 1, ch 7, 273.

becoming the circuit judges that we know today but 'ultimate authority was the King's alone'.[40] This slowly came to be seen as an adjudicative rather than administrative function, but it is clear that the prerogative of justice was originally rooted in the ordinary executive administration of the country, itself also a function of prerogative.[41] Pollock quotes Maitland approvingly, who pointed out that 'a distinction between the doing of penal justice and the collection of the king's income is only gradually emerging. The itinerant judge of the twelfth century has much of the commissioner of taxes'.[42]

Classically, applications to the king for relief or a remedy were based on the redress of grievances which was heard personally in his presence. That jurisdiction extended eventually to the power of the highest court, sitting as a parliament, to give judgment beyond any precedent, which eventually morphed into an independent power to legislate. As McIlwain explains, this blurring of the modern distinct functions of executive, judicial and legislative is a feature of historical constitutional discourse, however jarring it may feel today.[43]

Dicey expresses some surprise at the speed with which the prerogative of justice was promulgated by the king's judges throughout the kingdom:[44]

> Any reader of the History of English Law by Pollock and Maitland may well be surprised at the rapidity with which the law of the King's Court became the general or common law of the land.[45]

The law of the king's courts replaced the bewildering variety of law found in the local courts whose authority was derived from regional, and therefore highly variable, local custom. Although there was 'an embarrassing gap between immutable reason and mutable law', as well as a tortuous relationship between 'custom and reason', what remains of customary law was necessarily absorbed by the king's judges into their reasoning.[46] John Austin says that 'till the legislator or judge impress them with the character of law, the custom is nothing more than a rule of positive morality'.[47] Maitland does not consider custom that was not so incorporated as being law at all.[48] The displacement of the local courts by the king's judges created a law *common* to the whole realm, hence (judicial) 'common law'. Thus – and this may be a surprise to modern readers – common law was *royal* law.

[40] J Goldsworthy, *The Sovereignty of Parliament: History and Philosophy* (Clarendon Press, 1999) 27.
[41] See further ch 10, pp 198–200.
[42] F Pollock, 'The King's Peace in the Middle Ages' [1900] vol XIII *Harvard Law Review* 177, 187.
[43] McIlwain (n 13) 164, 166–73, 'On the evidence of words', esp 169.
[44] Dicey (n 8) 378.
[45] Dicey (n 8) 378. 'If we date the organisation of our judicial system from the accession of Henry II, we might say that a great legal revolution was carried through in not much more than a century' (at 379).
[46] G Burgess, *The Politics of the Ancient Constitution* (Palgrave, 1992) 46, 48.
[47] J Austin, *Province of Jurisprudence Determined* (John Murray, 1832), Lecture VI, 421.
[48] Maitland (n 6) 342.

Hearn concurs, pointing out that 'the business of the latter [King's] Court seems to have rapidly increased'.[49] Dicey gives the example of the Privy Council to illustrate the origin and close connection between the Crown and the courts as originally *executive* bodies in his comparison with the French *droit administratif*:

> [T]he 'judgments' of the Privy Council, even when acting through its judicial committee, though in reality judgments, are in form merely humble advice tendered by the Privy Council to the Crown. This form, which is now a mere survival, carries us back to an earlier period of English constitutional history ...[50]

Dicey correctly points out that the development of the prerogative of justice *qua* legal determinations, rather than mere administration, in many ways post-dates the development of other important prerogatives such as foreign affairs, declaration of war and the ownership of property. That is why, as Colin Munro points out, common law judicial decisions 'recognise' prerogative powers, rather than common law being the *source* of prerogative power, as some erroneously claim:[51]

> Strictly speaking the prerogatives are recognised, rather than created, by the common law.[52]

As Dicey explains, the prerogative of justice started as an executive, administrative power of the monarch that over a long period of time was transferred to the king's judges and slowly transformed into an adjudicative function:

> [T]he growth of our whole judicial system may historically be treated as the transference to parts of the King's Council of judicial powers originally exercised by the King in Council ... [with] the exertion, during the earlier periods of English history, by the King's Council, of hardly distinguishable judicial and executive powers.[53]

One might add 'legislative' powers to the list of barely distinguishable powers given that the judicial and legislative functions also historically 'blur together'.[54] Blackstone concurs with the claim that judicial common law is wholly and originally sourced in the monarch and the prerogative of justice, pointing out that 'our kings have delegated their whole judicial power to the judges of their several courts'.[55] This was a slow process, as Jeffrey Goldsworthy notes:

> During the thirteenth and fourteenth centuries ... the barons never attempted to use regular judicial procedures to compel the King to accept their demands ... They knew

[49] Hearn (n 1) 266.

[50] Dicey (n 8) 247.

[51] Harris (n 25) fn 6, relying on Lord Scarman, *Council of Civil Service Unions v Minister for the Civil Service (GCHQ)* [1985] AC 374, 407.

[52] C Munro, *Studies in Constitutional Law*, 2nd edn (Oxford University Press, 1999) 256; Kershaw (n 6).

[53] Munro (n 52) 246–47.

[54] McIlwain (n 13) 126–27, quoting Alston's analysis of the views of Sir Thomas Smith.

[55] Blackstone (n 15), text to fn 90.

> that the common law afforded them no remedy because it was the King's law and judges were his judges.[56]

Hearn asserts that it 'is therefore from the Crown that all jurisdictions in the kingdom emanate' and explains how the judges even as far back as Henry I began the process of 'bringing the authority of the *Curia Regis* within the reach of all parts of the country'.[57] He goes on to detail how under Henry II ordered that the 'justices of the *Curia Regis* … should hear and determine all the writs of the kingdom, not leaving the King's Court but remaining there for that purpose' and that 'an appeal lay from the New Court to the Great Council'.[58]

Hearn further points to the 'register of these writs' that was 'kept in the Chancery, and formed one main foundation of the Common Law in civil cases'.[59] Edward I carried on Henry II's reforms and discontinued the concurrent original jurisdiction of the House of Lords. This was supposed to be merely 'temporary, and not a permanent renunciation of its jurisdiction' but the 'original jurisdiction of that Council was lost by desuetude'.[60] Hearn concludes that the 'Court thus established marks the origin of our present judicial system'.[61] He continues in the same vein:

> In the reign of Edward III, the Court of King's Bench became, like the Common Pleas, stationary; and the organization of our judicial system was complete. Such seems to me to have been the origin of our Common Law Courts. They sprang from the *Magnum Concilium*,[62] the Great National Assembly of England, of which they exercised the authority and by which their judgments were revised.[63]

The modern source of judicial legal authority is rather different and is considered in chapter five.

The Prerogatives of Suspending or Dispensing with the Law, Pardon, Immunity and Peace

Further examples of the blurred boundaries that characterise the royal prerogative abound. One such is the set of legal powers, and legal consequences, that flow from the fact that the monarch remains immune from suit in their own courts. The famous phrase distilling this norm is that 'the king can do no wrong'.[64] It is

[56] Goldsworthy (n 40) 26.
[57] Hearn (n 1) 65 and 266.
[58] ibid 267.
[59] ibid 268.
[60] ibid.
[61] ibid.
[62] Literally: 'Great Council'.
[63] ibid 269, 271.
[64] See further, M-F Fortin, *The King Can Do No Wrong: Constitutional Fundamentals, Common Law History, and Crown Liability* (Oxford University Press, 2024).

difficult to envisage any clearer evidence of the original royal roots of 'common' law than the fact that the Crown remains technically outside the jurisdiction of the ordinary courts.

> [N]o suit or action can be brought against the king, even in civil matters, because no court can have jurisdiction over him …[65]

Even the fact that the monarch has immunity in his or her own courts can be traced back to the original point and purpose of prerogative which is the power to deal with property as the monarch sees fit. It will be recalled that English law traditionally fastens on remedies not on rights. Since the origin of the prerogative of justice was the application for a remedy to the monarch from the tenant, the judicial focus on remedies makes complete sense when understood in this historical context. It is understandable that the monarch would not themselves be subject to the jurisdiction of the courts. Instead, any 'remedy' granted by the monarch would be discretionary and *ex gratia*.

> The King is the vicegerent and minister of God on earth: all are subject to him; and he is subject to none but to God alone.[66]

Indeed, there is even evidence that the inability to secure a remedy against the king might be the origin of the rule that the king can do no wrong. Chitty points out that where there is no remedy, there can be no wrong in the first place:

> The law will presume that the subject cannot have sustained any such personal wrong from the Crown because it cannot afford any adequate remedy: and want of right and want of remedy are the same thing in law.[67]

Many will be familiar with the Latin phrase *ubi ius ibi remedium* which means 'where there is a right, there will be a remedy'. English law has always operated in reverse. Where there is a remedy, only then can there be said to be a right, at least originally.[68] Thus the Latin phrase should probably be reversed in English law: *ubi remedium, ibi ius*. Dicey quotes Mr Justice Stephen with approval, who pointed out that

> the maxim that there is no wrong without a remedy … would be more intelligibly and correctly stated if it were reversed so as to stand 'where there is no legal remedy, there is no legal wrong'.[69]

This demonstrates a highly pragmatic and suitably positivist attitude to the existence of rights at common law. The icing on the cake is the fact that one of the most

[65] Blackstone (n 15) Book 1, ch 7, 242. Blackstone's point applies also to the Crown.
[66] ibid.
[67] J Chitty, *A Treatise on the Law of the Prerogatives of the Crown: And the Relative Duties and Rights of the Subject* (Butterworth, 1820) 340.
[68] The author is grateful to Paul Craig for making the point in correspondence that over time the judiciary developed novel rights without reference to remedies.
[69] Dicey (n 8) 53–54; *Bradlaugh v Gossett* (1884) 12 QBD 271, 285.

important and redolent phrases in English constitutional law – the king can do no wrong – may have also originated in this unique methodological approach exhibited by the common law judges.

Closely connected to the fact that the monarch is immune from suit because the courts are *his* courts, is that he has the power to pardon offenders via the still-available prerogative of pardon and used to have the power to suspend the application of the law – a power put into abeyance by Article I, Bill of Rights 1689. This also must be understood in the context of the fact that the common law courts were the King's courts, and all crime was, and in a way still is, an offence against the King's peace – as Lord Justice Watkins succinctly pointed out in *Bentley*:

> The exercise of mercy by the Crown appears to have become firmly established in the middle ages, with the infringement of the King's peace emerging as the basis for criminal liability. Since major felonies were invariably capital, and pleas to self-defence had not developed, judicial procedure produced inflexible and unsatisfactory results. Use of the prerogative relieved those results.[70]

It will be recalled that to this day prosecutions are brought by, or can be taken over by, the *Crown* Prosecution Service and all criminal cases are currently *labelled* as '*Rex v*' (or, under the previous monarch, '*Regina v*'). Compare, for example, US nomenclature: '*The People v* …'.

This power leads us again to the crucial prerogative of the monarch's duty to keep the peace but this time in general terms, rather than just as underpinning the provision of justice. Blackstone provides one of the clearest pieces of evidence of the existence of this prerogative in the literature. The prerogative of the king's peace is rarely discussed in a purely *domestic* context, instead being mentioned frequently in conjunction with the prerogative of war in the foreign affairs realm.[71] The frankly startling reference in *Northumbria* to the 'scarcity of references in the books to the prerogative of keeping the peace',[72] might usefully be contrasted with the fact that Blackstone and others mentioned this prerogative in some detail. This appears to have been wholly overlooked. In one sense, the whole of criminal law flows from the prerogative of keeping the peace, as Blackstone makes clear:

> All offenses are either against the king's peace, or his crown and dignity; and are so laid in every indictment … all affronts to that power, and breaches of those rights, are immediately offenses against him … He is therefore the proper person to prosecute for all public offenses and breaches of the peace, being the person injured in the eye of the law.[73]

[70] *R v Secretary of State for the Home Department, ex parte Bentley* [1994] QB 349, 357.

[71] *R v Secretary of State for the Home Department, ex parte Northumbria Police Authority* [1989] QB 26, 58.

[72] ibid. Lord Justice Nourse, of course, made clear that there is 'an unspoken assumption' that keeping the peace does in fact exist as a prerogative.

[73] Blackstone (n 15) Book 1, ch 7, 268. See also CK Allen, *Hamlyn lectures: 'The King's Peace'* (Stevens & Sons, 1953) 33.

Pollock pointed out that 'every indictment for a criminal offence' once required the phrasing 'against the peace of our Lady the Queen' in order to be valid.[74] Pollock also explains how when Edward I ascended to the throne, he was abroad 'on the crusade'.[75] The 'king's council' ended the practice that the death of the monarch suspended the law by 'forthwith' causing 'his peace to be proclaimed throughout the kingdom'.[76] It is suggested that this is clear evidence of the foundational nature of the king's peace to the jurisdictional authority of the courts, and their origin in royal prerogative.[77] As Maitland states, the 'idea of law is from the first very closely connected to the idea of peace'.[78]

In the days before the full development of criminal law, and particularly in the context of defences, pardons were a mechanism to secure justice where someone was convicted technically but did not merit the conviction. Pardon did not vacate the conviction but this power to dispense with the effects of the law by obviating the punishment links umbilically to the prerogative of justice. It also only makes real sense if Blackstone's claim that the king is the injured party in all criminal cases is taken seriously. This also demonstrates the close connection between prerogative and land, addressed further below, because the original doctrine of escheat ensured that any offender convicted of a serious offence forfeited their property to the Crown.[79] It was Henry II who persuaded the country that serious crimes were offences against him and needed to be heard in his courts. It is thus not difficult to see how criminal law has its roots in keeping the King's peace.

The overlapping and interwoven nature of the prerogatives of pardon, immunity, dispensing with the law and keeping the King's peace can all be grounded in the basic connection of prerogative with land. If this is accepted, any attempt to carve out a separate non-prerogative, historical source of legitimacy and legal authority for the courts in some undefined alternative source called 'common law' would fail to account for the inescapably intertwined nature of the prerogative of justice with a host of other linked prerogatives.

It is suggested, therefore, that Dicey's definition remains a useful starting point for analysis. This is not least because it is fundamentally accurate, save that he does not express it in wide enough terms because he refers only to powers. Royal prerogative is all the non-statutory residual powers, duties and immunities of the Crown. Anything done on behalf of the Crown without statutory authority is a function of the remaining powers left to the Crown from its ancient, organic and plenary prerogative powers. In the sense of a separate *a priori* alternative

[74] F Pollock, 'The King's Peace' (1885) 1 *Law Quarterly Review* 37.
[75] Pollock (n 42) 185.
[76] ibid.
[77] ibid.
[78] FW Maitland, *The Constitutional History of England: A Course of Lectures* (Cambridge University Press, 1908) 108.
[79] SFC Milsom, *Historical Foundations of the Common Law* (Butterworths, 1969) 355.

source of plenary judicial power and legal authority, 'common law' does not exist. Historically, common law was *royal* law.

Dicey's definition, however, does not go far enough. A residual legal power possessed by the monarch is too vague a definition to deal with some of the modern complexities in the use of the concept, not least as a legal power conferred on the executive and now frequently judicially reviewable. A fresh explanation is necessary, and that requires us to trace some of the history of prerogative and further explore its connection to land.

Estates in Prerogative

The previous section considered the classic Diceyan definition of prerogative. This definition remains, it is suggested, the most useful starting point for the definition of prerogative that is prevalent in modern constitutional discourse. The history of prerogative power is perhaps best understood by returning to its roots as the reciprocal of the 'suit and service' which was the 'duty of attendance at the lord's court, whether it met for administrative or judicial purposes' as well as other core aspects such as military service.[80] These notions were themselves linked to property and the rights of owners of land. Many of the standard, historical, set of prerogatives become easier to understand when contextualised as part of the fundamental importance of *land* in medieval culture, politics and law.

> Land was wealth, livelihood, family provision, and the principal subject-matter of the law. To begin with, moreover, land was also government and the structure of society … Lordship, the Latin *dominium*, is to us an ambiguous word, because to us the concepts of ownership and jurisdiction are distinct … The rights of a great landowner were not over empty land but over the people who worked the land …[81]

The Crown has long had the power to declare war, conduct foreign affairs and diplomacy, defend the realm, requisition property in time of war, raise taxes to fight such wars and make treaties at the end of wars, or otherwise. All these prerogatives were ancillary to the Crown's ultimate stewardship of the realm, a realm which was the personal property of the Crown. Furthermore, all other land is held of the Crown in the sense that all property owners are either joint or common 'tenants' of the Crown.[82] Prerogative and land have always been intertwined. It follows that examining the nature and definition of prerogative inescapably requires consideration of how it relates to land as a matter of legal history.

[80] WS McKechnie, *Magna Carta* (James Maclehose and Sons, 1914) 67.
[81] Milsom (n 79) 88.
[82] *R v Hampden (Ship Money)* (1637) State Trials 825, 1226 per LCJ Finch. Also St John, Counsel for Hampden at 445.

The Prerogative of Justice and the Relationship to Land

The prerogative of justice is umbilically connected to stewardship of land. It is a necessary aspect of being a lord of the manor that the king, *qua* feudal owner, 'dispensed justice among his tenants just as any baron or freeman (landholder) dispensed justice'.[83] This was a core and essential element of administering the realm. This further demonstrates the fundamental, existential connection between prerogative and land. Simpson points out that 'amongst the duties of the feudal lord was the duty to hold a court for his tenants in which their disputes could be determined'.[84] Nor was the power to dispense justice originally limited to the monarch. McKechnie points out that 'practically every holder of land in England came to be also the holder of a court for the inhabitants of that land'.[85] Inevitably, a multiplicity of local, county and other jurisdictions emerged.

Henry II laid in train the reforms to 'convert the County Courts to Royal Courts … and to reduce all manorial or private Courts to insignificance … this policy ultimately met with success'.[86] That success can be seen by virtue of the fact that the full label for the courts in the UK is the '*Royal* Courts of Justice'.[87] The original meaning of a 'court' was the court of the king or lord where he decided how to run his estate. His power to do so was a function of his position as the lord of the manor, which in this case was his kingdom. As Blackstone points out, 'the king is considered in domestic affairs … as the fountain of justice and general conservator of the peace of the kingdom'.[88]

As part of the power to 'hold court', the monarch had the power to administer the realm, dispense with the law, grant pardons, set up new courts, mitigate the effects of the law and appoint servants to run the affairs of state. The original source for the jurisdictional authority of the royal courts of justice was therefore the prerogative of justice. It is suggested that the more recent, but long accepted, aspects of the prerogative slowly developed over time, as the concept of governance changed, such as appointing ministers, approving Bills, granting honours, making *ex gratia* payments, claiming treasure and organising the civil service.[89]

All these prerogative powers are umbilically and inescapably connected to the stewardship of land with the Crown as the ultimate authority responsible for both administration and adjudication. In that sense, the prerogative is best seen as growing from a single source of power but then being refined over time into different, connected, aspects of an overarching administrative power, like

[83] McKechnie (n 80) 80.
[84] AWB Simpson, *A History of Land Law*, 2nd edn (Clarendon Press, 1986) 25.
[85] McKechnie (n 80) 79.
[86] ibid 87.
[87] A Tomkins, *Public Law* (Oxford University Press, 2003) 53. A Tomkins, *Our Republican Constitution* (Hart Publishing, 2005) 120.
[88] Blackstone (n 15) Book 1, ch 7, 266. Allen (n 73) 27–35.
[89] See, for example, *ex parte C* (n 23) on ex gratia payments – also *Council for the Civil Service Unions v Minister for the Civil Service* [1985] AC 374 on the civil service prerogative.

the branches of a tree. This analogy was approved specifically by Dicey, endorsing John Reeves. Dicey said that Reeves' arguments 'undoubtedly rest on a sound basis of historical fact' despite being put on trial at the insistence of the House of Commons:[90]

> Among other statements for the publication of which he was indicted, was a lengthy comparison of the Crown to the trunk, and the other parts of the constitution to the branches and leaves of a great tree. This comparison was made with the object of drawing from it the conclusion that the Crown was the source of all legal power.[91]

Seen through the prism of its original source in the monarch's ownership of land, royal prerogative as the original source of judicial legal authority becomes much easier to understand. For Dicey, then, 'the Crown was the source of all legal power'.[92] It was from that source that judges drew their authority originally.

The delegation to the judges of the king's prerogative to administer justice was, it is suggested, the first example of the effective delegation of legal authority to exercise prerogative power. Originally, the decisions of the courts were treated as mere 'advice' to the Crown.[93] The monarch wielded the actual decision-making power, both legally and politically. Over time, however, it became clear that judges were empowered to grant legally binding and enforceable remedies in cases that came before them. The idea that the delegation of powers under prerogative to judges could eventually transition from administration to adjudication, and therefore be a matter of law, points to the possibility of a different way of now conceiving the modern relationship between the *executive* and the Crown. The latter relationship is currently normally couched in the language of advice, just as judicial pronouncements once were, and Privy Council decisions still are. The seeds of this novel approach germinate from recalling that the judges were originally a species of administrator, like the modern government. This was before their function developed from being executive in nature to become judicial in nature.

Is it Possible to Analyse Prerogatives in Terms of Different Estates?

Legally and structurally, it is suggested that the conceptual architecture of land law could provide one fruitful way to begin to understand the nature of the different interests in prerogative powers in the modern era. This relates in part

[90] Dicey (n 8) 420; J Reeves, *Reeves' History of English Law from the Time of the Romans, to the End of the Reign of Elizabeth* [1603] (Murphy, 1880).

[91] ibid.

[92] ibid.

[93] Although the treatment, to this day, of decisions of the Judicial Committee of the Privy Council as 'advice' to the Crown is perhaps instructive.

to the fact that the critical Cardinal Convention requires that prerogatives are exercised on the advice of the prime minister or Cabinet. It is not really satisfactory for there to be vagueness about the *legal* status of such advice, which there clearly is. Conventions are famously not technically legally binding, nor even legal in nature.[94] Nor is it theoretically clear, frankly, how advice to the monarch can be judicially reviewable in court if its provision is not somehow legal in nature.

Decisions of ministers advising the Crown on the exercise of prerogative powers were historically always immune from judicial review. That is now but a distant memory.[95] On the contrary, it is now clear that only prerogatives that raise issues of the highest policy are intrinsically immune from review.[96] It is unacceptable for the persistence of a fiction that ministerial advice on the use of a prerogative power is exercised purely as a matter of non-legal conventional advice when it is frequently judicially reviewed and, on occasion, quashed. If the advice is not legal in nature, what, exactly, is being quashed as a matter of law if an applicant successfully challenges advice given to the Crown by the government? How can decisions made under the treaty prerogative power be held to be non-justiciable as high (political) policy advice to the Crown in one case, but when such decisions conflict with a statute it immediately becomes a *legal* power that can declared to be *ultra vires* in another?[97] *Ultra vires* means, is defined as, acting outside the *legal* powers available. Advice given in accordance with constitutional convention is non-legal. How is this circle to be squared?

Freehold and Leasehold of Prerogative

The beginnings of the answer to the conundrum posed in the previous subsection requires further consideration of the legal relationship between prerogative and land. Rather than considering early prerogative power as being 'plenary' or 'sovereign' as we might classify near absolute power in modern language, it would probably be more accurate to consider that the king *historically* had unrestricted ownership and possession of prerogative. In a sense, prerogative power was originally a legal attribute or extension of land ownership. Central to this idea is the claim that, like land, there can be different 'estates' in prerogative.[98] In other words, there can be more than one legal bearer of different legal aspects of prerogative power – just like land.

[94] *Attorney-General v Jonathan Cape Ltd* [1976] QB 752, 765.

[95] *Council for the Civil Service Unions v Minister for the Civil Service (GCHQ)* [1985] AC 374.

[96] *Miller II* (n 24); *R v Secretary of State for Foreign and Commonwealth Affairs, ex parte Everett* [1989] QB 811; *R v Criminal Injuries Compensation Board, ex parte Lain* [1967] 2 QB 864.

[97] *R v Secretary of State for Foreign and Commonwealth Affairs, ex parte Rees-Mogg* [1994] QB 552; *Miller I* (n 13).

[98] C Harpum, S, Bridge and M Dixon, *Megarry and Wade: The Law of Real Property*, 8th edn (Sweet & Maxwell, 2019) 3-001.

We can apply this idea immediately to the conferral on judges of the power to grant remedies on behalf of the king. The birth of common law could be said to have occurred when it became clear that the judges had accrued a *legal* power to adjudicate on disputes and grant remedies. At that point, it could be argued, it could be logical to suggest that, purely by analogy, something like the 'freehold' in the prerogative of justice was held by the king and the judges held something like the 'leasehold'. It took a long time for it to be accepted that the monarch had perhaps thereby forfeited the right to sit in judgment in court himself.

On this view, the monarch conferred on the judges a long-term *leasehold* of the prerogative of justice. The judges eventually acquired exclusive rights of possession or, perhaps more accurately in legal reality, they acquired the right to exercise the legal power to adjudicate under the prerogative of justice. Viewing prerogative in this way arguably bolsters the argument that historically prerogative powers held by the Crown were somewhat akin to a freeholder no longer in actual possession of prerogative 'property'. On this view, the 'freehold' in the vast majority of prerogative powers could be said to have slowly but inexorably transferred to, and is now held by, the Crown. The government would hold the 'leasehold'.

Whilst the analogy with freehold and leasehold in land *prima facie* interesting and potentially valuable purely for illustrative purposes, in the end it remains at best only an analogy. This is in part because importing all the intellectual baggage that would come with the use of language from private law would be regressive, not least because shaking off the inappropriate use of private law language in public law has been the work of decades in public law. The analogy is useful, however, in one important sense which is that it demonstrates that there can be more than one type of legal norm derived from the same legal architecture or concept. So, for example, parliament possesses statutory legislative power and confers executive legal powers. Both types of legal norm derive their legitimacy and authority from parliament. This is helpful when we consider an alternative way in which we can divide up prerogative power that has resonance with more familiar public law concepts, which will be discussed below.

Legislative, Executive and Judicial Aspects of Prerogative

Rather than considering prerogative by analogy with the different legal estates in land, a better approach might be that prerogative power has legislative, executive and judicial aspects. This directly answers the conundrum of judicial review of executive decisions under prerogative that is currently poorly served by the language of 'advice' and 'convention'. All public lawyers are familiar and comfortable with the different legal aspects of statutory power. There is a sharp distinction drawn between the legislative aspect of statute, which is the province of parliament, and the executive aspects of statute, which is the province of the government. Parliament is the bearer of legislative powers. The government is the bearer of statutory executive powers conferred by parliament. The neatness of the distinction is illustrated by the differential treatment of the two aspects by the courts. The legislative aspect of statutory power is outside the jurisdiction of the courts. Challenging the legislative authority of a statute rightly remains a judicial taboo.

By contrast, the executive aspect of statutory power is policed by the courts through judicial review. The doctrine of *ultra vires* reinforces the role of the courts in ensuring that the intention of parliament is properly implemented by the government in its exercise of the executive aspect of statutory power. Ironically, the concept of judicial review for *ultra vires* action originates in the principle that the king can do no wrong. Thus executive errors, for which they were personally liable, were the responsibility of ministers acting outside the powers conferred on them.[99]

If provisions of Acts of Parliament can be understood as having both legislative and executive aspects, then it is suggested that royal prerogative can be similarly viewed. Indeed, royal prerogative can be seen, on close inspection, to have not only legislative and executive aspects but also judicial aspects. The bearer of the legislative aspect of prerogative is the Crown. The very fact that prerogative has a legislative aspect arguably explains, by analogy with statute, why the courts have hesitated about extending their jurisdiction to include reviewing the *legislative* aspects of the Crown's prerogatives. This struggle can be seen, paradigmatically, in the case of *Bancoult*.[100] In that case, the UK Government used prerogative power to permanently exclude Chagossians from their island home. It was with barely disguised reluctance that the House of Lords was forced to consider whether the plenary legislative power of the prerogative governing the Chagos Islands was justiciable.

Whilst the panel split on other issues in the case, the House was unanimous in holding that the plenary prerogative was justiciable. The core argument that persuaded Lord Phillips to reach this conclusion was that prerogative powers did not have the same level of democratic and representative mandate possessed by statutory powers granted by parliament to the government. He pointed out that even though the prerogative 'Orders in Council in certain important respects resemble Acts of Parliament', a crucial difference was the 'unique authority Parliament derives from its representative character'.[101] Importantly, he pointed out that an 'exercise of the prerogative lacks this quality; although it may be legislative in character, it is still an exercise of power by the executive alone'.[102]

[99] De Smith and Brazier (n 9) 134.
[100] *R (Bancoult) v Secretary of State for Foreign & Commonwealth Affairs* [2008] UKHL 61, [2009] AC 453.
[101] ibid [34].
[102] ibid.

The distinction drawn by Lord Phillips is important. Although the plenary power in relation to ceded colonies is technically legislative in nature, the fact that it was exercised by the executive alone, not by parliament, means that it was *treated* as effectively an exercise of executive power in this case. There are other examples of quasi-legislative powers being conferred on the executive in the modern constitution, but by parliament. Known as secondary legislation, they are controversial. They are also judicially reviewable.[103] Nonetheless, this case is perhaps somewhat challenging for the claim made in this book that the Crown – defined by its legislative prerogative powers – remains outside the jurisdiction of the courts. Perhaps it would be better to treat this example as effectively the exercise of *secondary* legislative prerogative powers by the executive.

It may be that this case must be confined to its facts due to the very unusual situation of being forced to address the mechanics of a prerogative that operates wholly outside the boundaries of the United Kingdom. It is therefore doubtful whether the case genuinely undermines the arguments as to the status of the legislative aspect of prerogative in domestic law and for the Crown as the bearer of that legislative power. In any event, given that the legislative aspects of prerogative in the domestic sphere are fixed and residual, rather than plenary as in *Bancoult*, it is questionable how relevant judicial review of the legislative aspect of prerogative could ever be in the future.

Some of the difficulties in classifying legislative and executive aspects of prerogative were perhaps illustrated in a fascinating section of Lord Rodgers' judgment in *Bancoult* where he points out that the applicant could have brought an action in the Scottish courts instead of the English courts.[104] This was precisely due to the 'wholly different pre-existing law and procedures in England and Scotland' in relation to the Crown.[105] As Tomkins points out, Lord Jauncey made clear that 'actions could be brought as of right in Scotland, whereas in England it was necessary to proceed by petition of right'.[106] The fact that Lord Rodgers felt forced to reference the possibility of an action being brought in the Scottish courts might be thought to illustrate the level of judicial discomfort with the judicial intervention in this case as a matter English law.

It is therefore suggested that it would be useful to draw a distinction between the executive and legislative aspects of prerogative power. The former are conferred on ministers, and the latter, for all intents and purposes, remain outside the jurisdiction of the courts and are technically possessed by the Crown, which also sits outside the jurisdiction of the courts. Prerogative powers cannot be expanded.[107] The legislative aspect of prerogative is akin to a set of statutory

[103] See further, the Donoughmore Committee, Report of the Committee on Ministers' Powers, Cmd 4060/1932.

[104] ibid [106].

[105] A Tomkins, 'Crown Proceedings, Remedies and Liability of the Crown' in A McHarg and T Mullen (eds), *Public Law in Scotland* (Avizandum Publishing, 2006) 275.

[106] *British Medical Association v Greater Glasgow Health Board* 1989 SC (JL) 65, 94.

[107] *BBC v Johns* [1965] Ch 32, 79, per Diplock LJ.

powers that are historically fixed. This flows logically from the claim that parliament in effect *adopted* the remaining prerogative powers centuries ago.

If this model is accepted, then it is much easier to comprehend how judicial review can be brought against the exercise of those executive prerogative powers that are not 'high policy'. 'High policy' prerogatives remain inherently non-justiciable.[108] For justiciable prerogatives, on the other hand, the aspect of prerogative power exercised by the executive is revealed to be a *legal* power, conferred by the Crown. It is not helpful to describe the exercise of judicially reviewable executive power conferred by the Crown on the government as 'advice' in some unexplained non-legal sense. It is not 'advice'. It is a legal power.

In summary, then, Dicey's definition of the prerogative as encompassing all non-statutory powers of the Crown remains by some distance the most useful and descriptively accurate starting point in analysing the royal prerogative, although a fuller definition would also encompass duties, immunities and privileges of the Crown. Dicey's definition must therefore be adjusted slightly to include these aspects. Relatedly, but slightly downstream of this broad approach, the advent of judicial review of the government in exercising legal powers under prerogative is best explained by discarding the language of non-legal 'advice' and embracing the idea that the conferral by the Crown of executive prerogative powers on the executive is now reviewable unless the issue is one of high policy.[109] The next chapter will consider the important alternative definition proffered by Blackstone and how that can be reconciled with Dicey's definition and how Locke's insights affect the meaning and operation of royal prerogative.

[108] *Everett* (n 96).
[109] ibid.

3

Refining the Definition of Prerogative

Introduction

The two most popular definitions of prerogative given by Dicey and Blackstone are frequently thought to be in conflict. This book argues, in contrast, that they are entirely reconcilable. In short, this is because prerogative is both the residue of the plenary power once held by the monarch as well as a set of powers held exclusively by the Crown today. The previous chapter addressed Dicey's definition.[1] The definition given by Blackstone is the focus of the first section of this chapter. The latter sections address the definitional contribution made by Locke in relation to the use of prerogative in extremis.

Blackstone's Definition of the Royal Prerogative

Blackstone gave a much cited alternative definition of the royal prerogative:[2]

> By the word prerogative we usually understand that special pre-eminence, which the king hath, over and above all other persons, and out of the ordinary course of the common law, in right of his regal dignity. It signifies, in its etymology, (from prae [before] and rogo [I ask]) something that is required or demanded before, or in preference to, all others. And hence it follows, that it must be in its nature singular and eccentrical; that it can only be applied to those rights and capacities which the king enjoys alone, in contradistinction to others, and not to those which he enjoys in common with any of his subjects: for if once any one prerogative of the crown could be held in common with the subject, it would cease to be prerogative any longer. And therefore Finch lays it down as a maxim, that the prerogative is that law in case of the king, which is law in no case of the subject.

In the modern era, Wade has argued that Blackstone's seemingly narrower definition of the prerogative is more apposite than Dicey's broader definition, which grounds all governmental exercise of non-statutory powers ultimately in prerogative. Wade claimed, correctly, that a true prerogative must be exclusive to the

[1] AV Dicey, *Introduction to the Study of the Law of the Constitution*, 8th edn (Macmillan, 1927) 421.
[2] W Blackstone, *Commentaries on the Laws of England* (1753) Book 1, ch 7, 239.

Crown.[3] Where Wade went wrong – and this is addressed in later chapters of this book – is in thinking that prerogative powers being exclusive to the Crown was in any sense in conflict with Dicey's definition. Reconciling Blackstone and Dicey's definitions is the work of this chapter and the next.

Blackstone and the Common Law

Blackstone's definition is fundamentally informed by his position as a leading defender of the common law view of the constitution. The traditional view, defended in this book, is that originally the king was 'the fountain of justice'.[4] The monarch's judges imposed his royal law and made it common to the land, hence the label 'common law'. Common law, in fact royal law, was derivative of, and subordinate to, the monarch. The subordination of law to the monarch is the reason why one of the prerogatives of the Crown is, and to an extent remains, the Crown's immunity in the courts. The common law view, led by Blackstone, inverts the traditional approach. Instead of the monarch being the fountain of justice from whom all law is derived, the common law is treated as being the *starting point* of the discussion, with the remainder of law subordinate to it or in some sense drawn from it. As an analysis of how English law arrived in its modern state, this view is mistaken.

The definition given by Blackstone is strongly redolent of the novel approach promulgated by the common law narrative. This is hardly surprising given Blackstone's life-long hagiographical, indeed almost mystical, stance towards the common law. The first sentence of his definition above gives the erroneous impression that the common law is 'the ordinary course', as in the *default* source of law, and makes the prerogative exceptional. The framing of prerogative and common law in this way is entirely at odds with the way the law appears in fact to have developed. Most crucially, it denies the label of prerogative to any power possessed by the Crown where there happens to be a similar legal power held by 'subjects' of the Crown that looks analogous. Blackstone cites no case law in support of this startling claim, but instead quotes 'Finch' as authority, an issue addressed further below.

Blackstone is entirely correct to point out that the prerogative is a 'special pre-eminence'. Indeed, the king was the fountain of justice and law so the other legal powers the monarch possessed are hierarchically superior to judicial common law. They are 'out of the ordinary course of the common law' only in that sense.[5]

[3] W Wade, 'The Crown, Ministers and Officials: Legal Status and Liability' in M Sunkin and S Payne, *The Nature of the Crown: A Legal and Political Analysis* (Oxford University Press, 1999) 24, 30.

[4] Per Lord Jones, *Ship Money (R v Hampden)* (1637) State Trials 825 at 1184: 'we are the [the king's] judges deputed, but our judgment flows from him. Judgment is settled in the king, he is the fountain of justice, from whence all other proceeds'.

[5] Blackstone (n 2).

As Blackstone states, royal prerogative is, in a sense, 'demanded before' and 'in preference to' all common law legal powers.[6] These two claims are also relatively uncontroversial if they simply mean that prerogative powers are distinct from the common law, which they are.

One less controversial matter can be dealt with quickly. If Blackstone meant by 'singular and eccentrical' that the prerogative is a unique set of special powers, then that is entirely correct. It certainly does not follow that a prerogative 'in its nature' must be 'singular and eccentrical', if that is taken to mean prerogative is a series of *individuated* powers, and it would be a stretch to try to interpret Blackstone that way. On the contrary, the prerogative was originally a *plenary* set of powers that have been slowly and painstakingly eroded over centuries by various constitutional settlements and the actions of particular individuals such as Sir Edward Coke, whose vision sometimes outpaced the actual legal rules.[7]

The relationship between prerogative and judicial common law has been dynamic and contested for centuries. One can but admire the subtlety of the significant intellectual move from the historic reality that the Crown is the original source of all law, to the erroneous view that the default legal starting point is 'common law' from which apparently the Crown derives its authority in some unexplained way. The shift is reasonably easy to see, but only once the highly questionable inversion of the historic relationship between the Crown and common law is noted and rejected.

The Origin of Common Law Rights of Subjects

As we have seen, the common law derives from the royal prerogative of justice. This has important implications for the source of jurisdictional authority of the courts.[8] The fact that the Crown could set up courts using the royal prerogative of justice was confirmed by the Lord Chief Justice in *ex parte Lain*:

> Indeed, the writ of certiorari has issued not only to courts set up by statute but to courts whose authority is derived, inter alia, from the prerogative.[9]

This may also be briefly illustrated by considering one of the themes of part I, which is the concept of land. Brian Simpson points out that but for two crucial concepts, 'there could have been no common law as we know it'.[10] The first 'is the idea that in some sense, all free tenants were the King's tenants'.[11] This flowed from

[6] ibid.

[7] See further M Loughlin, *Foundations of Public Law* (Oxford University Press, 2010) 376. See also J Goldsworthy, *The Sovereignty of Parliament: History and Philosophy* (Clarendon Press, 1999) 111–17 and 122–23 discussing difficulties with Coke's arguments; G Burgess, *The Politics of the Ancient Constitution* (Palgrave, 1992) 30 and 58.

[8] Addressed further in ch 5.

[9] *R v Criminal Injuries Compensation Board, ex parte Lain* [1967] 2 QB 864, 881.

[10] AWB Simpson, *A History of Land Law*, 2nd edn (Clarendon Press, 1986) 25.

[11] ibid 26.

the oath taken by all land-owning men in 1086 by which they became his men 'even against their own lords'.[12] The second, argues Simpson, is that the 'king is the fount of all justice'.[13] This meant that cases against a lord could be moved to the king's court by subjects if the lord 'will not do them justice'. Simpson goes on to say that the consequent 'rise of the royal common law of land … started as a mere system of royal judicial review … [but] became a take-over'.[14]

The (royal) common law courts therefore *extended* a series of property rights, and indeed obligations, which were, in a sense, held solely by the king, to freeholders – those who owned land. Simpson says that it was the 'invention of the common law … [that] produced … the invention of proprietary rights in land'.[15] The source and origin of those rights was the royal prerogative of justice. Indeed, it could be argued that whatever rights were conferred on the king's subjects were parasitic on, or derived from, the original rights and obligations of the Crown as to property.

The slow generation and creation of property rights for everyone other than the Crown in no way diminishes the fact that the original possessor of rights and obligations related to land was the Crown itself. As those rights were shared, replicated or adapted by the judges and conferred on subjects, those subjects acquired new legal rights. They acquired those rights from the Crown, indirectly, through the royal judges. They did not derive them from any transcendental 'Common Law'. The conferral of 'shadow' or parasitic property rights on subjects by the Crown's judges was just the beginning.

As the royal courts extended their jurisdiction, they slowly developed the law in other areas such as contract and 'uses', which became trusts. Eventually this extended throughout other areas we recognise today, from tort law to restitution and even constitutional law. The Crown's original and umbilical relationship with land exists without needing the permission of the judges or the conferral of any rights on the Crown by them. Ordinary citizens can make contracts and buy property because, in part, the king conferred such legal powers on ordinary people through his courts. As derivative legal powers reverse engineered from writ-based applications for remedies, they are not the *same* legal powers as prerogative powers. Furthermore, as part II will argue, the powers of Crown *servants* to make contracts and buy and sell property operate in *public*, not private law, while the analogue power of ordinary citizens to do these things operates in private law.

It is often argued, as Dicey points out, that modern public law was derived, in a sense, from private law. The better historical view is that all law was really *public* law before the split between public and private law as we understand it today. Royal common law started as an application to the king for a remedy via writ. That was 'public law' in all relevant senses in this discussion because it was overtly

[12] ibid.
[13] ibid.
[14] ibid 36.
[15] ibid 37.

an exercise of public power at the behest of the monarch or the monarch's judicial servants. It then slowly settled into a set of 'private' law rights before the third phase of developing modern 'public law' (especially the rise of judicial review) occurred for the most part in the second half of the twentieth century.

The power of the contrary and erroneous common law narrative is such that the proposition can be taken seriously – as literally and legally true – that legal powers of the Crown in relation to land (or otherwise) are conferred or derived *from the courts at common law*, a notion that is wholly ahistorical. Instead, the power to deal with property is the *progenitor* of the prerogative of justice and therefore judicial common law, because dispensing justice was an aspect of feudal lordship over land.

Blackstone claims that 'rights and capacities' of the Crown are not 'any longer' prerogative in nature if the king 'enjoys [them] in common with any of his subjects'. It is true that the king could sue, but not be sued. Furthermore, he had numerous litigation advantages including that time did not run against him and he could sue in any court.[16] The position of the king in his personal, private capacity is outside the scope of this work, and must be distinguished from the Crown, which cannot sue or be sued directly.[17] Nonetheless, to interpret Blackstone as suggesting that the Crown shares legal powers with subjects would be to misstate the very roots, basis and history of justice in English law.

Blackstone claims that 'once any one prerogative of the crown could be held in common with the subject, it would cease to be a prerogative any longer'. This is a confusing line by Blackstone because ordinary people do not hold any prerogative powers. It is therefore difficult to see how a prerogative of the Crown could ever 'be held in common with the subject'. The unique status and immunity of the Crown can even be seen in the very structure of judicial review proceedings. This further illustrates the distinction between the Crown and ministers. In judicial review, the Crown formally brings the action against the minister on behalf of the applicant. This incidentally conclusively demonstrates that the Crown in some sense has a legal capacity distinct from ministers/departments. The relationship between the latter and the Crown remains governed by prerogative. It also demonstrates that the structure of English law is rooted in the application for remedies from the Crown. The absurdity, or 'incongruity' of conflating the Crown and ministers acting in their official capacity was well illustrated by Lord Denman CJ, who was quoted in *M v Home Office*:

> The prerogative remedies could not be obtained against the Crown directly … because there would be an incongruity in the Queen commanding herself to do an act, …

Novel legal rights generated by courts and conferred on subjects are therefore simply derivative legal rights whose creation was implicitly licensed by the

[16] J Chitty, *A Treatise on the Law of the Prerogatives of the Crown: And the Relative Duties and Rights of the Subject* (Butterworth, 1820) 244–45.

[17] The Crown Proceedings Act 1947 is considered in ch 8.

monarch for the smooth running of the legal system as it develops over time. In a sense, the monarch started the process and let it run on. The *Crown's* exercise of any legal powers it possesses is always an exercise of prerogative because the monarch's historical legal rights and powers predate the justice system in any event. It follows that Dicey was completely correct to point out that *any* legal power possessed by the Crown that is not based on statute is a prerogative power of the Crown and that remains the case to this day.

Derivative rights held by ordinary citizens at common law are enforceable in the common law courts by judges whose original source of legal authority was the royal prerogative of justice. Blackstone is right to note that all powers exercised by the Crown are 'out of the ordinary course of the common law'. That is because they are prerogative in nature. As we shall see in part II, ministers may exercise common law powers, once appointed under prerogative, but ministers are clearly distinct from the Crown, not least because they are personally liable. The relationship between ministers and the Crown is governed by prerogative. Once disaggregated in this way, the relevant legal relationships are not complex. It follows that Dicey and Blackstone are both correct.

Which the King Enjoys Alone

Blackstone only cites one source for his claim that the prerogative cannot include legal powers of the king that are held 'in common with' ordinary citizens. The source cited by Blackstone is 'Finch, L. 85' which is less than helpful for anyone who wants to check this source.[18] Wade suggests a solution to the minor puzzle of Blackstone's source, stating that 'Blackstone then quotes *Chief Justice* Finch' (emphasis added), and in the footnote Wade cites 'Finch, Law, 85'.[19] The most (and perhaps only) famous pronouncement of Chief Justice Finch is his explosive judgment in the *Ship Money* case.[20]

The argument that Blackstone meant Chief Justice Finch in the *Ship Money* case might be thought to be bolstered by the fact that there are further references made to 'Finch' in the same chapter of Blackstone that could correlate with parts of Chief Justice Finch's *Ship Money* judgment. So, for example, the reference to 'who shall command the king' in Blackstone can be cross-referred to where Chief Justice Finch says 'none other can share with him in his absolute power'.[21] Another example is where Blackstone says that where an heir is attainted of treason, ascension to the throne 'would purge the attainder' – Chief Justice Finch says that Acts

[18] Blackstone (n 2) 239. The same reference can also be seen in the Project Gutenberg version available free online: www.gutenberg.org/files/30802/30802-h/30802-h.htm.

[19] HWR Wade, 'Procedure and Prerogative in Public Law' (1985) 101 *Law Quarterly Review* 180, 191.

[20] *R v Hampden (Ship Money)* (1637) *State Trials* 825, 1215–43.

[21] ibid 1226; Blackstone (n 2) 242.

'cannot bar a succession nor can [the king's powers] be attainted by them … no Act of Parliament can bar a king of his regality'.[22]

One searches the remainder of Finch's judgment in vain for any reference to the claim that the prerogative must be exclusive to the Crown and not shared with others. Further investigation into who exactly is Blackstone's 'Finch' is therefore necessary. A little historical digging reveals that there was a no less important Sir Henry Finch who was the *father* of Chief Justice Finch. Finch senior wrote a well-regarded legal treatise published in the early seventeenth century entitled '*Nomotexnia*'. In another version of Blackstone's chapter found by this author, the first reference to Finch's work states that the title is "*Law; or a Discourse thereof* which not an unreasonable translation of '*Nomotexnia*'.[23]

The Sources of Blackstone's Definition

Sir Henry Finch

It seems then that Wade may have latched onto the wrong source and Blackstone was referring not to *Chief Justice* Finch who decided *Ship Money* in 1638, but instead to *Sir Henry* Finch, whose legal treatise on English law in four parts was published in 1613. The passages referred to by Blackstone are in Book Two. The other references correlate well with the extracts cited by Blackstone in his chapter. It is unsurprising that Blackstone relied on this source because on reading his work, it is immediately clear that Sir Henry Finch is a dyed-in-the-wool defender of common law. This is an important factor to bear in mind when considering his arguments because, as we shall see, his common law bias skews his analysis.

The crucial passage from *Nomotexnia* is on the nature of the prerogative and merits full exposition, especially as Wade did not appear to know or have referred to the correct source.

> But in them all it must be remembered, that the king's prerogative stretcheth not to the doing of any wrong; for it groweth wholly from the reason of the common law, and is as it were a finger of that hand, although is much differing in fashion (as the head and the body can never be of one proportion) that if you set them in parallels together, you shall find it to be law almost in every case of the king, that is law in no case of a subject, and yet for all that they are not two, but one law: only the common law is as the *primum mobile*, which draws all the planets in their contrary course.[24] (Underlined emphasis added)

[22] ibid 1235.

[23] W Blackstone, *Commentaries on the Laws of England* (1765–9), reprinted in in G Jones, *The Sovereignty of the Law* (Macmillan Press, 1973) 91.

[24] H Finch, Book Two of *Nomotexnia* (1613) 85.

Sir Henry Finch's view of the prerogative raises a number of issues. The first and by far the most serious issue, is that Blackstone has *misquoted* Finch, seemingly for his own purposes. Blackstone claimed that

> Finch lays it down as a maxim, that the prerogative is that law in case of the king, which is law in no case of the subject.[25]

However, Finch did not say that. Finch said that 'you shall find it to be law *almost* in every case of the king, that is law in no case of a subject' (emphasis added).

The most important aspect of the word 'almost' in that sentence is that it is an entirely understandable gloss on the prerogative at the time it was written when almost all judges and commentators adopted a pose of exaggerated respect for the majesty of the king and the inappropriateness of interfering in his affairs, including his prerogative powers. This can be seen, for example, where Chief Justice Finch (Sir Henry Finch's son) in the *Ship Money* case a generation later protests at the vulgarity of being forced to pry into issues surrounding the prerogative of the king:

> [Y]et I may say, such a ravelling and diving into the king's revenue, and secret estate of princes, and what succeeding kings may be, or may do, it doth not well become these present times … but our example, I hope, shall be a bar hereafter, and our care shall be to prevent it.[26]

No less important than the attitude of contemporary commentators and judges to the prerogative are the implications for Blackstone's argument. It is perfectly understandable for Sir Henry Finch to be taken to treat as of minor importance those prerogative powers where the judges have developed parallel or analogous legal remedies for ordinary people in the common law courts. Far more important for a commentator such as Finch would be the regal prerogatives such as foreign affairs, defence of the realm and other such matters of high policy. If this is accepted, then Blackstone's decision to omit the 'almost' from the quotation becomes even more questionable. The source that he cites for his claim, Finch, appears to admit that prerogatives are indeed exclusive to the monarch, that only he can exercise them, and that they are not shared with ordinary people because they are as different as 'the head and the body'.

Finch also admits (because of the 'almost') that there are equally examples of prerogative powers that are analogous with, but clearly distinct from, the ordinary legal powers and rights in judicial common law that are available to citizens. Finch acknowledges that prerogative and common law run 'in parallels together'. One example would be making *ex gratia* payments of public money and the parallel (but wholly distinct) power of citizens to give away their own money, discussed further in part II. So prerogative and common law are wholly distinct, even where there are parallels between them on occasion. It is suggested in part II that it would

[25] Blackstone (n 2) 239. As it happens, Goldsworthy mentions another, comparatively trivial example of poor practice (Goldsworthy (n 7) 181).

[26] *Ship Money* (n 20) 122.

be a serious mistake to equate *ex gratia* payments with anything that ordinary people can do.

A further example would be the king's personal immunity from suit. This example must first recognise the highly complex relationship, but nevertheless 'distinct capacities', of the king and the Crown.[27] The Crown cannot sue or be sued. Nonetheless, and perhaps in parallel with ordinary citizens, the king in body natural could *bring* actions against others, and Chitty sets out his special evidential privileges in doing so.[28] The king could not and cannot be sued, however, and that shows how distinct the king was (and still is) from everyone else. Jurisdictionally, therefore, such actions in a sense ran 'in parallel' to ordinary common law actions. There are no legal powers 'held in common'.[29]

Far from supporting Blackstone's claim that prerogative legal powers that are analogous with common law 'would cease to be a prerogative any longer', Finch inadvertently seems to confirm the view that prerogative powers with common law equivalents or analogies are *still prerogative powers*. This is also a problem for Wade, addressed in chapter seven. It might also be argued that Finch is implicitly admitting that prerogative is 'senior' to common law powers because the 'head' is obviously more important than the 'body', notwithstanding his brazen attempt to refashion, even reconstitute, the relationship between prerogative and common law in favour of the latter. Finch is clearly, therefore, a strong defender of the common law narrative, which persists to this day. Further evidence for this lies in his claim that the king's prerogative 'stretcheth not' to doing any wrong. This is some distance from the original idea that the king himself could *do* no wrong. It should be mentioned, to be clear, that the latter concept was a valuable innovation and had the happy consequence of generating ministerial responsibility.

Incidentally, Finch is simply wrong to claim that the prerogative 'groweth wholly from the reason of the common law'. The opposite was the case. The common law, to coin a phrase, groweth wholly from the royal prerogative of justice. As Lord Crawley put it, 'The first regal prerogative is this, that containeth all the rest: That the king may give laws to his subjects'.[30] Finch also claims that the 'common law is *primum mobile* [first mover]' such that all other law is in its orbit. This is not only highly revealing of his common law mentality but also flatly inconsistent with Lord Crawley in *Ship Money* who states unequivocally that 'the king is the first mover'.[31] Crawley even uses the same planetary analogy to say the exact opposite to Finch thus perhaps demonstrating the common law bias of the latter: 'the prime mover is the king. It is observed that every planet but one hath a little orb by itself that moveth in its petty compass … the king is the first mover.'[32]

[27] E Kantorowicz, *The King's Two Bodies: A Study in Mediaeval Political Theology* (Princeton University Press, 1957) 12, 344, 358.

[28] Chitty (n 16) Chs XII and XIV.

[29] Blackstone (n 2).

[30] *Ship Money* (n 20) 1083 (a colon replacing a comma for sense).

[31] ibid.

[32] ibid.

Lord Berkeley also said that 'I never read nor heard that Lex is Rex; but it is common and most true that Rex is Lex'.[33] Finch further argues that prerogative and ordinary law are 'not two but one law'.[34] Perhaps ironically, this is correct in one sense but the actualité, with which Finch is somewhat economical, is the opposite of his view that the common law is the '*primum mobile* which draws all the planets'. Chapter five discusses in more depth the claim that the king was in fact the first mover through his prerogative of justice. He was originally the source of the common law, not the other way round. Despite these errors, Finch's work remains useful not just as the butchered source of Blackstone's definition. It is also useful because of his admission that the Crown's prerogative can still be a prerogative even where it is analogous with an ordinary judicial common law power. A close examination of his contribution is also helpful because it would seem to strengthen the claim that the Crown only possesses prerogative powers.

'I Never Read or Heard that Lex was Rex; but it is Common and Most True that Rex is Lex'[35]

In the modern world there is no doubt that 'Lex is Rex'. The rule of law constituted by the absolute supremacy of Acts of Parliament as well as the domestic enforceability of court orders is widely accepted in the modern constitution, even if the President of the Supreme Court was recently sufficiently moved to feel it necessary to reiterate that the 'mutual trust' between the government and the courts 'depends on the Government's compliance with court orders' as 'one of the core principles of our constitution'.[36] Lord Berkley's claim in *Ship Money* that he had 'never read or heard the Lex was Rex' is therefore wholly jarring to modern ears. So jarring, perhaps, that some contemporary modern scholars have gone to some trouble to attempt to locate an alternative narrative in seventeenth century case law.

Paul Craig is a leading example.[37] He has argued that 'the two central seventeenth-century authorities were both the work of Coke: *Prohibitions del Roy* ('*Prohibitions*') and the *Case of Proclamations* ('*Proclamations*').[38] He also argues that the courts consistently defended parliament against the monarch claiming that 'the principal beneficiary of the court's judgment [in *Prohibitions*] was, of

[33] ibid 1098.

[34] Finch (n 24).

[35] *R v Hampden (Ship Money)* (1637) State Trials 825, 1098, per Lord Berkley.

[36] *Craig v Her Majesty's Advocate (for the Government of the United States of America)* [2022] UKSC 6, [46], per Lord Reed.

[37] P Craig, 'Prerogative, Precedent and Power' in C Forsyth and I Hare (eds), *The Golden Metwand and the Crooked Cord: Essays in Honour of William Wade QC* (Oxford University Press, 1998) 65.

[38] ibid (1607) 12 Co Rep 63, (1611) 12 Co Rep 74.

course, Parliament' although he fairly concedes that 'it should not be thought … that Parliament always emerged victorious from the court-room'.[39]

Proclamations concerned two royal proclamations: the first was in relation to the construction of new buildings in London and the second related the production of starch from wheat. *Prohibitions* related to a jurisdictional turf war between the common law and ecclesiastical courts. The then Archbishop Bancroft sought the intervention of the King to resolve the dispute because 'the Judges are but the delegates of the King' so he claimed that the King could take on 'what causes he shall please … and may determine them himself'.[40] It would be a mistake to pass over Coke's summary of the submissions made by counsel for Bancroft in his note of the case because it is highly revealing. Coke famously claimed in his report of the case, not published for decades, that he told the king to his face that he was insufficiently expert to intervene. Alan Cromartie plausibly, and perhaps too mildly, suggests that Coke may have 'exaggerated somewhat'.[41] What is remarkable is the fact that the proposition that the King could still intervene *in extremis* was clearly legally tenable, because it was reported by Coke as having been argued by counsel in front of him, as late as the seventeenth century. Indeed, that this was still legally conceivable is confirmed by Lord Crawley, decades later, who held that one of the prerogatives, which he sets out in a list, is 'that the last appeal be to the king'.[42]

It might be thought that intervening to resolve *jurisdictional* disputes might be the one area where a residual power could have made sense, perhaps. Indeed that might be the very aspect of the prerogative of justice that counsel for Bancroft could be understood as referencing, although that is admittedly speculative. Such speculation is arguably bolstered by a House of Commons Briefing Note in 2017.[43]

> Moreover certain royal functions could be exercised only in certain ways. The common law courts were the King's courts and only through them could the King decide questions of title to land and punish felonies. Yet the King possessed a residual power of administering justice through his Council where the courts of common law were insufficient.

Dicey goes further, although he freely acknowledges the importance of the outcome:

> [N]othing can be more pedantic, nothing more artificial, nothing more unhistorical than the reasoning by which Coke induced or compelled James to forego the attempt to withdraw cases from the Courts for his Majesty's personal determination.[44]

[39] P Craig (n 37) 68–69.
[40] *Prohibitions* (1607) (n 38).
[41] A Cromartie, *The Constitutionalist Revolution* (Cambridge University Press, 2006) 211.
[42] *Ship Money* (n 20) 1083.
[43] G Bartlett and M Everett, 'The Royal Prerogative' Briefing Paper No 03861, House of Commons Library (17 August 2017) 5.3. See also D Torrance, 'The royal prerogative and ministerial advice', Briefing Paper CBP9877, 8 July 2024.
[44] Dicey (n 1) 18.

Nonetheless the possibility of actual regal intervention to resolve a dispute over jurisdiction seems to have become less conceivable through the seventeenth century. This was perhaps evidenced by Lord Coke's continuing turf wars with the ecclesiastical courts throughout his career. There were no less bitter battles with Lord Chancellor Ellesmere (which Coke and the King's Bench lost) and a number of 'other vessels of the king's authority'.[45] These were not resolved by the king intervening judicially.

Paul Craig's claim as to the perceived importance of the *Proclamations* case may be doubted. David Kershaw wryly notes that 'modern courts treat Coke's position "as the most respected of our authorities" – although it took 366 years to obtain its first citation'.[46] It certainly was not cited in *Ship Money*. Hearn points out that there 'can be little doubt that the King once exercised in person his judicial will'.[47] He gives examples of Henry III 'especially in the Exchequer' and even Edward IV 'in the latter part of the fifteenth century'. He does, however, caveat these examples by saying 'they were probably rather of an executive than of a judicial nature'. This point has rather less force than might first appear as it will be recalled that the sharp boundary we now draw between executive and judicial was rather less clear in previous centuries. Hobbes is considerably more critical of Coke, claiming that he deliberately et out to 'diminish, as he endeavours to do throughout his Institutes, the King's authority, or to insinuate his own opinions among the people for the law of the land'.[48]

Paul Craig's analysis has been criticised by Tomkins.[49] Tomkins claims that *Ship Money* and other constitutional cases that peppered the decade leading up to the Civil War were 'of the highest constitutional significance'. Thomas Poole is also sceptical of the importance of *Prohibitions* and *Proclamations*. He says that the two cases were 'dwarfed by other prerogative case of the period', although they were 'by no means insignificant', which is faint praise indeed. Poole even goes so far as to point out that *Proclamations* 'was more of a legal consultation than a judgement' and that '*Prohibitions* was even less of a real case than *Proclamations*'. He also points out that 'the judicial opinion [in *Proclamations*] seems to have had very little impact on subsequent practice'.[50] In other words the king carried on issuing proclamations notwithstanding Coke's claim that he had held that they were illegal. Doubts over Coke's alleged judicial denial of the right of the king to issue such proclamations has reached as high as the UK Supreme Court.[51]

[45] Burgess (n 7) 211.

[46] D Kershaw, 'Revolutionary Amnesia and the Nature of Prerogative Power' (2022) 20(3) *International Journal of Constitutional Law* 1071, 1081 citing *Laker Airways Ltd v Department of Trade* [1977] 2 All ER 182, 192 per Lord Denning MR.

[47] W Hearn, *The Government of England* (Longmans, Green, Reader, and Dyer, 1867) 66.

[48] T Hobbes, *Discourses*, collected and edited by W Molesworth, vol VI (John Bohn, 1840) 62.

[49] A Tomkins, *Our Republican Constitution* (Hart Publishing, 2005) 70ff. T Poole, *Reason of State: Law, Prerogative, and Empire* (Cambridge University Press, 2015) 23ff.

[50] Poole (n 49) 23–24.

[51] *R (Miller) v Secretary of State for Exiting the European Union* [2017] UKSC 5, [2018] AC 61, [2017] 2 WLR 583, [44]: 'Although this statement may have been controversial at the time …'.

It is also important to reiterate that these alleged judgments were not published for many decades and 'among many other problems', their 'accuracy has been debated'.[52] Neither were cited in *Ship Money*. Poole argues that *Ship Money* and the *Five Knights* case 'are two of the most significant cases ever decided by English courts' because they were 'flashpoints within a crisis of legitimacy that led to civil war'.[53] The *Five Knights* case was certainly a flashpoint, as it concerned forced loans backed by imprisonment, but in terms of political impact *Ship Money* – a judgment of all 12 judges running to hundreds of pages – arguably stands alone as the constitutional case of the millennium. Its enormous significance was not lost on the judges themselves. Lord Crawley rightly described it as 'one of the greatest cases that ever came in judgment before the judges of the law'.[54] The Lord Chief Justice of the Court of Common Pleas, Lord Finch, described the case as 'the greatest case that ever came in any of our memories, or the memory of any man'.[55] It is strongly arguable that the case was the moment that members of parliament realised that a legal route to achieving their goals was closed. The judiciary had effectively declared for the king. The civil war started soon after.

The 12 judges in *Ship Money* all gave judgment, mostly at great length. The great majority of them defend a view of law and the authority of the courts that is predicated on the idea that the monarch, Rex, was hierarchically superior to – indeed the very source of – the law, Lex. In stark contrast, the judgments in *Proclamations* and *Prohibitions*, relied on heavily by common law constitutionalists, are single authored and somewhat doubtful in authenticity. There is no doubt that, as Sedley puts it, 'history was on Coke's side' so from a modern perspective the two cases seem ahead of their time. Nonetheless, it is suggested that *Ship Money* is significantly more useful for any historical understanding of the genealogy of prerogative. It also provides powerful evidence that the prerogative of justice was originally at the head of the river that is common law. It may be less relevant today, but English law used to believe that Rex was Lex, not the other way round.

Whose Common Law?

There is another interesting example of a wrinkle in the common law narrative surrounding the source and topography of the common law. Blackstone claims that the prerogative is that 'special pre-eminence, which the king hath, over and above all other persons, and out of the ordinary course of the common law'. Loughlin points out that the first part of Blackstone's definition is drawn from a

[52] TFT Plucknett, 'Genesis of Coke's Reports' (1941–1942) 27(2) *Cornell Law Quarterly* 190, 212; JH Baker, 'Coke's Note-Books and the Sources of his Reports' (1972) 30 *Cambridge Law Journal* 59, 78.
[53] Poole (n 49) 28; (1627) 3 *State Trials* 1.
[54] *Ship Money* (n 20) 1078.
[55] ibid 1217.

version given by Dr John Cowell but with a surprising variation, first spotted by Holdsworth.[56] It will be recalled that Blackstone's definition is 'that special pre-eminence, which the king has, over and above all other persons, and out of the ordinary course of *the* common law' (emphasis added).[57] Loughlin says:

> Dr John Cowell, Law Interpreter (1607) defined the prerogative as 'that especial power, pre-eminence, and privilege that the king hath in any kinde, over and above the ordinarie course of the common law, in the right of his crowne'. Cited in WS Holdsworth, A History of English Law (London: Methuen, 1924), vol 5, 22. Holdsworth notes that 'Blackstone copied from it [sc. Cowell] his definition of the Prerogative, with only a slight (though a very crucial) verbal alteration'.[58]

The 'slight (but crucial) verbal alteration' is that Cowell *in fact* said 'over and above the ordinarie course of *his* common law' (emphasis added). Holdsworth was right to call the alteration 'crucial'. The change of the phrase '*his* common law' to '*the* common law' is remarkable. The doctored version provides implicit support for Blackstone's erroneous claim that the common law is an *independent* and self-contained set of legal concepts and treating it as such allows for Blackstone and later generations to claim that prerogative is in some sense a function of common law not, as is the reality, the other way around. This substantially undermines the credibility of the Blackstonian narrative in relation to the status and importance of the common law.

The original version of the definition substantially supports the interpretation defended in this book. If royal prerogative are legal powers and privileges of the king 'over and above the ordinarie course of *his* common law', that strongly suggests that Cowell, the author of the original definition, fully understood that common law was and is the product of the decisions of the king's judges operating solely under the aegis of, and with the legal authority bestowed by, the king. The very fact that Blackstone felt it necessary to *alter* the definition to try to bolster his claim reveals the serious weakness of his argument, at least in relation to common law. Far from being a neutral and objective account of the law, it is clear that Blackstone had a clear agenda to promote a partisan conception of the 'common law' which is at best ahistorical and at worst, entirely false. The monarch's prerogatives are legal powers 'over and above the ordinarie course' of *the monarch's* common law. It is clear, therefore, that Blackstone materially altered Finch's definition of prerogative when generating his own definition. None of this undermines the core aspect of his definition of prerogative as exclusive to the Crown which remains useful and reconcilable with Dicey's definition.

[56] M Loughlin, *Foundations of Public Law* (Oxford University Press, 2010) 381, fn 30; WS Holdsworth, *A History of English Law* (Methuen, 1924) vol 5, 22.
[57] Blackstone (n 2).
[58] Loughlin (n 56).

Reconciling the Blackstone Definition with Dicey

Unfortunately, Blackstone does not supply an example of a legal power 'held in common' with ordinary people so the reader is left to speculate as to what could constitute a legal power possessed by the Crown, even in theory, that could be held 'in common with the subject'. It is actually quite challenging to identify an example of a legal power possessed by ordinary citizens that the Crown holds in common with them. At the time Blackstone was writing, of course, it was plain that the Crown could not sue or be sued in, say, contract or tort. This was precisely why the Petition of Right slowly developed to circumvent the immunity of the Crown at judicial common law. The Crown Proceedings Act 1947 lay long in the future. It would seem, then, that the most obvious examples that a modern commentator might suggest as common law powers potentially possessed by the Crown, ie those deriving from contract and tort, could not have been what Blackstone was considering.

Nor is it possible to look to *ex gratia* payments or other prerogative powers of the Crown for an example of a power 'held in common'. This is examined further in chapter seven. Finally, this chapter has already considered and rejected the idea that property rights of the Crown could be said to be 'in common' with property rights of the subject, especially when it is considered that all land is held of the Crown in the first place so the idea that there is equivalence between the nature of the legal relationship of the Crown to land with that of ordinary citizens is not tenable. It is of course also true that *servants* of the Crown deal in land through sales and purchases, as well as leases and the like but those are decisions for which they are personally liable. Such transactions do not involve the Crown in legal transactions at judicial common law at all. Indeed, as discussed in part II, the Crown itself operates entirely outside the jurisdiction of the common law courts to this day.

This chapter has therefore considered, and rejected, all of the obvious potential ways in which it might thought possible to salvage any reading of Blackstone's definition of royal prerogative power that means the Crown 'held in common' any powers with subjects. Furthermore, if we distinguish the Crown from the king,[59] it is clear that the Crown cannot sue, never mind be sued, in the ordinary courts at all. On close examination, therefore, it is suggested that the 'powers-held-in-common' cupboard is entirely bare. This means that it is possible to reconcile Dicey and Blackstone's definitions by the simple expedient of suggesting that the Crown possesses *zero* judicial common law powers and therefore all non-statutory legal powers of the Crown were, and are, prerogative powers.

[59] This monograph is not concerned with the position of the monarch in his or her private capacity.

Prerogative in Extremis: John Locke

The important aspect of John Locke's definition of royal prerogative for our purposes is his consideration of its use in emergency or exceptional situations.[60] Locke's brief analysis of the concept of prerogative in his Second Treatise seems quite strident, even extreme, in its one-sided attribution of quite extraordinary power to those who wield prerogative in a community constructed on Lockean lines. There is no detailed or strict definition of prerogative in Chapter XIV of the Second Treatise where Locke considers prerogative power. His comments are quite discursive. He does, however, make clear how his conception of prerogative is supposed to function:

> This power to act according to discretion, for the public good, without the prescription of the law, and sometimes even against it, is that which is called prerogative.[61]

Locke restates that prerogative may be used in a way that is contrary to established laws more than once – a concerning claim to modern eyes:

> Nay it is fit that the laws themselves should in some cases give way to executive power …[62]
>
> [P]rerogative can be nothing but the people's permitting their rulers to do several things, of their own free choice, where the law was silent, and sometimes too against the direct letter of the law, for the public good …[63]

These claims are followed up later in the chapter by an even more alarming claim. Locke says that if there is ever any dispute over whether 'a thing claimed as a prerogative' power is in question, then there is an easy way to test the answer:

> the tendency of the exercise of such prerogative to the good or hurt of the people, will easily decide that question.[64]

It is, to put it mildly, a bold proposition that those who govern can simply break the law and appeal to what they argue is the 'public good' to justify doing so. For Locke 'a good prince … cannot have too much prerogative'.[65] Locke's only remedy for such behaviour is an 'appeal to heaven', which is code for a return to the state of nature. Fortunately, it is possible to contextualise this apparently extreme reading of Locke, because he makes repeated references to the requirement of an emergency as a prerequisite for the exercise of such powers.[66] The example of pulling 'down an innocent man's house to stop the fire' perhaps expresses this

[60] J Locke, 'Second Treatise', in *Two Treatises of Government* [1689], edited by P Laslett (Cambridge University Press, 1988), ch XIV ('Of Prerogative').
[61] ibid para 160.
[62] ibid para 159.
[63] ibid para 164.
[64] ibid para 161.
[65] ibid para 164.
[66] ibid para 160.

framing most clearly.[67] This purported limit to the extent of the power perhaps shows that Locke should only be read narrowly. Furthermore, Locke indicates that he is referring to those scenarios where the exigencies of the situation mean that 'the municipal law has given no direction, till the legislative can be conveniently assembled'.[68]

These troubling statements by Locke speak to an era of limited regulatory coverage, particularly in the area of emergency powers. That era has now passed. In the United Kingdom, for example, the Civil Contingencies Act 2004 ('CCA 2004'), s 22(3) confers powers on the executive to make regulations in an emergency 'which may make provision of any kind that could be made by Act of Parliament or by the exercise of Royal Prerogative'. The specific provision to include prerogative seems superfluous when the conferral of parliament powers means the executive could make any law whatever, but the breadth of the provision means that any possible historical usage or example of the prerogative would also be covered by regulations under this Act. In other words, prerogative has now effectively been superseded, entirely, in emergency situations.

The provisions of CCA 2004 are so controversial that they were not even deployed in the Covid-19 pandemic. Instead, regulations were passed under the Public Health (Control of Diseases) Act 1984. This was despite the fact that when the relevant provisions under the latter Act went through parliament, it was stated that 'measures made under the 1984 Act' were supposed to be 'minor in scope and effect'.[69] Obviously, the drastic national lockdowns and other measures decidedly were not minor either in scope or effect.[70] The author has argued elsewhere that these regulations were *ultra vires* for that and other reasons and that if the pandemic was not a qualifying emergency for CCA 2004, then it is difficult to see what could ever be.[71]

This example perhaps opens the way to considering if prerogative could ever be relevant in an emergency. Given the sheer breadth of CCA 2004, this may seem to be a futile exercise, especially as under s 22(3), in the highly unlikely event that the strict terms of the Act were ever thought to create problems in a serious emergency, any actions that appeared to draw on residual prerogative powers would also be covered by the Act. Nonetheless, there may be value in setting out a hypothetical scenario, even if it is only illustrative in close to unimaginable circumstances.

The use of powers under CCA 2004 is regulated by a requirement under s 27(1) that ministers lay any regulations passed under the Act before parliament and that

[67] ibid para 159.
[68] ibid.
[69] E Haves, 'Coronavirus Bill: What Emergency Powers Does the Government Already Have?' House of Lords Library (23 March 2020), lordslibrary.parliament.uk/coronavirus-bill-what-emergency-powers-does-the-government-already-have/.
[70] See further R Craig, 'Of Virus and Vires: Lockdowns, Vaccine Mandates and Role of the Courts' [2023] 6 *European Human Rights Law Review* 579.
[71] ibid.

'the regulations shall lapse' after seven days unless each House of Parliament passes a resolution approving them'.[72] It will be recalled that there was a period in 2020 before parliament went online, when the exigencies of the pandemic situation meant that parliament could not sit at all. That problem has been solved with the facility to sit online. It would therefore require an emergency sufficiently serious for MPs to be unable to meet online, or in person, after seven days, to approve and renew the emergency regulations. Only then could Locke's analogy of the government acting *in extremis* be remotely relevant. It is crucial to emphasise that this would *still* not be a genuine exercise of prerogative but instead would be a *statutory* action predicted and authorised by s 22(3) until parliament could urgently approve a renewal of the regulations authorising executive action. Even in the most extreme circumstances, prerogative would not be relevant, and the relevant powers must be treated as having gone into abeyance.

Somewhat related to the issue of extreme emergencies is the work of the security services. In an important Court of Appeal case in 2021, known as *Third Direction*, the definition given by Locke made a surprise appearance in the judicial reasoning.[73] The court relied on Locke's arguments to hold that the security services have the legal 'power … to run agents who participate in criminality', despite such behaviour being legally prohibited and therefore, by definition, *ultra vires*.[74] The court cited *dicta* by Viscount Radcliffe in *Burmah Oil* who quoted John Locke's claim that 'the essence of a prerogative power … is … to act for the public good where there is no law, or even to dispense with or override the law where the ultimate preservation of society is in question'.[75] The court then purported to ground the original legal basis for the work of the security services in a an unpersuasive amalgam of the prerogatives of defence of the realm in time of war and keeping the peace.[76] Controversially, the court sought to justify the use of prerogative in ways that clearly frustrated the execution of provisions of various Acts of Parliament, in seeming breach of the Bill of Rights 1689.[77]

When Rex was Lex, the idea that the king could go against the strict law for the common good might have made some sense. Now that Rex and Lex have in a sense inverted, and Lex is now Rex, the Lockean definition of prerogative as being available to be used in breach of the law must be reconsidered. The

[72] Section 27: 'Parliamentary scrutiny (1) Where emergency regulations are made (a) a senior Minister of the Crown shall as soon as is reasonably practicable lay the regulations before Parliament, and (b) the regulations shall lapse at the end of the period of seven days beginning with the date of laying unless during that period each House of Parliament passes a resolution approving them.'

[73] *Privacy International and others v Secretary of State for Foreign and Commonwealth Affairs and others* [2021] EWCA Civ 330, [2021] 2 WLR 1333. See further pp 213–14.

[74] R Craig and G Phillipson, 'Protecting National Security by Breaking the Law? Prerogative, Statute and the Powers of MI5' (2022) 85 *Modern Law Review* 1274.

[75] *Burmah Oil Company (Burma Trading) Ltd* [1965] AC 75, 118.

[76] *Privacy International* (n 73) [80]–[83].

[77] See further Craig and Phillipson (n 74).

problems faced by the Court of Appeal in attempting to retrospectively underpin the actions of the security services have thankfully been overtaken by a new statute that authorises relevant activities in this area.[78] Nonetheless, it is important to emphasise that the reasoning that seemed to justify *ultra vires* behaviour by the state cannot survive the advent of the modern requirement which mandates that state officials must locate legal authority for their actions. That means that identifying a valid use of prerogative must start by asking, as Lord Reid did in *Burmah Oil*, 'how was it used in former times and how has it been used in modern times?' so that 'the proper approach is a historical one'.[79] Locke's analysis of the use of prerogative in emergencies or other extreme situations is thus very much of its time. Nonetheless, this case illustrates that it can have an impact in the modern constitution.

Another example of Locke's potential continuing influence is his role in directly or indirectly underpinning those who claim that the government retains a residual power to act without obvious legal authority. Elliott suggests that, unlike local government, central government must retain a residual power to act even where there is no visible legal authority.[80] Elliott and Thomas are clear that this power cannot be used in a way that contradicts the law or rights, so this residual authority is but a pale shadow of the more extreme Lockean claims. This example is not so much 'in extremis' as simply the claim that the government can somehow operate without restriction where there appears to be no obvious legal authority. It is difficult to avoid the conclusion that the argument made by Elliott and Thomas contains an echo of the controversial idea that the monarch must have a reserve ability to act *in extremis*. This issue, sometimes referred to as whether the government possesses any third source powers, is discussed in more depth in chapter nine.[81]

The remainder of Locke's analysis of prerogative is perhaps less controversial. He manifestly regards prerogative as broader than simply a power to be used in extremis for emergencies. He specifically lists the more prosaic prerogative power of calling parliaments in general and specifically 'the precise time, place and duration'.[82] He also appears to list the power to prorogue parliament ('a legislative that depends upon his will for their convening') as a prerogative power, which is also scarcely, if ever, an emergency matter.[83] He further cites the distinctly mundane and non-emergency power of pardon against conviction for criminal offences. He justifies this because 'even the guilty are to be spared where it can prove no prejudice to the innocent'.[84] Finally, he accords to the executive the power

[78] Covert Human Intelligence Sources (Criminal Conduct) Act 2021.
[79] *Burmah* (n 75) 101.
[80] M Elliott and R Thomas, *Public Law*, 5th edn (Oxford University Press, 2024) 181–83.
[81] See ch 9, pp 180–82.
[82] Locke (n 60) para 167.
[83] ibid para 168.
[84] ibid para 160.

to dissolve parliament, which is close to the opposite of an emergency situation.[85] These observations are useful confirmation of some of the core prerogative powers. Nonetheless, as we have seen, where Locke differs from standard accounts in relation to emergency actions *in extremis* under prerogative, his analysis has now been rendered otiose in the light of total statutory coverage of the field of emergency powers.

[85] ibid para 156.

4

Can Prerogative Affect the Common Law?

Introduction

Wade provides a novel definition of royal prerogative that is primarily based on his reading of Blackstone's definition. The main purpose of this chapter and further in chapter seven is to explain the ways in which the two limbs of Wade's definition are erroneous. Wade claims that a true prerogative must both 'produce legal effects at common law' and 'be … unique to the Crown'.[1] The first limb is addressed in this chapter and the second is addressed in part II. The latter discussion comes after a chapter detailing a novel definition of the Crown. That new definition logically precedes consideration of what powers are unique to it.

There are significant difficulties with Wade's interpretation of Blackstone's definition. This is important because Wade's definition has been gaining increasing currency in the case law.[2] Indeed, Wade, and his co-author Forsyth, refer to two major and relatively recent cases in their textbook where Wade's interpretation of Blackstone's definition has been followed.[3] Both cases are considered in detail in part III. Chapters two and three argued that Dicey's and Blackstone's definitions of prerogative can be reconciled: royal prerogative comprises all non-statutory legal powers, rights, duties and immunities of the Crown and those powers are exclusive to the Crown. Indeed, the Crown can usefully be defined as the bearer of the remaining prerogative powers.

As we have seen, Blackstone claimed that the prerogative label 'can only be applied to' legal powers and rights 'which the king enjoys alone' and that if a legal power was held by the Crown 'in common with any of his subjects' then it would 'cease to be a prerogative'.[4] Judicial common law legal powers in contract, tort and property would naturally spring to mind as obvious examples of legal powers seemingly (but not actually) held by the Crown 'in common' with citizens.

[1] HWR Wade, 'Procedure and Prerogative in Public Law' (1985) 101 *Law Quarterly Review* 180.

[2] See, for example, *R v Panel on Take-overs and Mergers, ex parte Datafin plc* [1987] QB 815 at 848.

[3] W Wade, C Forsyth and J Ghosh, *Wade & Forsyth's Administrative Law*, 12th edn (Oxford University Press, 2022) 42, referring to *R v Secretary of State for Health, ex parte C* [2000] HRLR 400 and *Shrewsbury & Atcham Borough Council, Congleton Borough Council v The Secretary of State for Communities and Local Government* [2008] EWCA Civ 148.

[4] W Blackstone, *Commentaries on the Laws of England* (1753), Book 1, ch 7, 239.

Ostensibly, therefore, there is a significant difference between Dicey and Blackstone. This is because legal powers of the Crown that are not exclusive to the Crown but are apparently shared with ordinary subjects are not, for Blackstone, prerogative powers. Wade builds on this apparent distinction between Dicey and Blackstone to argue that all legal powers that he claims are possessed by the Crown at common law, which he defines very broadly, are not, by definition, prerogative powers.

The gap between Dicey's and Blackstone's definitions is, however, more apparent than real. It is only possible to claim that the Crown has *two* sets of non-statutory legal powers (ie prerogative powers and judicial common law legal powers), if there are indeed judicial common law powers possessed by the Crown. The last chapter denied that the Crown possesses judicial common law powers. The ordinary legal rights of citizens were *derived* from the Crown dispensing justice through its judges. It makes no sense to ascribe ordinary legal rights to the Crown precisely because its legal powers are free-standing and, originally, sovereign rather than derivative. Unsurprisingly, the Crown, to this day, is unable to sue or be sued directly in court in contract or tort cases. Instead, ministers sue, or are sued, in their personal capacity, albeit their position is now statutorily underwritten by the Crown through the Crown Proceedings Act 1947.[5]

If the previous paragraph is accepted, then the Crown does not directly possess any legal powers at judicial common law. In those circumstances, all legal powers of the Crown are indeed exclusive to the Crown and the definitions given by Dicey and Blackstone can be entirely reconciled. It will be recalled that Blackstone did not actually identify any legal powers that were allegedly shared between the Crown and ordinary citizens. Moreover, in Blackstone's time it was crystal clear that the Crown operated outside the jurisdiction of the ordinary courts in exercising all of its prerogative powers. Thus it is possible (even obvious) that the Crown possesses exclusively prerogative powers and for all non-statutory legal powers of the Crown to be prerogative in nature. It is pleasing to be able to reconcile the definitions of prerogative given by Dicey and Blackstone, two giants of our intellectual constitutional heritage.

Wade's argument is diametrically opposed to the position defended in this book. His starting point is to accept Blackstone's definition and prefer it where it appears to conflict with Dicey's definition. In particular, Wade argues that the Crown possesses, and exercises, a number of legal powers at common law and those powers are not prerogative powers. He further argues that some powers classically treated as prerogative powers, such as signing treaties, are not in fact prerogatives because they do not have any effects at common law. All these claims are mistaken.

Wade therefore frames his analysis of the meaning and definition of prerogative through the prism of judicial common law. This is puzzling precisely because, as suggested in chapter three, 'common law' is simply a label for judicial decisions

[5] Discussed further in ch 8.

determined originally under the aegis of the prerogative of justice. Common law therefore itself is the product of the exercise of prerogative powers. Wade argues not only that alleged judicial common law powers of the Crown cannot be prerogatives, but also that alleged 'prerogatives' that operate outside the jurisdiction of the courts and do not therefore affect common law judicial decisions, are not really prerogatives at all. This is bewildering. It considers the definition of prerogatives from entirely the wrong end of the common law telescope. It makes no sense to claim that prerogative legal powers of the Crown can only be valid prerogatives if they, in some unexplained sense, *affect* common law which is itself derived from the prerogative of justice.

This chapter, as well as chapter seven, will argue that nearly all the claims Wade made about the prerogative are erroneous or unhelpful. His arguments are predicated on centring a conception of the 'common law' that is inconsistent with a rational modern understanding of the development, context and functioning of the legal system from a contemporary perspective. It will be suggested in this chapter that Wade was wrong to exclude treaty prerogatives and the like from the category of prerogative legal powers because they do not produce legal effects at common law. Chapter seven will argue that prerogative powers that are, to varying degrees, arguably somewhat *analogous* to common law legal powers possessed by ordinary citizens are no less prerogatives for all that. They are exercises of *public* power for a start, so equating them to private law legal powers of ordinary citizens is flawed *ab initio*.

Wade's argument that the Crown has a series of judicial common law powers, such as making contracts or conveying property, follows logically from his stance that the Crown shares legal powers with ordinary citizens. Chapter seven will focus on the claim that some legal powers of the Crown are 'shared' with ordinary citizens by arguing that whilst some powers may initially appear analogous, they are fundamentally different in source and nature: powers exercised by government ministers in public law are intrinsically and conceptually distinct from analogous powers exercised by ordinary citizens in private law. It is suggested that it is only servants of the Crown and ministers who have arguably been subjected to judicial common law jurisdiction, not the Crown itself, and that the relationship between ministers of the Crown and the Crown is the aspect that is governed by prerogative.

This chapter first sets out Wade's understanding of the royal prerogative in detail and his justification for the alternative, extremely narrow, definition that he defends. Wade's argument that prerogatives must affect common law in order to be true prerogatives is rejected, not least because the law long ago established that prerogative powers *cannot* affect rights at common law. The implications of this stance are further explored by considering a debate between Gavin Phillipson and David Feldman around the time of the *Miller I* litigation.[6] Next, the

[6] *R (Miller) v Secretary of State for Exiting the European Union* [2017] UKSC 5, [2018] AC 61, [2017] 2 WLR 583, [47] ('*Miller I*').

chapter considers whether the exercise of prerogative can have *any* legal effects, even if prerogative cannot be used to affect common law. It is suggested that legal effects *can* be identified, indirectly. It is suggested that prerogative and common law should be understood as being separate legal domains. Finally, the chapter argues that prerogatives without legal effects at common law are still prerogatives.

Wade's Definition: Two Limbs

Wade's definition purported to build on Blackstone's definition:

> The two tests for a genuine prerogative power seem to me to be:
>
> a) Does it produce legal effects at common law, and
> b) Is it unique to the Crown and not shared with other persons?[7]

The first limb of this test was entirely invented by Wade, who cited no source in academic writings or judicial authority for it. The second limb of this test is Wade's interpretation of Blackstone's test. Just before setting out his definition Wade lays out his core argument in its defence.[8]

> The royal prerogative consists of a bundle of miscellaneous powers and rights which are inherent in the Crown and in no one else. The power to summon and dissolve Parliament, to create a peer, to pardon a convicted criminal, to create a common law corporation – these are familiar examples of prerogative powers which are unique to the Crown and are possessed by no subject. At the same time the Crown possesses the powers of an ordinary person, for example the power to make contracts, to convey land, to transfer chattels or money, and so forth. But no one would maintain – or I had better say, should in my opinion maintain – that these latter powers are prerogative, since they are possessed by all and sundry …
>
> [Dicey's definition] is the loose meaning of 'prerogative' which has commended itself to the courts in recent years … But its accuracy is clearly questionable. There is nothing whatever 'prerogative' about the making of a government contract or an *ex gratia* payment by a government department. The Crown can do such things because anyone and everyone can do them and it has no need of any 'singular or eccentrical' power for the purpose.
>
> If the distinction between the true prerogative and the ordinary powers of the Crown had been observed, the *GCHQ* case might have taken a very different course … I would venture this is not a prerogative power at all, but merely the ordinary power which everyone has to employ servants and to tell them what to do … It is of course true, as several of the judgments emphasised, that in law the Crown can dismiss its servants at pleasure … but the likely basis of this position is not any particular power, prerogative or otherwise, but a specific rule of law that the service of the Crown is not contractual …

[7] Wade (n 1) 180.
[8] ibid 191–2.

> What is sauce for the civil servants may equally be sauce for ministers. Books on constitutional law, when they expound the royal prerogative, almost always begin by quoting Blackstone, but … I wonder why the prime minister and equally the Crown's other ministers, should in law be in any different position from the civil servants at GCHQ … The Crown's powers over ministerial appointments, I would therefore maintain, derive from a combination of ordinary personal powers and statutory designations, and are not truly prerogative at all.

In summary, Wade makes a series of claims:

- Prerogative powers are exclusive to the Crown.
- True prerogatives include summoning parliament and creating peers but not those that have no legal effects such as making treaties or deploying the armed forces.
- The Crown possesses the same, non-prerogative, legal powers as an ordinary person.
- The powers exercised in *GCHQ*[9] were not prerogative powers but a matter of ordinary employment law.
- Ministers, including the prime minister, are in no different position to an ordinary employee.

It appears that the one of the driving forces behind Wade's main article setting out his definition of the prerogative was his concern about the effect of drawing bright lines between public law and private law. Much of his analysis can be read as an overt attempt to remove any boundaries between powers that belong to the Crown and powers of ordinary citizens, which Wade clearly believes should be dealt with in identical ways by the courts. As he argues:

> Public law and private law have always been enmeshed together in the English system, giving it a unitary character which has been one of its strengths.[10]

This might be one reason why Wade is so keen to restrict the ambit and importance of royal prerogatives in the narrow sense in which he defines that concept so that all ordinary exercises of superficially similar allegedly common law legal powers would come to the same court. Wade in any event believes prerogatives that pass his two tests are non-justiciable; hence if those powers are laid to one side, it would indeed be the case that if Crown legal powers and legal powers of citizens were the same, they would be treated identically by the courts.[11]

It is clear from the same article that Wade was dismayed at the effects of drawing a bright line between public and private law actions which led to repeated trips to the then House of Lords on purely procedural points. This happened in a series of cases (including *O'Reilly v Mackman* most famously), trying to

[9] *Council for the Civil Service Unions v Minister for the Civil Service (GCHQ)* [1985] AC 374.
[10] ibid 184.
[11] ibid 197.

determine which cause of action should have initiated proceedings.[12] Wade leads the reader through the procedural implications with his characteristically winning and self-deprecating prose.[13] He defends the traditional common law approach that all proceedings should be heard before the same court, which indeed had been the case before the effect was felt of the Order 53 reforms to judicial review that he traces. However, it is possible to agree with Wade that it is a strength of English common law that there are not rigid dichotomies between public and private law actions, without doing such violence to the basic definition of the prerogative. A more nuanced approach is preferable.

Wade appears to have been driven by the urge to incorporate the vast majority of legal powers of the Crown into a judicial common law framework, and to exclude many of the residual legal powers from legal consideration by the courts altogether, whether because they were not legal powers as they had no effect on common law or because they were simply non-justiciable. Unfortunately, this leads him into a series of extremely tangled and difficult arguments as he tries to fit the square peg of prerogative into the round hole of judicial common law.

In one sense, Wade's position can be interpreted consistently with one of the core claims of this book – that all royal prerogative powers are exclusive to the Crown. The controversy lies in what legal powers are included within the definition of prerogative in the first place. Unhelpfully, however, Wade's mission to narrow and restrict the definition leads him, for example, to the absurd position of claiming that the Prime Minister is literally *employed* by the Crown, like a private citizen, which suggests that he or she could in theory sue for wrongful or unfair dismissal. This is not sustainable and examples like this seriously weaken the efficacy of Wade's arguments, at a minimum in relation to ministers.

The liability of ministers does, however, provide strong evidence for the outcome Wade desires which is that all nominally private law actions involving the government come to the ordinary courts. This has been achieved by the fact that a minister of the Crown can be sued for breach of contract following the Crown Proceedings Act 1947. In addition, judicial review of the exercise of most prerogatives is now available.

It appears, therefore, that Wade's fears of creating a dichotomy between public and private law were unfounded. Nonetheless, he presses his suggestions that: first, where the Crown seems to have the same or very similar powers that all of us possess at common law, those powers are not prerogative; second, his narrow set of 'true' prerogatives are non-justiciable; and third, that prerogatives must affect common law and those that have no legal effects are not truly prerogatives at all.

[12] *O'Reilly v Mackman* [1983] 2 AC 237. See also *Wandsworth v Winder* [1985] AC 461 and *Davy v Spelthorne Borough Council* [1984] AC 262.

[13] ibid 180–190.

Wade: Prerogatives must Affect Common Law

Wade claims that genuine prerogatives must have legal effects at common law. He cites no actual judicial authority for this novel claim. This must immediately cause some doubt over his purported test for prerogative powers. Wade does cite some alleged *academic* support for his argument. Wade points out that Blackstone had seen the treaty prerogative as a valid example of prerogative (unsurprisingly perhaps) but then claims that

> Maitland duly put him [Blackstone] right, pointing out that 'a treaty made by the king has in general no legal effect whatever' and that it was a mistake to classify the treaty power with true prerogatives such as the power to make war and peace.[14]

Had Maitland in fact drawn the distinction between the treaty prerogative and 'genuine prerogatives' that Wade claims, Wade's argument would indeed be bolstered given Maitland's eminence and multiple insights – but Maitland says no such thing. Maitland does indeed disagree with Blackstone, but only in respect of Blackstone's argument that the treaty is 'binding on the whole community'.[15] Maitland simply says 'a treaty made by the king has in general no legal effect whatever'.[16] Nowhere does Maitland claim that the prerogative of treaty-making is not a 'true' prerogative – on the contrary, his entire commentary is predicated on the validity of this prerogative as a genuine Crown power *even though* it has no legal effect at common law. Maitland's analysis, far from supporting Wade, wholly contradicts his argument.

Maitland even makes clear that his critique of Blackstone must be tempered by the fact that 'it is fair to Blackstone to point out' that the legal inefficacy of the treaty prerogative in law 'was not so clear in his own day'.[17] This is even more problematic for Wade's argument. If it is indeed the case that *historically* the treaty prerogative actually could have had some domestic legal effects, then Wade's argument is wrong even on his own terms. This is before considering the implications of the fascinating fact that the judges appear to have decided, over time and for their own unexplained reasons, that such legal effects should be brought to an end. As we shall see, the better view is probably that any domestic legal effects of the treaty prerogative were only effective within the prerogative 'domain'.

It seems therefore, that the Wadean criterion that prerogatives must have legal effects at judicial common law sprang Athena-like, fully formed, from Wade's head. It might be thought somewhat puzzling that this requirement is postulated as a *necessary* element in the definition of the prerogative, particularly as it seems to be a confusing and unnecessary aspect of Wade's argument. It might fairly

[14] Wade (n 1), 194.

[15] Blackstone (n 4), 257 (referenced in FW Maitland, *The Constitutional History of England: A Course of Lectures* (Cambridge University Press, 1908) 424 at fn 3).

[16] Maitland (n 15) 424.

[17] ibid 425.

be asked why Wade thought it was necessary, and he never explains his reasoning for suggesting this novel requirement. His exposition of the point may be found here:

> In the first place, the prerogative consists of legal power – that is to say, the ability to alter people's rights, duties or status under the laws of this country which the courts of this country enforce. Thus when Parliament is dissolved under the prerogative it can no longer validly do business. When a man is made a peer, he may no longer lawfully vote in a parliamentary election. When a university is incorporated by royal charter, a new legal person enters the world. All these legal transformations are effected in terms of rights, duties, disabilities, etc, which the courts will acknowledge and enforce. The power to bring them about is vested in the Crown by the common law, so it clearly falls within the definition of the royal prerogative as 'the common law powers of the Crown'. But when the Government cancels the designation of Laker Airways by making a communication to the Government of the United States under the terms of an international agreement, that has no effect under the law of this country whatsoever and has nothing to do with any power conferred by common law or recognised by British courts. It may be, as the Court of Appeal held, an act prohibited by a British statute. But it is not an act of power in any British constitutional sense, since it involves no special power that a British court will recognise. Whatever powers the Government may have had under the Bermuda Agreement were powers in the sphere of international law, and their capacity to make the Agreement came not from common law but from their status in international law as an international person. In the *Laker Airways* case the Attorney General claimed that the Crown was entitled to cancel the designation under the royal prerogative, and there was much talk about prerogative in the judgments. But if there was no power, in the correct legal and constitutional sense, there was no prerogative either. There was merely a piece of administrative action on the international plane.[18]

In attempting to replicate, or at least try to guess at, the *process* of Wade's thinking, it is important to remember that he was also captured, at least in this area, by an overarching common law mentality. Common lawyers believe that common law is the foundation of legal thinking and legal reality. Common law is the yardstick by which other law is assessed.[19] As Sedley claims, the legal system in general is 'an ocean of common law with islands of statutory provision'.[20] For Wade, unless an alleged 'law' operates and has effect in court it is not properly labelled 'law' at all. The view is mistaken because there are numerous legal norms that operate outside the jurisdiction of the ordinary courts.[21] As we saw

[18] HWR Wade, *Constitutional Fundamentals (Hamlyn Lectures, 32nd series)* (Stevens and Sons, 1980) 58–60.

[19] Some even think, mistakenly, that parliamentary sovereignty is determined by the courts and therefore is a doctrine of the 'common law'. See, for example, LJ Laws, 'Illegality: The Problem of Jurisdiction' in M Supperstone and J Goudie, *Judicial Review*, 1st edn (Butterworths, 1992).

[20] S Sedley, 'The Sound of Silence: Constitutional Law Without a Constitution' [1994] *Public Law* 270, 273.

[21] See, for example, *R v Lord President of the Privy Council, ex parte Page* [1993] AC 682 and *R (Cart) v Upper Tribunal* [2012] 1 AC 663, discussed further below.

in chapter one, common law is correctly defined as simply the accumulation of judicial decisions – nothing more.

Are Prerogatives without Common Law Effects Still Prerogatives?

Wade's claim that some prerogatives are not true prerogatives because they have no direct legal effects at common law ignores the fact that prerogative *predates* common law which itself is a derivative of the prerogative of justice. Prerogatives of the Crown clearly existed before the old baronial courts were replaced by royal common law. They may be archaic and conceptually distinct from the prerogative of justice, but that does not mean that they are not legal in nature regardless of their effect or otherwise at judicial common law in some cases.

The next major problem for Wade is that his controversial view flies in the face of centuries of consensus. All judges and academic commentators before Wade took it as obvious that powers such as signing treaties, conducting foreign affairs, and the relations between the United Kingdom and other governments were clearly exercises of prerogative legal power. It is necessary therefore to examine what led Wade to make the mistaken claim that only norms that are enforceable in common law courts can properly be considered to be legal in nature.

The first and best example of legal norms that are not common law norms is the original power of the Crown to set up new courts, such as the Star Chamber. Such courts, by definition, were not part of common law because they competed with it and yet they produced *legal* norms. The most famous example of this is of course the establishment of the courts of Equity under the Lord Chancellor, discussed in chapter five.[22] The existence of the courts of Equity definitively disproves the claim that the only legal norms in England and Wales are derived from common law. This seriously undermines Wade's argument.

Other Valid Legal Norms

Wade's error can be further demonstrated by illustrating other examples of valid domestic legal norms that are not part of common law, or to put the point more precisely, are outside the jurisdiction of the ordinary courts. We will see below that there are some legal rights in the prerogative field that are not common law rights and that can be removed by prerogative power as in *GCHQ*.[23] Legal parliamentary privilege is another example. Yet another is the University Visitor's

[22] See pp 96–97.
[23] *GCHQ* (n 9) and pp 82–84.

jurisdiction discussed at length in the case of *Page*.[24] In that case, a senior judge acted as a visitor to hear a complaint by a university lecturer who had been made redundant. A judicial review of the Lord President of the Privy Council failed because he had an exclusive jurisdiction that was not within the power of the senior courts to review. It is clear therefore that there are legal norms that are valid, yet not within the jurisdiction of, and not enforceable in, the ordinary courts. Universities set up by royal charter have their roots in royal prerogative. Blackstone confirms that the writ of the king's bench does not stretch as far as the university jurisdictions:

> In places of exclusive jurisdiction, as the two universities, indictments must be delivered to the courts therein established by charter, to be tried ...[25]

A similar argument can be made following the case of *Cart* where it was held that the Upper Tribunal could not be judicially reviewed unless the issue qualified under the 'second appeal criteria' as a matter of general public importance.[26] Other less important issues would not be within the jurisdiction of the ordinary courts. This demonstrates, again, that there are some valid legal norms that are not within the jurisdiction of the common law and not enforceable in those courts. The roots of this separate jurisdiction are statutory.

It follows therefore that it is perfectly possible for there to be valid legal norms in England and Wales that are not enforceable in the ordinary courts. Wade is therefore wrong to insist that prerogative powers that have no direct effect on the common law are not true legal prerogatives for that reason.

Tracing Wade's Intellectual Process

Once the erroneous common law mentality is understood as the prism through which Wade was considering his definition of prerogative, it is possible to envisage one way in which he may have arrived at his startling, and mistaken, definition. The starting point for understanding prerogatives is that unlike conventions (for example), prerogatives are *legal* in nature. This is a baseline assumption that every first-year law student is taught. Wade may then have asked himself what exactly distinguishes conventions from laws. This is also an obvious and well-known constitutional principle. Conventions are not legal in nature *because they cannot be enforced in court*. This is the key, it is suggested, to understanding Wade's assertions. He started from a few well-known and accepted premises. Prerogatives

[24] *R v Lord President of the Privy Council, ex parte Page* [1993] AC 682.

[25] W Blackstone, *Commentaries on the Laws of England* (1765–69), edited by Hardcastle Browne (St Paul West Publishing, 1897), Book 4, ch 24, 695.

[26] *R (Cart) v Upper Tribunal (Public Law Project and another intervening)* [2011] UKSC 28, [2012] 1 AC 663, [94].

are legal norms. Conventions are non-legal norms. The *reason* conventions are not *legal* norms is precisely, and only, because the courts do not enforce them. Wade appears to have leapt to the conclusion that prerogatives, in order to be legal norms, must therefore be enforceable in the common law courts and have legal effects at common law.

Unfortunately for Wade's argument, the label 'legal norm' is not confined to norms enforced in common law courts. Another way of putting the same point is that Wade appears to have conflated the narrow definition of common law *qua* judge-made law with the common law as 'higher norms' forming the metaphysical ocean from which statutes are mere exceptions. For Wade to be right, he must prove that non-statutory legal norms can *only* exist if enforced by common law courts. Not only was he a long distance from proving that much more radical claim, he did not even *argue* for it. He simply conflated common law judicial decisions and all non-statutory law and asserted that only norms enforced by common law courts could be legal norms.

Wade was already primed to exclude huge swathes of commonly alleged prerogatives under his version of the Blackstone test, which insists that only prerogatives that are exclusive to the Crown are truly prerogatives. By adding his second criterion, he was able to exclude huge further swathes of prerogatives that, in his view, were also misclassified, including treaty-making and foreign affairs. This rather begs the question as to exactly what such powers are if they are not prerogatives. They are not statutory powers. They are not part of the common law because, by Wade's definition, common law powers must be enforceable in the ordinary courts. They are not, apparently, prerogative powers. They are not, in fact, *legal* powers at all.

Yet every year, the government carries on the mechanics of international diplomacy and other actions without, according to Wade, any legal basis in domestic law for doing so. The closest Wade comes to categorising the power is as an 'administrative action'.[27] The problem with this is that actions by the executive generally require legal underpinning.[28] Furthermore, as we shall see in part III, administration is itself a prerogative power of the Crown. Joseph Raz emphasised the necessity for legal underpinnings for governmental action in *The Authority of Law*:

> It is said that the rule of law means that all government action must have foundation in law, must be authorized by law.[29]

[27] Wade (n 18).

[28] *R v Somerset County Council ex parte Fewings* [1995] 1 All ER 513, 524. There is serious debate over whether executive action *always* requires a legal basis that is discussed in ch 9. That section also deals with the equally vexed question of the status of some ancillary and fairly trivial powers used in the context of statutory powers, such as making lists etc.

[29] J Raz, 'The Rule of Law and its Virtue' in *The Authority of Law: Essays on Law and Morality* (Oxford University Press, 1979) 212. It is true that Raz suggests that the latter phrase 'seems to amount to an empty tautology', but as Harris' discussion perhaps shows, it would seem that far from being empty, the point needs to be spelled out explicitly (see part III).

Tomkins argues that 'all government powers (of whatever description) need positive legal authority: the government may do nothing without prior legal authority'.[30] Loughlin defines the rule of law in similar terms:

> The principle of the rule of law in the English system is founded on the rule of judicature. It means, in essence, that every exercise of public power must have a lawful source of authority …[31]

On this view, the fact that according to Wade, acting in the international plane is not rooted in legal prerogative power means that positive, legal authority is needed for any government action at the international level. As was seen in *Miller I*, the absence of an identifiable legal basis for executive action at the international level means such action requires fresh legislative authority.[32] Wade's argument would mean that the executive has no *legal* basis for acting at the international level and binding the UK to treaties with other sovereign states, one of the Crown's most crucial functions. This is extremely difficult for Wade's argument: exactly what legal power would be being judicially reviewed, as a matter of law, in cases where the treaty prerogative is in the frame?[33]

Interaction with Statutes

Wade's view that prerogatives that have no legal effects at common law are not true prerogatives can also be shown to be wrong when prerogatives interact with statutes. Prerogatives that do not have legal effects on common law are still treated as *legal* powers when statutes are affected. This can be seen, paradigmatically, with the treaty making prerogative because it is normally not justiciable in court, and therefore falls foul of Wade's definitional fiat as not being a prerogative power. However, the treaty prerogative becomes immediately justiciable *as a legal power* if it is purportedly exercised in a way that frustrates the intention of parliament in any statute, as was powerfully illustrated in *Miller I* but also in *Laker Airways*.[34] In the latter case, in which the government purported to exercise the treaty prerogative power to, in effect, render nugatory statutory UK landing rights possessed by the airline, Lord Justice Lawton approved

[30] A Tomkins, 'The Authority of *Entick v Carrington*' in A Tomkins and P Scott, *Entick v Carrington: 250 Years of the Rule of Law* (Hart Publishing, 2017) 183.

[31] M Loughlin, 'Evolution and Gestalt of the state in the United Kingdom', http://eprints.lse.ac.uk/81516/, [51].

[32] *Miller I* (n 6). It is of course the case that the court held that fresh legislative authority was necessary because of the *legal effects* that would inevitably accrue if Article 50 was triggered. See also *Entick v Carrington* in contrast with *Malone*.

[33] For example, *R v Secretary of State for Foreign and Commonwealth Affairs, ex parte Rees-Mogg* [1994] QB 552 and *ex parte Molyneaux and Others* [1986] 1 WLR 331.

[34] *Miller* (n 6).

the Attorney-General's uncontested and blunt statement that the power was a prerogative power. The AG had argued that

> there was nothing in the Act of 1971 which curbed *the prerogative rights of the Crown* in the sphere of international relations. (emphasis added)[35]

The judge went on to hold, contrary to the AG's argument, that the government could not 'use the Crown's powers in this sphere in such a way as to take away the rights of citizens'.[36]

While Wade could argue that *Laker* was wrongly decided, the decision of the Supreme Court in *Miller I*, repeatedly referred to 'the prerogative power to make treaties' and upheld the ratio of *Laker* to the effect that

> ministers could not exercise *prerogative powers* at the international level to revoke the designation of Laker Airways under an aviation treaty as that would have rendered a licence granted under a statute useless.[37] (Emphasis added)

Thus, both *Laker* and *Miller I* identified the prerogative of treaty making as a legal power whose exercise frustrated relevant statutes and was hence unlawful. In light of this case law, it is simply not tenable to argue that the treaty making prerogative is not a legal power and not a royal prerogative power. It is both. A non-justiciable legal power (in domestic common law courts) is still a legal power. It is just that its exercise cannot be reviewed by the courts unless it is exercised in a way that conflicts with an Act of Parliament, in which case it is clearly justiciable as the exercise of a legal power.

As the next section shows, Wade indeed has it completely back-to-front: with the possible exception of royal assent, prerogatives are *not* capable of altering or affecting the common law, a stance, explicitly endorsed by the Supreme Court in *Miller I*.

Comparing Wade's Definition with Other Case Law

In *Rayner*, it was held by the then House of Lords that 'the Royal Prerogative, whilst it embraces the making of treaties, does not extend to altering the law or … depriving individuals of rights'.[38] This quotation suggests that, for Lord Oliver at least, the common law courts have decided that the prerogative could not be used in a way that altered the law or took away any rights. These dicta were approved in *Miller I*.[39] The problem is immediately apparent when it is

[35] *Laker Airways v Department of Trade* [1977] QB 643, 727–28.
[36] ibid 728.
[37] *Miller I* (n 6) [51] and [55].
[38] *JII Rayner (Mincing Lane) Ltd v Department of Trade and Industry (Tin Council)* [1990] 2 AC 418, 500.
[39] *Miller I* (n 6).

contrasted with Wade's definition: Wade's position is directly contradictory to the case law.

In *Bancoult*, Lord Hoffmann stated that: 'since the 17th century the prerogative has not empowered the Crown to change English common law or statute law'.[40] *Miller I* also held that 'the exercise of [prerogative] powers must be compatible with legislation and the common law'.[41] They also approved Lord Parker of Waddington in *The Zamora* who held that the 'idea that the King in Council, or indeed any branch of the Executive, has power to prescribe or alter the law to be administered by Courts of law in this country is out of harmony with the principles of our Constitution'.[42]

Thus, numerous authorities establish that the prerogative cannot be used to alter the law or affect rights at common law, flatly contradicting Wade's proposition that any exercise of the prerogative *must* affect common law. If therefore we measure Wade's definition against the case law, it would seem to follow that *there are no prerogatives*. Since that is an absurd claim, Wade's definition could therefore be dismissed outright. Whilst this might be tempting, it would be a mistake. Instead, as the next section will show, Wade is right to claim that prerogatives can have effects that are recognised by the courts, but those effects are not necessarily legal effects *at common law*.

Can Prerogative Powers have *Any* Legal Effects?

In the course of the first *Miller* litigation, the question arose as to whether the prerogative could be used to take away common law rights. As it turned out, the courts relied on the impact of the mooted exercise of the prerogative on statutes, in particular statutory rights under the European Communities Act 1972 and other Acts, so the question of taking away common law rights receded somewhat in importance. Notwithstanding this fact, however, a striking debate was conducted on the UK Constitutional Law Association blog between Feldman and Phillipson on this question.[43]

Feldman cited a number of authorities in support of his claim that the prerogative could indeed be used to take away common law rights – on which he based a broader argument that the prerogative could take away rights generally. One case he cited was *Bancoult* which concerned the use of plenary prerogative powers on a ceded colony in a way which removed rights from inhabitants.[44] Feldman

[40] *R (Bancoult) v Secretary of State for Foreign & Commonwealth Affairs* [2008] UKHL 61, [2009] AC 453 at [44].

[41] *Miller I* (n 6) at [44] and [45] quoting Lord Coke CJ in *Case of Proclamations* (1610) 12 Co Rep 74.

[42] *The Zamora* [1916] 2 AC 77, 90.

[43] See ukconstitutionallaw.org/2016/11/08/david-feldman-brexit-the-royal-prerogative-and-parliamentary-sovereignty/ and ukconstitutionallaw.org/2016/11/25/gavin-phillipson-the-miller-case-part-1-a-response-to-some-criticisms/.

[44] *Bancoult* (n 40).

claimed that the decision to eject the resident Chagossians using the prerogative was evidence that the prerogative can be used to remove rights. Phillipson disagreed with Feldman on the extent, if at all, to which prerogative could be used to take away legal rights. He countered Feldman's arguments on *Bancoult* by observing that the particular power referred only to ceded colonies and *not* to the law of England and Wales, pointing out that Lord Hoffmann expressly drew this distinction in *Bancoult* itself.[45]

Phillipson was correct to distinguish domestic common law rights because they are not affected by the exercise of a prerogative power outside the United Kingdom. Indeed, the very fact that the contested issues in that case concerned the validity of a prerogative action rather serves to bolster the claim that common law and prerogative are separate dominions in legal terms. *Bancoult* did not raise any common law rights issues precisely because all the decisions in that case fell under the aegis of prerogative of foreign affairs exercised outside England and Wales and only related to the particular circumstances of a ceded colony.

Feldman was, however, correct to claim that the prerogative *could* be used to remove the right to reside in the Chagos Islands from the applicants in *Bancoult.* What is in doubt is the *status* of that 'right' to reside in those islands. It is arguable that any so-called rights conferred by prerogative are in any event contingent and *discretionary* in their conferral and continued enjoyment. Whether the label 'rights' is even appropriate at all must be in doubt. So, for example, there is no *right* to a pardon, or mercy, or *ex gratia* payments, or a peerage. None of these examples are rights that can be held or exercised by any citizen. These are indulgences granted at the discretion of ministers. Phillipson's scepticism about the validity of 'rights' at common law that can be affected by prerogative is therefore justified.

Feldman also cited the example of the prerogative of requisitioning property in time of war. This example is also less than satisfactory because that prerogative, in domestic law, was put into abeyance by statute, as the *De Keyser Hotel* case held.[46] By contrast, as the case of *Burmah Oil* showed, this prerogative persists when exercised abroad, although a requirement to pay compensation was rather unexpectedly imposed by the House of Lords in that case.[47] This was controversially and retrospectively reversed in the War Damages Act 1965 which reversed the obligation to pay compensation for property destroyed in Rangoon during World War II. It would seem, therefore, that the prerogative of requisitioning property in time of war can provide no support for Feldman's argument.

Perhaps Feldman's best example, however, is the case of *GCHQ*.[48] The right to be consulted before a major change in the terms and conditions under which the civil servants worked at *GCHQ* look very much like a set of rights that are

[45] Per Lord Hoffmann (n 40).
[46] *Attorney General v De Keyser's Royal Hotel* [1920] AC 508, HL.
[47] *Burmah Oil Company (Burma Trading) Ltd v Lord Advocate* [1965] AC 75, HL.
[48] *GCHQ* (n 9).

protected by the common law courts. Crucially, however, the rights that were reviewed were *public* law rights. The House of Lords held that the civil servants had a procedural right to consultation before the changes to their terms and conditions was imposed. Phillipson picks up this point, pointing out that the civil servants who worked for the government did not have any private (common) law rights to lose because they are 'in a *sui generis* class, regarded as dismissible at will'.[49] The rights that the courts held were possessed by the civil servants were *not* private common law rights – at best they were public law duties owed by the government.

Feldman might counter that the distinction between public and private law rights is irrelevant in proving that the common law courts accept that prerogative can be used to alter the legal terms and conditions of *GCHQ* workers, which looks very much like being able to 'affect' the law using prerogative in a Wadean sense. The crucial distinction, however, is that the relevant legal rules had nothing to do with common law rights. The decision by the courts to impose rules analogous to natural justice and *ultra vires* on prerogative powers does not suddenly make those powers part of the common law. Instead, the legal reality is that the courts imposed judicial review rules on the separate domain of prerogative law. The rules may converge, but that does not make prerogative become part of common law. Rather, there are two legal dominions, both now supervised by a judiciary determined that exercises of executive power should be constrained by rules of fairness and legality in order to promote and protect the rule of law.

It might even be suggested that the very fact that it is clear that the prerogative can be used at the discretion of the executive in such startling ways in respect of civil servants being dismissed at will, serves to brighten the red line between the prerogative dominion and the common law dominion. It is now established law that the prerogative cannot be used to alter the common law or affect common law rights. It is no less clear that if no common law rights or rules are at stake, the prerogative can be used in ways that very clearly affect civil servants and others in ways that would be impossible if the interaction was governed by common law. This suggests that the dismissal of civil servants at will is part of the prerogative dominion, separate from common law. The delicate question is how the courts manage the situations where the two dominions intersect. It is suggested that exercises of public prerogative power are *recognised by*, but are not part of, common law.

Miller I

The delicacy and difficulty of the relationship between prerogative and common law dominions is well illustrated by a curio in the *Miller I* judgment in the

[49] Phillipson (n 43).

Supreme Court. The court grappled with the fact that some exercises of prerogative appeared to have some legal effects at common law. Indeed, as Payne points out

> every act will have a legal effect somewhere along the line, for instance the giving away of money by the Crown will, as Diplock LJ said, have the legal effect of entitling 'the recipient to retain the money'. The granting of a passport will have the legal effect of entitling that person to use the passport.[50]

The acceptance by the majority in *Miller I* that prerogatives can have legal effects was clearly in tension with the general claim, accepted by the court, that prerogative 'cannot change the domestic law' and the approval of Lord Oliver's dicta in *Rayner* that 'depriving individuals of rights' is not possible using prerogative.[51] The majority held that this 'does not mean that such an exercise is devoid of legal consequences'.[52] They gave two examples:

> The first is where it is inherent in the prerogative power that its exercise will affect the legal rights or duties of others. Thus, the Crown has a prerogative power to decide on the terms of service of its servants, and it is inherent in that power that the Crown can alter those terms so as to remove rights … The Crown also has a prerogative power to destroy property in wartime in the interests of national defence[53]

The majority conceded that these examples did indeed 'affect individual rights' but 'the important point is that it does not change the law, because the law has always authorised the exercise of the power'.[54] This attempt to restrict the meaning of the rule that prerogatives cannot affect common law rights to where *the law* is changed is not sustainable precisely because the court was elsewhere explicit that prerogative cannot take away rights where the law remains unchanged. The better view, perhaps, is that the 'rights' in question in the quotation are *not common law rights.* That is why they can be altered and 'deprived' using prerogative. Understood this way, it would remain the case that prerogative cannot take away common law rights, nor alter the common law. The most obvious example would be working in the service of the Crown with the ever-present possibility of immediate dismissal without recourse.

There are possibly some minor legacy prerogative powers that have fallen into disuse which could breach this judicially imposed bright-line prohibition on the exercise of prerogative powers against the common law – and now HRA-protected – rights of individuals, such as pressing men into the Navy. Another example might have been requisitioning property in time of invasion but that has now also been superseded by statute in the same way that the right to tax directly has been put into abeyance by the Bill of Rights 1689. It will be recalled that these minor

[50] S Payne, 'The Royal Prerogative' in M Sunkin and S Payne, *The Nature of the Crown* (Oxford University Press, 1999) 84–85.
[51] *Miller I* (n 6) [52], [56]; *Rayner* (n 37) 500.
[52] ibid [52].
[53] ibid.
[54] ibid.

examples illustrate that *originally* the Crown certainly had the power to interfere in common law rights, but it was precisely this kind of unaccountable power that was a proximate cause of the Civil War and then the Glorious Revolution that helped to terminate the exercise of such powers, not least by the courts over time insisting that prerogative could not override common law rights. Since common law was originally sourced in the royal prerogative of justice, it is scarcely surprising that the Crown was originally able to override common law rights at will. Indeed, that was the whole point of the dispensing prerogative that was put into abeyance by Article I of the Bill of Rights 1689.[55]

The second example given by the majority in *Miller* is extremely useful in establishing how best to treat exercises of prerogative power that do indeed affect rights and have legal effects more generally.

> The second category comprises cases where the effect of an exercise of prerogative powers is to change the facts to which the law applies. Thus, the exercise of the prerogative to declare war will have significant legal consequences: actions which were previously lawful may become treasonable (as in *Joyce v Director of Public Prosecutions* [1946] AC 347), and some people will become enemy aliens, whose property is liable to confiscation. Likewise, in *Post Office v Estuary Radio Ltd* [1968] 2 QB 740 the Crown's exercise of its prerogative to extend UK territorial waters resulted in the criminalisation of broadcasts from ships in the extended area, which had previously been lawful.[56]

The majority held that this kind of exercise of prerogative 'has not created or changed the law, merely the extent of its application'.[57] This also seeks to limit the rule about prerogative legal effects to a narrow restriction on exercising prerogative in a way that creates or changes the law rather than affecting legal rights. This would appear to leave open the possibility of prerogative being used to affect rights. The problem for this argument is that the court elsewhere specifically held that prerogative is incapable of 'depriving individuals of rights'. Reconciling these contradictory *dicta* requires some careful unpicking.

A declaration of war has some dramatic legal consequences for 'enemy aliens' who would normally be entitled to the protection of their property rights at common law. Furthermore, the criminalisation of conduct that was previously lawful by prerogative fiat is dramatic evidence that prerogative can have common law legal effects. It might be thought, then, that the fact that the ordinary courts enforce the legal consequences of the exercise of legal prerogative powers that at least some prerogatives can take away legal rights at common law. Not so. This would be to conflate the common law and prerogative domains.

[55] Article I, Bill of Rights 1689 refers to the 'pretended' power of dispensing the law. This can be understood generally as referring to the attempt by the King to *extend* the undoubted prerogative power, which still exists, to pardon and grant mercy to include a *general* power of dispensing the law.
[56] ibid [53].
[57] ibid.

Treating Exercises of Prerogative as a Question of Fact at Common Law

It is suggested that a better approach would be to treat the prerogative domain as analogous to a separate legal jurisdiction, with issues arising under it treated as questions of fact when considered in the common law courts, as happens with, say, issues of French law in private international law cases. This would keep strictly separate those situations where prerogative has serious effects on people *within* the prerogative domain. The consequential legal effects of those exercises of prerogative power at common law would be *ancillary* to the exercise of prerogative power in the prerogative domain.

An illustrative example may assist. In *R v Naguib*, it was held that factual evidence as to whether the defendant had been lawfully married in Egypt was necessary before a defence could be raised to a charge of bigamy in England.[58] The matters of Egyptian law were treated as a question of fact, but the resolution of those questions had dramatic consequences on the defendant's arguments that he had not committed bigamy as a matter of domestic law in the UK. In other words, factual evidence as to the law in an alien jurisdiction had *considerable legal effects at common law* and on the rights of the defendant. Even though the questions of Egyptian law had those legal effects, that did not mean that Egyptian law somehow became part of the common law or that Egyptian law could alter change or 'affect' domestic common law, or 'take away' rights. The *effect* of the previous marriage, however, was to 'take away' the right of the defendant to marry in the UK.

A declaration of war under the prerogative ought to be treated as an issue of fact in the same way as the marital status of Mr Naguib in Egypt was a question of fact. If war is declared, various legal consequences would occur for enemy aliens at common law. Likewise, in the event of a territorial extension using prerogative, pirate radio stations would incur legal consequences at common law because as a matter of fact they were now within the relevant territory for the purposes of prosecution. If this is accepted, then the problems raised in these two difficult paragraphs in *Miller I* melt away. The rights affected by prerogative action had clear effects at common law, but those effects flowed purely from the common law recognising the validity of those prerogative actions as a matter of fact and determining the legal consequences at common law. In addition, the debate between Phillipson and Feldman can be resolved. Feldman was right to argue that the prerogative can be used in ways that can deprive individuals of 'rights' in certain circumstances – to be clear, this would only be 'rights' in the prerogative domain even if there are then ancillary common law legal consequences. Equally, Phillipson was right to argue that none of the examples given actually evidence any ability of the Crown to alter common law itself, or to affect *common law* rights directly.

[58] *R v Naguib* [1917] 1 KB 359.

An exercise of prerogative power can affect common law rights only because the common law *recognises* the fact of a prerogative action in the same way it would recognise, as a question of fact, something that happened as a matter of law in Egypt.

A parallel analysis can also deal with a number of other prerogatives. Passports can be issued or refused by the executive and the factual question of whether an individual has a valid passport will trigger various legal consequences at common law.[59] A peerage, one of Wade's favourite examples, also triggers various legal consequences including the loss of the right to vote in general elections. This can safely be treated as a question of fact if it ever became an issue in common law legal proceedings. Wade himself provides a number of examples of where prerogatives do have eventual legal effects at common law. Until 2011, a good example was the power to dissolve parliament. This was technically exercised by the monarch (on advice) and had legal effects at common law, not least the proroguing of parliament and causing writs to be issued to bring about elections in each constituency. Dissolution also removed the right of sitting MPs to continue to as MPs for the time being, which is a clear removal of their rights, and their right to continue to draw a salary if they lose the ensuing election. These consequences, however, are the *consequential* effects of the exercise of prerogative power, rather than the prerogative itself directly removing common law rights. They are also all clearly actions in public law.

The power to pardon is another example of an apparent effect on common law which on close inspection is not. It is a legacy aspect of the ancient prerogative power of the Crown to dispense with the law, the excessive use of which was put into abeyance by Article 1, Bill of Rights 1689. As de Smith and Brazier put it:

> It would seem that a pardon may be granted before conviction; but this power is not exercised. The line between pardon before conviction and the unlawful exercise of dispensing power is thin.[60]

It might be thought that the line between pardon *after* conviction and a *de facto* use of the dispensing power is no less svelte. Consistently with the argument in this section, the prerogative of pardon does not technically vacate conviction at common law or change common law rights because it is in fact an *indulgence* granted at the discretion of the Crown rather than a change in the legal status at common law of the beneficiary of the *de facto* dispensation. The distinction is indeed a narrow one, but the common law conviction does not change.

> [T]he effect of a free pardon is such as, in the words of the pardon itself, to remove from the subject of the pardon, 'all pains penalties and punishments whatsoever that from

[59] In fact, recent work by Paul F Scott suggests that passports do have some legal consequences that are recognised by the common law courts and therefore even according to Wade's definition should be considered as true prerogatives: PF Scott, *The National Security Constitution* (Hart Publishing, 2018) ch 4. See further ch 9, pp 190–92.

[60] S De Smith and R Brazier, *Constitutional and Administrative Law*, 6th edn (Penguin, 1990) 138, fn 121.

the said conviction may ensue,' but *not to eliminate the conviction itself*.[61] (Emphasis added)

On the other hand, the issuing of a pardon can have a fairly dramatic effect on the convicted person, who is released if they are in prison, but only as an ancillary consequence of the pardon. Of course, posthumous or significantly delayed pardons have no such visible effects. It could be argued that the power to restore the *de facto* freedom of the convicted person is because the prerogative power in such cases is a residue of the Crown's *judicial* power which is now exercised on the advice of ministers. This further raises issues about the sometimes porous boundary between the executive and judicial function.[62] The *effect* of the release, of course, is that the freed person can thenceforth exercise the liberties of a free person in society to do anything that is not prohibited.

Changing or Altering Common Law Using Prerogative

It is worth recalling that the example above of the ancient prerogative power to suspend or dispense with the law demonstrates that the removal of the power to alter common law via prerogative is a comparatively recent innovation. It is certainly more recent than the *Case of Proclamations* which is why excessive reliance on *dicta* from that case is arguably inappropriate, not least because it preceded the Glorious Revolution.[63] Historically, the Crown could, and did, disapply the common law, and statutes, at will. After all, the king was originally 'the fountain of justice'.[64] Furthermore, as we saw earlier in the chapter, it was by no means clear in Blackstone's time that the treaty-making power had no legal effects at common law. It may be that those effects were solely in the prerogative domain, in accordance with the arguments in the previous section, but, as Dicey somewhat coyly suggested, it is 'even open to question whether the treaty-making power of the executive might not in some cases override the law of the land'.[65]

Indeed, the whole of the dispute in the famous *Ship Money* case in 1638 centred on whether the prerogative could be lawfully used to insist that subjects should be required to fund the building of new ships. A clearer example of prerogative being used to affect common law rights would be hard to find, even with the caveat that

[61] *R v Foster* [1985] QB 115, 130.

[62] See further R Craig, 'Black Spiders Weaving Webs: The Constitutional Implications of Executive Veto of Tribunal Determinations' (2016) 79 *Modern Law Review* 166, 171–73. The author is grateful to Gavin Phillipson for the suggestion that this power could be a residual aspect of the Crown's *judicial* powers.

[63] *Case of Proclamations* (1610) 12 Co Rep 74.

[64] Per Lord Jones *Ship Money (R v Hampden)* (1637) State Trials 825, at 1184: 'we are the [the king's] judges deputed, but our judgment flows from him. Judgment is settled in the king, he is the fountain of justice, from whence all other proceeds'.

[65] *Walker v Baird* [1892] AC 491, 497. AV Dicey, *Introduction to the Study of the Law of the Constitution*, 10th edn (Macmillan, 1959) 310.

property in the ship technically remained with the donees of the funding.[66] More difficult was where money was paid in lieu. Lord Jones specifically held that his decision in favour of the king turned on the fact that money paid in lieu went to the Admiralty not the king.[67] It is worth noting that neither *Proclamations* nor *Prohibitions* were cited in *Ship Money*, which perhaps demonstrates why the modern fetishisation of *dicta* in those cases is somewhat questionable, given the seismic importance of *Ship Money* at the time and subsequently.[68] It might be thought that the advent of the Bill of Rights 1689 and the fact that the prerogative power of suspending or dispensing with the law was thereby put into abeyance has probably settled the matter. It is important not to forget, however, that the prerogative of pardon could be seen in one sense as a residual legacy of the dispensing power.[69]

There is, however, one important prerogative which has survived the purge and could be argued changes and alters the common law. That is the prerogative of royal assent. It is in reality exercised by ministers. It is virtually inconceivable that it would ever be exercised by the monarch personally, although this is irrelevant to its technical legal status.[70] When royal assent is granted to a Bill, that certainly changes common law (and statute for that matter), so it follows that prerogative, in conjunction with the consent of the two Houses, *can* be used to take away rights and has legal effects at common law. It may be that the fact that the royal assent prerogative is, in a sense, folded into the process of passing an Act of Parliament with the consent of both Houses significantly limits the impact of this particular example. It remains the case, however, that this prerogative is clear evidence that the inability of prerogative to change common law is not pre-ordained but has in fact been imposed by the judiciary *ex post facto*.

In brief summary, therefore, Wade was wrong to claim that a true prerogative was one that affected common law, not least because case law makes clear that prerogative cannot affect common law. Matters are arguably different in relation to the exercise of prerogative within its own domain, which should be recognised and treated as a question of fact by the ordinary courts. The exercise of prerogative is discretionary and confers no rights on those affected. In that sense, the case law stating that prerogative cannot affect common law rights is completely accurate. Nonetheless, prerogative norms are legal in nature, notwithstanding that many operate outside the jurisdiction of the ordinary courts for much of the time. Chapter five will consider the architecture of the legal system as a case study of how royal prerogative was foundational to the structure of the modern constitution.

[66] *Ship Money* (n 64).

[67] ibid, Lord Jones.

[68] ibid: '[I]t is as great a case as ever came to be advised on before judges', per Lord Jones, 1181.

[69] There is a respectable alternative view that the dispensing power was inappropriately extended from the pardon power which led to it being squashed in the Bill of Rights as a 'pretended' power. This is beyond the scope of this book, however, and will have to await a fuller treatment in due course.

[70] Ministers have not advised refusal of royal assent since 1707.

5

Constitutional Architecture

Introduction

English law now starts with Parliament. This book has argued that there are only two sources of ultimate legal authority: statute and prerogative. Kershaw has gone further, arguing that following the Glorious Revolution, prerogative powers were effectively adopted, authorised and then delegated to the Crown by parliament.[1] This book does not go that far, although Kershaw's claims cohere with the core arguments and viewpoint defended in this book. This chapter takes up Kershaw's implicit invitation to address the fundamental architecture of the constitution. It does this by considering what has happened to the prerogative of justice, arguably the most important domestic prerogative historically. It argues that the Judicature Acts 1873–75 put that prerogative into abeyance when parliament created the modern courts which are, as a result, now wholly statutory bodies with wholly statutory jurisdictions. Thus, the source of ultimate authority for the overwhelming majority of the legal norms applicable in this country, ie statute and judicial common law, is now parliament.

Acceptance of this framing of the constitutional architecture would be, in many ways, a pleasing vindication of the democratic centrality of parliament in the modern constitution. It would also be a pragmatic recognition of the result of the Civil War and who instigated and promulgated the Glorious Revolution. The Roundheads won. The Cavaliers lost. Parliament defeated the Crown. These historical realities have political, legal and constitutional consequences.

To put the central point another way, at the time of the Glorious Revolution Parliament subordinated royal prerogatives to its final and supreme authority. Thus, we can say with fair confidence that the source of authority for statutes and judicial common law is now manifestly traceable back ultimately to parliament. We can also say (more circumspectly) that one can either follow Kershaw in formalising the prerogative as powers now delegated by parliament to the Crown, or simply regard them as a set of legacy powers now generally *subordinated* to parliament's authority. The choice is, in the end, probably a question only of degree, although the latter option has greater explanatory power.

[1] D Kershaw, 'Revolutionary Amnesia and the Nature of Prerogative Power' (2022) 20(3) *International Journal of Constitutional Law* 1071.

The constitutional ructions of the seventeenth century did not leave the judges untouched. *Ship Money* was the constitutional case of the millennium.[2] That case dragged the judges into the political fray. They picked the wrong side. This was perhaps unsurprising given that the authority of the judiciary originated in the prerogative of justice. One aspect of that prerogative was the power to remove judges from office. Judicial tenure was at the whim of the monarch. When Charles I referred the case to the judges, there is little doubt that he believed that he who pays the piper calls the tune. Judges served at the pleasure of the king, just like ministers and other advisers, because they were originally administrators before their role changed to one of adjudication.

The Revolution changed everything. This should be no surprise. Parliament made clear in the Act of Settlement 1701 that the power under the prerogative of justice to remove a judge from office was no longer in the hands of the Crown. That aspect of the prerogative power went into abeyance and the judges were thenceforth to serve *quamdiu bene se gesserint*.[3] Under the 1701 Act, judges may be removed from office by an Address of both Houses, placing that crucial power onto a statutory footing. This was the first stage in a longer process of fundamental changes to the constitutional architecture of the United Kingdom and in particular, at least for our purposes in this chapter, to the foundations of the judiciary.

It is important to examine where the courts now fit into the constitutional architecture since the Revolution. Tomkins' insightful and persuasive analysis of the historic duality of Crown and Parliament are formative of the claims in this book about the ultimate sources of legal authority in the constitution.[4] This section builds on Tomkins' arguments about that duality but draws a diametrically opposed conclusion about where the source of the legal authority of the courts now lies. Tomkins argues that 'the courts are in some sense part of, or dependent on the Crown, and are not independent of it'.[5] This was certainly true historically. It is no longer true now. The courts may now be almost entirely independent, subject to the 1701 Act, but they are ultimately accountable to, and now constituted by, parliament. This chapter explains how the most important prerogative of all – the prerogative of justice – was put into abeyance by statute.

The Modern Source of Judicial Legal Authority

The original source of legal authority for the courts was the prerogative of justice. This chapter argues that this is no longer true because the modern source of legal authority for the courts is now parliament. The courts are now acting as wholly statutory bodies when they generate common law. Crucially, it is not being suggested

[2] *Ship Money (R v Hampden)* (1637) *State Trials* 825.
[3] '[F]or as long as they may conduct themselves properly'.
[4] A Tomkins, *Public Law* (Oxford University Press, 2003) ch 2.
[5] ibid 54.

that valid legal rules derived from judicial decisions are now somehow themselves statutory in nature. That would be to ignore the fact that judicial common law forms a discrete source of legal norms. The issue addressed in this section is the source of ultimate legal *authority* for the legal norms that are laid down by the ordinary courts. That source used to be prerogative. It is now parliament.

For many legal powers, the source of authority is not in doubt. Parliament provides the legal and legitimate authority for statutory powers of the executive. The Crown is the source of legitimate authority for the exercise of prerogative powers although, as we shall see, Kershaw argues that the *authority* for the residual prerogative powers was granted by parliament after 1689, and delegated to the Crown.[6] There are a large set of legal powers, duties and obligations derived from judicial decisions at common law. The courts once derived their authority from the Crown. Now they derive their authority from parliament. Either way, judges have always drawn their authority to make legal decisions from a superior legal body. The courts explicitly now derive their legal authority from parliament. The Crown is now legally subordinated to parliament. Parliament does not draw its legal authority from anywhere else. There is no superior legal body to parliament.

Tracing the Source of Judicial Authority

Chapter one suggested that common law has as many as four different meanings depending on the context. The primary meaning, it is suggested, is that common law is the collected series of judicial decisions held together by the doctrine of precedent. That case law cannot itself be the source of the legitimate authority of the judiciary. As was claimed in chapter one, to argue to the contrary would be to commit a constitutional solecism no less egregious than the periodic undergraduate mistake of claiming that the source of the authority and supremacy of parliament can be located in statutes such as the Bill of Rights 1689. Such an argument would be circular. It would conflate the product of the authority with the source of that authority.

Instead, it must be explained to the mistaken devotee of the Bill of Rights 1689 that the authority of parliament is derived from the consensus of the officials in the system, not any particular Act, in accordance with the insightful claims made by HLA Hart.[7] Parliamentary sovereignty is the supreme rule of the constitution, which means that it prevails over any competing legal norms within the system. Nor does it depend for its validity on any other legal norm, source or body. There are no higher legal norms from which it derives its legal authority. Instead, the ultimate Rule (or perhaps rules) of Recognition identifies that parliamentary sovereignty is the supreme rule.[8] This has been true since the Revolution in 1688.

[6] Kershaw (n 1).
[7] HLA Hart, *The Concept of Law* (Oxford University Press, 1961) ch VI.
[8] ibid 106.

The source of the authority of parliament is the Rule of Recognition as evidenced by official consensus.

Hart illustrates the absence of any higher legal norms above parliament by considering the validity of a 'purported by-law of the Oxfordshire County Council' whose validity is questioned. He points out that a 'a very familiar chain of legal reasoning' leads us to trace the validity of the by-law to a statutory order, from there to a statute and from there to 'the rule that what the Queen in Parliament enacts is law'.[9] At this point, he argues, 'we are brought to a stop in inquiries concerning validity: for we have reached a rule … [that has] no rule providing criteria for its own legal validity'.[10] This is the Rule of Recognition.

Legal norms laid down by the courts are different. Unlike parliamentary sovereignty since the Glorious Revolution, legal norms laid down by the courts have always derived their validity and authority from a further set of higher legal norms. So if we undertake the same 'very familiar chain of legal reasoning', but this time starting with a court order not a by-law, we are not 'brought to a stop' when we reach the High Court or Appeal Courts. On the contrary, we can nowadays manifestly identify criteria for the validity of the courts themselves in the statutes that now confer jurisdictional authority on those courts. Originally, the source of the validity of the remedies granted by the king's judges was the prerogative of justice, which conferred jurisdictional authority on the ancient courts. As we shall see later in this chapter, that is no longer true. The validity of court orders and decisions used to be derived from and dependent on a prerogative of the Crown, which was the source of a set of superior, non-judicial, legal norms conferring authority on those courts.

Before the Revolution, the source of validity of the Crown was similar to the source of validity of parliament after the Revolution. It was rooted in the consensus of the officials and the Rule of Recognition which identified that consensus. This can be illustrated by a curious story told by Sir Frederick Pollock, Ernest Kantorowicz and Sir Carleton Allen.[11] By an unhappy coincidence, Edward I was in Palestine when his father, Henry III, died in 1272. On a previous occasion in 1135 when the king died, Allen says 'there was a dangerous interval of abeyance of the King's Peace'.[12] Pollock says 'there was tribulation soon in the land, for every man that could forthwith robbed another'.[13] This is because it was once thought that the king's peace lapsed on the death of the king because 'his peace died with him'.[14] The king's peace was foundational to the criminal justice system.

[9] ibid 107.
[10] ibid.
[11] F Pollock, 'The King's Peace' (1885) 1 *Law Quarterly Review* 37, 49; CK Allen, *Hamlyn lectures*: '*The King's Peace*' (Stevens & Sons, 1953) 11; E Kantorowicz, *The King's Two Bodies: A Study in Mediaeval Political Theology* (Princeton University Press, 1957) 317.
[12] Allen (n 11) 11.
[13] Pollock (n 11) 49.
[14] ibid.

Matters were quite different in 1272 because, in contrast with the troubles of 1135, 'the great men of the realm, by a wise audacity, took upon them to issue a proclamation of the peace in the new king's name forthwith'.[15] Given that the prerogative of keeping the peace was partly constitutive of the justice system itself, this event is arguably a neat and practical illustration of Hart's Rule of Recognition.[16] This is because this real world example provides an illustration of the necessity for the agreement of the officials in constituting the ultimate rules of the system. In this case they authorised, implemented and enforced the legal system in the name of the king. There was therefore an official consensus to that effect in precisely the way Hart describes. The authority of the ancient courts was derived from the Crown. The Crown's authority derived from what was then the Rule of Recognition, itself validated by official consensus.

This explanation also has the ancillary benefit of dealing with a potential problem, identified by Hart, of establishing the validity of prerogative powers on the transition between monarchs historically.[17] If the king is the fountain of justice, what 'higher' law governs the transition between Rex I and Rex II? Hart's brilliant solution asserts that ultimately there needs to be recognition by the officials in the system of the supremacy of regal legal authority. This recognition of the legal authority of the monarch by the rest of the machinery of state persisted through multiple generations.

The Constitutional Status of the Courts

McIlwain explains how 'the King has his court in his Council, in his Parliament' and that 'the courts were still the Council, their acts were its acts, their judges were its members … the Council was the court and the court was the Council'.[18] The 'curia' was not 'at first … a judicial body at all', but in 'fact, its business was both judicial and legislative' because 'there was no clear distinction between legislative and judicial'.[19] It should also be noted that the Council was as much executive as judicial or legislative because the distinction with executive power was equally unclear, as McIlwain elsewhere points out.[20] Dicey likewise argues that historically 'judicial and executive powers' were 'hardly distinguishable' and that 'the

[15] ibid. The proclamation and discussion of it can be found in W Stubbs, *Select Charters* (Clarendon, 1888) 447–48.

[16] See further ch 10, pp 207–16 and ch 2.

[17] The famous Rex I/Rex II problem. Hart (n 7) 52–55. The author is grateful to John Finnis for raising this potential difficulty in a seminar discussing a draft chapter of this monograph in Oxford.

[18] CH McIlwain, *The High Court of Parliament and its Supremacy* (Oxford University Press, 1910) 23 and 25.

[19] ibid 30.

[20] ibid 21.

absolute … lawgiver was originally the Crown'.[21] As we saw in chapter one, Loughlin expresses the modern definitions in similar terms:

> The Crown-in-Council expresses governmental authority, the Crown-in-Council-in-Parliament signifies ultimate legislative authority …[22]

So the source of authority for ministers, courts and parliament originated with the monarch, and the boundaries between them were somewhere between blurred and non-existent. The 'authority' for all these institutions 'lay in the ancient jurisdiction of the Council itself'.[23] The authority and legitimacy of the Council derived from royal prerogative and the imprimatur of the monarch. English law started with the Crown.

It was not just the King's Bench that originated in the Crown. It is worth noting that Dicey argued that Equity constituted a separate jurisdiction from the ordinary law:

> Equity in England … constitute[s] a body of law which differs from the ordinary law of the land, and under certain circumstances modifies the ordinary civil rights of every citizen.[24]

The growth of the Equity jurisdiction eventually led to jurisdictional conflict with the common law of the King's Bench.[25] Dicey states that the courts of Equity also derived their original legal authority from royal prerogative, and therefore the Crown. This was because 'the [Lord] Chancellor, after all, was a servant of the Crown holding his office at the pleasure of the King':[26]

> There was a time in the history of England when the judicial power of the Chancellor, bound up as it was with the prerogative of the Crown, might have overshadowed the Courts of Law.[27]

The same was true of the original Assizes, the Star Chamber and the Court of Common Pleas, as well as the original King's Bench (the clue being in the name).[28] All judicial power was, then, originally rooted in the Crown and the prerogative of justice. Dicey even goes so far as to assert that:

> Judges … 'rather than the government, represent the august dignity of the State, or, in accordance with the terminology of English law, of the Crown'.[29]

[21] AV Dicey, *Introduction to the Study of the Law of the Constitution*, 8th edn (Macmillan, 1927) 371 and 67 (footnote).

[22] M Loughlin, policyexchange.org.uk/wp-content/uploads/2019/10/The-Case-of-Prorogation.pdf, 6–7; Dicey (n 21) 67 (footnote).

[23] ibid 25.

[24] Dicey (n 21) 253: 'Equity in England … constitute[s] a body of law which differs from the ordinary law of the land, and under certain circumstances modifies the ordinary civil rights of every citizen'. This lexical priority was confirmed in the Judicature Act 1873, s 25.

[25] A Cromartie, *The Constitutionalist Revolution* (Cambridge University Press, 2006) 212, 215; PD Halliday, *Habeas Corpus: From England to Empire* (Harvard University Press, 2010) 81.

[26] ibid 249.

[27] Dicey (n 21) 265.

[28] ibid 243, 249. See also WS McKechnie, *Magna Carta* (James Maclehose and Sons, 1914) 90.

[29] ibid 259. This perhaps fails to give due regard to the effect of the Judicature Act 1873 discussed later in this chapter.

Blackstone also believed that the courts of Equity were rooted in the prerogative of justice:

> [The King] has alone the right of erecting courts of judicature … And hence it is, that all jurisdictions of courts are either mediately or immediately derived from the crown, their proceedings run generally in the king's name, they pass under his seal, and are executed by his officers.'.[30] (Emphasis added)

Hobbes believed that the 'highest ordinary court in England is the Court of Chancery, wherein the Lord Chancellor … is the only judge'.[31] Halliday quotes Sir Matthew Hale who argued that 'all jurisdiction was originally translated into the crown'.[32] It is therefore unarguable that the jurisdictional authority of equity originally derived from the Crown. It is suggested that the same is also true for the common law, and for similar reasons, although it is accepted that tracing the pathway back to the Crown is slightly clearer in the case of equity.

The Effect of the Glorious Revolution

The Glorious Revolution permanently inverted the relationship between parliament and the Crown. It changed the supreme rule of the constitution, in the Hartian sense, which is why it was a revolution. Hart specifically warns that it is a mistake to conflate the supreme rule and the ultimate rule (also known as the Rule of Recognition).[33] The supreme rule is the rule that always prevails if it conflicts with any other rule. The ultimate rule is the rule that identifies the sources of valid legal rules. The rule of recognition identifies the supreme rule in the United Kingdom as being that whatever parliament enacts is law and overrides all other law. The ultimate rule also identifies other valid laws in the system. Sir Neil MacCormick gives a brief summary of the ultimate rule when he lists 'the recognised sources of law for the UK in rank order':[34]

> Acts of Parliament, acts of delegated legislation so far as interpreted to be *intra vires* and precedents of the higher courts themselves ranked hierarchically.[35]

A fuller list might include ecclesiastical law, prerogatives and possibly the University Visitor jurisdiction but that is not important for our purposes here.[36] The important point here is to note that the rules of recognition can change without there being a revolution.

[30] W Blackstone, *Commentaries on the Laws of England* (1753), Book 1, ch 7, 239.
[31] T Hobbes, *Discourses*, collected and edited by W Molesworth (John Bohn, 1840).
[32] Halliday (n 25) 140.
[33] Hart (n 7) 106; see R Craig, 'A Simple Application of the Frustration Principle: Prerogative, Statute and Miller' (2017) *Public Law (Brexit Special Issue)* 25, 45–46.
[34] N McCormick, *Questioning Sovereignty: Law, State, and Nation in the European Commonwealth* (Oxford University Press, 1999) 87–88.
[35] ibid 88.
[36] *R v Lord President of the Privy Council, ex parte Page* [1993] AC 682.

One example of such a change relates to devolved assemblies. The list given by McCormick would need to be updated to include legal rules laid down by those assemblies. These novel sources of valid legal norms were inserted into the hierarchy of norms by the devolution Acts, thus changing the Rule of Recognition.[37] The rule that Acts of Parliament prevail over other legal rules (the supreme rule) is clearly not the same as the list of all recognised sources of legal rules (the ultimate rule). Changing the supreme rule is revolutionary. Changing the ultimate rule, without changing the supreme rule, is not revolutionary. When the Supreme Court in *Miller I* held that the ultimate rule – the Rule of Recognition – had not changed as a result of the UK's membership of the European Union, they actually meant that the *supreme* rule had not changed.[38] Membership manifestly changed the rules of recognition because it created a new source of valid legal norms in the United Kingdom, even if it was parliament that conferred that validity on EU norms. The Rule of Recognition, the ultimate rule, changes with surprising frequency. The supreme rule only changes when there is a revolution.

Before the Revolution, all legal validity was traceable back to the Crown, which sat at the apex of the system. The remedies granted by the courts were on behalf of the Crown and the Crown legislated through prerogative or with the acquiescence of parliament. As Lord Crawley pointed out in *Ship Money*, 'the last appeal be to the king'.[39] After the Revolution, the supreme rule changed. The last word passed to parliament and whatever parliament laid down was final. The new settlement constituted and recognised parliament as the supreme legal body, identified by the Rule of Recognition.

By contrast, the source of the authority and validity of the decisions of the ordinary courts remained the Crown. These roots are important. Nonetheless, there has been an important further change that has occurred since the Glorious Revolution. It took place in the 1870s. The prerogative courts, rooted in the prerogative of justice and ultimately the Crown, were abolished by a hugely important, but often overlooked, series of Acts of Parliament that created and constituted a brand new system of ordinary courts, as Maitland explains:

> At last came the Judicature Acts of 1873 and 1875 … The old courts were abolished, Chancery, Queen's Bench, Common Pleas, Exchequer, also the Court of Probate, the Court of Divorce, and the Court of Admiralty. In their place was put a High Court of Justice with a Court of Appeal above it … the divisions of the High Court are utterly different things from the old independent courts.[40]

In doing so, parliament put the prerogative of justice into abeyance. The basis of the legal authority of the court system in the prerogative of justice was brought to

[37] Scotland Act 1998, Northern Ireland Act 1998 and the Government of Wales Act 1998.

[38] *R (Miller) v Secretary of State for Exiting the European Union* [2017] UKSC 5, [2018] AC 61, [2017] 2 WLR 583 ('*Miller I*') [60].

[39] *R v Hampden (Ship Money)* (1637) State Trials 825, 1083.

[40] FW Maitland, *Equity: A Course of Lectures* (Cambridge University Press, 1936) 15.

an abrupt end. Instead, the jurisdiction of the new High Court became statutory. It was conferred on it by the Judicature Acts 1873–75. This was a significant change to the Rule of Recognition because it fundamentally altered the source of authority of the ordinary courts. All roads led to the regal Rome. That is not the case any longer. Now, all paths point to the people's parliament.

This does not mean that judicial decisions somehow changed their nature qua common law. The set of judicial decisions known as common law is conceptually distinct as a class of legal norms from the statutory foundations of the modern court system, just as the appointment of ministers under prerogative is conceptually distinct from an action against the government for breach of contract.[41] Nonetheless, the legal and legitimate authority for the common law is now rooted in parliamentary authority, not the Crown.

Nick Barber claims that the authority of common law is not the monarch but 'the local customs of the people'.[42] Although he admits that the 'king created the courts that applied the common law', he denies that common law norms were created by the courts, claiming instead that the king 'was not the originator or legitimator of the common law' because common law was in fact 'grounded in customs applied by the judges'.[43] Barber does not explain the origin of these alleged customary legal rules, nor how the regularisation and 'standardisation' of the law across the country was anything other than a royal takeover as they 'replaced diversity'.[44] At most, the king's judges *absorbed* any residual trace elements of customary law, derived from local courts and the like, into the hegemonic set of legal norms now known as 'common law' but which could easily and more accurately have been labelled royal law. Barber's claims are flatly inconsistent with the core arguments in this book and must be rejected if the points made here are accepted.

The process by which any genuine legal norms derived from custom were absorbed or replaced by the King's courts took many centuries.[45] The legal validity of customary law was in any event conferred by the Crown as Sir Robert Filmer points out, quoted in McIlwain:

> It is not the being of a Custom that makes it lawful but then all Customs, even evil Customs, would be lawful; but it is the Approbation of the supreme Power that gives a legality to the Custom …[46]

The claim that judicial authority or common law is somehow rooted in 'custom' is therefore a non-starter. Judges make common law in the narrow sense of generating

[41] See further part II.
[42] NW Barber, *The United Kingdom Constitution: An Introduction* (2021) 31.
[43] ibid.
[44] ibid.
[45] CH McIlwain, *The High Court of Parliament and its Supremacy* (Oxford University Press, 1910) 44–45.
[46] ibid 96.

valid legal norms through precedent. The source of their legitimate legal authority was the Crown and is now parliament. The details of the transfer of jurisdictional authority are explored further below. The jurisdictional authority of the ordinary courts is now wholly statutory.

Prerogatives as Delegated Powers from Parliament

Kershaw offers a radical alternative explanation for the source of the authority of prerogative power in modern times.[47] He claims that the Glorious Revolution in 1688 was a decisive break with the previous constitutional settlement and that the invitation by the 'Convention Parliament' to William and Mary to take the throne could not be retrospectively validated after they were appointed.[48] For Kershaw, this was a genuine revolutionary hiatus and he marshals considerable evidence from Maitland and others as to the impossibility of reconciling the events around the Glorious Revolution with any pre-existing constitutional principle.[49]

For Kershaw, the victory of the Roundheads over the Cavaliers, of parliament over the monarchy, followed by the removal of James II from the throne, had even more revolutionary consequences than generally accepted. These unprecedented events meant that whatever legal powers possessed by the monarch *after* 1688 were held at the behest of, and solely by the grace of parliament.[50] For him, such powers are now *delegated* legal powers conferred by parliament and can be removed at the whim of Westminster. Kershaw claims the remaining prerogatives were 'delegated from a parliamentary sovereign' to William and Mary on sufferance and *pro tempore*.[51]

It is not necessary to go as far as Kershaw does to explain the events of the late seventeenth century. Pragmatically, prerogatives are now held only for as long as parliament remains content with the *status quo*. They can be put into abeyance at any time by parliament. Further, if all prerogative powers are already, in a sense, a species of delegated statutory power, that might be thought to reduce the significance of decisions by parliament consciously and deliberately to put particular prerogatives onto a statutory footing. It possibly also elides the real differences between the exercise of prerogative and statutory powers. In the end, as mentioned earlier, the question is probably a matter of degree.

The issue of the prerogative of justice was not considered by Kershaw but, as we have seen, his arguments are entirely consistent with the claims in this monograph.

[47] D Kershaw, 'Revolutionary Amnesia and the Nature of Prerogative Power' (2022) 20(3) *International Journal of Constitutional Law* 1071.
[48] ibid 1074.
[49] ibid 1075.
[50] ibid 1098.
[51] ibid 1102.

If all prerogative power post-1688 was possessed by the Crown through the implicit – or for Kershaw, the *direct* authorisation of parliament – it is no great stretch to suggest that the prerogative of justice was also implicitly or directly authorised by parliament after 1689. Either way, the ordinary prerogative courts continued to be rooted in the Crown until the momentous changes brought about by the Judicature Acts 1873–75.[52]

The status and purpose of the Act of Settlement 1701 is relevant because the Act contains a provision which states that judges have tenure 'quamdiu se bene gesserint',[53] and only permits the removal of judges if there is an Address of Both Houses. This makes judicial tenure contingent on continuing parliamentary approval. It is suggested that the prerogative of justice can be disaggregated into various elements which necessarily includes the power of dismissal of judges. The latter power was clearly held by the Crown before the Glorious Revolution. The 1701 Act put the power of dismissal onto a statutory footing and that aspect of the prerogative of justice went into abeyance.

The remainder of the prerogative of justice remained implicitly delegated to the Crown until the Judicature Acts, addressed below. The effect of the Judicature Acts was to put the remainder of the prerogative of justice into abeyance by deliberately creating brand new statutory courts. At all times, the legal authority of the various courts that have variously existed in our history can be seen to derive from a higher set of legal norms.

The Judicature Act 1873

The *current* source of the jurisdictional authority of the courts is radically different from the historic source of the jurisdictional authority of the courts which was the Crown. A seismic change in the constitution was brought about by the Judicature Act 1873 ('the 1873 Act') and in particular s 16 of the Act. This Act, and others passed at this time, receive surprisingly little attention in modern discourse. The Judicature Acts fundamentally altered the judicial system in the UK, famously placing the courts of common law and equity into one single system. Understanding the other effects of the 1873 Act that are more relevant to this book involves using two principles set out in chapter six: the abeyance and frustration principles. This section suggests the 1873 Act has put the prerogative of justice into abeyance.

The 1873 Act abolished the previous courts and invented a brand new 'High Court'. Parliament constituted it as a superior court of record and conferred original jurisdiction on it. The High Court, and appeal courts, are wholly statutory

[52] See ch 3, pp 51–54.

[53] '[F]or as long as they may conduct themselves properly'.

bodies deriving their legal authority and jurisdiction from parliament. The crucial sections for our purposes are below.

> Long title:
>
> An Act for the constitution of a Supreme Court, and for other purposes relating to the better Administration of Justice in England; and to authorise the transfer to the Appellate Division of such Supreme Court of the Jurisdiction of the Judicial Committee of Her Majesty's Privy Council.

Sections 3, 4, 5 and 16 state, in part:

> 3. [the pre-existing courts]
>
> … shall be united and consolidated together, and shall constitute, under and subject to the provisions of this Act, one Supreme Court of Judicature in England.
>
> 4. [the High Court]
>
> … shall have and exercise original jurisdiction …
>
> 5. All the Judges of the said Court … shall be addressed in the manner which is now customary in addressing the Judges of the Superior Courts of Common Law.
>
> [Senior judges] shall continue to be appointed to the same respective offices, with the same precedence, and by the same respective titles, and in the same manner, respectively, as heretofore.
>
> 16. Jurisdiction of High Court of Justice.
>
> The High Court of Justice shall be a Superior Court of Record, and, subject as in this Act mentioned, there shall be transferred to and vested in the said High Court of Justice the jurisdiction which, at the commencement of this Act, was vested in, or capable of being exercised by, all or any of the Courts following; (that is to say,)
>
> (1.) The High Court of Chancery, as a Common Law Court as well as a Court of Equity, including the jurisdiction of the Master of the Rolls, as a Judge or Master of the Court of Chancery, and any jurisdiction exercised by him in relation to the Court of Chancery as a Common Law Court;
>
> (2.) The Court of Queen's Bench;
>
> (3.) The Court of Common Pleas at Westminster;
>
> (4.) The Court of Exchequer, as a Court of Revenue, as well as Common Law Court;
>
> … [(5)–(11) omitted]
>
> The jurisdiction by this Act transferred to the High Court of Justice shall include (subject to the exceptions herein-after contained) the jurisdiction which, at the commencement of this Act, was vested in, or capable of being exercised by, all or any one or more of the Judges of the said Courts, respectively, sitting in Court or Chambers, or elsewhere, when acting as Judges or a Judge, in pursuance of any statute, law, or custom, and all powers given to any such Court, or to any such Judges or Judge, by any statute; and also all ministerial powers, duties, and authorities, incident to any and every part of the jurisdictions so transferred.

The first point to note is that the High Court of Justice, which forms a new 'Supreme' Court, is a newly created statutory body that did not exist before 1873.

The status of 'Superior Court of Record' is expressly conferred on it by statute. The extensive jurisdiction of the High Court is *constituted* by the Act and the judicial common law or prerogative jurisdiction has gone into abeyance as the new High Court entirely supersedes the old system.[54] Importantly, and examining the actual wording of the provisions, the Act *transfers* and *vests* (s 16) in the High Court 'every part' of the jurisdiction which had previously been 'vested in, or capable of being exercised by', a number of listed prerogative or 'common law' courts such as the Court of Queen's Bench and the High Court of Admiralty, for example. The importance of the ending of the jurisdiction of the old courts by the Act is difficult to understate. Furthermore, all the pre-existing courts disappeared as a function of this Act. The decision by parliament to abolish all the previous law courts and constitute a new Supreme Court is powerful evidence, it is suggested, that parliament intended to displace the original source of the jurisdictional authority of the old courts entirely and substitute a statutory source for the jurisdiction of the court system thenceforth.

The Act divided the High Court into a number of divisions that were labelled in ways that corresponded with the previous system but that does not affect the sheer novelty of parliament's actions. The source of validity post 1873 was reconstituted entirely and was from that time onwards grounded in statute. It was as if the cathedral of judicial common law was dismantled and transported, brick by brick, and rebuilt on completely new and different foundations on parliament's side of the Rubicon between Crown and parliament.

It is also crucial to note that the draftsman specifically stated that any jurisdiction 'capable of being exercised' by the old courts was caught by this section. This must include any further development of judge-made law in the future. Furthermore, in the final paragraph of s 16, the draftsman makes clear that the jurisdiction being removed from the old courts included *any* jurisdiction possessed by judges of any of the courts listed 'in pursuance of any statute, law, or custom'. This means that whether the previous jurisdiction of the courts is correctly defined as prerogative (as argued above), 'common law', custom or other legal basis, the jurisdiction of the courts was thenceforth firmly grounded in a statutory basis by this Act.

In addition, 'all powers given to any such court' are stated to be transferred. The section also says that all powers 'incident to any and every part of the jurisdictions so transferred' are placed onto a statutory footing. These statutory provisions are further evidence that included in the transfer is any power to develop, amend or change judge-made law in the future in the way that courts have always done in the UK. The transfer must also include any claimed 'inherent jurisdiction' or 'original

[54] That jurisdiction of course extends to private law as well as public law. This is to embrace a position set out by Paul Craig (P Craig, *UK, EU and global administrative law, foundations and challenges (The Hamlyn lectures)* (Cambridge University Press, 2015) 143) to the effect that parliamentary intent would need to be embraced as the basis of more than just public law – a position that he claims would be 'unlikely to be shared by scholars in private law, criminal law and international law, who do not conceive of their subject in this manner'. The author respectfully disagrees.

jurisdiction' previously held by the old courts. In terms of the wording in the statute, it is difficult to see how parliament could have made clearer its intention to replace, or displace, the previous grounding of the jurisdiction of the courts in the Crown and when it 'transferred' the 'jurisdiction, which, at the commencement of this Act, was vested in … all, or any one or more of the Judges of the said Courts'. Parliament thereby clearly intended to substitute a statutory source for the jurisdiction of the judicial system as a whole.

It is suggested that any claim that there exists a residual prerogative jurisdiction that is available to judges is unsustainable in the face of such clear statutory language. This can also be seen by the use in s 16 of the wording 'capable of being exercised by' the judiciary. Prior to the Judicature Act, the jurisdiction conferred via the prerogative of justice on the courts was the entirety of the jurisdiction that they were 'capable' of exercising. By expressly conferring that jurisdiction anew, but this time via statute, it is suggested that parliament deliberately constituted an entirely new basis for the court system. Finally, the first line of the long title also confirms the sheer novelty of what was done. Parliament makes clear that the purpose of the Act is the 'constitution' of an entirely new court, the 'Supreme Court', by statutory fiat which entirely replaced the previous system and therefore, and as a matter of logic, displaced the original prerogative of justice which supplied the constitutional basis for the old court system.

It follows, therefore, that the previous jurisdictional basis of the courts before the 1873 Act, which was the royal prerogative of justice, has now gone into abeyance and been wholly replaced by a statutory jurisdiction. This book has argued that the ancient jurisdiction was specifically based on the prerogative of justice and the abeyance principle must therefore apply. However, even if somehow there were to be some other arguable jurisdictional basis for judicial common law other than prerogative, that basis must also necessarily be superseded by the 1873 Act as a function of parliamentary sovereignty because statutory law is superior to all other law and supersedes it. In other words, the administration of justice was put onto a statutory footing and when statute is passed, it necessarily supplants any previous legal basis entirely.

Even if the link between judicial common law and the historic prerogative of justice was somehow once inexplicably, and silently, severed by the judges (contrary to the argument in this book) statute supersedes common law in precisely the same way as it does prerogative. Hence, whatever the nature of their previous jurisdiction, the courts are now statutory bodies under the aegis of Parliament and their jurisdictions are entirely statutory. There is no residual 'common law' jurisdiction. If there ever was a 'higher-order' common law that somehow conferred legal authority on the old courts, that has now been replaced by statutory authority. The better view is that common law means the set of all judicial decisions, and that cannot form the basis for the authority of the judiciary without conceptual circularity and contradiction. One might well ask a sceptic to identify which case severed the courts from their historic jurisdiction derived from prerogative, and established any alleged historic 'common law' jurisdiction of the courts.

Dicey's Response to Blackstone: The Crown Setting Up Courts

Dicey was heavily influenced by the work of Bagehot, who had transformed the way in which the constitution was viewed by focusing heavily on what really happened, pragmatically, rather than the theoretical and strict legal position. This sometimes led Dicey to go too far in his move away from some of Blackstone's explanations for the workings of the legal system. One vivid example of this relates again to the constitutional underpinnings and legal basis of the court system.

As discussed above, Blackstone correctly claimed that the king alone possessed the right to set up courts, which is obviously part of the royal prerogative of justice and incidentally provides further powerful evidence of the original roots of the courts in prerogative.[55] Until the appellate courts were placed on a statutory footing, the power to set up new courts logically must have included setting up various courts of appeal, as indeed Blackstone confirms.[56] Dicey was scathing about the claim by Blackstone that the Crown still theoretically possessed the power to set up courts, including appeal courts. Dicey first quotes a passage where Blackstone claims that the monarch is the 'general conservator of the peace [who] … has the right of erecting courts by his authority … derived from the Crown'.[57] Dicey then dismisses Blackstone's view, saying 'here we are in the midst of unrealities or fictions'.[58] He goes on to pour withering scorn on the idea that anyone other than parliament could set up new courts:

> Neither the King nor the Executive has anything to do with erecting courts of justice. We should rightly conclude that the whole Cabinet had gone mad if to-morrow's Gazette contained an order in council not authorised by statute erecting a new Court of Appeal.[59]

The question of whether the Crown retained the power to set up courts by Dicey's time is far more nuanced than Dicey allows and his heavy criticisms of Blackstone were too strident. It is undoubtedly the case that historically the Crown had the power to set up new courts and did so on a number of occasions, including the court of common pleas, the courts of Equity and, infamously, what became the Star Chamber. In theory, therefore, the Crown retained the power to set up new courts using the royal prerogative of justice.

At first glance, Dicey's point is unarguably correct. The Cabinet could not 'erect a new Court of Appeal' overnight. The reason they could not do so, however, requires a little explanation. There is no doubt that the Crown could set up courts with appellate powers as a matter of history. Crucially, however, it is strongly

[55] Blackstone (n 30).
[56] ibid [257].
[57] ibid.
[58] Dicey (n 21) 11.
[59] ibid.

arguable that the royal prerogative of justice could not be used to set up new appellate courts after 1873 because the Judicature Act 1873, s 4 set up a permanent Court of Appeal with appellate jurisdiction over the High Court which itself had jurisdiction over the lower courts:

> The said Supreme Court shall consist of two permanent Divisions, one of which, under the name of 'Her Majesty's High Court of Justice,' shall have and exercise original jurisdiction, with such appellate jurisdiction from inferior Courts as is herein-after mentioned, and the other of which, under the name of 'Her Majesty's Court of Appeal,' shall have and exercise appellate jurisdiction, with such original jurisdiction as herein-after mentioned as may be incident to the determination of any appeal.

It is a matter of statutory construction as to whether parliament intended to prevent the prerogative of justice being used after this Act to create new courts with appellate jurisdiction. It is suggested that this section is a comprehensive and clear expression of parliamentary intent that thenceforward, appellate jurisdiction would be exercised by the statutory Court of Appeal constituted by the Judicature Act 1873. It would appear, therefore, that whilst Dicey was technically correct to claim that the Cabinet could not set up a new Court of Appeal, this was because parliament had put the prerogative power to do so into abeyance by the Judicature Act 1873, rather than because the Crown *originally* lacked any power to do so.[60] The claims in this chapter are significantly bolstered by observations made by Lord Phillips in *Cart*:

> The Judicature Act 1873 (36 & 37 Vict c 66) marked the assumption by Parliament of responsibility for the infrastructure necessary for the administration of justice. A new hierarchy of courts was created, including a High Court and a Court of Appeal. The common law powers of the King's Bench were vested in the High Court.[61]

A very interesting question remains when considering the creation of tribunals and other bodies for the allocation of compensation or resources at the behest of the executive. The more an administrative body set up by the executive appears to exercise quasi-judicial rather than purely administrative functions, the more it might appear to be encroaching on the territory and jurisdiction of the courts and the modern statutory basis for their jurisdiction. The government cannot lawfully advise the Crown to exercise the prerogative in way that frustrates or is inconsistent with an Act of Parliament, which is why care must be taken in considering the quasi-judicial status of administrative bodies that become more and more formalised in their processes, and even their internal appeal processes.[62]

If pressed too far, it might be thought that a tribunal set up via prerogative to allocate compensation may cross the line between the prerogative of making *ex gratia* payments and the prerogative of setting up a court which is now in

[60] R Craig (n 33) 25.
[61] *R (Cart) v Upper Tribunal (Public Law Project and another intervening)* [2011] UKSC 28, [2012] 1 AC 663, [65].
[62] ibid.

abeyance. Relatedly, how tribunals straddle the awkward boundary between executive and judicial functions in analysing the case of *Evans* is discussed by the author elsewhere.[63]

In brief summary, then, the constitutional architecture radically changed following the Glorious Revolution. After 1688, royal prerogative was implicitly or directly authorised by parliament so that prerogatives from then on were authorised and, for Kershaw, delegated on the authority and imprimatur of parliament. The aspect of the prerogative of justice relating to dismissal of judges was put into abeyance by the Act of Settlement 1701. More significantly, the Judicature Acts abolished the old courts whose authority was rooted in the Crown and created the High Court, Court of Appeal and other bodies whose authority was and remains entirely grounded in parliament. Pleasingly from a democratic point of view, all judicial roads now lead, directly or indirectly, to the parliamentary Rome.

Part I: Conclusion

Part I has sought to reconcile the two competing definitions of prerogative set out by Dicey and Blackstone and put prerogative into its modern constitutional context. It argues that all prerogatives are exclusive to the Crown and that all residual non-statutory powers exercised by the Crown are rooted in prerogative. Prerogative has its roots in land and contains legislative, executive and judicial aspects. Prerogative can no longer be used in emergencies contrary to the law, *pace* Locke, and cannot affect common law, *pace* Wade. The foundational prerogative of justice was once the source of the legitimate authority of the courts, but a series of Acts have resulted in the modern courts being wholly statutory bodies whose authority, validity and legitimacy is now entirely derived from parliament. This is as it should be, in a democracy.

[63] R Craig, 'Black Spiders Weaving Webs: The Constitutional Implications of Executive Veto of Tribunal Determinations' (2016) 79 *Modern Law Review* 166; *R (Evans) v Attorney General* [2015] UKSC 21, [2015] 1 AC 1787, [2015] 2 WLR 813 (SC).

PART II

The Crown

6

The Crown and Common Law

Introduction

Part II defends the claim that the Crown has no so-called 'common law' powers. This claim flows logically from the argument made in previous chapters and throughout this book that the terms 'prerogative powers' and 'non-statutory legal powers of the Crown' are synonymous. Indeed, this monograph goes further and claims that the Crown should be defined, at its core, as the legal bearer of the remaining prerogative powers.[1] Indeed, the Crown might best be considered as simply a set of complex, interacting rules governing the exercise of prerogative power such that the concept of the Crown is an example of the fiction theory usually discussed in relation to the issue of corporate identity.[2] It might even be a paradigm example of where there is no clearly identifiable, pre-existing legal entity sitting behind a set of interlocking legal norms. Instead, it might better to assess the set of remaining prerogatives on their own terms and only then consider the Crown as the nominal bearer.

This novel core definition of the Crown as the bearer of the remaining prerogatives must therefore be treated with a little caution. This is because there are strong Hartian arguments that no simple, or single, definition is really possible because the term can have different meanings depending on the context.[3] So, for example, the Crown can frequently refer to the government and the executive, or sometimes to the body technically bringing a criminal prosecution or sometimes to the realm as a whole, especially internationally. Nevertheless, the *core* definition defended in this monograph is arguably reflected in the wise, and surprisingly overlooked, words of Lord Simon in *Town Investments*.

> The term 'the Crown' is therefore used in constitutional law to denote the collection of such of those powers as remain extant (the royal prerogative), together with such other powers as have been expressly conferred by statute on 'the Crown'.[4]

As discussed in chapter one, the phrase 'common law' has different meanings in different contexts.[5] It is usually possible to discern which meaning is intended in

[1] Albeit with some extra powers expressly conferred by statute.

[2] M Wolff, 'On the Nature of Legal Persons' (1938) 54 *Law Quarterly Review* 494, 505.

[3] HLA Hart, 'Definition and Theory in Jurisprudence' in *Essays in Jurisprudence and Philosophy* (Oxford University Press, 1983) ch 1. See further below.

[4] *Town Investments Ltd. and Others v Department of the Environment* [1978] AC 359, 397.

[5] See ch 1, pp 13–16.

the particular circumstances. The same could equally be said about the Crown. It might be useful to differentiate some of those meanings. One example might be when the term is used to represent the nation as a whole. In such circumstances, it might be better to relabel the Crown in that context as 'Crown-in-Realm'. Another example would be when the Crown is used to represent the prosecution – perhaps 'Crown-as-Prosecutor' would be clarificatory. The remainder of this chapter focuses on the core meaning of the concept defended in this book, which is that the Crown is best understood as the legal bearer of the remaining prerogative powers.

If all non-statutory legal powers of the Crown are prerogative powers, it follows logically that the Crown has no common law powers. This flows from the claim defended in this monograph that common law powers and prerogative powers are conceptually distinct. It will be recalled that common law powers are those powers that the courts in effect created and linked to the remedies sought by applicants to those courts.[6] The courts effectively conferred those legal powers on applicants. They are thus distinguishable from historic powers of the monarch. The judges originally administered the prerogative of justice on behalf of the monarch when they toured the country asserting, and confirming, his regal authority over the populace.

The fact that the original jurisdiction of the courts derived from the prerogative of justice means, therefore, that the idea that prerogative powers form part of the common law created by the courts fundamentally misunderstands the structure, nature and history of English law. Furthermore, this chapter will argue that the Crown continues to operate entirely outside the (necessarily limited) jurisdiction of the ordinary courts and to this day cannot sue or be sued. Nor does the Crown itself, in contrast with its servants or agents, enter any contracts. Technically, the Crown itself has no personality at common law.[7] The relationship between the Crown and its servants was originally, and to a large extent is still, governed by prerogative. As discussed in earlier chapters, the broad definition of prerogative that is rooted in Dicey's work has received heavyweight approval in the case law culminating in *Miller I*, where the majority held that the 'Royal prerogative encompasses the residue of powers which remain vested in the Crown'.[8] This powerful and recent statement from the highest court is entirely consistent with the definition of the Crown defended so far. Those powers are exclusive to the Crown, as Blackstone argued.[9]

In a book chapter in 2015, Lord Sales, a Supreme Court judge, argues that the Crown does have common law powers.[10] He draws a distinction between

[6] See further ch 2, pp 35–36.

[7] *M v Home Office (CA)* [1992] QB 270, 301.

[8] *R (Miller) v Secretary of State for Exiting the European Union* [2017] UKSC 5, [2018] AC 61, [2017] 2 WLR 583 ('*Miller I*'), at [47].

[9] W Blackstone, *Commentaries on the Laws of England* (1753), Book 1, ch 7, 239. See further ch 3, pp 54–55.

[10] Lord Sales, 'Crown Powers, the Royal Prerogative and Fundamental Rights' in H Wilberg and M Elliott (eds), *The Scope and Intensity of Substantive Review* (Bloomsbury, 2015) 361.

'prerogative powers' and 'common-law powers', which he defines as those powers that 'the Crown enjoys in the same way as every other person, by virtue of it having legal personality'.[11] He claims that 'rights common to the Crown and everyone else are not aspects of the prerogative' and that this 'appears now to be accepted at the highest level', citing recent case law.[12] He claims that Dicey's definition 'conflates' these two categories.[13] Lord Sales' arguments provide a sophisticated foil for the exploration in this chapter of the relationship between Crown, prerogative and common law.

Part II aims to demonstrate some of the difficulties that may be caused by adopting Lord Sales approach, and in particular if the courts were to approve the claim that the Crown possesses 'common law' powers. It addresses his claims both conceptually and from a pragmatic legal point of view. Potential problems include blurring the boundaries between public and private power and failing to work with the grain of the ancient principle that servants, agents and ministers must bear the legal responsibility for their official decisions. The issue, then, is a significant but by now familiar problem: there is serious lack of clarity as to the legal basis for Crown powers that are not based on statute. Is it correct to describe all such actions as fundamentally traceable to, indeed defined by, prerogative as a matter of law, or are there two distinct legal categories of non-statutory legal powers possessed by the Crown: prerogative and 'common law'? If the Crown is properly defined as the legal bearer of prerogative powers, then the former is correct, and the latter must be rejected.

Lord Sales is right to point to an interesting conundrum for judges addressing executive actions that are not rooted in statute. On the one hand, there are legal powers that are *sui generis*, universally agreed to be based on prerogative, such as creating peers. In these scenarios, there is no analogous legal power that could be exercised by private citizens, and therefore no sense in claiming that such a legal power is shared with them by the Crown. On the other hand, when the government enters a contract, that would appear at first sight to be a correlative legal analogue with when an ordinary citizen enters a contract. These are the powers that Lord Sales labels as 'common law' powers.

The legal basis for entering contracts as between government ministers and citizens is radically different, however. This is because ministers entering such contracts are doing so in their formal capacity and on behalf of the government. Their position in that government is officially a function of the prerogative of appointing ministers. Those ministers are directly, and traditionally personally liable for any breaches of those contracts. A decision by a minister to enter a contract in their official capacity therefore involves an aspect of prerogative power that inescapably requires the deployment of *public* power. The minister must act

[11] ibid.
[12] ibid 362.
[13] ibid.

lawfully subject to the quite different legal standards and norms imposed on public officials that bear no relation to general contractual transactions in private law. A conceptual chasm therefore separates such legal scenarios from ordinary contracts by private citizens.

Part II defends the claim that the Crown has no common law powers in stages. First, it addresses the vexed question of defining the Crown itself, which is the purpose of the first chapter in this part. This includes an examination of the views of Wade and Lord Sales on whether the Crown should be seen as a corporation sole. The next chapter addresses the claim that the Crown has legal powers at common law. Blackstone and Wade's claims to this effect are analysed. It is frequently assumed that the Crown now has some kind of formal legal status at common law. This claim is questionable, not least because it is the *minister* or *government department* who is actually sued by citizens aggrieved at some action or decision of the government, not the Crown itself – and in fact this practice continues to this day. This is a crucial distinction, frequently elided, that has important implications.

It is therefore suggested that the Crown has a *sui generis* legal status, not least because it has 'resisted all efforts to grasp its essence in unambiguous terms'.[14] Kantorowicz mentions that it was treated 'for some purposes of taxation or jurisdiction or administration' as 'quasi-corporate *ad hoc*' in 'late mediaeval England' which for our modern purposes simply begs the question as to its actual status and definition today.[15] Whilst the Crown now formally, and statutorily, stands behind defendants in cases brought against government ministers and departments, that is not the same as saying the Crown itself exercised any legal powers at common law in such cases. The more important question for our purposes surrounds the status of the Crown at judicial common law and the effect of the Crown Proceedings Act 1947 ('CPA 1947'), which is addressed in the final chapter of part II. The prism through which the issue of the Crown's status at common law is examined throughout this chapter is the prerogative that stands behind the making of contracts by government officials.

The final chapter of part II also claims that the better view of the relationship between the Crown and ministers in such circumstances is that any litigation involving ministers acting in their public capacity is best described as a 'disguised public law' claim, even when the litigation appears to be a solely private law action. This is because the ostensibly private law action presupposes that the minister's decisions are *intra vires*. It may seem odd that quasi-public law actions can be heard in private law but, as is well known, English is law is famously pragmatic about where legal proceedings are heard.

[14] E Kantorowicz, *The King's Two Bodies: A Study in Mediaeval Political Theology* (Princeton University Press, 1957) 382.

[15] ibid.

Problems with Defining the Crown

The issue of state liability for wrongs was always going to be a somewhat delicate issue in a country where the king can do no wrong. Matters were complicated by the fact that the Glorious Revolution relocated the centre of gravity of executive and legislative power into one body. As Mark Graber put it, 'institutional power after 1648 and 1688 flowed to Parliament, the institution on the winning side of the English revolution'.[16] The major constitutional changes in relation to the locus of executive power over the centuries are what led to Maitland's ingenious constitutional conundrum as to who owes the national debt. No satisfactory answer has been suggested so far.[17] Maitland's apparent constitutional paradox serves as a serious warning against attempts to provide a neat, single answer to the issue of defining the Crown because of its polymorphous nature. Tomkins makes a similar point:

> [T]he Crown is a label that can be used to mean different things in different contexts. Sometimes it refers to the 'person of the sovereign', sometimes to an institution of government and sometimes to 'the entire collective of sovereign and ministers' … One of the reasons why 'the Crown' has no neat and tidy legal definition is because it is a term that may be used to refer to a number of legally and politically different entities.[18]

Relatedly, and no less problematically, when dealing with wrongs there is an intensely human desire to find, or manufacture, a responsible entity at the apex of the pyramid to hold to account – and not just with wrongs. Austin famously, and with an obvious nod to Hobbes, insisted that behind every constitution there must be a legally unlimited single sovereign power.[19] Hart demolished this trope and in forcing us to confront the reality of our complex system, infinitely improved our understanding of it.[20]

It is an error to consider the Crown as coterminous with the state (outside of the international context). In the domestic sphere, the state necessarily includes important institutions such as, for example, the Scottish Parliament, the Tribunal Service and divers Local Authorities.[21] On no sensible understanding of the Crown can these bodies be said to form part of it. The spectre of the Crown caused

[16] M Graber, '*Ship Money*: The Case that Time and Whittington Forgot', University of Maryland Francis King Carey School of Law Legal Studies Research Paper, No 2020-06, http://ssrn.com/abstract=3545486, 7.

[17] F Maitland, 'Moral Personality and Legal Personality', *Collected Papers* (Cambridge University Press, 1911) 318.

[18] A Tomkins, 'The Crown in Scots Law' in A McHarg and T Mullen (eds), *Public Law in Scotland* (Avizandum Publishing, 2006) 263 64.

[19] J Austin, *Province of Jurisprudence Determined* (John Murray, 1832), Lecture VI; T Hobbes, *Leviathan* [1660], edited by Richard Tuck (Cambridge University Press, 1991) ch XVIII.

[20] HLA Hart, *The Concept of Law* (Oxford University Press, 1961) ch IV.

[21] J McLean, *Searching for the State in British Legal Thought* (Cambridge University Press 2012) 140. HM Moore, 'Liability for Acts of Public Servants' (1907) 23 *Law Quarterly Review* 12, generally but especially 13–14, 16–17 and 21–23.

significant complications for the courts. McLean details the challenges faced by the courts in attempting to deal with changing circumstances as society modernised and various public, and private, bodies and institutions sprung up and faded away over time. She describes the 'formalistic' turn taken by the courts as they sought to narrow the immunities they had perhaps mistakenly conferred on some public bodies by including them within the Crown.[22]

Notwithstanding her sober assessment of the serious difficulties of locating a single entity which could be labelled as the 'state' as such, McLean nevertheless at points hints at a lingering desire to find a single, or at worst collective, 'real will' for the purposes of legal liability.[23] In a section headed 'A common will to do wrong', she claims that the 'most prominent question in the domestic common law [is] … how to locate a legal person to sue'.[24] The problem with this argument is that in her attempt to locate a single or collective will, in order satisfy the urge to ascribe legal and moral responsibility, she is chasing a chimera. As Harold Laski so memorably put it, 'the state cannot be sued because there is no state to sue'.[25]

It is fair to acknowledge that the title itself, 'Searching for the State in British Public Legal Thought', arguably suggests that McLean thinks the search may ultimately be futile. Nonetheless, the idea of 'searching' for the state presupposes that *finding* a 'state' might be good, if it were possible. This suggests a residual itch to locate a morally responsible entity to blame, subject to 'moral opprobrium' and sue.[26] This is not McLean's *general* view. Her primary approach is the opposite, emphasising that the state should not be seen as 'a single *personne morale*, but rather as a diffuse and variegated complex of entities whose "unity" is created by the application of shared 'public law' norms'.[27] McLean's general approach is thus wholly consistent with this book's analysis of the variegated meanings of the Crown, depending on the context.

The incipient and frequent desire to locate a single 'will' is reminiscent the approach taken by Bentham and others who have a strong focus on finding 'real persons' and 'real powers' in order to impose liability.[28] In other words, Bentham's focus on finding a 'real' defendant springs from an instinctive desire to find a 'will' at an institutional level. Bentham's solution is to insist on locating responsibility, and therefore fault in some sense, at the personal level. This approach was of course mirrored by the courts who, when it was relevant, also insisted that a servant of the Crown be located before liability could be established.

[22] McLean (n 21) 141–46, quoting S Anderson, 'Public Law' in W Cornish and others (eds), *The Oxford History of the Laws of England* (Oxford University Press, 2010) vol. XI, 370, also 214–16 and generally ch 5.
[23] McLean (n 21).
[24] ibid 214.
[25] H Laski, 'The Responsibility of the State in England' (1918-19) 32 *Harvard Law Review* 447, 450.
[26] McLean (n 21) 229.
[27] ibid 167.
[28] ibid 4, fn 11 referencing J Bentham, *A Fragment on Government*, W Harrison (ed) (Basil Blackwell, 1948).

It would be better, it is suggested, to adopt the approach of Martin Wolff who argued for a 'fiction theory' for corporations in his analysis of the 'nature of legal persons'.[29] This approach contains 'concealed wisdom' because it is flexible enough to accommodate differing scenarios where 'no uniform answer' can be given.[30] It does this, in large part, because it 'allows certain bodies to be treated as persons in some respects and non-persons in others'.[31] It is the flexibility that is so attractive in considering the concept of the Crown, precisely because the Crown is so amorphous and chameleonic in different circumstances having undergone, as Dicey put it, a 'transformation [that] was based on the constant use of fictions'.[32] If the methodology of identifying an entity and only then considering action, responsibility and remedy is reversed, the alleged corporate nature of the Crown diminishes drastically as an issue. Remedies are sought against the government and the courts then determine if that remedy should be granted. If a justiciable prerogative power is exercised inappropriately as a matter of public law, then a remedy should be granted regardless of whether it is possible to identify a responsible will or entity.

Hart's Alternative Approach

McLean's methodology and approach are arguably consistent with Hart whose penetrating analysis argues that, pragmatically, public law (and law generally) now comprises a highly intricate set of rules ascribing liability in certain complex circumstances that vary in context.[33] This is also entirely consistent with Wolff's approach. No single or collective institutional will exists. This does not prevent sensible and just remedies being awarded to litigants seeking remedies for wrongs done by various public institutions, ascribing blame or adopting fictions as far as is strictly necessary and no more. In classic style, the common law solutions to these problems are pragmatic and aimed at the lowest level of abstraction, which is the relevant department, not 'the state' or Crown as a whole.[34]

As a general rule, English common law historically started with remedies for wrongs and reverse engineered from that point to the minimum extent necessary to get to a pragmatic result. Common law has little time for the metaphysics of law. Instead, it is suggested, it would be better start with the notion of remedies, as is traditional in common law.[35] From this starting point, solutions to wrongs done by different public institutions can be fashioned pragmatically and incrementally, as

[29] Wolff (n 2) 505.
[30] ibid 504, 505.
[31] ibid 511.
[32] AV Dicey, *Introduction to the Study of the Law of the Constitution*, 8th edn (Macmillan, 1927) 465–66 (footnote 2).
[33] Hart (n 3), esp 21–26.
[34] C Sunstein, 'Incompletely Theorized Agreements' (1995) 108 *Harvard Law Review* 1733.
[35] And as argued above, see ch 2, pp 35–38.

we shall see further below. This methodology is preferable to the alternative which is to locate some kind of entity that 'wills', label it as part of the 'Crown', identify its alleged decisions, decide those decisions are wrong in some sense, and only then identify an appropriate remedy. Starting with remedies, by contrast, is much more consistent with the kind of pragmatic, solution-focused, positivistic framework that is characteristic of the common law over centuries. It is important to acknowledge that understanding the history and development of common law in terms of remedies is not the whole story. Common law judges have also innovated in multiple other ways to fashion solutions to difficult cases and grant remedies as a result. Common law may have started by reasoning backwards from remedies, but it quickly learned to reason forwards on occasion as well.[36]

The instinct for holding someone directly, morally, responsible for errors is deeply embedded in human psychology. This drive struggled against the longstanding principle that the king can do no wrong, itself arguably a function of now-outdated beliefs in divine ordination and the risks, pragmatically, involved in any subject standing up against the monarch directly. The efforts to avoid attaching blame to the king led to a norm developing that an adviser was held liable instead of the monarch for wrongful acts causing harm to other. One of the oldest and most important constitutional doctrines is the notion of ministerial responsibility. This grew out of the core principle of royal inerrancy because it became established that if anything did go wrong, it must be the responsibility of bad advisers and bad advice, not the responsibility of the king. One side effect of this kind of moral chicanery is that it creates a split between morality and normal constitutional developments. In other words, it might be thought that one of the reasons why the constitution is so positivist is because of the historical chasm separating what most people would have regarded as the actual, regal, moral responsibility for various mistakes and the quite different allocation of *legal* liability. It is not controversial to assert that when dealing with matters of high politics, a significantly more nuanced approach to questions of morality might sometimes be required.

Breaches that would normally sound in contract law against the king's advisers instead only gave rise to a claim under the Petition of Right. Over time, as we have seen, this gave rise to a practice of government departments putting forward a nominal defendant in litigation against the government, even if that person had little involvement in the issue. The government would underwrite the costs and any damages. This became more and more unworkable until the point where legislation was required to remedy the situation. Crucially, the statutory allocation of departments to become the nominal defendants, replacing individuals, leaves unresolved the issue of state or Crown liability in generic terms. Indeed, the Crown continues to be outside the jurisdiction of the courts.[37] It might therefore

[36] The author is grateful to Paul Craig, who made this point emphatically – and correctly – in correspondence.

[37] *M v Home Office (HL)* [1994] 1 AC 377.

be thought that the actual historic common law approach of ascribing state liability to a nominated defendant rather tends to support the claim that identification of a transcendental 'will' or single entity at fault was never of much concern to the courts. What matters is securing an appropriate remedy for a worthwhile applicant, in the interests of justice.

Rather than identifying a particular 'will', then, the Hartian vision of a system of legal rules that provide a functionally effective remedy in accordance with differing sets of norms in different circumstances is the better approach. If the rules are breached then a quashing order or damages are awarded without any necessity to identify or blame the state, an individual or any particular collective or single 'will'. The key effect of this pragmatic solution-focused approach is that it significantly undermines the drive to define, semantically, a single meaning of 'state' or 'Crown' for the purposes of constitutional or administrative law. There is no need to do so, because there is no necessity for there to be a defined entity of this kind for the purposes of securing remedies for those who are affected by erroneous decisions of public bodies. Attempting to *define* the state or the Crown as a specific entity with a single 'will' is revealed, on close inspection, to be an unhelpful distraction.

Hart also argued against attempts to define concepts such as the State, by drawing an analogy with something that 'corresponds' to the label in the physical world. In such cases, analysis that attempts to impose analogous rules originally designed for real persons, for example, on concepts such as a corporation (or the 'Crown') risk obscuring more than they illuminate.[38] In other words, the analogies may fail. It is probably better to abandon these attempts to analogise between the Crown and other concepts. The Crown is *sui generis*. Complicated questions have arisen as to whether a *legally created* 'will' is even theoretically capable of doing wrong because it seems contradictory for an entity that only exists within a nominally just legal system to be empowered to commit wrongs.[39] Hart is withering in his criticism of such simplistic approaches.

What is fascinating about Hart's analysis of attempts by others to locate simple, semantic definitions of concepts such as the state was that he casts a particularly cold eye over attempts that insist on real world correlates. He demands, in stark contrast, that we consider the concepts in their full context, which may be very different depending on the circumstances. It may well be that we ascribe moral and legal liability to real individuals in private law, predicated on notions of will, choice and moral culpability rooted in many centuries of philosophical argument about human nature and deontology. There is no necessary reason why the same moralistic, anthropomorphic, approach is appropriate for ascribing legal liability to public bodies – on the contrary in fact.

[38] Hart (n 3) 46–47.
[39] ibid.

The problem, of course, is that as we have moved away from personal liability of Crown servants, we risk falling between two stools. The nominated defendant solution was slowly perceived to be unworkable, leading to CPA 1947, discussed in chapter eight. The relentless search for a responsible 'will' was therefore forced to abandon the nominated defendant. Advocates of what might be termed the 'will' approach proceeded to start looking for a 'will' at the institutional level. This project was doomed to failure. The better approach, it might be thought, would be to focus on whether the regulatory structure now provides adequate, real-world remedies for wrongs. The conclusion of this chapter suggests that this desirable outcome, post CPA 1947 and *M v Home Office*, has been functionally achieved.

Conflating Public and Private Law

Dicey took inordinate pride in the fact that the High Court drew no distinction between private citizens and public officials even when dealing with purely administrative acts – praising the 'absolute supremacy of the ordinary law of the land'.[40] He regarded this as evidence of compliance with the core rule of law principle of equality before the law. He further criticised the French system for its alternative approach which treated public officials differently from private citizens. One of the most important features in the development of public law in this country in recent decades has been the recognition that Dicey was wrong on this point and the French were right. It makes no sense to treat the exercise of power by public officials indistinguishably from private citizens. This is to take nothing away from the point that one beneficial side effect of this approach was to establish quasi-state liability considerably earlier in English law than on the continent.[41]

The twentieth century saw the development, with many fits and starts, of a separate system of administrative law, focused on judicial review of executive action, that was and remains quite distinct from private law actions between individuals. The general failure of common law to give proper effect to the distinction between public law and private law has been pointedly critiqued by Loughlin.[42] It has taken many decades for the creeping realisation to crystallise that the French were right to distinguish, formally, public and private law matters. This was somewhat ruefully admitted in the Donoughmore Committee report in 1932, which in

[40] Dicey (n 32) 325.

[41] McLean (n 21) 209. Scottish law took a different course than England and Wales on this issue: see *British Medical Association v Greater Glasgow Health Board* 1989 SC (HL) 65 at 94, and the Crown Suits (Scotland) Act 1857, well discussed in A Tomkins, 'The Crown in Scots Law' in A McHarg and T Mullen (eds), *Public Law in Scotland* (Avizandum Publishing, 2006) 270–71. Unlike English law historically, under Scottish law the Crown can be sued as of right.

[42] M Loughlin, 'The State, the Crown and the Law' in M Sunkin and S Payne, *The Nature of the Crown: A Legal and Political Analysis* (Oxford University Press, 1999), esp 69–70.

one sense may be thought to have fired the starting gun for the modern development of public law provision in English law.[43]

It should be noted, however, that the apparent moribund state of judicial review in the early twentieth century belies the activity of the judiciary in the more distant past. Indeed, a recent book by Paul Craig argues that previous centuries developed principles of judicial review not radially dissimilar to today.[44] He argues that therefore Lord Diplock's view that 'progress towards a comprehensive system of administrative law' was the 'greatest achievement pf the English courts' in his lifetime might in the end have been more restorative than innovative.[45] As J Stuart Anderson points out, 'the Commissioners of Excise controlled a large modern statutory agency, efficient and effective' from the eighteenth century onwards.[46] Furthermore, 'excisemen were treated as officers in relation to the public' and were thus in a sense public officials but at the same time 'the relationship between commissioners and excise was one of employment'.[47]

As discussed in chapter two, English law was not always understood as being entirely 'private' law.[48] On the contrary, the fact that the law focuses on remedies secured from the king's judges means that, in a sense, English law started as *public* law because it was the king's officials, his judges, who were intervening in disputes and enforcing the king's law. The hegemonic victory of the royal courts in imposing a law 'common' to the whole land eventually came to be understood as a system of private law and private remedies, from which private rights developed parasitically. The third, and by far the most recent stage, is the rise of a separate regime of public law adjudication which was delayed by decades, if not longer, by Dicey's influence. One example of the long-term effect of Dicey's mistake is that, astonishingly, it was not until 2000 that a separate Administrative Court was established.

During the long centuries where private and public law were not properly distinguished, the status of the Crown in private law was somewhat anomalous. The Crown was and remains outside the jurisdiction of the royal courts. Servants of the Crown, and in particular ministers, were held personally liable for legal wrongs committed by the executive but the Crown itself was immune. What is so fascinating about the rise in a separate public law regime is that it appears to have roughly coincided with a significant challenge to the traditional, orthodox immunity of the Crown at common law. In other words, just at the point where the development of a separate public law regime could in theory have been married

[43] Report of the Committee on Ministers' Powers (Donoughmore Committee), Cmd 4060/1932, 112.

[44] P Craig, *English Administrative Law since 1550* (Oxford University Press, 2024). Unfortunately, the timing of the publication of this monograph and Paul Craig's book meant that there was not sufficient time available for this monograph to be able to engage with its core ideas, still less to do the arguments justice.

[45] *R v Inland Revenue Commissioners, ex parte National Federation of Self-Employed and Small Business Ltd* [1982] AC 617, 641.

[46] Anderson (n 22) 343.

[47] ibid 343–44.

[48] See ch 2, pp 44–45.

up again with the Crown as the appropriate vehicle through which to consider the exercise of such public powers, the system, at almost the same time, pushed to draw the Crown in some sense *within* the aegis of private law from which it had been excluded for so long.

This coincidence, and the unhelpful attempt to marry the concept of the Crown to the emerging realm, is well discussed, and to some extent lamented, by McLean.[49] The judicial refusal, however, to broaden the concept of the Crown to include public authorities generally is perhaps not hugely surprising. This would have meant that railway companies, myriad municipal corporations and trading entities and even 'organizations for profit' might have had to be included within the concept of the Crown.[50] The difficulties and ripple effects of the attempts by the courts to grapple with the implications of the 'formalistic turn' adopted by the courts in relation to the Crown in this context culminated in the changes made by CPA 1947.[51]

The concept of the Crown developed over time alongside considerable efforts to ascribe a legal personality to it. Three options have commonly been mooted and are considered in more depth below. First, that the Crown should be treated as a natural person. Second, that it should be treated as a corporation sole – in other words as a legally artificial entity with one member only at a time. Third, that it should be treated as a corporation aggregate, in other words a collection of legal personalities, especially corporations sole, that fluctuate over time. It is quite ironic to see this mangling of the concept of the Crown in an attempt to shoehorn it into one or other of these *private* law categories at roughly the same time that the legal powers of the Crown, ie royal prerogatives, were in principle being subjected to judicial review as a matter of *public* law.

More importantly for the purposes of the remainder of this chapter, it will be suggested that the attempt to constitute the Crown as a legal entity *at judicial common law* was always misguided and should be abandoned. In particular, it is suggested that the Crown defies categorisation in any of the three ways mooted. This is precisely because it predates the common law, formerly possessed plenary powers and is, to this day, immune from the jurisdiction of the courts. The definition and meaning of 'the Crown' is always contextual and its meaning, like other concepts, can shift depending on the circumstances, as Hart persuasively argued.[52]

As the technical holder of legislative prerogative powers, the Crown remains an important legal entity but attempting to confine its definition to one or other of the three typologies commonly suggested is to miss a great deal of nuance and also fails to appreciate the Crown's amorphous nature.

[49] McLean (n 21) 143.
[50] ibid 149–59.
[51] ibid 163.
[52] Hart (n 3).

Crown as Corporation

Lord Sales' View that the Crown Should be Viewed as a Corporation Sole

In his recent chapter on common law powers, Lord Sales has set out a contrary view, claiming that there 'is not much doubt that classification of the Crown as a corporation sole is the correct legal view'.[53] He further claimed that this view 'has the considerable authority of Coke, Blackstone, Maitland and, in modern times, Sir William Wade behind it'.[54] The next subsection deals with the arguments put forward by Coke and Maitland. The chapter thens turn to Wade before considering the proper place of the Crown at common law explained by John Howell, who draws on Blackstone. It will be argued, *pace* Lord Sales, that the Crown cannot be classified as a corporation, either sole or aggregate, not least because it is outside the jurisdiction of the ordinary courts but also because it is *sui generis*.

Coke and Maitland

It is probably best to start with Coke who might reasonably be thought to have caused as much trouble as help in the development of English law.[55] Coke's original analysis was caught up in what Maitland calls 'metaphysical – or we might say metaphysiological – nonsense' which preoccupied commentators for centuries, concerning whether the king had two 'bodies' or not: one body natural and one body corporate.[56] Maitland elegantly fillets Coke, amongst others, by pointing out the serious confusion in a conceptual framework that purportedly conferred corporate sole status on the Crown but simultaneously, for example, required all court cases to be restarted on the demise of the monarch.[57] It will be recalled that historically, justice was administered on behalf of the king who nominally even continued to sit on the Bench even when not physically present.[58] When a judge

[53] Lord Sales (n 10) 364.

[54] ibid.

[55] See for example the voluminous literature demolishing the entire corpus of Coke's arguments about Magna Carta, for which he is most famous – for example, WS McKechnie, *Magna Carta*, 2nd edn (Glasgow, 1914). See also J Goldsworthy, *Parliamentary Sovereignty: Contemporary Debates* (Cambridge University Press, 2010) 18–19 and J Goldsworthy, *The Sovereignty of Parliament: History and Philosophy* (Clarendon Press, 1999) 122–23, quoting Cromartie as arguing that Coke was 'embarrassingly extreme'. Hobbes even accuses Coke of citing long overruled law for his own purposes and to 'diminish … the King's authority', which is about as serious an accusation as could possibly be made at that time (T Hobbes, *Discourses* [1681], collected and edited by W Molesworth, Vol VI (John Bohn: 1840) 62).

[56] FW Maitland, 'Crown as Corporation' (1901) 17 *Law Quarterly Review* 134; Kantorowicz, (n 14).

[57] ibid 135–36.

[58] J Chitty, *A Treatise on the Law of the Prerogatives of the Crown: And the Relative Duties and Rights of the Subject* (Butterworth, 1820), 244; McKechnie (n 55) 385.

dies mid-case, the litigation obviously has to be restarted. Hence, the death of the monarch traditionally led to the necessity for all litigation to be recommenced.

The confusion is caused because it makes no sense for court cases to have to be restarted because the monarch has died and at the same time demand that the Crown should be considered as a corporation sole. The whole point of treating the Crown as a corporation sole would be to remove the necessity for all court cases to be restarted on the death of the monarch because the corporation would simply continue post-demise. Nonetheless, as Maitland pointed out, on the 'demise of the Crown … all litigation not only came to a stop but had to be begun all over again'.[59] The fact that cases were still restarted even as late as the accession of Queen Victoria is a fatal blow to the claim that the Crown is properly to be treated as a corporation sole as a matter of legal history. It is also a fascinating codicil to a core claim of this book which is the historical roots of the ordinary courts are in the Crown rather than any mythical, higher 'common law'.[60] Restarting all cases rather suggests that the umbilical cord between the Crown and the courts may not have been entirely cut, at least until that rule was abolished. If the link between the courts and the Crown had been severed centuries ago, why would litigation need to restart as late as the nineteenth century?

Lord Sales is certainly correct that Maitland stated in his first paragraph that 'we now say that the Crown is a corporation' but this is a prelude to Maitland's delivery of a series of hammer blows against the idea that the Crown is a corporation *sole* including describing Coke's idea as 'sterile and unprofitable'.[61] Instead, he argues that 'our sovereign lord is *not* a "corporation sole" but is the head of a complex and highly organized "corporation aggregate of many"' (emphasis added).[62] Indeed he argues that 'such is the destined fate of all corporations sole'.[63] He also says 'the suggestion that "the Crown" is very often a repressed or partially recognized corporation aggregate is forced upon us' when we look at the language of judges 'when they … are not feeling the pressure of old theories'.[64] Lord Sales is right to say that Maitland was a supporter of the claim that the Crown is a corporation of some kind, but not that he was a supporter of the Crown as a corporation sole. Maitland thought the Crown was a corporation aggregate. Thus, it would be fair to say that Lord Sales may very well argue for the Crown to be considered as a corporation sole, but he can cite less academic and other support than might first appear.

Maitland also pointed out just how much remedial legislation in Victorian times was required to try to mitigate some of the deleterious effects of the demise of the previous monarch in other areas of the law.[65] If the Crown was a corporation

[59] Maitland (n 56) 131, 136.
[60] Goldsworthy (2010) (n 55) ch 1 'The myth of common law constitutionalism'.
[61] Maitland (n 56) 144.
[62] ibid 140.
[63] ibid 146.
[64] ibid 139.
[65] ibid 136–37.

sole, this legislation would have been unnecessary because the corporation sole, as an artificial person that does not die, would continue notwithstanding the death of the monarch. The fact that the legislation was unavoidable necessarily contradicts the claim that the Crown should properly be considered a corporation sole. Reliance on Coke as authority for the idea of the Crown as corporation sole is an entirely plausible reading of Coke, so Lord Sales is correct to that extent, but Coke's reasoning leaves a great deal to be desired – as these examples perhaps demonstrate. Perhaps it would be best to classify this element of Coke's work as another example of what Harrison Moore memorably calls his 'maledictions' and move on.[66]

Wade's View on the Corporation Sole Debate

Wade certainly supports the idea of the Crown as corporation sole, although his defence of the idea is somewhat confusing. This is perhaps shown when he discusses the Crown and the Queen in an unhelpful way – first distinguishing the two terms, then seemingly eliding them:

> In truth, 'the Crown' means simply the Queen, though the term is usually confined to her in her political or constitutional capacity. She has plenty of legal personality, both as a natural person and, according to a long line of authority, as a corporation sole … The Crown's legal personality is obvious from the fact that it can convey land and make contracts without statutory assistance.[67]

It is possible that Wade chose to define the Crown as a corporation sole precisely because the Crown might appear, at first sight, to have some kind of legal status at common law following CPA 1947 and it is not sensible to think that it is genuinely possible to treat the Crown (as opposed to the Queen personally) as a natural person. Nonetheless, Wade is simply wrong to describe the monarch as a corporation sole. His analysis unfortunately elides the monarch and the Crown and disregards the important distinction between the monarch and the Crown which has been explained so painstakingly by Kantorowicz.[68] Many of the immunities and privileges possessed by the monarch historically devolved also onto the Crown but the crucial distinction is that the Crown itself was never brought within the jurisdiction of the ordinary courts. It is the Crown that matters from a public law point of view, not the monarch. It is no accident that the modern judiciary nowadays refer to the 'Crown-in-Parliament', rather than the 'King-in-Parliament'.[69]

[66] HM Moore, 'The Crown as Corporation' (1904) 20 *Law Quarterly Review* 351, 352.

[67] W Wade, 'The Crown, Ministers and Officials: Legal Status and Liability' in M Sunkin and S Payne, *The Nature of the Crown: A Legal and Political Analysis* (Oxford University Press, 1999) 24.

[68] Kantorowicz (n 14).

[69] *R (Jackson) v Attorney General* [2005] UKHL 56, [2006] 1 AC 262, [2005] 3 WLR 733, [2005] 4 All ER 1253, [9].

It is perhaps worth pointing out that the power of the monarch to convey and deal with land long predates the detailed rules of property law slowly developed over centuries by the common law judges. Hence to argue that the personal historic property rights of the monarch necessitate that the Crown has legal personality at common law is to conflate two unrelated issues. As argued in chapter two, the development of the judicial common law rules of property law are best understood as intertwined with the extension and development of the original royal prerogative of justice. In other words, the remedies granted by the king's judges were granted as a delegated function of the monarch's primary duty to dispense justice as the feudal lord and landowner. The contrary notion of the monarch, or the Crown, appearing as an *applicant* to the courts for a remedy is to misunderstand the relationship between the monarch and the courts. The judges were the kings' men, as Ship Money proved beyond all doubt. As Lord Jones put it, 'we are his judges deputed, but our judgment flows from him … he is the fountain of justice … he is the supreme judge'.[70] The majority of judges in *Ship Money* found for the king, despite the implications for confirming the existence of a power to take property without the consent of parliament, annually, for an alleged emergency for which there was not time to call parliament.

Wade also refers to another a type of legal power that he said is possessed by the Crown, and that he wrongly claimed to be shared with ordinary people, which is the power to make contracts. On close inspection, and contrary to Wade's claim, it is far from clear that the Crown itself can 'make contracts'. Instead, it might be thought the Crown had historic prerogative powers to administer the realm, including appointing servants or agents under prerogative. It is those servants who actually enter contracts and other transactions.[71] It is important to make clear that disaggregating the function of the Crown and the function of ministers in entering contracts is central to the arguments put forward by this entire book because it speaks directly to the claim that the Crown is *defined* as the bearer of prerogative powers and entering contracts is not a prerogative power.

A more obscure variation of this argument might be the idea that historically the Crown in no sense entered contracts (not even through its servants) but in fact exercised a prerogative power to *requisition property or money* (as long as that did not amount to a tax) and pay *ex gratia* compensation or donate property in return.[72] Either way, 'making contracts' with the Crown has long been held to be addressed, where necessary, by litigation against *servants* of the Crown through the ancient procedure of Petition of Right because the Crown was, and remains, immune. Such contracts, and litigation, were not therefore with, or

[70] *Ship Money (R v Hampden)* (1637) State Trials 825, 1184. See further ch 2, pp 34–37.

[71] Private transactions by the monarch in their personal capacity are outside the scope of this work. Wade suggests that the old law still applies, including the possibility of a Petition of Right. W Wade, C Forsyth and J Ghosh, *Wade & Forsyth's Administrative Law*, 12th edn (Oxford University Press, 2022) 663.

[72] See further below on contracts and the effect of CPA 1947.

against, the Crown itself and this alternative approach is how the law actually developed.

It is obvious that the Crown cannot really be treated as a natural person for all the reasons that led the common lawyers to try to construct a solution to practical legal problems by developing the notion that the king has two 'bodies'.[73] The Crown is not, and never has been, an ordinary person. It is an artificial legal entity that lies outside the jurisdiction of the courts.[74] Indeed, the concept of the Crown was *invented* as an attempt to create a separate artificial legal entity separate from the monarch qua natural person.

In the unlikely event that treating the Crown as a natural person at common law is ever seriously contemplated, it should be done by an Act of Parliament. The model for this might possibly be found by considering the status of local councils who are now, by statute, treated as individuals with the power to do 'anything that individuals generally may do'.[75] If legislation was required for the relatively minor matter of the legal status of local councils, it might be thought necessary for parliament to legislate if the capacity of natural person were to be conferred on the Crown.

Furthermore, it is difficult to reconcile Wade's description of the Crown as a corporation sole with his simultaneous commitment to the continuing 'immunity' of the Crown in the ordinary courts that he describes as a 'compromise, which is well suited to a state, which is both a monarchy and a democracy'.[76] If the Crown is immune from judicial common law, it cannot also be a 'corporation sole' subjected to the jurisdiction of the common law courts. Corporations sole are constructs of the common law. If the Crown operates outside the common law, it makes no sense to force the concept within the straitjacket of common law.

Wade argues that the intention of parliament in CPA 1947 was to 'remove the Crown's immunity in respect of tort, contract and certain other liabilities, and to remove the 'lacuna in the rule of law' which had long been criticised'.[77] The lacuna was the consequence of the technical immunity of the Crown from liability. It should perhaps be noted that this immunity stands in sharp contrast to corporations, individuals and local authorities, *inter alios*. Happily, Wade goes on to endorse the long standing and sharp distinction between the Crown and ministers of the Crown that is also defended in this book.[78] The case of *Town Investments* had threatened this distinction, albeit with a strong dissent from Lord Morris, but it was emphatically reinstated by *M v Home Office*.[79] In the former case, the courts had treated the Crown and servants of the Crown as effectively

[73] Kantorowicz (n 14).
[74] *M v Home Office (HL)* [1994] 1 AC 377.
[75] Localism Act 2011, s 1.
[76] Wade (n 67) 31.
[77] Wade (n 67) 27.
[78] Wade (n 67).
[79] *Town Investments Ltd v Department of the Environment* [1978] AC 359, 377, 385. *M v Home Office (HL)* [1994] 1 AC 377.

the same but, famously, the latter case distinguished the two and, as Wade points out, thus vindicated the rule of law. This was because *M v Home Office* made clear that while the Home Secretary was not personally liable for contempt of court in that case, the impossibility of an injunction against the Crown did not extend to ministers as well.[80] Thus, courts could impose an injunction on ministers of the Crown in their official capacity as well as government departments, but not the Crown itself.

It seems therefore that it has simply been *assumed* that the Crown must be pigeon-holed within some common law legal category. The common law has, however, conspicuously failed to classify the Crown as any particular *type* of corporation successfully. It is also reasonably clear that classifying the Crown as a natural person makes no sense as a matter of public law precisely because natural persons operate in private law and the Crown does not.[81] Given the difficulties of classification of the Crown in common law, it would be better to go back to first principles and attempt to construct an alternative legal understanding of the role and function of the Crown, its use of, and legal relationship with, prerogative powers and a more accurate analysis of the relationship between the courts and the Crown. The remainder of this chapter attempts this task, and does so in a way that arguably better reflects the history and development of the law.

It is important to note that if the analysis in this chapter is accepted, and thus the Crown is seen to have a unique relationship with judicial common law, and technically sits outside its jurisdiction, then the importance of trying to classify the Crown as some kind of corporation or otherwise significantly diminishes.[82]

The Crown at Common Law

The concepts of natural person, corporation sole and corporation aggregate are *private law* concepts, and are fiendishly difficult, if not impossible, to map onto the concept of the Crown. This is well explained by Howell, who claims, persuasively, that 'the Crown is unique'.[83] Howell is highly sceptical about the classification of the Crown as a corporation sole, and highlights Blackstone's pertinent point that Crown does not even possess the 'very first powers' necessary to be a corporation sole, which are the powers to sue and be sued. The same fatal difficulty applies to the claim that the Crown could be a corporation aggregate. Howell is particularly scathing about the idea that the Crown can be seen

[80] The minister was held not to be liable personally because he had acted at all times on legal advice: *M v Home Office* [1994] 1 AC 377, 424.

[81] Natural persons can bring actions *against* public bodies, of course, but that is a separate matter entirely.

[82] This is to leave to one side the fact that the original source of the legal authority for common law was the prerogative of justice.

[83] J Howell, 'What the Crown May Do' (2010) 15 *Judicial Review* 36, [13], [30], [40], [44], [49], [98].

as a corporation, following Maitland's withering dismissal of the idea as having 'parsonified' the Crown.[84]

> Any attempt to treat the Crown as if it is like any other corporation is not sustainable … As Littledale J stated …, 'the King is altogether on a different footing from other corporations sole'. … Unsurprisingly, as Romer J once stated, the Crown differs 'in many respects' from other corporations sole.
>
> Indeed, simply looking at Blackstone's list of powers, which he and the judges in the *Case of Sutton's Hospital* thought were necessary incidents of incorporation, the Crown does not generally have the very first powers there mentioned as a matter of English law – the powers to sue and be sued.[85]

Howell goes on to point out that the case law contradicts the idea that the Crown has an easily understandable status at common law.

> As Lord Woolf has pointed out, 'even after the [Crown Proceedings] Act of 1947, [the Crown] cannot conduct litigation except in the name of an authorised government department or, in the case of judicial review, in the name of a minister'. It is also plain that as a matter of English law the Crown lacks the capacity to be sued …
>
> There is thus no necessary identity between the capacity of the Crown as a corporation and the capacity of other corporations.[86]

Howell's claim that the Crown is unique is convincing. The Crown is the bearer of a bundle of legal powers many of which certainly have no equivalent and, even more crucially, the fact that the Crown could not be sued historically meant that it was clearly outside the jurisdiction of the ordinary courts.[87] This significantly reduces the salience of the various attempts to classify the Crown by Lord Sales and others. It is also fatal for the claim that the Crown can be classified as a corporation aggregate, in particular because the Crown cannot sue or be sued. The *government* may be a corporation aggregate, but that is separate question. The following sections attempt to show that the Crown does not in fact exercise any judicial 'common law' powers and therefore there is no need to agonise over the pigeon-holing of the Crown within existing juridical constructs as a matter of common law. The Crown is *sui generis*.

The Crown: Towards a Definition

Three Wrong Definitions of the Crown

As we have seen, the definition of the Crown has historically oscillated between three different potential and contradictory meanings: the king, the government

[84] Maitland (n 56) 132.
[85] Howell (n 83) [27].
[86] ibid.
[87] See also JG Allen, 'The Office of the Crown' (2018) 77 *Cambridge Law Journal* 298.

and the state.[88] None of these three potential definitions of the Crown stands up to meaningful scrutiny. The Crown cannot be defined as coterminous with the state.[89] The latter concept is far too rich and broad to be equated with the Crown – 'too large' as Allen puts it.[90] Indeed, as Maitland famously pointed out, the Crown 'does nothing but lie in the Tower of London to be gazed at by sight-seers'.[91] A comprehensive definition of the state must include all the institutions of the country including the devolved assemblies, local authorities and parliament – none of which can sensibly be described as within any meaningful definition of the Crown. The Crown is too thin a concept to encompass the concept of the state in such a broad sense without significantly redefining the idea.

Maitland tried to institute the concept of 'Commonwealth' to encompass the broader notion of the state beyond simply the Crown, but his insightful idea has not gained acceptance.[92] The problem is difficult enough that the phrase 'the state' has found its way into some statutes and consequential case law, presumably to circumvent the difficulties with the Crown.[93] It is suggested that an alternative label to Commonwealth is needed in order to capture the concept of the state from a domestic point of view. Such a novel label would need to have more historic resonance than Maitland's suggestion of 'Commonwealth'. It is suggested that one possible option would be 'Realm'.

If it is felt that the concept of the 'Crown' cannot be discarded for historical reasons, another option might be to disaggregate the differing definitions of the concept of Crown. One element of the Crown is that aspect of the Crown that is contained within Crown-in-Parliament. It might then be worthwhile to separate out and label the domestic concept of the state as 'Crown-in-Realm', by contrast with Crown-in-Parliament which is clearly distinct from the state. The phrase Crown-in-Realm could be used as an overarching generic label for the state as a whole, encompassing the other institutions that are an inescapable part of the state. An alternative, perhaps more prosaic, label would be Crown-in-State, which would perhaps reflect the fact that some statutes refer to the concept of the 'state'.

The second common way that the label 'the Crown' is used in constitutional discourse is when it is equated with the government. This alternative usage of 'the Crown' is highly context-specific and cannot capture all the variegated uses of the Crown in public law. Indeed, for most purposes, there needs to be a sharp *distinction* drawn between the government and the Crown. Government ministers have huge swathes of statutory powers conferred on them by parliament. Those powers

[88] Tomkins (n 41) 263.

[89] See M Loughlin, 'The State, the Crown and the Law' in M Sunkin and S Payne (eds), *The Nature of the Crown: A Legal and Political Analysis* (Oxford University Press, 1999) 33 for an attempt to do so.

[90] Allen (n 87) 316.

[91] FW Maitland, *The Constitutional History of England*, edited by HAL Fisher (Cambridge University Press, 1980) 418.

[92] Maitland (n 56) 140.

[93] *Chandler v DPP* [1964] AC 763.

are conferred on them, or on government departments, in their official capacity as ministers. *M v Home Office* established that those ministers and departments could be injuncted and CPA 1947 has now been definitively interpreted as distinguishing the potential liability, and legal status, of ministers from that of the Crown.[94] It is also a longstanding rule that the Crown is not bound by statute unless the Act says so expressly. The same does not apply to ministers. Thus, the government and the Crown cannot be treated as synonymous generally, even though on occasion they are functionally treated as the same concept for some purposes.

Third, 'the Crown' is sometimes used because 'the king' immediately encounters the problem that the king has more than one capacity, memorably described by Chitty, among others, as the 'body natural' and the 'body politic'.[95] The king in his natural capacity can act in ways, and do certain things, that the Crown cannot do, such as get married, have children and die. More complex is the idea of the king in his body politic which could sometimes (historically), encompass the whole realm including parliament. This lack of clarity makes it problematic to equate the king in body politic with the Crown.

A Novel Approach to Defining the Crown

There are therefore serious, arguably fatal, difficulties with all the three classic potential meanings of the Crown: state, government and king. An alternative definition is needed. The starting point for a novel definition is the observation that in the modern world, and with some well understood exceptions, the category of prerogative powers is fairly well established and known.[96] The simple version of the definition suggested below also presupposes that the Crown does not, for example, enter contracts *itself*, the arguments for which are examined in the next chapter.[97] Too much focus on these admittedly important questions simply obscures, in this author's view, the debate over definition. For now, and it is hoped fairly uncontroversially, the broad category of prerogative powers is fairly stable, with some debate at the fringes.

If this is accepted, then a novel definition of the Crown can be attempted. Hitherto, the debate over the definition of the Crown has, understandably, focused on what it means as a matter of law, what powers it supposedly possesses and what it can do. Instead, it is suggested a more fruitful approach would be to reverse the methodology entirely. Rather than start with the Crown and argue over what it can do, it would be better to start with what can still be done using prerogative and reverse engineer the definition from there. In other words, if we start with

[94] *M v Home Office (HL)* [1994] 1 AC 377.
[95] Chitty (n 58), 205; Kantorowicz (n 14).
[96] House of Commons Public Administration Select Committee, *Taming the Prerogative: Strengthening Ministerial Accountability to Parliament* (HC 2003-04 422).
[97] See ch 7.

the prerogative powers (including duties etc) that we can identify and collate, the Crown can be simply defined as the legal bearer of the residual, remaining prerogative powers, privileges and duties. Dicey hints at something similar when he says that 'certain [prerogative] powers … are now left by law in the hands of the Crown, and are exercised in fact by the executive government'.[98]

This reverse methodology would significantly reduce the confusion in the literature so far surrounding the definition of the Crown. This definition would demonstrate, fairly easily and conclusively, why the Crown has no common law powers and no third source powers. Those are excluded, by definition, to the extent that they are not classified historically as prerogative – although this problem is addressed in more detail in later chapters. Slightly more difficult are the incredibly rare situations where parliament deliberately *confers* statutory powers on the Crown. This is rare precisely because such powers are normally conferred on ministers and departments, distinct from the Crown. Some statutes confer powers on the monarch directly, which also clouds the issue somewhat.[99] Nevertheless, if the basic, stable definition of the Crown is related to being the bearer of prerogative powers, parliament may confer new statutory powers on the Crown, such as giving statutory assent to bills of the Scottish parliament, if the Westminster parliament decides, in its wisdom, to do so. Parliament is, after all, a legally unlimited sovereign.

Who Owes the National Debt?

This new suggested definition of the Crown may point to a novel potential solution to the famous dilemma posed first by Maitland.[100] In a post Glorious Revolution world, Maitland asks rhetorically, which legal entity is in fact the debtor when the national debt is considered in the round? Historically, of course, the answer was easy. The king borrowed money and owed debts that accrued from those borrowings, secured on his property. That narrative cannot survive the civil war, the decision by parliament to take control of the purse strings, and the statutory removal from the monarch of the power to levy taxation.

Nor is it plausible to say that parliament owes the debt. In the short term, it is the executive that spends money, not the legislature, so it is difficult to claim that any overspend is a debt voluntarily and knowingly accrued by parliament. It also makes little sense to ascribe the debt to the state, however defined, because it is not plausible to argue that institutions such as local government, devolved assemblies, judiciary and other bodies are in some sense liable for the national debt. Another possibility is to claim that the government owes the debt. After all, it spent

[98] Dicey (n 32) 61.
[99] See, for example, the Scotland Act 1998, s 45(1): 'The First Minister shall be appointed by Her Majesty from among the members of the Parliament and shall hold office at Her Majesty's pleasure'.
[100] Maitland (n 17).

the money. This struggles with the fact that new governments frequently loudly proclaim their condemnation of the accrual of such debt by previous governments, which they blame for incurring it, and it stretches credibility that the government itself is the debtor for debts owed and accrued by previous governments of vastly different political hues. Furthermore, if debt is defined as the borrowing of money *against future revenue*, there is a sense that government debt is expenditure of money to be raised by future *parliaments* and cannot sensibly be said to be owed by the current government in any meaningful sense, especially for debt that sits on the book as gilts for generations.

It is tempting simply to ignore the question as having no clear answer. One potential solution may come from a close examination of the concept of the prerogative of revenue itself. It is clear that the prerogative of revenue has to a large extent been superseded by the core statutory changes that mean that only parliament has the legal right to levy taxation in the modern world. Taxation raised by statute is known as 'extraordinary' taxation and is distinguished from 'ordinary' revenue which, as Chitty and Blackstone explain in considerable detail and with some relish, is the revenue that historically accrued to the king from malt tax, excise duties, stamp duties and myriad other sources.[101] All these revenue streams, accrued to the king over centuries by the invention of wily advisers, were long ago assigned to the executive in return for the Civil List that funds the actual costs of the monarchy.

It might be thought that it follows that the right to *receive* (rather than *levy*) taxation was therefore also handed over to parliament. Not so. Dicey sets out a fascinating curio when he describes the daily collection by officials from the treasury of monies received from the public as taxation and its transfer from the bank of England to the Treasury.[102] It would appear, therefore, that while the prerogative of *levying* taxation has gone into abeyance, the aspect of the prerogative of revenue that relates to the *receipt* of taxation is still extant. In other words, the prerogative power to receive taxation is still in existence and effective, even if it is then formally handed over to the current government who is obviously politically, legally and in all other ways accountable for the expenditure of that revenue.

There remains, then, a sliver of prerogative power remaining in this context. It would make no sense to claim that the king still holds that prerogative. Indeed, that would be to reverse the result of the civil war, as Lord Templeman once famously said.[103] Nor is it technically legally accurate to claim that the *government* is the recipient of that revenue. On the contrary, we have seen that the revenue is formally *transferred* to the government after receipt. Who then receives the revenue? The answer is plain. Revenue is received by whoever retains that sliver of prerogative power relating to revenue that is not the right to levy taxation, or

[101] W Blackstone, *Commentaries on the Laws of England* (1753), Book 1, ch 8, 'Of the King's Revenue'; Chitty (n 58) ch XI.
[102] Dicey (n 32) 312–13.
[103] *M v Home Office (HL)* [1994] 1 AC 377, 395.

the right – and responsibility – for spending that revenue. Under the definition put forward in this chapter, the legal bearer of the remaining sliver of the revenue prerogative is, by definition, the Crown. So the Crown owes the national debt. Not the government, not the king and not the state. This example thus neatly illustrates why it is mistaken to equate any of those three definitions with the Crown. It further perhaps bolsters the definition suggested in this chapter as it arguably accurately captures who owes the national debt.

Definition of the Crown

It is suggested, therefore, that a simple definition of the Crown is that it is the bearer of the remaining prerogative powers that were once possessed by the monarch. The definition of the Crown given by Lord Simon, seemingly forgotten, can scarcely be improved upon. It was cited earlier in the chapter but bears repeating.

> The term 'the Crown' is therefore used in constitutional law to denote the collection of such of those powers as remain extant (the royal prerogative), together with such other powers as have been expressly conferred by statute on 'the Crown'.[104]

The next chapter builds on this definition by considering the implications for two scenarios: where prerogative power looks very much like an ordinary common law power and secondly where a government action looks completely indistinguishable from a prerogative power. In the first scenario, it is suggested that the two powers should be carefully distinguished. In the second scenario, it is suggested that it is not in fact the Crown but rather its servants that exercise the relevant non prerogative power – and prerogative is only relevant for the appointment of that servant to the relevant office.

[104] *Town Investments* (n 79) 397.

7

Prerogatives are Exclusive to the Crown

Introduction

Having defined the Crown as the bearer of prerogative powers possessing no common law powers, it is now necessary to consider the second limb of Wade's definition. Wade claims that the set of prerogative legal powers is far smaller than many might think, comprising only those powers that Wade believes can genuinely be said to be exclusive to the Crown. This chapter therefore considers whether prerogatives that look ostensibly similar to common law powers should be treated as being common law powers exercised by the Crown, as Wade argued. It addresses two types: first legal powers that look similar by analogy, such as *ex gratia* payments; second, powers and liabilities such as those in contract and tort that are seemingly exercised by the Crown and look indistinguishable from those exercised by ordinary people.

Blackstone's definition was the basis for Wade's claim that a genuine prerogative must be 'unique to the Crown and not shared with other persons'.[1] Wade argues that whenever a prerogative power, seemingly exercised by the government, looks sufficiently similar to a legal power possessed by ordinary citizens, then that power is no longer a prerogative power. Instead, Wade claimed that such a power should be understood as a common law legal power. This can only mean that he believed that such powers have somehow been conferred on the Crown by the judiciary, in the way that the common law courts have indirectly conferred legal powers on ordinary people over the centuries by granting *remedies* to them and thereafter generating causes of action such as those in contract and tort. Unpacking and debunking this claim therefore requires us to consider the relationship between powers and remedies.

English law started with the granting of remedies by the Crown (originally the monarch). Over time, this was delegated to the judges on behalf of the Crown through the writ system. No writ, no remedy. The writ system was predicated on the applicant then working backwards from an application for a remedy to show that the facts of their case fitted within the straitjacket of the legal *prerequisites* before that remedy could be granted. It follows that common law, historically, has not been primarily concerned with 'rights', but with *wrongs*. Rights, and powers,

[1] HWR Wade, 'Procedure and Prerogative in Public Law' (1985) 101 *Law Quarterly Review* 180, 193.

are parasitic on *remedies* granted by judges, originally on behalf of the monarch, to members of the public against someone who has allegedly wronged them. Public law is about wrongs that are done to individuals by those *in power*. Individuals originally sought a remedy from the king through his judges against those who wielded power over them. Mr Justice Sedley (as he then was) put it memorably:

> Public law is not at base about rights, even though abuses of power may and often do invade private rights; it is about wrongs – that is to say misuses of public power.[2]

Thus, legal powers and rights indirectly conferred by the judges on ordinary citizens are in a sense *reverse engineered* from the remedies sought. Over time, a claimant had to satisfy various pre-requisites in order to justify the granting of a remedy. Those pre-requisites eventually became seen as common law rights and powers. English law focuses on remedies, not rights and powers, because the origin of legal actions in the royal courts is founded in application by ordinary people to the king's judges for a remedy. Rights and powers began their existence by being parasitic on remedies. This is to take nothing away from the subsequent creativity of judges in inventing new causes of action as part of the development of common law.

The same cannot remotely be said of legal powers of the Crown, which are *sui generis*, sourced in the Crown and were originally a plenary set of powers, rights, immunities and duties. It makes little or no sense to describe the Crown' legal powers as being parasitic on securing a *remedy* for itself, from itself, through its own courts. Remedies, it will be recalled, are the starting point for common law legal powers. Equally, any 'remedy' granted *by* the Crown was almost invariably *ex gratia*, originally at the discretion of the monarch and secondary to the exercise of the relevant prerogative power or duty. The false equivalence between judicial common law remedies and discretionary exercises of prerogative power with highly uncertain outcomes is a quirk of English law that is difficult to understand, and it is perhaps time to formally sunder any assumed, or manufactured, link between the two. They are chalk and cheese.

The basis of Wade's unevidenced claim that a prerogative legal power possessed by the Crown must – if seemingly 'shared' with private citizens – transform somehow into a common law power conferred by the courts is, to say the least, opaque. It immediately makes the assumption that the Crown is a legal entity at common law which is impossible to reconcile with the fact that not only can the monarch do no wrong but also the Crown cannot sue or be sued, as Blackstone pointed out.[3] But even if we leave to one side the fact that the Crown has always operated outside the jurisdiction of the common law courts, the proposition is a strange one on its own terms. Since prerogative powers predate the common law, it is incomprehensible why Wade thought that *any* legal power exercised by the Crown must be parasitically derived from previous judicial decisions granting remedies to citizens, which

[2] *R v Somerset County Council and ARC Southern Ltd* [1998] 75 P & CR 175, 183.
[3] This is dealt with in more depth in ch 6.

is what common law means. In short, his argument that the Crown has common law powers conferred by the judiciary does not withstand serious scrutiny.

Ex Gratia Payments

This chapter considers the sharp differences between prerogative powers of the Crown and judicial common law powers of ordinary citizens by examining the prerogatives of making *ex gratia* payments and engaging or dismissing Crown servants at will. This is because these prerogatives, and the older case law discussing them, help to highlight the legal chasm that separates prerogative powers exercised by the Crown and the actions of natural persons in private law. They also help to illustrate that these two prerogatives are indeed unique to the Crown and not shared with ordinary people.

Wade believed that the public award schemes under the aegis of the *ex gratia* prerogative constitute examples of a legal power that 'the Crown shares with its subjects;' hence that it is not a prerogative power at all.[4]

> There is nothing whatever 'prerogative' about the making of a government contract or *ex gratia* payment by a government department. The Crown can do such things because anyone and everyone can do them.[5]

On the Criminal Injuries Compensation Board ('CICB') itself he said this:[6]

> The Criminal Injuries Compensation Board is an instance of the practice, dear to the administrative heart, of doing things informally and extra-legally if means can be devised. This Board pays out several million pounds of public money annually to the victims of violent crime. But until recently it had no statutory authority. [The Board was made statutory by the Criminal Justice Act 1988.] Parliament simply voted the money each year, and the Board dispensed it under the rules of the scheme, which were laid before Parliament by the Home Secretary but had no statutory force. Nevertheless, by a feat no less imaginative than in the *Laker Airways* case, the courts assumed jurisdiction to quash decisions of the Board which did not accord with the rules of the scheme. In doing so, they described the Board as 'set up under the prerogative' [*R v Criminal Injuries Compensation Board ex p Lain* [1967] 2 QB 864, at 881, 883]. But one essential of 'prerogative', if I may be forgiven for saying so, is that it should be prerogative. Its etymology means that it should be some special power possessed by the Crown over and above the powers of an ordinary person, and by virtue of the Crown's special constitutional position.
>
> … Now if we apply this test to the constitution of the Criminal Injuries Compensation Board, it is surely plain that the Government, in establishing it, was merely doing

[4] W Wade, 'The Crown, Ministers and Officials: Legal Status and Liability' in M Sunkin and S Payne, *The Nature of the Crown: A Legal and Political Analysis* (Oxford University Press, 1999) 24, 30.

[5] Wade (n 1) 191.

[6] HWR Wade, *Constitutional Fundamentals (Hamlyn Lectures, 32nd series)* (Stevens and Sons, 1980) 58–60.

> what … any of us could do if we had the money ready to hand. We could set up a board, or a committee, or trustees with authority to make grants according to whatever rules we might please to lay down. Thousands of foundations or trusts have been set up in the exercise of exactly the same liberty that the Government exercised in the case of the criminal injuries scheme. So far as the Crown came into the picture at all, it was exercising its ordinary powers as a natural person, which of course include power to transfer property, make contracts and so on. [Footnote: In *R v Panel on Take-overs and Mergers ex p Datafin* plc [1987] QB 815, at 848, Lloyd LJ expressed his agreement with this argument.] Blackstone was quite right, in my opinion, in saying that such powers are not prerogative at all.

It follows from the arguments made thus far that these claims by Wade are seriously questionable. It is of course correct to say that any natural person may *give away* their money or property to others as a matter of private law, but Wade appears to assume that this is legally identical to the executive making a discretionary award using taxpayers' money to a victim of crime who has no other recourse. The latter is an issue of formal public policy, involving the use of taxpayer's money for which ministers are entitled to seek political credit – or suffer political loss – in parliament and at general elections. To liken that to a private gift would be seriously strained, because when considered carefully there are important differences between the two situations.

On the one hand, public discretionary award schemes are a public benefit to the community as a whole, using public funds and designed to accrue political benefit to the government and more widely as a public good. On the other hand, a private gift is designed to achieve whatever personally motivates a private person to donate money which can be a myriad of reasons including admiration, pity and reputational salvation. In addition, the only legal regulation of gifts by private persons is through deeds and wills.[7] It is important to note in delineating the significant differences between the two situations that neither of the latter two examples of formal gift giving in private law have any public law equivalent.

If a private person wants to give away a significant sum of money formally and irrevocably as a matter of law, that can be done by a straightforward gift, either individually or after deciding to 'set up a board or a committee' to help the donor distribute the funds. It can also be done more technically, as Wade also points out, by creating a private trust or making a charitable donation. This is quite different from the legal requirements for valid and lawful discretionary payments by the government or delegated public bodies, not least because the legal rules as to creation, regulation, unwinding and terminating of trusts and charities are significantly different from the public law *ultra vires* and natural justice rules surrounding the discretionary distribution of public funds. Equally, the donation of money via a simple gift generates no legal consequences in terms of impropriety of purpose and other factors that can vitiate the payment of public moneys.

[7] Designation of charitable status affects how such gifts are taxed, which is an issue of public law but lies outside the scope of this book. Some gifts can incur taxation obligations generally.

There is another way in which public award schemes are radically different from private law '*ex gratia*' settlements. A formal discretionary award by the government in the criminal injuries context means a payment of public money to someone who has been a victim of crime but has no prospect of redress from the perpetrator, who truly *owes* the victim compensation. It follows therefore that a straight comparison with an '*ex gratia*' settlement in private law, which is defined as being a payment of money expressly without the admission of any legal liability, is inappropriate. When the government pays out to victims of criminal injuries that is *ex gratia* in the sense of 'a discretionary publicly funded award' and *not* in the sense of a private person paying out a sum of money voluntarily without any admission that she did anything wrong as a matter of strict law. It would make no sense to argue that the government, when paying out for criminal injuries, did so to avoid admitting *wrongdoing*.

In contrast, *ex gratia* settlements of legal disputes in private law in the narrow sense of voluntarily making a financial payment without admitting doing anything wrong, when made by private citizens, almost invariably take place in private law as part of a formal contract when legal proceedings between the parties are compromised and where all the loose ends are tied up and the parties agree a settlement. It is a very long way from public discretionary awards to victims of crime who have nowhere else to turn.

The final categorial difference is of course that the funding for such *ex gratia* governmental compensation is derived from taxpayers' money, voted on by parliament through the Appropriation Acts and is an exercise of *public* power. Payments made *ex gratia* are limited by all the standard grounds of judicial review. The mistake of comparing the two, as Wade does, can be most clearly seen by considering the *remedies* available, or sought, in both scenarios. The argument for equivalence could only begin to make sense if a private gift, for example, could be *quashed* in judicial review proceedings on any of the standard public law grounds and remitted to the gift-giver. Even putting the suggestion in these terms reveals the error in equating the two situations.

Gifts and decisions to compromise legal claims by natural persons in private law should be sharply *distinguished* from governmental discretionary award schemes in public law. Indeed, the conflation of the two scenarios demonstrates how the wrong end of the legal telescope is being deployed. If the law is generally viewed as concerning the exercise of rights and powers, the two situations look superficially similar, (except of course one situation involves public money and political accountability). If the law is instead, and with more historical accuracy, considered through the prism of the *remedies* sought, the chasm between the two scenarios is immediately apparent. Consider, for example, a proprietary interest *in rem*, or a remedy *in personam* in private law through a resulting or constructive trust. Such a hypothetical remedy for a failed private law scheme has few obvious commonalities with seeking the remedy of a quashing order or mandatory order in public law following, say, a decision of a public body tainted by a real possibility of bias or a decision made for an improper purpose. Public expenditure and a private gift have little or nothing in common, legally speaking.

Case Law Supporting Wade

It is important, however, to address the fact that Wade has Court of Appeal authority in support of his position. In *Datafin*, the question arose as to the source of power for the Panel on Takeovers and Mergers, a non-statutory regulatory body.[8] In considering this question Lord Donaldson MR observed, somewhat wryly, that 'the panel is a truly remarkable body, performing its function without visible means of legal support'.[9] Lord Justice Lloyd remarked:

> [Counsel] submits that there has never been a case when the source of the power has been other than statutory or under the prerogative. There is a certain imprecision in the use of the term 'prerogative' in this connection, as Professor Sir William Wade makes clear in another Child & Co. Oxford Lecture, 'Procedure and Prerogative in Public Law' *(1985) 101 L.Q.R. 180*. Strictly the term 'prerogative' should be confined to those powers which are unique to the Crown. As Professor Wade points out, there was nothing unique in the creation by the government, out of funds voted by Parliament, of a scheme for the compensation of victims of violent crime. Any foundation or trust, given sufficient money, could have done the same thing. Nor do I think that the distinction between the Criminal Injuries Compensation Board and a private foundation or trust for the same purposes lies in the source of the funds. The distinction must lie in the nature of the duty imposed, whether expressly or by implication. If the duty is a public duty, then the body in question is subject to public law.[10]

This case does not directly concern royal prerogative, because the Panel's authority was not rooted in prerogative, so it need only be addressed very briefly. What the case does, arguably, illustrate is just how important it is to focus on *remedies* in English law. The extension of public law jurisdiction in this case was undoubtedly novel, but as Forsyth famously argues, the common law has long regulated monopoly powers.[11] This case has similar overtones. Labelling such powers as 'public' powers was justified on the grounds that the unique self-regulatory mechanisms that had grown up organically would otherwise have required statutory regulation – as had happened in other countries.[12] Lloyd LJ held that 'power exercised behind the scenes is power nonetheless'.[13]

Crucially, however, what was being sought in this case was a public law remedy from the courts. The court held that the power, influence and importance of the Panel on Takeovers and Mergers meant that it in effect exercised powers that were monopolistic and quasi-public and therefore the case should be treated as a matter of public law. Indeed, the very remedy sought in this case, that of *certiorari*,

[8] *R v Panel on Take-overs and Mergers ex parte Datafin plc* [1987] QB 815.
[9] ibid 834.
[10] ibid 848.
[11] C Forsyth, 'Of Fig Leaves and Fairy Tales: The Ultra Vires Doctrine, the Sovereignty of Parliament and Judicial Review' (1996) 55 *Cambridge Law Journal* 122, 124–27.
[12] *Datafin* (n 8) 835–36, per Lord Donaldson MR.
[13] ibid 849.

arguably bolsters the claim that a sharp distinction should be drawn between ordinary claims in private law and specialised public law claims. It is not possible to seek *certiorari* for a private gift. Since the views of Lloyd LJ views on the definition of prerogative were not material to the decision, they were clearly *obiter*. The judge was right to say that prerogative comprises 'those powers which are unique to the Crown' and, as argued already, the fact that a foundation can give away money is conceptually quite distinct from the distribution of public money. The key to understanding the difference, as previously suggested, is to look at the remedies sought.

The Importance of *Ex Parte Lain*

This section considers the seminal case of *Lain* in the Divisional Court in more detail. It is the classic prism through which to consider the prerogative of *ex gratia* payments in public law.[14] In *Lain*, the government scheme for criminal injuries was set up under the royal prerogative. A police widow claimed under the scheme. The issues raised in the case surrounding judicial review of prerogative are beyond the scope of this work. For our purposes here, the first point to note is that the analysis of Lord Chief Justice Parker, Mr Justice Ashworth and Lord Justice Diplock (no less) in *Lain* is entirely reliant on the Diceyan approach defended in this book. It is also perhaps worth noting that the powerful membership of this court was in part why *Lain* was treated as being so seminal later in *GCHQ* – which of course included Diplock LJ on the panel.[15]

As discussed above, Wade's approach is confusing because it conflates a private gift or contract with a formal government compensation scheme. Recall Wade's argument.

> [I]f we apply this test to the constitution of the Criminal Injuries Compensation Board, it is surely plain that the Government, in establishing it, was merely doing what … any of us could do if we had the money ready to hand. We could set up a board, or a committee, or trustees with authority to make grants according to whatever rules we might please to lay down.[16]

By contrast, Parker CJ in *Lain* said that the scheme was 'set up by executive government, i.e., under the prerogative' and Diplock LJ said that the government's legal authority to set up the scheme 'is not derived from any agreement between Crown and applicants but from instructions by the executive government, that is,

[14] *R v Criminal Injuries Compensation Board, Ex parte Lain* [1967] 2 QB 864. The traditional label of '*ex gratia*' will be maintained in the rest of this book due to its likely familiarity for readers.

[15] *Council for the Civil Service Unions v Minister for the Civil Service (GCHQ)* [1985] AC 374, 399 (per Lord Fraser of Tullybelton), 407 (per Lord Scarman), 411 (per Lord Diplock) and particularly 418 (per Lord Roskill).

[16] Wade (n 6) above.

by prerogative act of the Crown'.[17] These are orthodox, even banal, claims – at least pre-Wade.

What pervades the reasoning of the three judges in *Lain* is a strong sense that they were treading on an area that was both outside statute (obviously) but also outside the realm of judicial common law. Ashworth J made this point explicitly:

> It was contended by Mr. Bridge that before this court has jurisdiction to entertain an application for an order of *certiorari*, it must be shown that the tribunal in question has either been constituted by Act of Parliament or derives its jurisdiction from common law … In the present case it is plain that the board does not derive its jurisdiction from common law, and it is equally plain that it has not been constituted by Act of Parliament.[18]

It is important to note that deriving 'jurisdiction from common law' means that the source of legal authority for many such bodies in previous case law lies in judicial common law.[19] But not in this case. Ashworth J was correctly identifying the central point that the source of the legal authority to make *ex gratia* payments is *not* common law but instead the *ex gratia* prerogative which is wholly different. Until *Lain*, it was clear that those exercising administrative powers under the aegis of royal prerogative were outside the jurisdiction of the courts. It is also noteworthy that Ashworth J straightforwardly assumed that prerogatives are not part of the common law.

Blackstone provides no less compelling evidence, pointing out that accountability for the exercise of prerogative was solely in the political realm:

> In the exertion therefore of those prerogatives, which the law has given him, the king is irresistible and absolute, according to the forms of the constitution. And yet, if the consequence of that exertion be manifestly to the grievance or dishonor of the kingdom, the parliament will call his advisers to a just and severe account.[20]

It is true that subsequent court decisions encroached on this separate and self-contained area of law by imposing – without explicit statutory authorisation – some of the grounds analogous to judicial review onto decisions taken under the aegis of royal prerogative.[21] This jurisdictional extension might mistakenly be thought to bring prerogatives 'within' judicial common law in some sense.

The better view, it is suggested, is that the courts' regulation of prerogative powers is an entirely separate and self-contained branch of judicial review. Conceptually speaking, it makes much more sense to regard the regulation of executive prerogative power by the courts along similar lines as normal judicial review as the *convergence* of the domain of prerogative law with the common law

[17] *Lain* (n 14) 881, 883.

[18] ibid 871.

[19] Examples of such bodies include 'fellowships … partnerships and unincorporated associations' which are 'not recognised in law has having separate corporate existence'. J McLean, *Searching for the State in British Legal Thought* (Cambridge University Press, 2012) 48.

[20] W Blackstone, *Commentaries on the Laws of England* (1753) Book 1, ch 7, 251.

[21] *GCHQ* (n 15).

rules not *conversion* of prerogative into judicial common law. Prerogatives are *recognised and regulated* but not *sourced in* judicial common law. Approaching the issues in this way would also help to explain how prerogative can appear to affect legal rights without altering common law – an issue addressed in chapter four.[22]

One slightly tricky issue is that there might be thought to be a fine line between making *ex gratia* payments and setting up a new administrative, bordering on quasi-judicial, body to determine those *ex gratia* payments. The Crown cannot use the *ex gratia* prerogative to revive the prerogative of justice itself so as to create, in effect, a new judicial body of whatever kind. As noted in chapter five, the prerogative of justice, which includes the power to create new courts, is now in abeyance following the Judicature Act 1873.[23] However, the boundary between new administrative bodies operating under a set of rules, and the institution of a new 'court' may be tricky to locate on occasion.

It is difficult to reconcile Ashworth J's clear statement of the law in *Lain* with Wade's claim that the determination of *ex gratia* payments by the government-constituted board is grounded in some kind of judicial common law power.[24] Diplock LJ also picked his way carefully past Ashworth J's point that the power to make *ex gratia* payments using public funds is obviously not a power at judicial common law shared with private citizens, noting that there had been no previous occasions since 'the 17th Century' to extend the supervisory jurisdiction of the court over novel executive bodies 'whose ultimate authority to decide matters is derived from any other source [than statute or judicial common law]'.[25] He meant prerogative, of course, because the ordinary courts have long assumed that they had jurisdiction over all other bodies, whether they derived their jurisdiction from statute or judicial common law, and have acted accordingly. What was so novel here was that the board derived its authority from neither source. The source of the Board's authority was prerogative.

Diplock LJ also said that the novel scheme 'was no more than a reversion to the ancient practice of government by Royal Proclamation'.[26] It is not easy to discern quite how Royal Proclamations to underpin a governmental *ex gratia* compensation scheme involving a public body operating in public law and paying out public money are supposed to relate, as Wade argues, to an individual's freedom to make gifts in private law. In addition, it might be thought that issuing Royal Proclamations looks rather like an exercise of royal prerogative.

Wade attempts to draw attention away from this difficult aspect of the case for him by focusing on the fact that the ostensible issue in *Lain* was whether *certiorari* was available against the compensation board, saying: 'There need have been no confusion with the prerogative – it was simply a question of the ambit of the

[22] See pp 82–84.
[23] See pp 101–04.
[24] Wade (n 1) 191.
[25] *Lain* (n 14) 884.
[26] ibid 886.

remedy of certiorari.'[27] The problem with this argument is that by attempting to shift the analysis to the *remedy* Wade simply weakens his case further. Against what decision, taken under what power, was *certiorari* sought? The answer is a decision by a public body exercising public, legal, discretionary, prerogative powers, funded by taxpayers' money, that it was claimed failed to properly compensate the widow of a police officer for the injuries he had suffered, and for which she had no other recourse in private law.

Public law and private law are different beasts, and it does no good to conflate them in the sense of trying to *harmonise* the rules. Could Wade have cited an example of *certiorari* being sought against a private citizen for any kind of gift under any circumstances? Obviously not. Even on Wade's own terms, then, focusing on *certiorari* does not help his case. More importantly, viewing this issue through the prism of *certiorari* in fact helps to illustrate the chasm between the public law issues raised in this case and the sharp distinction between such issues and those raised in private law actions. The High Court is a court of original jurisdiction, created entirely by statute, so the issue was whether that court could extend the application of judicial review to include the CICB even though it did not have statutory or judicial common law underpinnings. The court decided that it could and quashed the decision.

Diplock LJ addressed another sharp distinction between this case and private law cases. He noted that the applicants have no *right* to any compensation but points out that

> it does not follow that a determination of the board in favour of an applicant is without any legal effect upon the rights of the applicant to whom it relates. It makes lawful a payment to an applicant which would otherwise be unlawful.[28]

This demonstrates a further stark distinction between making an *ex gratia* payment and the lawfulness of a gift in private law. A private gift requires the possession of no legal power and is treated as lawful unless the gift can be shown to have been vitiated for some reason. By contrast, the government and the Crown's ministers must show positive legal authority for their actions under the principle suggested by Laws LJ in *Fewings*:

> For private persons, the rule is that you may do anything you choose which the law does not prohibit … the freedoms of the private citizen are not conditional upon some distinct and affirmative justification for which he must burrow in the law books … But for public bodies the rule is the opposite … any action to be taken must be justified by positive law.[29]

Thus, an award of public money made by the government is presumptively *ultra vires* and unlawful *unless* it was done pursuant to lawfully exercised positive

[27] Wade (n 1) 198.
[28] ibid 888.
[29] *R v Somerset County Council ex parte Fewings* [1995] 1 All ER 513, 524, per Lord Justice Laws. See also ch 7, p [207] – also ch 5, p [157].

public law power. Public officials have an obligation to operate within public law constraints. Private citizens owe no such obligation, and their gifts are subject to no such presumption.

Crucial for Lord Parker CJ in *Lain* was that the board was 'clearly, therefore, performing public duties'.[30] Indeed, it was this factor that convinced him that the court had the power to supervise the board at all. This again undermines the claim that there is no difference between *ex gratia* payments in public law and a natural person donating money in private law where there no public law implications, duties, or powers at stake. Judicial review of a decision of a body only lies when that body is a public one. Equating gifts made in private law with the exercise of discretionary prerogative powers by ministers who are politically responsible to parliament is, on close inspection, untenable.

Crown Servants and the GCHQ Case

Another reason why *Lain* is commonly regarded as being so important is because it was treated in the no less seminal case of *GCHQ* as the liminal moment when royal prerogative was first judicially reviewed.[31] Judicial review of prerogative in general terms is outside the scope of this chapter and book but *GCHQ*'s importance for our purposes relates to the discussion in that case of the legal relationship between the Crown and servants of the Crown which was at all times rooted in prerogative.

The case concerned the terms and conditions of civil servants working at *GCHQ*, which were unilaterally altered by the minister using prerogative powers. Of course, Wade considered that neither *Lain* nor *GCHQ* actually concerned royal prerogative at all. Indeed, he proudly detailed how he believed that he had directly influenced Lord Diplock in *GCHQ*, saying that Lord Diplock 'guarded himself against basing civil service discipline on the prerogative' and quoted Lord Diplock as specifically holding that the legal relationship between Crown and civil servants 'might equally be the consequence' of civil servants being dismissible at will:

> [This could be the result,] for entirely different reasons, of a rule of constitutional law whose origin is to be found in the theory that those by whom the administration of the realm is carried on do so as personal servants of the monarch who can dismiss them at will, because the King can do no wrong (per Lord Diplock, *GCHQ*).[32]

A power to dismiss Crown servants at will, without recourse to the ordinary courts, because the 'king can do no wrong' is a pretty succinct description of a

[30] *Lain* (n 14) 882.
[31] *GCHQ* (n 15).
[32] Wade (n 4) 30–31; Lord Diplock, *GCHQ* (n 15) 409.

prerogative power.[33] This is somewhat ironic, because Wade claims he could 'recognise in those words the substance of a conversation which I had with Lord Diplock shortly before the decision'. Wade mistakenly appeared to be under the impression he was describing some kind of 'common law' – and therefore private – power, although his reasoning on this point is somewhat opaque. It is not clear why Wade thought dismissal of Crown servants, paid from the public purse, is a private law issue. It is, to put it mildly, hard to analogise private employment contracts with the power of ministers, who are primarily accountable to parliament, to engage and dismiss (usually senior) Crown servants *at will* and, frequently in politically controversial circumstances, because the king was historically immune from suit in his own courts.[34]

Wade even goes further and claims that ministers and even the prime minister are 'employed' as a matter of private law ('I wonder why the prime minister and equally the Crown's other ministers, should in law be in any different position from the civil servants at GCHQ').[35] This striking claim at least has the merit of consistency, if nothing else. At this point, even the fiercest defender of Wade must surely pause. It would appear that Wade is so strongly ideologically committed to shoe-horning anything that looks remotely like an employment relationship into common law that he would even include ministers and the prime minister into that category. This is in stark contrast to other leading experts. Anne Twomey, for example, straightforwardly and unequivocally treats the appointment of the prime minister as a reserve prerogative power in her magisterial review of such powers.[36]

The position of the prime minister and the underlying prerogative basis for the prime minister's appointment is so core to the functioning of the political constitution that the attempt to deny that such a paradigm prerogative is indeed a prerogative must cast doubt on Wade's whole position. It is not tenable to claim that the appointment of the prime minister of His Majesty's government on the grounds that this person is best placed to command the confidence of the House of Commons could seriously be argued not to be a prerogative power.[37] Is a prime minister eligible to bring unfair or wrongful dismissal proceedings if they lose their job? The suggestion alone refutes the idea.

The mischief Wade appears to be aiming at is the possibility that all cases concerning the Crown would need to be decided by judicial review, but this is a fanciful objection.[38] The courts have long since adopted a purely pragmatic

[33] Dismissal of Crown's servants is logically and conceptually distinct from private 'servant'/employment or contractual relationships, for the reasons set out elsewhere in the book – the fact that private 'servants' ie employees in private law are now treated totally differently rather tends to prove that point.

[34] www.theguardian.com/politics/2020/feb/29/priti-patel-home-office-chief-resigns-unfair-dismissal, accessed 3 May 2021.

[35] Wade (n 1) 192.

[36] A Twomey, *The Veiled Sceptre: Reserve Powers of Heads of State in Westminster Systems* (Cambridge University Press, 2018) 120–25.

[37] See further Twomey (n 36) ch 3 ('Appointment of Chief Minister').

[38] Wade (n 1) 197.

approach at the procedural level to cases that mix public and private law.[39] There is no reason why matters that raise few or no public law questions cannot continue to be heard outside the Administrative Court as raising issues that are at most *analogous* with private law. The legal underpinnings of such 'disguised' public law proceedings are considered in the next chapter.[40]

We have seen, therefore, that Wade's insistence that the only true prerogatives are those Crown legal powers that have no common law analogues for ordinary citizens does not withstand serious scrutiny. On the contrary, his attempts to reclassify a series of Crown powers, including *ex gratia* payments, as common law powers must be rejected. Non-statutory legal powers of the Crown are *exclusive* to the Crown, not least because the source of its legal powers has nothing to do with the common law, ie case law. *GCHQ* provides significant and material further support for the claim in this chapter that prerogative powers such as appointing ministers, senior civil servants and the prime minister at will are exclusive to the Crown, are residual public prerogative powers, and cannot be equated with private powers at judicial common law. Ministers and other public officials who are dismissible at will by the Crown cannot be likened to private sector employees on any sensible view of the legal realities. Wade went wrong in attempting to reconcile the norms of public and private law in this area.

Alleged Common Law Powers of the Crown

The last section considered in detail Wade's mistaken claim that *ex gratia* payments and appointing the prime minister, are not in fact prerogative powers because such powers are analogous to powers exercised by ordinary citizens at common law. It was argued, *contra* Wade, that these powers should be sharply *distinguished* from common law powers such as gifts or employment relationships on numerous grounds, not least because both prerogative powers involve the exercise of public power with serious constitutional or financial implications that equivalent actions at private law do not possess. It is important to keep in mind a key distinction between the two legal scenarios, which is the radically different remedies available in these areas of law. Viewed through this prism, the error of conflating the two legal categories is much easier to see.

The last section, in short, considered examples of prerogatives that at first glance look as if they overlap with powers possessed by ordinary people but, on closer inspection, are categorically different from the legal powers of ordinary citizens. The perhaps more difficult question considered in this section relates to actions taken, apparently by the Crown, that appear *completely indistinguishable* from powers exercised by private citizens at common law. The most obvious

[39] *Roy v Kensington & Chelsea FPC* [1992] 1 AC 624.
[40] See pp 163–64.

examples are the power underpinning the authority granted to ministers to enter contracts and to sue, or be liable, in tort.

Lord Sales believes that the definition of prerogative powers should be confined to powers that have no analogue for ordinary citizens. This leads to his suggestion that the Crown also has 'common law powers' including powers, for example, to make contracts. For Lord Sales, the claim that the Crown enters into contracts is proof positive that the Crown operates within common law and is a legal entity at common law just like natural persons or corporations.[41] One immediate problem for Lord Sales' argument is that, on close inspection, the relevant legal powers of the Crown associated with government contracts and alleged torts relate solely to the *vires* of the minister's role. This is a function, arguably, of the prerogative power of appointment which gives the minister the right to exercise the executive aspect of the prerogative of administration. This arguably constitutes a liminal question before the terms of the contract are even in play. The purpose of this section is to disaggregate the relevant legal questions.

This chapter therefore argues that these examples do not genuinely challenge the central claim of this book that all non-statutory legal powers of the Crown are prerogative powers precisely because the Crown is properly defined as the bearer of the remaining prerogative powers and therefore *confers* on ministers their status as such and the power to conduct the administration of the realm.[42] The short version of why the central claim remains untouched is because the Crown does not in fact, to this day, exercise those common law legal powers *itself*. Instead, when examined closely, it can be seen that legal liability at common law is in fact dealt with by ministers or departments or others who actually entered the contracts or committed the torts for the purposes of the litigation. The historical position was set out by Dicey who made crystal clear that ministers were *personally* liable in English law:

> The Minister or servant of the Crown who thus takes part in giving expression to the Royal will is legally responsible for the act … Now supposing that the act done is illegal, the Minister concerned in it becomes at once liable to criminal or civil proceedings in a Court of Law … the Crown can act only through Ministers … who thereby become not only morally but legally responsible for the legality of the act in which he takes part.[43]

Wade agrees:

> [A]gainst the king, the law had no coercive power. But this immunity never extended to the Crown's servants … ministers and officials of all kinds, high or low, are personally liable …[44]

[41] The claim by Lord Sales that the Crown should be seen as a corporation sole is discussed at pp 123–25.

[42] JG Allen, 'The Office of the Crown' (2018) 77 *Cambridge Law Journal* 298, 300.

[43] AV Dicey, *Introduction to the Study of the Law of the Constitution*, 8th edn (MacMillan, 1915) 211–12.

[44] W Wade, C Forsyth and J Ghosh, *Wade & Forsyth's Administrative Law*, 12th edn (Oxford University Press, 2022) 654–55.

Terence Daintith and Alan Page put the point succinctly when they say 'ministers are the actors in government who bear both legal and political responsibility'.[45] Historically, the minister or, if necessary, the Attorney General,[46] would be sued personally for damages and, if they lost, the minister would in practice then have their costs and liability ultimately underwritten by the Treasury (whose own 'origins lie in prerogative') because they were acting in their role as minister appointed through an exercise of prerogative.[47] Ultimate Treasury responsibility is rooted in the fact that 'no expenditure can properly be incurred without the approval of the Treasury' and 'in the field of finance, therefore, the United Kingdom executive is unitary not pluralist'.[48]

Further evidence of the chasm separating the Crown from any meaningful connection with the jurisdiction of the common law can be seen in the resolute refusal to permit the Crown to be sued directly. This led, for example, to Mr Entick suing Mr Carrington, one of the King's Messengers, rather than the Crown itself. The case is known as *Entick v Carrington* not *Entick v Rex*, or even *Entick v Attorney-General*.[49] As McLean points out, this split between the continuing immunity of the Crown and personal liability of ministers and servants has deep roots, but *de facto* achieved the kind of state liability in practice which other countries struggled to impose. Indeed, she describes the 'English solution' as 'in many ways ahead of its time'.[50] It permitted representatives of the state to be sued without in any way threatening the system itself, because the Crown was outside the jurisdiction of the courts.

Ahead of its time or otherwise, more recent developments have seen the counterparty to contractual obligations tending to be a government department. As Daintith and Page point out, when a new department is created by statute, 'it is common to incorporate the Secretary of State, usually in the form of a corporation sole, so that the department can hold property, enter into contracts, and sue, and be sued in its own name and not that of the Crown'.[51] Daintith and Page therefore confirm that it is not the Crown that is party to the contract. It is the department, incorporated or not, which headed by a minister. That minister owes their position to the royal prerogative of appointing ministers.

> One of the most obvious expressions of [the Crown's] significance … is the fact that the business of government is carried on in its name by ministers and civil servants who are all servants of the Crown … the Crown is also the source of the executive's prerogative powers.[52]

[45] T Daintith and A Page, *The Executive in the Constitution* (Oxford University Press, 1999) 325.
[46] JM Jacob, *The Republican Crown* (Dartmouth 1996) 68.
[47] Daintith and Page (n 45) 113.
[48] ibid 177, 118.
[49] Entick sued Carrington when his 'seditious literature' was seized by the King's Messengers. *Entick v Carrington* (1765) 19 St Tr 1030.
[50] McLean (n 19) 205–29.
[51] Daintith and Page (n 45) 33.
[52] ibid 27.

The increasingly unsatisfactory conceptual underpinning of the running of formal litigation was evidenced, for example, by an unsavoury practice documented by Daintith and Page. They note that less scrupulous departments on occasion deliberately induced 'the settlement of a claim on terms which the complainant would otherwise probably not have accepted' by threatening not to underwrite the 'actual wrongdoer'.[53] Indeed, it could be argued that one of the primary purposes of the Crown Proceedings Act 1947, addressed in the next chapter, was to stop this kind of sharp practice by replacing a prerogative discretion to make what were in reality *ex gratia* prerogative payments with a formal statutory obligation.

Ministerial Posts as Personal Sinecures

The Westminster Review of 1876 explains that 'for a long period of history, the emoluments of Ministers were derived from poundage and the use of public moneys in official hands'. Aylmer confirms that 'the old administrative system' was characterised by 'the remuneration of officials by means of fees, gratuities and perquisites, as much as, often more than, by salaries, stipends or wages from the Crown' as well as 'the regarding of office as a private right or interest, rather than as a public service'.[54] In other words, the ministers treated public revenue as their income and defrayed the costs of employing clerks and others against that income, retaining any residue.[55] This was then replaced by a fixed salary for the 'great posts of Government' which was then supplemented by 'exacting fees from the public'.[56] Included within this incredible system was the fact that the 'sale of subordinate posts became a recognised source of revenue to a Minister'.[57] The flip side, perhaps ironically, was that there was fairly tight control over the size of the civil service because the costs came directly out of the minister's pocket which, as the Westminster Review puts it somewhat laconically, 'precluded any undue extravagance' in the employment in service of the department.

It was only the 'absolutely incorruptible' Mr Pitt who ended the 'practice of converting ministerial posts into sources of revenue for Ministers', which Cohen, with admirable understatement describes as 'the peculations which had been common in earlier times'.[58] The separation of public and private interest was underpinned by statutory conversion of civil servants from 'being servants of a minister to servants of the Crown'.[59] It is hardly surprising that Dicey conceptualised

[53] ibid 71–2.

[54] GE Aylmer, 'From Office-Holding to Civil Service: The Genesis of Modern Bureaucracy: The Prothero Lecture', *Transactions of the Royal Historical Society* Vol 30 (1980) 91, 92.

[55] ibid 464.

[56] ibid.

[57] ibid.

[58] *The Westminster and Foreign Quarterly Review* (1876) Vol 105, 464. E Cohen, *The Growth of the British Civil Service 1780–1939* (Frank Cass & Co, 1965) 20.

[59] Jacob (n 46) 85.

ministerial legal responsibility in private law terms when traditionally ministers appeared to regard themselves as possessing 'sinecures' and their employees had no public status and no connection to the Crown at all, for centuries.

> Until the passing of this Act, these employees were simply private clerks to the Minister intrusted with the office, and in his service. They obtained pay for their work out of the fees which he received from such members of the public as had business with the department, and they were destitute of any public status whatever … Out of this fund the Minister defrayed the working expenses of his department, and he retained as his perquisite any balance that was left. For a long period of history, the emoluments of Ministers were derived from poundage and the use of public moneys in official hands … the practice of exacting fees [and] … the sale of subordinate posts became a recognised source of revenue to a Minister.[60]

In effect, then, ministerial offices were run as small private businesses with divers sources of income, tasks to accomplish, and assistants to hire and fire through 'patronage' that was not remotely thought of, or treated as, public service by the civil service as understood from a modern perspective.[61]

Emmeline Cohen points out that 'sale of office was common', citing the example of 'Sir Charles Middleton' who 'estimated in 1786 that he received on average 300 guineas annually from premiums on the appointment of clerks' which 'was not considered an abuse at the time'.[62] Indeed, such practices were 'nothing that could be reasonably objected to in days when seats in Parliament had a market value throughout the country'.[63] Resistance to the changes were in part driven by concern that it could reduce the ministerial sense of direct, personal responsibility for the department. Crucially, for our purposes, the modern conception of civil servants as public servants working for the Crown is a startlingly recent innovation.

How the Civil Service became Crown Servants

A step change occurred when it became clear that business, and workload, was expanding beyond the available funds at the same time that the practice of charging fees 'fell off'.[64] This led to the Public Salaries, etc Act 1810 (50 Geo III c 117) which determined that the deficit should be made up out of 'the Civil List of the sovereign'. This made the former employees of the minister into servants of the sovereign. This stop-gap solution was then altered again by the Civil List Audit Act 1816 which transferred liability for these salaries to the Consolidated Fund. According to the Westminster Review, this in effect 'created a Civil Service of the Crown'.[65]

[60] *Westminster Review* (n 58) 464; 50 George III, c 117.
[61] Cohen (n 58) 21 and 24.
[62] Cohen (n 58) 25.
[63] *Westminster Review* (n 58) 466.
[64] ibid 465.
[65] ibid.

One unfortunate side effect of these reforms was to give ministers patronage without personal fiscal responsibility. This had the immediate and predictable side effect of an explosion in personnel numbers as ministers lobbied the Treasury for extra clerks whose roles could be leveraged for their personal advantage – and not just amongst the aristocracy. Inevitably the 'Civil Service of the Crown became the epitome of the intellectual weakness of the nation'.[66]

> Families ennobled through law or trade deemed the public service a sphere of inactivity suited to their incapables, and gladly quartered them on the national exchequer … Petty tradesmen … true to the principle of barter, made their electoral support contingent upon the promise of a place for some local hopeful.[67]

The famous Trevelyan-Northcote report catalogued the abuse of the public purse, insisted on appointment on merit, and led directly to the famous Order in Council of 1855 which is the foundation of the modern Civil Service.[68]

Dicey's Description of the Traditional Civil Service

The convoluted history of the Civil Service, and the machinations that led to the reforms, is all quite alien, even shocking, to modern eyes. Nonetheless, it is an inescapable backdrop to understanding why Dicey analysed constitutional law in ostensibly private law terms. As we saw in chapter two, Dicey famously claimed that the beauty of English law was that everyone came to the same court, regardless of their status or position. He contrasted that with the French system which had separate courts for the executive. What is less commonly realised is that the system of government prior to 1816 was, in essence, almost completely privatised at the operational level.

It therefore made absolute sense for Dicey to point out that a minister is inescapably and personally liable in private law for their actions. This was not some counterintuitive peccadillo by Dicey, trying to shoehorn public law concepts into private law pigeonholes. On the contrary, the reason that Dicey pointed to remedies in private law against the minister was because at that time it was a completely accurate reflection of how government was actually run. This significantly undermines the claim that the Crown is the counterparty in transactions and litigation between the government and others. This was plainly untrue in Dicey's time and previously.

[66] ibid 467.
[67] ibid 467.
[68] *Report on the Organisation of the Permanent Civil Service, Together with a Letter from the Rev. B. Jowett* (Parliamentary Papers 27, 1854) (p 4: 'Admission into the Civil Service is … for the unambitious, and the indolent or incapable … public service suffers in both internal inefficiency and public estimation'). Order in Council (21 May 1855) and multiple further such including Order in Council (4 June 1870), discussed in K Fielding, 'Carlyle's unpublished comments on the Northcote-Trevelyan Report' *Carlyle Annual*, No 10 (1989), 5, 7. Daintith and Page (n 45) 62–63 particularly highlight Civil Service Order in Council 1995.

The claim that the Crown historically had any plausible connection with the making of contracts by ministers, departments and officials is therefore untenable. The only relevance of the Crown to the running of public administration was through the prerogative of appointment of ministers who were thereby technically responsible for exercising the executive element of the administration prerogative. The crucial aspect for our purposes was that ministers were appointed under royal prerogative and remain dismissible at will. This inescapable fact has its roots in the historic reality that administration was originally the responsibility of the monarch. To this day, senior ministers are appointed to the Privy Council, thus cementing their status and role as advisers to the monarch on the administration of the country.

The chasm separating the Crown from contracts entered by ministers and departments therefore explains why it was uncontroversial for Dicey to say ministers were personally liable in private law for their decisions. It is also fatal for the claim that the Crown itself enters contracts or commits torts. What about the claim that the Crown Proceedings Act 1947 constituted the Crown as a legal entity at common law?[69] The next chapter argues that it did no such thing.

[69] T Cornford, 'Legal Remedies against the Crown and its Officers' in M Sunkin and S Payne, *The Nature of the Crown: A Legal and Political Analysis* (Oxford University Press, 1999) 245: 'The Crown Proceedings Act abolished the petition of right and other archaic modes of proceeding against the Crown, and put the Crown, in most respects, on the same footing as an ordinary subject for the purposes of proceedings in contract and tort'.

8

Crown Proceedings Act 1947

Introduction

Part II of this book has sought to disaggregate the concept of the Crown from ministers who are legally responsible for governmental actions at common law. Ministers owe their position to their appointment made under the prerogative of appointing ministers. As Dicey made clear, ministers are personally liable in contract and tort for their decisions and actions. The Crown does not itself enter contracts or commit torts. Instead, the Crown stands behind the minister. Originally, through the prerogative of *ex gratia* payments, the Crown subsidised the minister's costs and defrayed the financial consequences of decisions made by governments. This pragmatic *pro tempore* solution eventually ran out of road, leading to the Crown Proceedings Act 1947 ('CPA 1947').[1] This Act put onto a statutory footing, albeit in a 'narrow and piecemeal' way, the developing Crown practice of voluntarily underwriting the decisions and policies of ministers of the Crown.[2] The purpose of this chapter is to explain how 'narrow and piecemeal' was the approach taken by the drafters of the Act.

This chapter argues that the structure, intention and effect of CPA 1947 vindicates one of the central claims of this book, which is that the Crown and prerogative are taxonomically coterminous. The Act formalised the Crown's hitherto effectively voluntary obligation to underwrite the actions of ministers at common law but left untouched the core of the relationship between Crown and ministers. It thus implicitly confirmed the Diceyan orthodoxy that ministers are liable for their actions at common law, as well as for the actions of their department, and the Crown remains outside the jurisdiction of the ordinary courts. Even after the Act, the only non-statutory role of the Crown was to authorise ministers as servants of the Crown under royal prerogative. The statutory obligations imposed on the Crown by the Act did not affect the prerogative of ministerial appointment, nor the conferral of executive administrative prerogative powers on ministers, nor even the personal liability of ministers at common law.

[1] J McLean, *Searching for the State in British Legal Thought* (Cambridge University Press, 2012) 227; J Jacob, 'The Debate Behind an Act: Crown Proceedings Reform, 1920–1947' (1992) *Public Law* 452.

[2] ibid 228.

The Background to the Crown Proceedings Act 1947

As a matter of history, the starting point in analysing CPA 1947 must again be the familiar rule, and fundamental prerogative, that the king can do no wrong. Harold Laski lambasted what he argued were the pernicious effects of this deep-rooted legal rule over a century ago.[3] His core objection was that no compensation was available in general against public institutions for any wrongdoing. He argued that this was because 'the British Crown covers a multitude of sins'.[4] He claimed that this would be 'intolerable', but for the fact that 'the English have a genius for illogical mitigation'.[5] He was referring, of course, to the personal liability of servants of the Crown, and the fact that their liability was underwritten by the Crown. Nobody designing a constitution from scratch would ever construct a system that operated in this way. Nonetheless, the mitigation of the legacy features of the constitution which resulted in the organic solutions painstakingly developed to accommodate the changing political and constitutional realities are key to understanding how and why the Act was passed.

Laski's 'illogical mitigation' is an elegant reference to the fact that, as McLean points out, English law managed to find a pragmatic solution to the problem of immunity that bedevilled continental and domestic law by attaching liability to servants of the Crown personally.[6] Laski also pointed that despite these innovations, 'ministers are not the Crown'.[7] Laski's insights predate the case law culminating in *M v Home Office* but are wholly consistent with the outcome. Laski disagrees that moral fault is essential to establishing appropriate legal regulation and liability, suggesting that requiring moral fault is unnecessary:

> It is a matter not less of political than of economic experience that the enforcement of liability for fault, *often indeed, without it*, is the only effective means … [for] the payment of our [society's] due debts'.[8] (emphasis added)

The payment of compensation is the quintessential example of the allocation of liability by a court. For it to be done on a no fault basis, or at least on the basis that ascribing fault to the state is irrelevant, is arguably to confirm that there is no necessity for a 'will' or entity with moral responsibility or blame. The historic rule of royal inerrancy clearly grounds the immunity of the Crown at judicial common law. Since common law was originally rooted in the royal prerogative of justice, the immunity of the monarch in his or her own courts is entirely to be expected. Nor can it be any surprise that the same immunity was extended to the Crown, even though a consensus slowly developed that the Crown was not a synonym for the

[3] H Laski, 'The Responsibility of the State in England' (1918–19) 32 *Harvard Law Review* 447.
[4] ibid 447.
[5] ibid 449.
[6] McLean (n 1) 205–09.
[7] Laski (n 3) 450.
[8] ibid 451–52.

monarch.[9] On the issue of immunity, Lord Woolf was unequivocal in *M v Home Office*:[10]

> The prerogative remedies could not be obtained against the Crown directly as was explained by Lord Denman C.J. in *Reg. v. Powell* (1841) 1 Q.B. 352, 361: '... because there would be an incongruity in the Queen commanding herself to do an act ...'.

The argument does not need to be repeated that the notion of 'the Queen commanding herself to do an act' presupposes that the source of the ultimate jurisdictional and legitimate authority for the granting of remedies by the courts was originally rooted in the monarch. Furthermore, as Maitland pointed out, the Crown is a 'personality our law does not formally or explicitly recognise', and 'is not ... among the persons known to our law'.[11] By contrast, the monarch in his or her private capacity had legal status sufficient to bring actions and was granted numerous advantages in litigation. In essence, the monarch had the benefit, but not the burdens, in his or her own courts.[12] Whether this 'half-in/half-out' status means the monarch can genuinely be said to be within the jurisdiction of the ordinary courts is perhaps doubtful, and for our purposes, unimportant. By contrast, the Crown certainly is not within the jurisdiction of the ordinary courts because it cannot sue or be sued.

The Court of Appeal in *M v Home Office* confirmed Maitland's claims and held that the Crown has no legal personality at common law.

> Proceedings for contempt can only be taken against a person or body with a sufficient legal personality. As neither the Crown nor the Home Office has any legal personality, no such proceedings can be brought ... for present purposes it suffices to note that [CPA 1947] did not give 'the Crown' or government ministries legal personality.[13]

It is notable that the Court of Appeal was overruled in the House of Lords on the legal status of the Home Office, but *not* on the legal status of the Crown. It might have been technically more accurate for the Court of Appeal to have said that the Crown has no legal personality *at common law* but the point made in the above extract is critically important. It is plain that the Crown has legal status *of some kind* as the bearer and source of legal prerogative powers such as signing treaties, making *ex gratia* payments, requisitioning property in time of war and conducting foreign affairs. What is crucial is that this legal personality was and remains entirely *outside* the jurisdiction of the common law courts.

[9] E Kantorowicz, *The King's Two Bodies: A Study in Mediaeval Political Theology* (Princeton University Press, 1957) 337–46, esp 341.

[10] *M v Home Office* [1994] 1 AC 377, 415. Discussed in detail by M Loughlin, 'The State, the Crown and the Law' in M Sunkin and S Payne (eds), *The Nature of the Crown: A Legal and Political Analysis* (Oxford University Press, 1999) ch 3.

[11] FW Maitland, 'The Crown as Corporation' (1901) 17 *Law Quarterly Review* 131, 136 and 138.

[12] J Chitty, *A Treatise on the Law of the Prerogatives of the Crown: And the Relative Duties and Rights of the Subject* (Butterworth, 1820) ch XIV.

[13] *M v Home Office (CA)* [1992] QB 270, 301.

The House of Lords therefore differed from some of the reasoning of the Court of Appeal in *M v Home Office*, when it held that a distinction could be drawn between the Crown and a department or minister of the Crown. The latter could be held in contempt in their official capacity, but importantly for our purposes, Lord Woolf held that the Crown remained immune in the courts.[14] Lord Woolf also pointed out that the Crown was in a peculiar position even after CPA 1947:

> On the other hand, even after the Act of 1947, it [the Crown] cannot conduct litigation except in the name of an authorised government department or, in the case of judicial review, in the name of a minister.[15]

It is only fair to point out that Lord Woolf also said that 'at least for some purposes, the Crown has a legal personality. It can be appropriately described as a corporation sole or a corporation aggregate … The Crown can hold property and enter into contracts'.[16] The purpose of the remainder of this chapter is to challenge Lord Woolf's *obiter dicta* claim that the Crown can hold property and enter contracts at judicial common law. The serious difficulties of his previous claim, which Woolf hedged, as to whether the Crown can be considered as a corporation sole or aggregate, notwithstanding Lord Sales' heavyweight claim that the Crown is a corporation sole, have been considered above in chapter six.

In order to understand Lord Woolf's *obiter* claim that the Crown can 'hold property and enter into contracts' it is necessary to recap how the law developed in this area. The king, and the Crown, originally had immunity from the jurisdiction of the common law courts, for obvious reasons – they were the king's courts exercising the king's prerogative of justice and granting remedies on the king's behalf. Unfortunately, the immunity of the Crown in its own courts left stranded many subjects who would otherwise have valid claims against servants of the Crown, for example for breach of contract.

As discussed in chapter six, the practice then grew up of permitting aggrieved persons to sue servants of the Crown *personally* using a writ called a 'Petition of Right' instead of suing the Crown directly, because that was impossible. If a minister lost such a case, it became accepted practice for the Crown to indemnify the minister using the prerogative of *ex gratia* payments.[17] As a prerogative, there was in theory a residual discretionary power to refuse to indemnify the minister or servant but the power to refuse was never exercised in practice, even if that was it

[14] *M v Home Office* (n 10) 424. To be fair, this must mean that *Town Investments* is doubtful on this point, as Wade makes clear in his chapter – see W Wade, 'The Crown, Ministers and Officials: Legal Status and Liability' in M Sunkin and S Payne, *The Nature of the Crown: A Legal and Political Analysis* (Oxford University Press, 1999).

[15] ibid.

[16] ibid, per Lord Diplock and Lord Simon of Glaisdale respectively in *Town Investments Ltd v Department of the Environment* [1978] AC 359.

[17] J Jacob, *The Republican Crown* (Dartmouth, 1996) 71–72.

on occasion to induce settlement – wholly inappropriately.[18] Arguably this regular practice could be seen as a constitutional convention.[19]

It might be thought that if the Crown is defined as the legal bearer of prerogative powers, and some prerogative powers can now be judicially reviewed, it is no longer correct to say that the Crown is outside the jurisdiction of the ordinary courts. This would be mistaken. For a start, as discussed above, the highest court confirmed that that the Crown remains outside its jurisdiction in *M v Home Office*, in 1994, long after *GCHQ*. Furthermore, even after the apparent extension of the jurisdiction inherent in imposing judicial review limits on some prerogative powers, that does not bring the Crown within the jurisdiction of the courts any more than judicial review of the exercise by ministers of statutory powers brings parliament within the jurisdiction of the courts. Judicial review of executive powers conferred under prerogative is distinct from the legislative aspect of prerogative held by the Crown.

The Crown Proceedings Act 1947

McLean explains that the system of nominating individuals to act as defendants on behalf of the Crown became increasingly unworkable over time. A turning point occurred in the case of *Adams v Naylor*, where the House of Lords 'unmasked the full extent of the fiction' entailed in the traditional approach.[20] In this case, children were harmed in a poorly marked minefield on Crown land. The case turned on a statutory point, but the issue of the nominated defendant troubled some of the judges. The army officer put forward as a defendant on behalf of the Crown was 'treated as the occupier of the land' even though it 'was not suggested he was in possession of the minefield'.[21] The problem was also that tortious liability could only be found against the occupier. Furthermore, the officer appeared 'neither to have been at the top nor the bottom of the ladder of responsibility'.[22] His position as defendant against the action, instead of the Crown, was therefore an obvious fiction.

Both Lord Simonds and Lord Uthwatt called for reform by legislation. Lord Uthwatt decried the practice of the parties 'by agreement to have the matter dealt with on the footing, proved to be false, that the defendant was in occupation of the land in question'.[23] Lord Simonds referred to a draft Bill already circulating as well

[18] ibid.

[19] I am grateful to Gavin Phillipson for the insightful suggestion that this may have formed a constitutional convention. It would seem to satisfy all three limbs of Jennings' test. WI Jennings, *The Law and the Constitution* [1933], 5th edn (University of London Press, 1960) 136.

[20] McLean (n 1) 227. *Adams v Naylor* [1946] AC 543. The application was also out of time, incidentally.

[21] ibid 554–55.

[22] ibid 881.

[23] ibid 555.

as 'the protracted labours of a committee appointed by Lord Birkenhead'.[24] This case finally, and perhaps inevitably led to the reforms instituted by CPA 1947.[25] Joseph Jacob addresses the decades of serious political arguments and debates that led up to this Act, explaining well the difficulties raised and the caution with which the issue was approached.[26] A wholesale reform it was not. Rather, the minimum necessary was done to overcome the problems caused by cases such as *Adams v Naylor* where the fiction of nominating someone to stand as defendant was most obviously exposed.

As we saw earlier, McLean describes CPA 1947 reform as 'partial' and having a 'narrow and piecemeal quality'.[27] The first point to note about the Act is that nowhere does Parliament expressly confer a legal personality on the Crown as a corporation of any kind or as a natural person, as the Court of Appeal in *M v Home Office* has specifically confirmed.[28] On the contrary, as McLean points out, it 'allows direct liability only in very limited named circumstances' and 'only holds the Crown vicariously liable for the actions of *individuals*'.[29] Any reading of the Act as constituting the Crown as a legal personality of some kind *within the jurisdiction of the common law* must therefore be argued for, rather than simply assumed, because 'the statute does not concede as a *general proposition* that the Crown is capable of "willing to do wrong"'.[30] In other words, the statute absolutely does not create a legal entity at common law that is capable of being liable as a legal and moral entity per se.

If any such reading is arguable, it would only be one possible interpretation of CPA 1947. There is another possible reading, and it is more plausible. It could also be mentioned that nowhere in CPA 1947 does the Act confer on the Crown the power to enter contracts *itself*. It has long been accepted that the Crown operates through its servants and ministers in such matters. This often overlooked point is crucial to the discussion in this section. Section 1 of the Act provides:

> Where any person has a claim against the Crown after the commencement of this Act and, if this Act had not been passed, the claim might have been enforced, subject to the grant of His Majesty's fiat, by petition of right … [then] the claim may be enforced as of right; *and without the fiat of His Majesty*, by proceedings taken against the Crown … [emphasis added]

The first point to note about s 1 is that it proceeds on the basis that claimants could have theoretically valid claims against the Crown before the Act but that

[24] ibid 553.

[25] J Jacob, 'The Debates Behind an Act: Crown Proceedings Reform, 1920–1947' (1992) *Public Law*452. See also J Jacob, *The Republican Crown* (Dartmouth, 1996) ch 6.

[26] ibid 452.

[27] McLean (n 1) 227 and 228.

[28] *M v Home Office (CA)* [1992] QB 270, 301: 'the Crown Proceedings Act 1947 … did not give "the Crown" or government ministries legal personality'.

[29] McLean (n 1) 228 (emphasis in the original).

[30] ibid (emphasis in the original).

the *enforcement* of those claims would previously have proceeded by a Petition of Right because the courts have no jurisdiction over the Crown. The Crown did not appear to have any legal personality at judicial common law before the Act because it is this very Act that generated the power to sue 'the Crown' (later interpreted by the courts to mean its servants) in the first place.[31] In theory, it is only if the Crown could be sued directly in the ordinary courts that the question of its legal personality might need to be determined as a matter of common law. Whether CPA 1947 was intended to create a legal personality for the Crown is quite another matter, but it must be reemphasised that it is clear in the drafting of this Act that the Crown had no legal personality at common law *before* the Act. The Act proceeds on that assumption.

The first section of CPA 1947 therefore assumes that subjects have always had putative claims 'against the Crown' but that they were unenforceable against the Crown itself but instead were enforced as against the *servants* of the Crown via the petition of right procedure. The use of the word 'Crown' in this section must therefore continue to mean 'a claim against [the servants or agents acting on behalf of] the Crown' for the purposes of any actual litigation. Indeed, this is how such litigation is in fact conducted to this day. The law reports are not littered with cases in the form '*Smith v Regina*' or '*Smith v Rex*'.

The phrase 'proceedings against the Crown' must therefore logically be interpreted as meaning in reality 'proceedings against [ministers or departments on behalf of] the Crown'. This was eventually made clear in *M v Home Office* in 1994 which drew a critical distinction between the Crown and servants of the Crown. The same modern distinction between the Crown and servants of the Crown also renders irrelevant much of the discussion in previous decades and centuries about the legal status of the Crown as an undifferentiated legal entity. Since we now expressly distinguish the concept of the Crown from ministers and servants of the Crown, any alleged status of the Crown at judicial common law must be examined in light of *M v Home Office*. The crucial point is that the retention of the liability of servants of the Crown at common law entrenches the judicially accepted principle that the Crown is outside the jurisdiction of the courts to this day. The Crown itself is not a legal personality at common law and is not subject to the jurisdiction of the common law.

Section 2 of CPA 1947 deals with tortious liability.

> [T]he Crown shall be subject to all those liabilities in tort to which, if it were a private person of full age and capacity, it would be subject:
>
> (a) in respect of torts committed by its servants or agents;
> (b) in respect of any breach of those duties which a person owes to his servants or agents at common law by reason of being their employer; and
> (c) in respect of any breach of the duties attaching at common law to the ownership, occupation, possession or control of property …

[31] *M v Home Office* (n 10).

Section 2 would appear to bolster the interpretation suggested in this chapter because it states that the liabilities imposed on the Crown are those for which it would be liable *if* 'it were a private person of full age and capacity'. That is far from saying that the Crown is *constituted* as a private person of full age and capacity by the statute. In fact, it is flatly contradictory to such a claim. Further, it strongly suggests that the Crown is not, and cannot be, a natural person because there would then be no need to mandate it be treated *as if* it were a private person.

A good illustration of the importance of the distinction between ministers and the Crown drawn in *M v Home Office* is the effect of CPA 1947 on occupiers liability torts. For the purposes of the Act, the minister in their official capacity must be deemed to be the occupier for liability purposes and the Crown stands behind them. This is far more satisfactory than the previous system of a named individual nominally standing in as the defendant. Maintaining the distinction between Crown and minister post *M v Home Office* would preserve the intention of the Act which was to fix the problems of nominal defendants, without treating the Crown as occupier for legal purposes directly.

McLean concurs, arguing that CPA 1947 'excludes direct liability of the Crown in tort' and that the 'section does not recognize any originating fault in the Crown … The actions and omissions of individuals (but not their mental states) are instead *attributed* to the Crown'.[32] McLean bemoans the fact that 'vicarious liability, so conceived, is a means by which to give the victim an alternative avenue of redress but, conceptually at least, does not carry the same level of moral opprobrium as direct liability'.[33] She goes on to conclude that at 'least as it is framed, the Crown Proceedings Act 1947 is a repudiation of "real will" theories'.[34] Since 'real will' theories are of questionable value in a system primed to award remedies against the government for wrongs, the drafter's decision is to be welcomed.

It is also very difficult to see how s 2 could be construed as constituting the Crown as a *corporation* of any kind. This is because the wording imposes statutory liability *equivalent* to a private person – rather than a corporation. Indeed, it could even be argued that s 2 is fatal to the claim that the Crown should be treated as a corporation at judicial common law, precisely because liabilities equivalent to a private person *of full age and capacity* are imposed, which is incompatible with the idea of the Crown being a corporation.

It is also worth noting that the Crown is treated differently to private employers. As Wade makes clear, 'the Crown shall not be liable unless the servant or agent would themselves have been liable'.[35] This provides the Crown with an exemption

[32] McLean (n 1) 229 (emphasis in the original).
[33] ibid.
[34] ibid 230.
[35] W Wade, C Forsyth and J Ghosh, *Wade & Forsyth's Administrative Law*, 12th edn (Oxford University Press, 2022) 656.

from the normal rule that defences available to the servant are not available to the employer unless the employer is also entitled to them personally. It is suggested that this differential treatment provides further evidence that the Crown is supposed to remain outside the jurisdiction of the courts. Instead, the Crown continues simply to *underwrite* the liability of its servants. This is because, unlike private employers, the Crown anomalously accrues any exemption possessed by its servants.

Rule of Law Implications?

It might be thought that the above reading of CPA 1947 raises some rule of law implications because, following this approach, it would appear that the Crown continues to operate wholly outside the jurisdiction of the ordinary courts, and, as McLean points out, the Act leaves a number of gaps due to the narrow drafting.[36] McLean explains how the courts effectively 'circumvented' those gaps over time by imposing a 'duty of care to the public in administrating statute'.[37] This would appear to be in the finest traditions of incremental common law development. So successful has this process been that McLean highlights only minor residual problems from the narrowness of the drafting. She mentions the famous example of who owes the national debt and also claims that it is not clear 'who is responsible for future generations'.[38] These are not major issues. In other words, the incremental approach, without the need for identifying a single will or entity representing the state has not prevented the courts from ensuring that liability, and therefore justice, are served appropriately.

The potential rule of law critique that the Crown still operates outside the jurisdiction of the courts would also risk making the mistake that Lord Wilson warned about in *Evans* of conflating the rule of law with the rule of the courts.[39] It is clear following CPA 1947 and *M v Home Office* that the *government* is now rightly subject to the rule of law in all material respects.[40] The fact that the Crown operates outside the jurisdiction of the common law courts is neither here nor there because decisions of government departments, represented by their Secretaries of State are now reviewable by the courts and any wrongs are righted. This is true whether the issue concerns statutory powers or when exercising prerogative powers on behalf of the Crown (other than 'high policy' prerogatives).[41] It is also worth noting that this structure would provide a logical explanation for how prerogative remedies against ministers and departments could originally have been granted by the

[36] McLean (n 1) 228–29.
[37] ibid 231.
[38] ibid 239.
[39] *R (Evans) v Attorney General* [2015] UKSC 21, [2015] 2 WLR 813, [154].
[40] *Pace* Wade's gentle warning about the *enforcement* of a court order against ministers of the Crown which, it is hoped, will never need to be tested. *Craig v Her Majesty's Advocate (for the Government of the United States of America)* [2022] UKSC 6, [46].
[41] *R v Secretary of State for Foreign and Commonwealth Affairs, ex parte Everett* [1989] QB 811, 817.

Crown as a matter of strict technicality, even though those remedies have since been placed on a statutory footing.[42]

It could also be argued that CPA 1947, s 21 entrenches and endorses the exceptional status of the Crown because it lays down that no orders for specific performance or recovery of land may be made against the Crown, but instead 'declaratory' orders would be made. The Act also makes clear (in s 21(2)) that no relief may be granted against an officer of the Crown 'which could not have been obtained in proceedings against the Crown'. The fact that mere declarations are mandated by s 21, as well as the limits imposed in s 21(2), provides further strong evidence that the Crown itself was *not* supposed to be brought within the jurisdiction of the ordinary courts by the Act.

It might be thought that mere 'declaratory' orders were deliberately chosen for s 21 precisely because they would have no legal effect. It is to be presumed that in such cases, the government would remedy the situation *ex gratia* to respect the law as laid down in the declaration. Further, the refusal in s 21 to impose specific performance obligations on the Crown could be read as a deliberate shielding of the Crown from any substantive legal consequences at judicial common law by keeping the Crown outside the purview of the common law courts.

This interpretation is considerably reinforced by Lord Woolf's speech in *M v Home Office* because he very carefully makes clear that only ministers of the Crown are affected by the decision, not the Crown itself.[43] The continued immunity of the Crown itself at judicial common law also reflects what Wade called the 'compromise, which is well suited to a state which is both a monarchy and a democracy'.[44] It is suggested, therefore, that the vexed question of the Crown's alleged legal personality at common law can now be laid to rest – because it is in fact a non-question. One might as well enquire as to the legal personality of parliament at common law. CPA 1947 does not place the Crown under the jurisdictional supervision of the common law courts, and this was made crystal clear in *M v Home Office*.

'Disguised Public Law Actions'

It will be noted that Dicey did not use 'the Crown' in the quotation cited earlier defining the royal prerogative and the powers that accrue to the executive as a result. Instead, he referred to 'executive government'.[45] Could it not therefore be

[42] Judicature Act 1873, s 16 and Senior Court Act 1981, s 31. There are interesting questions about the legal basis of the advice to the Crown given *by the judges* on the exercise of this particular prerogative power. Normally ministers advise the Crown. Of course, travelling circuit judges were the original executive centuries ago, so it may not be that controversial.

[43] *M v Home Office* (n 10) 424.

[44] Wade (n 14) 32. Importantly, the monarch has no actual power.

[45] 'Every act which the executive government can lawfully do without the authority of the Act of Parliament is done in virtue of this prerogative.'

countered that the *executive government* certainly enters into contracts at judicial common law, even if the Crown technically does not, and that this is *de facto* indistinguishable from the idea that 'the Crown' effectively enters into contracts at common law? Such a claim would miss the legal authority underpinning the actions of the executive government acts in entering those contracts. It also fails to account for the distinction now drawn by the courts between the Crown and servants, ministers or departments acting on its behalf. Chapter nine will show that there is an oft-overlooked prerogative power which this book has labelled the 'administration prerogative', which operates to underpin the ordinary day-to-day management of affairs by the Crown, or rather by its servants on behalf of the Crown.

Ministers and servants of the Crown gain their legal authority to act administratively from the executive aspect of the administration prerogative. It is therefore a *prerequisite* for any ostensibly 'private law' activities undertaken by servants of the Crown to be valid that the administration prerogative has been lawfully exercised beforehand. In a sense, therefore, all actions of the Crown, and servants of the Crown, that are not based on statute are indeed done 'in virtue of this prerogative'.[46] The entry into such contracts – or the conveyance of land – by servants or ministers of the Crown is therefore in fact a *mixed* question of public law and private law.

Now it is perfectly true that as a matter of convenience the court system may choose to investigate claims against servants or ministers of the Crown by determining the issues in what ostensibly *look* like purely private law proceedings. English law is famously pragmatic on such matters, as Dicey pointed out.[47] This should not be allowed to obscure the legal reality that there is an inescapable public law element in such proceedings. Such actions are 'disguised public law' proceedings' where an ostensibly private law action is *underpinned* by a prerogative power authorising the action. In the vast majority of cases, the public law underpinning will pass unnoticed and unmentioned in the proceedings. This should not be allowed to obscure the fact that the public law element is inescapably present in such litigation.

Analogy with Ultra Vires Local Council Decisions

A useful analogy that may help to illustrate the disguised public law actions within some private law claims can be seen in the case of *Crédit Suisse v Allerdale Borough Council*.[48] Allerdale Borough Council wanted to build a swimming pool

[46] AV Dicey, *Introduction to the Study of the Law of the Constitution*, 8th edn (Macmillan, 1927) 421.

[47] See also *Roy v Kensington and Chelsea FPC* [1992] 2 WLR 239, [1992] 1 All ER 705 and *Dennis Rye Pension Fund v Sheffield City Council* [1998] 1 WLR 840 which softened, if not entirely removed, the 'bright line' distinction drawn by Lord Diplock in *O'Reilly v Mackman* [1983] 2 AC 237.

[48] *Crédit Suisse v Allerdale Borough Council* [1997] QB 306.

for residents but was severely restricted by statute in its ability to borrow money to fund construction.[49] In order to circumvent these restrictions, the council embarked on an 'ingenious scheme' to set up a company 'off balance sheet'.[50] This was 'designed to avoid the statutory controls on local authorities'.[51] The company borrowed around £6 million from Credit Suisse. The council guaranteed the loan to the company which resulted in a more favourable interest rate for the loan. The loan was supposed to be paid off by the sale of time-share units but when that failed, the company went into liquidation. The bank sought to enforce the guarantee against the Council.

The Court of Appeal held that the Council had no statutory power to give such a guarantee for the company's borrowing. This was notwithstanding the fact that the court held that the action was 'a private law claim albeit against a public authority'.[52] The Council's decision to give a guarantee was also an improper purpose. The bank's claim therefore failed for reasons that had nothing to do with contract law, or indeed private law at all. The claim was a disguised public law action and turned entirely on the *vires* of the council's action. Lord Justice Neill said that the effect of the *ultra vires* action of the council were the same as 'those which flow where one of the parties to the contract lacks capacity'.[53]

Another example of where the public and private aspects of a series of decisions were disaggregated is the infamous interest rate swaps litigation, which also concerned imaginative accounting methods used by councils to try to circumvent statutory borrowing limits. Even when the looming disaster was brought to its attention by the auditor, the 'council continued to insist on the legality of its activities' and gave 'the clear impression … [it] had played the markets and won'.[54] This claim was undermined when interest rates then nearly doubled. This market speculation was brought to an abrupt halt by the case of *Hazell v Hammersmith and Fulham LBC*.[55] The auditor had a statutory power to bring a judicial review against the council under the Local Government Act 1982, s 19. As the litigation got under way, the banks who were involved in the transactions were permitted to intervene to try to protect their position. The House of Lords held that all the transactions were *ultra vires* and therefore void *ab initio*. The banks could not enforce the contracts.

Litigation was then brought by Westdeutsche Landesbank against Islington Council which had been similarly engaged in *ultra vires* swaps activity. The sums were so huge that this litigation was for the difference between the compound and simple interest of the net sums possessed by the council during the key period.[56]

[49] Local Government Act 1972, Sch 13.
[50] *Crédit Suisse* (n 48) 333 and 358.
[51] ibid.
[52] ibid 343.
[53] ibid.
[54] D Campbell-Smith, *Follow the Money* (Penguin, 2008).
[55] *Hazell v Hammersmith and Fulham LBC* [1992] 2 AC 1.
[56] *Westdeutsche Landesbank Girozentrale v Islington LBC* [1996] AC 669.

The litigation was wholly private, being an action for money had and received because the relevant contracts were all void *ab initio* due to the *ultra vires* actions of the council as had been established in *Hazell*.

It is suggested that an analogy can be drawn between the position in public law of the council decision-makers in these cases and ministers of the Crown. The difference is that statute establishes the legal capacity of councils whereas prerogative underpins the official capacity of ministers. Where a council acts *ultra vires*, that vitiates the contracts they enter *ab initio*, thus demonstrating the disguised public law nature of any consequential litigation. Similarly, if ministers were to act in a way that vitiates their capacity to make those contracts *qua* minister, that could have serious consequences for the validity of those ostensibly private law contracts. In neither case does it make sense to argue that the legislative body that *confers* the capacity to enter the contracts is a *party* to those contracts. In other words, it makes no more sense to say that the Crown enters contracts than it does to say that Parliament enters contracts.

It is suggested, therefore, that it is wrong to claim that the Crown has *judicial common law* powers to enter into contracts or buy and sell property. Instead, the Crown possesses prerogative powers, including the administration prerogative, that legally underpin, and therefore authorise, servants and ministers of the Crown to engage in what look at first like private law transactions but are in fact disguised public law actions. If, for example, a minister were surreptitiously to enter a series of contracts on behalf of the Crown with a close friend and business partner or in some other highly capricious or bad faith way, that would be treated completely differently to a situation where a private person decided to enter a series of contracts with a close friend and business partner, or acted in other ways that would be *ultra vires* if done by a public official.[57]

Public or Private Law?

English law, as Loughlin has pointed out, has long been held back by Dicey's proud insistence that all actions come before the same court.[58] Commentators have pointed to the fact that this has meant that 'public law' has been treated as a branch of private law with private law concepts being transplanted in unhelpful ways into the public law realm. Indeed, the example of the misuse of the private law concept of 'corporation' has been a core issue in this chapter. It could even be argued that part of the problem with classifying the Crown as either a corporation sole or corporation aggregate is precisely because both those concepts were originally derived from, and rooted in, different aspects of the theoretical concept of the

[57] See, for example, *Porter v Magill* [2002] 2 AC 357 for a useful analogy. There may be personal liability issues for those involved, as *Porter* demonstrated.

[58] Loughlin (n 10) 69–70.

Crown that developed over time. This illustrates how odd it is to then try to map those derivative private law concepts back on to the Crown. Trying to shoehorn the Crown into one or other definition of a corporation is like trying to classify a dinosaur as either an iguana or an eagle.

In reality, however, what has hampered the development of public law is not that all law was historically private law but, instead, that all law has historically been *public* law, as discussed in chapter two.[59] Baked into the foundations of the law is the historic fact that judicial common law started as a set of processes whereby ordinary citizens sought relief, and remedies, from the king's judges. English law traditionally fastens on remedies, not rights or principles – as Lord Wilberforce once so memorably pointed out.[60] The remedies were granted by the grace of the king through his judges. In that sense, all legal disputes were therefore, in a sense, public law. Over time, the breadth of the coverage gave common law the veneer of a comprehensive system of private law rights. Only then was it realised that a sub-category of specialised public law needed to be developed, but that was only done slowly and late.

The exercise of public power, and the expenditure of public money, is an entirely separate area of law to private law and the fact that some of the rules look similar is strictly irrelevant. Public law and private law need to be kept strictly *conceptually* separate regardless of which actual court such issues are heard in, which is unimportant. Ministers enter contracts and are legally responsible for them. Ministers have the power to enter those contracts as a result of the executive authority they accrue by being appointed by the Crown under prerogative. Since, therefore, the Crown operates solely through prerogative, as well as some statutory powers, it is clear that the Crown has no judicial common law powers.

Part II: Conclusion

The perhaps somewhat contentious claim made in part II is that contrary to some judicial *dicta* as well as considerable academic comment, the Crown does not in fact possess any 'common law' powers, particularly in the areas of contract and tort. Instead, the Crown possesses only prerogative powers, and indeed is best defined by that legal fact. This deceptively simple starting point has required some careful unpicking of different academic and judicial detours that have occurred in this area of law. As shown in part I, it is arguable that the problem started all the way back with Blackstone's definition of royal prerogative which was extended and further refined by Wade. Wade's definition wrongly assumes that the Crown shares legal powers with ordinary citizens at common law.

[59] See pp 51–54.

[60] *Davy Spelthorne BC* [1984] AC 262, 276: 'English law fastens, not upon principles but upon remedies'.

Part II has suggested that the legal powers of the Crown are unrelated to common law, in the sense of judicial decisions of the court of Queen's Bench and connected appeal courts. Indeed, prerogative powers of the Crown in fact predate the very origins of such judicial decisions. To root other prerogatives in the prerogative of justice or its derivative set of judicial 'common law' precedents makes no logical or legal sense. Furthermore, to claim that the Crown had alleged common law legal powers *conferred* on it by the courts in the way that such powers have been conferred on citizens is also illogical and confusing. It is also flatly contradicted by legal history because litigation for unlawful executive action has always been against servants and ministers of the Crown, rather than the Crown, or the monarch, directly. The Crown, as distinct from ministers or departments, remains immune from the jurisdiction of the courts to impose an injunction to this day.[61]

Rather than focusing on the intricacies of the alleged common legal powers of the Crown, the final chapter of part II has instead focused on the Crown Proceedings Act 1947. It has been suggested that nothing in the Act constitutes the Crown as a legal personality of any kind at common law. The previously vexed question of the status of the Crown as a corporation or natural person at common law may thus be firmly put aside as a red herring.[62]

It was further claimed that actions of ministers that *appear* to be the subject of purely private law claims are in fact 'disguised public law' claims because the validity of, for example, any contractual agreements made by ministers presupposes that they have acted *intra vires* under the administration prerogative. Thus, a clear conceptual separation can be kept between public and private law matters, even if claims are heard in what appear to be purely private law proceedings. The conclusion of this chapter is simple: Dicey was correct in claiming that all lawful actions of the executive government that are not based on statute 'are done in virtue of' the royal prerogative. It follows, therefore, that the Crown has no common law legal powers. Part III considers the linked claim that the Crown also has no third source or non-legal powers. It therefore seeks to reframe the case law in that area to integrate those cases into a prerogative-based analysis.

[61] *M v Home Office* (n 10) 409–10.

[62] This leaves to one side the miniscule number of statutory powers conferred directly on the Crown, as opposed to ministers of the Crown.

PART III

Third Source

9

The Myth of Third Source Powers

Introduction

Third source powers (or freedoms) may be loosely defined, according to Harris, as those actions that the Crown can lawfully undertake that are not based on prerogative or statute.[1] The claim that there are no such third source powers or freedoms will come as no surprise in the light of the arguments in part II which made the closely related claim that the there are no *common law* powers possessed by the Crown. If the latter claim is true, then the claim that the Crown has no third source powers must follow inexorably, even apodictically, because for many commentators they are effectively the same.[2]

The challenge to third source powers (or freedoms) in this chapter follows logically from one of the main claims in this book which is that there are only *two* ultimate sources that can, and do, confer validity on legal norms in this country: prerogative and parliament. As discussed in chapter four, all actions by the Crown must be authorised by law, so it is further suggested that all powers of the Crown are necessarily *legal* powers.[3] Thus, this chapter will also argue that not only does the Crown have no 'freedoms', it also has no 'non-legal' powers.

If the arguments in relation to third source or other powers in this chapter are accepted, then the definition of prerogative defended in this book would be bolstered. All non-statutory Crown powers are prerogative powers. The converse is equally true and exhaustive. All prerogative powers are exclusive legal powers of the Crown. Putting the same point in yet another way (and leaving to one side the miniscule number of *statutory* powers of the Crown), the terms 'Crown powers', 'prerogative powers', 'legal powers of the Crown' and '*intra vires* actions of the Crown' are all synonymous. These claims flow inexorably from the argument that the Crown is the legal bearer, or repository, of royal prerogative powers. As chapter six argues, one of the novel claims in this monograph is that it would be preferable to undertake a Copernican reversal of the relationship between the Crown and prerogative. Rather than attempting to define the Crown and then ascribing

[1] B Harris, 'The "Third Source" of Authority for Government Action' (1992) 108 *Law Quarterly Review* 626.

[2] Lord Sales, 'Crown Powers, the Royal Prerogative and Fundamental Rights' in H Wilberg and M Elliott (eds), *The Scope and Intensity of Substantive Review* (Bloomsbury, 2015) 361.

[3] See pp 79–80.

prerogative powers to it, considerable clarification and simplification is achieved by reversing that methodology.

Therefore, not only does it make no sense to claim that the Crown has any common law powers, it is also suggested that the Crown does not possess any other types of powers, such as third source powers, non-legal powers or freedoms. Finally, and as a function of basic rule of law and constitutional principles, everything that the Crown does must have a legal basis. That basis can only, ultimately, be royal prerogative, save for some extremely rare examples of statutory powers conferred *directly* on the Crown (as opposed to *ministers* of the Crown). This chapter therefore examines two main arguments that contradict the positive claims made so far in this book. The first is the claim that the Crown possesses third source powers or freedoms. The second argument is that the Crown has various *non-legal* powers. The most important aspects of these claims derive from an alternative understanding of the definition of royal prerogative rooted in one reading of Blackstone as developed by Wade. As we saw in chapters four and seven, Wade contends that true royal prerogative powers are confined to such powers as are exclusive to the Crown, have legal effects at common law and have no equivalent at common law. This inevitably leaves a considerable gap for those powers ostensibly exercised by the government that, according to Wade, are *not* exclusive to the Crown. Wade in effect argues that such powers were better understood as being common law powers.

Harris has suggested an alternative label for these powers: 'third source powers'.[4] This catchy label has had considerable impact on this area of law and has been taken seriously by, or at least mentioned in, numerous academic legal textbooks.[5] Somewhat curiously, Harris has gone further in later work and described these powers as being 'residuary *freedoms*', claiming that, in essence, the government can do anything that is not prohibited by law.[6] He concedes, however, that whilst he terms them third source 'freedoms' they are frequently labelled as 'de facto or common law powers' by others.[7]

This chapter challenges virtually every aspect of Harris's analysis of the supposed category of third source powers. The first section considers the arguments made by Harris in favour of his suggested concept. After setting out a summary of his views, some problems with his claims are identified, not least of which is the reduction of the concept of prerogative powers to meaninglessness.

[4] Harris (n 1).

[5] See for example, M Elliott and R Thomas, *Public Law*, 4th edn (Oxford University Press, 2020) 173–75; H Fenwick, G Phillipson and A Williams, *Text, Cases and Materials on Public Law and Human Rights*, 4th edn (Routledge, 2017) 478/483; A Le Sueur, M Sunkin and JE Murkens, *Public Law: Text, Cases, and Materials*, 4th edn (Oxford University Press, 2019) 302, 304–07; A Bradley, K Ewing, and C Knight, *Constitutional and Administrative Law*, 17th edn (Pearson, 2018) 305.

[6] BV Harris, 'Government "Third Source" Action and Common Law Constitutionalism' [2010] 126 *Law Quarterly Review* 373.

[7] Harris (n 1) 651 fn 6. Also B Harris, 'The "Third Source" of Authority for Government Action Revisited' [2007] *Law Quarterly Review* 225.

Following Wade, Harris claims that those powers of the Crown that do not affect or override common law rights, such as treaty powers or foreign affairs, are not in fact prerogatives. It is suggested, as with Wade, that any definition of prerogative that does *not* include such powers as part of prerogative power is necessarily, and for that reason, fatally defective. The section goes on to consider the problems with the executive claiming a power or freedom that has no obvious source and challenges the claim that the concept of residuary freedom makes sense when applied to the executive as opposed to ordinary people. Finally, the section endorses Perry's critique of Harris, which in essence denies that third source powers can intelligibly be understood as 'freedoms' at all. They can only be understood as powers.

The second section of this chapter then turns to the question of whether the Crown can be said to possess any 'non-legal' powers or whether all powers of the Crown are necessarily legal powers. If the Crown does indeed possess non-legal powers then the definition of prerogative defended in this book would be non-exhaustive, because in addition to prerogative legal powers, which are necessarily legal, the Crown would also possess a set of non-legal powers that would also need to be accounted for in textbooks and the like. The claim that the Crown possesses non-legal powers is defended by Perry in the same article in which he demonstrates that Harris must be committed to the claim that all powers of the Crown must be *legal* powers.[8] This section of the chapter sets out to show that to the extent that Harris' theory is best understood as defending the claim that all powers of the Crown are in fact *legal* powers, then Harris' claim is correct on that point. Thus, all powers of the Crown are legal powers and should be labelled royal prerogative.

The third section of the chapter addresses the difficulty raised by Perry for this book's claim that the Crown only possesses legal powers: there are a number of mundane activities undertaken by government (such as writing memos and making ordinary administrative decisions) that do not appear to have, or even need, legal underpinnings. The suggested solution to this mini conundrum is that there is a mostly forgotten prerogative power – although it was mentioned by Chitty's standard treatise – that the Crown has a prerogative power to 'administer the government of the … realm' served by 'their officers and ministers'.[9] If this prerogative is properly understood, it may be thought to cover a wide range of minor administrative matters that would otherwise appear not to be underpinned by any legal authority. This then provides a useful prism through which to consider the administration prerogative, and the relevant case law, in chapters ten and eleven.

[8] A Perry, 'The Crown's Administrative Powers' [2015] *Law Quarterly Review* 652.

[9] J Chitty, *A Treatise on the Law of the Prerogatives of the Crown: And the Relative Duties and Rights of the Subject* (Butterworth, 1820) 7.

Third Source Freedoms

As Perry has argued, Dicey's definition of the prerogative as, in effect, comprising all non-statutory legal powers 'has come under stinging criticism'.[10] One major source of that criticism was a series of articles by Harris beginning with a well-known article in the *Law Quarterly Review* in 1992.[11] Harris claims that there is a set of hitherto unnoticed powers of the Crown which he labels 'third source' powers, and that these powers ground a number of actions by the Crown that are distinct from any prerogative powers.[12] He defines the latter extremely narrowly. In essence, his claim is that the Crown possesses considerable freedom as a natural person and those freedoms may be exercised by the government, in effect, as long as such exercise does not conflict with any statute or judicial precedent. These freedoms are the eponymous 'third source powers' which Harris claims form part of the 'common law'.[13] Harris also claims that prerogative powers, as he defines them, are part of the 'common law'.[14] This latter claim is plainly mistaken. For the 'prerogative in the narrow sense' to be a type of 'common law power' Harris would need to provide evidence of the source of such powers in case law, but he fails to cite any judicial decisions to substantiate this claim, because none exist.

Harris builds on the definitions of the prerogative given by Blackstone and Wade, and adopts the ahistorical common law perspective that was critiqued in previous chapters. His starting point is that a distinction should be drawn between what he terms 'the prerogative in the narrow sense' and 'the freedom which the government has to do anything that is not prohibited by law'.[15] It is clear that Harris regards the two categories as exhaustive. Either a particular power is a genuine prerogative under his definition, or it is a third source freedom.

'Overriding' Common Law

Genuine prerogatives, for Harris, are those prerogatives that are unique to the Crown and can be used to 'override' common law rights.[16] This means that Harris goes even further than Wade. Wade's test for a 'genuine' prerogative was whether its exercise produces 'legal effects at common law'.[17] Harris, by contrast, insists that prerogatives 'in the narrow sense' must be able to 'override common law rights'.[18]

[10] ibid.
[11] Harris (n 1).
[12] In a footnote, Harris says he could have labelled them 'common law' powers instead but that would be 'insufficiently precise' because that would include prerogative powers 'in the narrow sense'): ibid at fn 6.
[13] ibid.
[14] Harris (2007) (n 7) 226.
[15] Harris (n 1) 626.
[16] Harris (n 1) 627.
[17] HWR Wade, 'Procedure and Prerogative in Public Law' [1985] *Law Quarterly Review* 180, 193.
[18] Harris (n 1) 627.

This is much narrower even than the definition Wade set out for genuine prerogatives, which itself suffers from the serious problems highlighted in chapters four and seven.

One example of a Wadean prerogative that Harris might reject is *nolle prosequi*, which is the exclusive power of the Crown to stop prosecutions. Wade's definition probably includes this power as a prerogative because it affects the *application* of the law. Harris probably would not include it because it does not *override* any rights – this is because it only impacts on the defendant and whether they are prosecuted. Victims have no right at common law to insist on continued prosecution, so their rights are not 'overridden'. The same could be said about pardons, which are technically an indulgence and whilst they may or may not 'have legal effects at common law' in a Wadean sense, they certainly do not involve *overriding* any common law rights in the Harris sense.

This leads us to the first major problem with Harris' definition. He restricts even Wade's already very narrow definition of prerogative to an extreme degree by deciding to limit his definition to those prerogatives that *override* judicial common law rights. This is a problem precisely because it is established law, recently confirmed by the Supreme Court in *Miller I*, that prerogative cannot infringe or change, never mind override, 'any part of the common law, or statute law'.[19] The *Miller I* majority went on to say that 'the exercise of those [prerogative] powers must be compatible with legislation and common law'.[20] Using prerogative to *override* common law rights would flatly contradict *Miller I*, which does no more than restate longstanding and accepted law.[21] For example, Lord Hoffmann in *Bancoult* said for the majority that 'since the 17th century the prerogative has not empowered the Crown to change English common or statute law'.[22] Hence, were we to apply Harris's definition, the bizarre result would be that there would be *no genuine prerogative powers at all*, since it is clear law that prerogatives *cannot* override common law rights. Since Harris has also excluded from the definition of prerogatives traditional prerogative powers such as treaties and crown immunity, the number of genuine prerogatives 'in the 'narrow sense', according to Harris, must be zero. For Harris, therefore, all non-statutory legal powers are in fact third source freedoms.

Emptying the Concept of 'Prerogative' of All Meaning or Content

Harris's approach would thus empty the well-established legal concept of 'prerogative powers' of all content. To give just one example, the power to prorogue

[19] *R (Miller) v Secretary of State for Exiting the European Union* [2017] UKSC 5, [2018] AC 61, [2017] 2 WLR 583 ('*Miller I*'), [44]. See also [45] and [69].

[20] ibid [45].

[21] See *R (Bancoult) v Secretary of State for Foreign and Commonwealth Affairs (No 2)* [2008] UKHL 61, [2009] 1 AC 453, [44].

[22] ibid.

Parliament – the subject of the *Miller II* case[23] – does not affect, still less override, any common law rights. So, for Harris, prorogation is not a prerogative power. The Wadean claim, endorsed by Harris, that prerogative powers that do not have effects at judicial common law are not really prerogatives cannot withstand serious scrutiny. However, Harris goes even further than Wade and appears to exclude every generally accepted power historically exercised under prerogative from his definition.

It is no small irony that Harris appears to consider that *all* non-statutory executive legal powers can be lumped together in one category, whatever label might be given to it. It would seem that, in a strange way, he agrees with one of the core premises of this book – that there are ultimately in fact only *two* sources of executive legal authority, since there are no genuine 'prerogatives in the narrow sense' if his test is conscientiously applied. His argument might therefore be thought to have come full circle save for a matter of simple labelling. The two sources of executive authority, according to Harris, are statute and another source, which could perhaps fairly be defined for Harris as anything that the government is 'free' to do that is not based on statute.

However, this second category of executive action already has a long-established label: 'royal prerogative'. Although instead of being entirely 'free' to do what is not legally prohibited, the better view --not least on rule of law grounds – is that the executive has some residual *legal* powers that are increasingly strictly defined. If this is accepted, 'third source' powers may be seen as entirely mythical or at best a question of semantics.

Harris might respond that the difference between him and this author is that, for him, the legal powers (or 'freedoms') apparently possessed by the executive are derived from 'common law' not from prerogative. However, if 'common law' is defined as 'all non-statutory' law then we are simply returned to a semantic debate about the appropriate label for all non-statutory legal powers. In that debate, 'royal prerogative' has the clear advantages of being the more traditional label as well as being historically more accurate. If, by contrast, 'common law' is narrowly defined as judicial precedent, then Harris is plainly wrong because prerogative powers are not derived from judicial precedent – instead, courts have long recognised prerogatives as a *pre-existing* power.

Interestingly, Harris on some occasions appears close to resiling from his more restrictive definition. In the conclusion of his 1992 article, he argues that third source government action 'cannot *affect* rights created by law' (emphasis added).[24] This suggests that Harris may concede that the wider (Wadean) set of prerogatives that *can* 'affect' rights created by law could still be prerogatives in the 'narrow sense'. This would be contrary to Harris' original definition, which restricted narrow prerogatives to ones that can be used to 'override' common law rights.

[23] *R (Miller) v Prime Minister; Cherry v Advocate General for Scotland* [2019] UKSC 41, [2020] AC 373, [2019] 3 WLR 589, [2019] 4 All ER 299 ('*Miller II*').

[24] Harris (n 1) 651.

This wider definition, if Harris were to accept it, might bring, say, the prerogative power to declare war within his adjusted definition of valid actual prerogative powers. Obviously, this prerogative would not qualify under the original definition because it cannot be used to *override* any rights. It is not entirely clear which definition Harris ultimately defends and whether he would genuinely define all prerogatives out of existence by fiat. For the purposes of this chapter, nothing turns on this point because the focus here is on those powers that Harris classifies as ordinary 'third source' powers, not the boundary of what he would see as genuine prerogatives.

'Everything is Permitted Except what is Expressly Forbidden' and 'the Ram' Doctrine

Harris defends the controversial proposition that the government has the freedom to do anything that is not expressly contrary to the law. Although Harris labels this 'freedom' the 'third source' of governmental authority, he says that the label 'source' makes him 'slightly uncomfortable', since in his view it is a 'residuary freedom' rather than a source of legal power.[25] Harris claims that it is the 'consequence of the principle of legality that everything is legal that is not prohibited'.[26] Contrary to Harris' controversial take on the principle of legality, this famous axiom normally relates to the obvious claim that *private citizens* are, in a liberal society, free to do anything that is not expressly contrary to the law. There is a chasm between the claim that for private citizens 'everything is permitted except what is expressly forbidden' and the claim that the same is true *for the government*.[27] Another separate problem for Harris is that the principle of legality is also normally understood to be a principle of statutory interpretation rather than anything wider, as Lord Sales points out.[28]

It is difficult to see what relevance the residuary freedom principle has to legal authorisation for *executive* actions in a democracy with commensurate political accountability and for which lawful authority would appear to be a basic prerequisite under even the thinnest conception of the rule of law. Raz made this point succinctly in 1979:

> It is said that the rule of law means that all government action must have foundation in law, must be authorized by law … Actions not authorized by law cannot be the actions of the government as a government … government is, by definition, government authorized by law.[29]

[25] Harris (n 1) fn 6.
[26] ibid.
[27] *Malone v Metropolitan Police Commissioner* [1979] Ch 344, 357.
[28] Lord Sales (n 2) 385.
[29] J Raz, 'The Rule of Law and its Virtue' in *The Authority of Law: Essays on Law and Morality* (Oxford University Press, 1979) 212. See also ch 4, pp 79–80.

As is well known, some support for the idea that ministers have power to act freely unless contrary to statute appears in an infamous document called the 'Ram' memorandum, although it is surprisingly difficult to draw that conclusion from reading the actual text of the document, not least because it refers to 'powers' not 'freedoms'.

> [A] minister of the Crown … may, as an agent of the Crown, exercise any powers which the Crown has power to exercise, except so far as he is precluded from doing so by statute. In other words, in the case of a government department, one must look at the statutes to see what it may not do.[30]

This memorandum was considered in a House of Lords Select Committee report entitled 'The pre-emption of Parliament'.[31] The Committee held unequivocally that the 'Ram memorandum itself is not a source of law, and should not be considered one' and that it 'is not an accurate reflection of the law today'.[32] Worse still, the Committee found, the Ram memorandum has given rise to the 'Ram doctrine' which is the claim that 'ministers can do anything a natural person can do, unless limited by legislation'.[33] This further claim has received extremely heavyweight criticism. The Select Committee quoted evidence from Sir Stephen Sedley, a former Court of Appeal judge:

> What appears to be being made in Whitehall, out of Ram, is a fabrication. Ram never said what is attributed to him. His proposition that government can do anything reasonably ancillary to its explicit functions is completely unobjectionable, but it is nowhere near the proposition that appears to have been derived from it in Whitehall that Government can do anything that a private individual can do. The converse is the case.[34]

The Committee went on to quote Sir Jeffrey Jowell:

> Sir Jeffrey Jowell thought that equating the powers of ministers with those of a private individual is "a constitutional heresy. Even if it were a settled convention, it would be overridden by a constitutional principle, which has higher authority: namely, the rule of law".[35]

The Committee concluded with a stark dismissal of the Ram doctrine:

> The description of the common law powers of the Crown encapsulated by the phrase 'the Ram doctrine' is inaccurate and should no longer be used.[36]

Sedley has subsequently weighed in to the debate again.[37] He describes the idea of third source powers as 'previously unrecognised form of authority which places

[30] https://publications.parliament.uk/pa/ld200203/ldlwa/30122wa1.pdf.
[31] House of Lords Select Committee on the Constitution,13th Report of Session 2012–13, 'The pre-emption of Parliament' (HL Paper 165), 1 May 2013).
[32] ibid [52] and [54].
[33] ibid [55].
[34] ibid [56].
[35] ibid [57].
[36] ibid [60].
[37] S Sedley, *Lions under the Throne: Essays on the History of English Public Law* (Cambridge University Press, 2015) 134–39.

the state on a par with the private individual and allows it to do anything that the law does not explicitly forbid'.[38] He implicitly supports the broader definition of prerogative that encompasses all non-statutory power when he argues that the third source power 'theory itself is arguably a jurisprudential version of the emperor's new clothes'.[39]

Lord Lester and Matthew Weait concur, arguing in a section entitled 'The constitutional illegitimacy of the Ram doctrine', that it would be contrary to the rule of law for the Crown to be permitted to do what is not prohibited. It would amount to 'constitutional and legal heresy'.[40] However, these thunderous criticisms have not settled the issue, or at least not yet. As will be seen in chapters nine and ten, the case law has havered somewhat about the nature of the powers available to ministers in this area. The purpose of part III is to argue that the critics of the Ram doctrine who are quoted in the Select Committee report are correct and that the legal powers of ministers are ultimately confined to two sources: prerogative and statute.

The Genesis of Harris' Third Source Idea

The primary source on which Harris bases his arguments is the peculiar and anomalous case of *Malone*.[41] In that case, an antiques dealer charged with handling stolen goods had his phone tapped by the Post Office on behalf of the police, without any entry onto his property. Mr Malone claimed that his rights of property and privacy had been breached without lawful authority, but the court held that he had no substantive rights that had been infringed, including any arising from trespass.

Oddly, the case was framed as turning on the question of whether any particular right of Malone's had been infringed, instead of what legal power authorised the state to tap Malone's phone. Indeed, it was the failure of the government to identify any clear legal basis for its actions that saw it lose the case in the European Court of Human Rights in Strasbourg.[42] In the domestic courts, however, Vice-Chancellor Megarry took a different approach. As the judgment makes clear, one turning point in the case was when the judge asked counsel for 'what positive authority was given by the law to permit people to smoke. Mr. Ross-Munro [counsel for Malone] accepted that there was none'.[43] A deal of trouble might have been averted if Mr Ross-Munro had instead replied: 'my lord, Her Majesty's Government does not smoke'. Thus, and most unfortunately and wrongly, the judge held that the

[38] ibid 135.
[39] ibid.
[40] A Lester and M Weait, 'The Use of Ministerial Powers Without Parliamentary Authority: The Ram Doctrine' [2003] *Public Law* 415 at 422.
[41] *Malone* (n 27).
[42] *Malone v UK* (1985) 7 EHRR 14.
[43] Lord Sales (n 2) 366.

government was free to do anything that was not prohibited by law. He added that 'England is not a country where everything is forbidden except what is expressly permitted. It is a country where everything is permitted except what is expressly forbidden.'[44] In addition, the judge stated:

> If the tapping of telephones by the Post Office at the request of the police can be carried out without any breach of the law, it does not require any statutory or common law power to justify it: it can lawfully be done simply because there is nothing to make it unlawful.[45]

The Rule of Law

There are serious rule of law implications for this approach. Indeed, Lester and Weait go so far as to claim that *Malone* 'does not correctly state the present state of the law' precisely because of the lack of a 'clear legal basis'.[46] Raz's compelling definition of the rule of law includes requirements that citizens know where they stand and can plan their life.[47] In Razian terms, how can a citizen 'effectively direct [their] life' or discover the law that is 'capable of guiding their behaviour' if they do not know the extent of the powers available to the government?[48] Furthermore, if there are a swathe of actions available to the government that have no legal basis then how can the courts identify and police the boundaries of such actions?

Mr Justice Laws (as he then was), in *Fewings*, put the opposite case to Megarry's argument with considerable force, as discussed in chapter three:

> For private persons, the rule is that you may do anything you choose which the law does not prohibit … But for public bodies the rule is [that] … any action to be taken must be justified by positive law.[49]

Elliott draws a sharp distinction between local authorities such as Somerset Council and central government for the application of the principle laid down by Laws. He claims that while Laws' maxim applies to the former, it does not apply to central government unless what the government is trying to do affects 'the legal rights … of others'.[50] In Elliott's view, therefore, the government retains a residual power to do anything not prohibited by law. There might be thought to be some tension for Elliott between the claim that the government in a liberal democracy is free to do anything not legally prohibited, when he has elsewhere

[44] ibid 357.
[45] ibid 367.
[46] Lester and Weait (n 40) 421.
[47] Raz (n 29) 213.
[48] ibid 220, 214.
[49] *R v Somerset County Council, ex parte Fewings* [1995] 1 All ER 513, 524. See also ch 4, p 144.
[50] M Elliott, *The Constitutional Foundations of Judicial Review* (Hart Publishing, 2001) 167–68, 170.

expressed serious concerns about the recent actions of the executive in the United Kingdom.[51] Elliott further claims that the government can act without positive legal authority because 'the Crown, as a natural person, may do all that other natural persons may do; and the government may, in the Crown's name, do those things too'.[52] As discussed in chapter six, it is not tenable to treat the Crown as a natural person.[53] The idea that it can be so treated also flatly contradicts the compelling evidence given by Lord Justice Sedley to the House of Lords Select Committee, discussed earlier.

It is difficult to see what principled justification there might be for the distinction drawn by Elliott. Why is political power wielded centrally conceptually distinct from political power wielded locally? Perhaps there is a concern that, in the absence of the freedom to do anything not specifically prohibited, the government might be hindered from acting to achieve some important but unstated goal. This has echoes of the Lockean approach discussed in chapter three.[54] It will be recalled that Locke argued that prerogative power included the power to act beyond the law in extreme situations where necessary. That extreme position is no longer tenable, but the idea that there is, or needs to be, a retained default power to act in certain situations is arguably a modern expression of the original Lockean sentiment. That residual power is significantly more restricted in the modern era, of course.

Indeed, this could also form part of an explanation for Elliott's perhaps somewhat surprising position in the *Miller I* litigation.[55] He argued that the European Parliamentary Elections Act 2002 did not create any vested statutory rights in citizens because such rights were always conditional on the government's power, via prerogative, to trigger the UK's exit from the European Union.[56] In that event, the 2002 Act would become 'spent' as its original purpose was only to 'entitle relevant individuals to vote in elections … to the European Parliament' if the UK was a member of the European Union.[57] Again, the echoes of a Lockean conception of prerogative as far less constrained in its usage than many others in the debate considered, including the majority of the UK Supreme Court, is noticeable.

Contrary to the residual power arguments made by Elliott, this chapter will argue that there are sufficient prerogative powers already to cover the government sufficiently for all general administrative matters that could crop up in the

[51] Elliott laments, for example, 'the increasingly confrontational approach that the Government is adopting towards legal constraints upon it and judicial enforcement of those constraints', publiclawforeveryone.com/2020/11/23/the-uk-constitution-under-pressure-a-lost-age-of-civility/.

[52] ibid.

[53] See ch 6, pp 125–28.

[54] See ch 3, pp 180–82.

[55] *Miller I*; M Elliott, 'The Supreme Court's Judgment in Miller: In Search of Constitutional Principle' (2017) *Cambridge Law Journal* 257–288; publiclawforeveryone.com/2016/11/21/article-50-the-royal-prerogative-and-the-european-parliamentary-elections-act-2002/.

[56] ibid Section II.C.

[57] ibid.

ordinary course of the government's duties. It is suggested, therefore, that the *Fewings* approach is to be preferred and the government must provide evidence of a positive legal authority for its actions, not least in order to comply with the most basic conception of the rule of law. It is perhaps worth distinguishing between the necessity for lawful authority from the necessity for statutory authority. The latter is only necessary when infringing on existing rights. Lawful authority, be it statutory or prerogative, is still necessary where no rights are infringed. *Malone* will be considered further in chapter ten, but in the context of judicial review of prerogative power.[58]

Legal Powers or Mere Freedoms

The claim that the Crown can exercise 'residuary freedoms' must thus overcome serious rule of law concerns. Harris admits his discomfort with the nomenclature of third source *powers* precisely because he claims to regard them as *freedoms* not powers. Yet his inability to identify an alternative label, and his admonition to 'compare' his label with the terms 'de facto or common law powers' is revealing.[59] It is tolerably clear that he could equally have labelled the powers as 'common law powers' but for his insistence that 'prerogative in the narrow sense can also be included within' common law.[60] This is a difficulty that is exposed by Perry as making his position unsustainable.

Perry highlights a logical gap in Harris' argument. There is a conceptual leap from not being prohibited from doing something and having the *power* to do something. Just because one is not legally prohibited from doing something does *not* mean one has the legal power to do that thing. Perry gives the example of minors not having the power to form binding contracts.[61] This does not prohibit a minor from entering a contract, but the legal system will not treat such a contract as binding, so in reality minors lack the legal power to form binding contracts. It follows therefore that the set of legal *powers* available to the Crown is necessarily smaller than the set of things it is in theory not prohibited from doing.

Since there are some things the Crown is not prohibited from doing that it has no legal power to do, it follows that it is logically mistaken to say that the Crown has the *power* to do everything that is not prohibited, which is what Harris wrongly claimed. Perry suggests 'repealing all the laws in France' as one example of something the Crown is not prohibited from doing but has no power to do, as well as 'making a will for you'. Perry is correct. For the executive, acting without an identifiable legal power is the very definition of *ultra vires*, although technically and strictly the latter only relates to statutory powers. It is, of course, unlawful for

[58] *Malone* (n 27).
[59] Harris (n 1) 651, fn 6.
[60] ibid.
[61] Perry (n 8) 656.

the Crown to act *ultra vires*. It may be that the *ultra vires* doctrine could be restated as holding that the executive is prohibited from doing what it has no power to do, enforced by judicial review remedies.

There is no private law equivalent for this limitation on the Crown in public law to actions that are underpinned by legal authority and this is, to put it mildly, another surprising example of where an attempt has been made to equate the Crown to a private individual for no obvious good reason. Similar evidence of mistakenly equating the Crown and private individuals was seen in chapter eight, and it is not clear why this erroneous equivalence has survived for so long in public law discourse.

Perry further points out that third source powers, for Harris,

> can only be a kind of *legal* power or authority, given that it is supposed to be the absence of any *legal* prohibition that generates the power or authority.[62]

He says it follows that 'Harris would seem to be committed to the claim that all the Crown's administrative powers are legal powers'.[63] In other words, it follows inescapably that if the powers alleged to be possessed by the Crown are derived from the absence of *legal* prohibition, then they must logically be *legal* powers.

Perry's argument is persuasive, although caution is necessary over some of his examples of things the Crown has no power to do. So, for example, the reason why the Crown cannot 'make a will for you' or give 'itself the power to make a will for you' is because the courts have in effect imposed restrictions on what were formerly *plenary and sovereign* prerogative powers.[64] These restrictions are based on examining historic usages and precedents and, to that extent, the Crown is indeed *prohibited* from using prerogative powers to make wills on behalf of citizens, and this immediately takes those examples outside Perry's framework.[65]

There are real world examples of the effect of the mistake of conflating an alleged freedom to do something with a legal power to do the same thing. Phillipson provides a useful illustration in a chapter on common law rights of freedom of assembly and association.[66] Phillipson points out that in *Murray v UK*, the Strasbourg court 'appeared to mischaracterise' the lack of *prohibition* on the police taking photographs of a suspect as a common law *power* to do so. This led that court to then hold that taking the photos was 'lawful under the common law'.[67] Phillipson points out this fails to satisfy the European Convention on Human

[62] ibid (emphasis in the original).

[63] ibid.

[64] *Miller I* [41].

[65] It is of course the case that the Crown used to possess very serious and important powers over estates on the death of any lord who was a direct tenant of the Crown. *Magna Carta* was in large part concerned with attempting to mitigate some of the effects of these powers. See, further, WS McKechnie, *Magna Carta*, 2nd edn (Glasgow, 1914).

[66] G Phillipson, 'Searching for a Chimera? Seeking Common Law Rights of Freedom of Assembly and Association' in M Elliott and K Hughes (ed), *Common Law Constitutional Rights* (Hart Publishing, 2019) 141–66.

[67] ibid 162; *Murray v UK* (1994) 19 EHRR 193, [88].

Rights, Article 8 requirement of a '*positive* legal basis' for the action. Worse still, when the matter came up again in domestic law, the domestic courts held that the Strasbourg decision was authority for the idea that the 'common law provided a positive police *power* to engage in surveillance'.[68] Levitation via bootstraps was apparently achieved.

As this chapter will go on to explain, the unfortunate confusion created by the judgment in *Malone* and its subsequent academic and judicial treatment has obscured the fact that the Crown can only exercise identifiable and identified positive legal powers, be they prerogative or statutory. There are no third source 'freedoms' possessed by the Crown. To the extent that *Malone* holds otherwise, it should be treated as being of limited persuasive authority. Notwithstanding the eminence of Vice-Chancellor Megarry, it was in the end only a High Court decision.

'Non-legal' Powers of the Crown

Perry is therefore right to conclude that Harris must be committed to the idea that Crown 'freedoms' are in fact legal powers. The logical corollary of this would be that servants of the Crown can only act based on identifiable legal powers, leaving aside legal duties and legal immunities for the purposes of this part of the discussion. It will be recalled from part II that Lord Sales simply assumes, correctly, that all powers of the Crown are *legal* powers. Thus, something of a consensus appears to be forming that the Crown only exercises, and possesses, *legal* powers. This author concurs with this virtual consensus. Prerogative powers are legal powers. The Crown is defined as the bearer of prerogative legal powers. However, the growing consensus is not universal: Perry goes somewhat further than Harris and claims that in addition to its legal powers, the Crown also has a series of 'non-legal powers'. Perry's claims are challenged in this section. The short summary is that an almost forgotten prerogative called the administration prerogative effectively addresses most of the issues he raises, and therefore the Crown does not possess any 'non-legal' powers.

Perry on Non-legal Powers

In support of his claims, Perry identifies a series of powers of the Crown that he claims are 'non-legal' powers including the powers to:[69]

- circulate written material (*ex parte C*);[70]

[68] Phillipson (n 66) 163.
[69] Perry (n 8) 661.
[70] *R v Secretary of State for Health, ex parte C* [2000] HRLR 400.

- consult with officials (*Shrewsbury*);[71]
- adopt policies and guidelines (*New College*);[72]
- make promises;
- issue apologies;
- communicate with foreign governments;
- place wiretaps (*Malone*);[73]
- issue passports.

The first six constitute aspects of the administrative prerogative available to the Crown, discussed further below and in the next chapter. Perry claims that they are powers but not *legal* powers and that they 'pose an unusual and serious threat to the rule of law'.[74] He further argues that 'the rule of law demands' that the Crown 'stop using these powers altogether'.[75] He says that the law 'cannot strip the Crown of its ordinary powers', and the 'Crown could be prohibited from using its ordinary powers, and while this would not make it impossible for the Crown to use these powers, it might discourage it' from using them.[76] It is not immediately obvious why, for example, issuing an apology or other such powers is a 'serious threat to the rule of law'.

If Perry is correct that such powers should be treated distinctly as 'non-legal' powers, this could be a minor exception to the rule that all the non-statutory powers of the Crown are prerogative legal powers. This chapter instead argues that such powers are inescapable and entirely legitimate aspects of the legal prerogative of administration. Analogous capabilities are possessed by councils pursuant to statute. They raise no rule of law concerns, *pace* Perry, in large part because they are essential elements in normal administration and form an integral part of a justiciable prerogative. In other words, they raise no rule of law concerns precisely because their usage by ministers and civil servants is authorised by virtue of a minister's lawful appointment to that role and the conferral on the minister of the relevant prerogative legal powers to administer the realm.

These aspects of governmental administration are arguably essential and uncontroversial aspects of the prerogative of administration, which does have legal effects and is a legal power. It is a mistake to disaggregate the different aspects of the prerogative of administration too far. The latter two examples on the list above are more difficult to classify as purely administrative powers. Both are considered further below.

[71] *Shrewsbury & Atcham Borough Council, Congleton Borough Council v Secretary of State for Communities and Local Government* [2008] EWCA Civ 148.
[72] *R (New London College Ltd) v Secretary of State for the Home Department* [2013] UKSC 51, [2013] 1 WLR 2358, [2013] 4 All ER 195.
[73] *Malone v Metropolitan Police Commissioner* (n 27).
[74] ibid 672.
[75] Perry (n 8) 670.
[76] ibid.

These supposedly non-legal powers are on top of the legal powers Perry ascribes to the Crown such as:

- making contracts;
- hiring staff;
- conveying property;
- making *ex gratia* payments.

As we have seen in earlier chapters, most of the items on the latter list are in fact carried out by ministers who are personally responsible in law and who occupy their position as a result of the prerogative of appointing ministers. The final one is indeed a prerogative power possessed by the Crown and is exclusive to it because only the government can create *ex gratia*, publicly funded, compensation schemes – as discussed in chapter seven. Thus, all of the valid legal powers listed above are either directly or indirectly referable to prerogative powers of the Crown. The Crown has no common law powers.

Perry's Definition of a Legal Power

The reason some of the powers such as making promises and issuing apologies are best described as 'non-legal', according to Perry, is because such powers do not fit within his definition of legal powers which is largely based on one given by Wade, but with an extra twist. A legal power, for Wade, is the 'ability to alter people's rights, duties, or status under the laws of this country which the courts of this country enforce'.[77] It will be recalled from chapter four that Wade's definition necessarily and wrongly excludes prerogatives such as treaty making from the category of legal powers possessed by the Crown. This is because the exercise of prerogative treaty powers cannot affect legal rights in domestic law unless incorporated and given legal force by statute.[78] Concerningly, it is not clear what status treaty-making has under Wade's, and Perry's, rubric.[79] Perry claims that 'most of the Crown's administrative powers' are not in fact legal powers but he says that the explanation for why 'takes some explaining' given that a number of these supposedly 'non-legal' powers can affect the legal duties or rights of relevant actors, especially the Crown.[80]

To illustrate why he thinks his 'non-legal powers' – which he also labels 'ordinary powers' – are not legal powers, Perry draws an analogy with the tort of assault by a private individual. Such an action *affects* the legal position of others, as well

[77] Perry (n 8) 660.

[78] *JH Rayner (Mincing Lane) Ltd v Department of Trade and Industry (Tin Council)* [1990] 2 AC 418, 476–77 per Lord Templeman.

[79] See ch 4, pp 75–77.

[80] Perry (n 8) 660.

as the tortious actor, but cannot be described as the exercise of any kind of 'legal power' because the duty to pay compensation is *imposed* on the tortious actor by the courts. It makes no intuitive sense to say that someone has a 'legal power' to commit a tortious assault for which they are found liable in damages.

In *Everett*, the court held that the Foreign and Commonwealth Office had failed to communicate its reasons for refusing to issue a new passport to someone subject to an arrest warrant who was residing in Spain.[81] Perry claims that, analogously, the wrongful failure of the government to provide reasons for refusing a passport in *Everett* is equivalent to the tortious assault scenario because the duties are *imposed* on the Crown by the courts and are not the exercise of any kind of *power*. Perry claims that the facts in *Everett* are legally analogous to an assault in tort because the Crown 'came under a duty to give reasons', but 'had not *intended* to come under that duty'.[82] In essence, therefore, Perry claims that non-legal powers are not legal powers because when the government, say, makes a promise, that is not done as a function of an exercise of a legal power. This is true, according to Perry, even if it results in a legal duty being imposed on the government. For Perry, just because some legal *effects* have resulted does not mean that a legal *power* has been exercised.

Perry goes even further than Wade's definition of a legal power because he insists on an extra element. What Wade is missing, according to Perry, is 'intentionality', without which the existence of mere legal effects is insufficient to constitute the exercise of a legal power. The relevant intention for Perry is to 'effect legal change'.[83] It is important to recognise that the issue of intention in a legal context is treated with some care in different situations by the law. Three examples will suffice. First, Raz points out that not every exercise of legal power requires intention. He gives a useful example, which is that one can inadvertently enter a contract.[84] This could be done, for example, by a car driver parking in the wrong place and not seeing the relevant signs that make clear that to park in that area means entering a contract with the car park owner. This is a clear example of an incontrovertible exercise of a legal power without intention. At best, intention is *imputed* to the inadvertent car driver who mistakenly parks the car in the wrong place.

A second example is given by Andrew Halpin who suggests the example of a 'maverick tramp' who intentionally commits a crime in order to be sent to prison to avoid bitter winter temperatures outside.[85] It is counter-intuitive to describe committing criminal offences, similar to the commission of torts, as the exercise of any legal power. So a clear intention, with direct legal effects, is not

[81] *R v Secretary of State for Foreign and Commonwealth Affairs, ex parte Everett* [1989] QB 811.
[82] ibid 662 (emphasis in the original).
[83] ibid 662.
[84] J Raz, *Practical Reason and Norms* (Oxford University Press, 1975) 104.
[85] A Halpin, 'The Concept of a Legal Power' (1996) *Oxford Journal of Legal Studies* 129, 142. Halpin credits WH Davies, *Supertramp*, for the idea, cited in N MacCormick, *H.L.A. Hart* (Stanford University Press, 1981) 73.

necessarily regarded as the exercise of a legal power. As a matter of policy and pragmatism, it makes sense to refuse to describe the maverick tramp as exercising a legal power.

Thirdly, there can be situations where a party enters a contract with full intentionality, apparently expecting it to be legally enforced, but the other party does not have the requisite counter intention. This is most often seen in family or friends situations. In such scenarios, the court sometimes holds, as a matter of policy, that it will not hold the contract to be binding because there was no, or insufficient, intention to create legal relations. Again, policy determines how such scenarios are regulated by the courts, rather than a blanket rule imposed by conceptual fiat.

It is clear, therefore, that the courts are cautious in their treatment of intention and there can be significant policy aspects to a decision to recognise, or on rare occasions simply to impute or ascribe, legally relevant intention in different contexts. Policy implications can also lead to a refusal to impute or ascribe a legal power despite evidence of a clear intention. The interaction between intention, legal effects and the exercise of legal powers is therefore not simple. Seemingly unintentional acts can on occasion be functionally treated as the exercise of a legal power. Seemingly intentional acts, with direct and contemplated legal effects can be dismissed as not being the exercise of any legal power. Seemingly fully intentional acts in exercise of a legal power can be treated as not having legal effects.

The Intention of Ministers or Civil Servants

Some of the powers listed as non-legal powers by Perry are in fact legal powers. So, for example, a minister or civil servant may make a promise, or decide on a policy, that they well know will create a procedural or substantive legitimate expectation. Such knowledge may result from formal or informal advice by civil servants, and in particular lawyers either internal or external to the department. In other words, if ministers promise that they or their department will do something, or promise to have a hearing before doing it, then that is an exercise of a legal power voluntarily undertaken. It clearly has legal effects, not least in the voluntary and intentional assumption of novel legal duties, and those legal effects were intended, or must be presumed to be intended, by the relevant department officials because they are presumed to want to act fairly in their official positions.

Perry might counter that a legitimate expectation to have a hearing or award a substantive benefit is *imposed* on the department by the court analogously with the imposition of a duty to give reasons in *Everett*. This would be fundamentally based on Perry's analogy with the imposition of a requirement to pay damages following a tortious action. The analogy fails in this case. It fails because it makes no sense for someone negligently or even intentionally to commit a tort *in order to* be liable for tortious damages, which they would then come under a duty to pay. Such damages are indeed imposed by the court. In stark contrast, it would make complete sense for a minister knowingly to accrue legally binding obligations following a promise or policy decision, and to do so for political benefit such as gaining or reinforcing a reputation for good administration, which allows people to plan their lives. This would be done knowing, or being advised or warned, that a financial or other legal obligation would inevitably, or even likely, ensue.

The allocation of resources, change in policy or other such decisions would be likely preceded by consultation, meetings and memos discussing the implications which could and should be seen as part of the necessary preparatory work prior to the exercise of the legal power. To focus solely on the potential for litigation and a court-ordered award is to miss the fact that not all legal issues end up in court or are litigated by or against the government. Where a cost is deliberately incurred, in the knowledge that legal obligations will most likely flow, it is difficult if not impossible to see how an analogy with tortious damages is apposite. Rather, these are fairly mundane examples of the exercise of a legal prerogative power. A better analogy for the ministerial decision-making process than an award for damages in tort might be the making of a future gift by deed.

It is entirely reasonable that circulated written material and consultations with civil servants could be consciously and intentionally undertaken in the knowledge that, if disclosed in later litigation for example, there could be legal consequences. Even if there were not direct legal consequences and no such consequences were necessarily intended, such discussions and meetings are an intrinsic part of the decision-making process and it is suggested that they form a seamless part of general administration. Engaging in general administration and governance very much does have intended or inevitable legal consequences in many cases. It therefore makes no sense to disaggregate part of that process in the way that Perry does.

Perry disagrees. He argues that 'the duties imposed by the rules of administrative law apply to the Crown whether it wishes them to apply to it or not'.[86] This is too quick. He would treat the accrual of legal obligations from a promise, policy or apology as *entirely* court imposed rather than the intentional exercise of a legal power with foreseeable and predictable legal consequences. Indeed, in many cases a minister may allocate a budget to cover the costs of any such change in policy or novel promise. This is arguably a paradigm example of the exercise of a legal power pursuant to the prerogative of administration. The allocation of financial resources is a quintessential exercise of a public legal power. Furthermore, Perry appears to ascribe to officials and ministers a willingness to breach their administrative law obligations that is unwarranted.

A further difficult example is that of formal apologies. These can also attract direct legal liability, which is why authorisation to give them is tightly controlled internally within the system. Such apologies are therefore done, or must be presumed to be done, intentionally – in the sense of a full awareness and

[86] Perry (n 8) 662.

forewarning of the likely legal consequences and accrued obligations. They are, in a very real sense, therefore 'intentional'. Whether that intention is explicit or, in a sense, imputed is not the issue. The issue is whether it is appropriate for the courts to treat the government as having intended the legal effects of its decisions. Of course it is appropriate. To treat these kinds of governmental decision-making processes as analogous with a tortious battery must be rejected.

This monograph has consistently argued that analogies with private law are problematic, as Perry's unhelpful tort analogy perhaps demonstrates. With that warning duly caveated, if an analogy with private law is desired, it might be more useful to recall the imputed intention to enter a contract example given by Raz earlier.[87] He gives the example of a contract where a driver inadvertently parks in a chargeable car park. The driver has no actual intention to enter the contract and incur the parking charge, but the contract remains valid and is treated as an exercise of a legal power. The requisite intention is imputed by the courts as a matter of policy given the potential problems that could ensue if those contracts were not enforced.

The latter analogy, it is suggested, would be far more apposite in considering the treatment of the governance and administration of the country than the tortious damages analogy proffered by Perry. Of course the courts should impute the requisite intention to government officials deliberately and knowingly making decisions with sometimes dramatic consequences in the lives of ordinary people. Intentional actions and policy decisions by officials and ministers, with foreseeable legal effects, ought to be treated as exercises of legal power. It is not obvious what practical negative consequences Perry believes would flow from the courts doing so.

Perry is therefore mistaken when he claims that there are significant rule of law consequences to his points about administrative acts by government officials that do not appear to have direct legal effects. He claims that 'it is inconsistent with the rule of law … for the Crown … to rule using powers not conferred by law'.[88] Circulating memos, consulting officials and setting policies are indeed aspects of governance, but they are intrinsic to the wider legal prerogative power of administration and raise no rule of law concerns at all. Such powers are conferred by law through the prerogative of administration. Ministers are held accountable politically for their administration of their departments and are subject to judicial review in the event that they act illegally, irrationally or in breach of natural justice. As *Everett* itself proved, only 'high policy' prerogatives are non-justiciable, unlike ones that involve 'mere administration'. It would perhaps be difficult to find a prerogative falling more squarely within the test for 'mere administration' than the prerogative of administration.

Even Perry's own prime example of passports is somewhat questionable. Recall that Wade said that issuing or refusing to issue passports is not an exercise of legal

[87] Raz (n 28).
[88] Perry (n 8) 670.

power because there is 'no effect on legal rights'.[89] Perry says that given passports *do* in fact alter legal rights and duties (in this case the duty to give reasons) then, according to Wade's own definition, passports ought to be classified as a legal power. Perry then turns this point on its head by claiming that issuing passports is *not* in fact a legal power because the duty to give reasons was not *intended* precisely because that duty was imposed by the courts. Thus he illustrates his argument that mere legal effects without intention do not mean there is a legal power.

Readers still following these conceptual twists and turns, gasping a bit perhaps, will see that Perry is right that if the government did not intend to incur the legal obligation to give reasons, then it is conceptually mistaken to claim that there is a legal power in play. This is to leave aside, for now, the imputed intention argument made above but this chapter will return to a further problem for Perry below. Where Perry goes wrong, however, is in missing the fact that the issue or refusal to issue a passport has a *number* of legal effects beyond duty to give reasons imposed by the courts.

As Scott has persuasively argued, the absence of a valid passport will make it effectively impossible to travel abroad, even if technically it is not an absolute legal requirement:

> [T]he better view is that the issuance and withdrawal of passports does affect legal rights, and so is a genuine example of a prerogative power even on Wade's restrictive understanding.[90]

Crucially, the government in *Everett* and other cases certainly intended to refuse or grant a passport to an applicant. If those intentional acts have broader legal effects outside administrative law remedies, and it is clear that they do, then clearly that was the intentional exercise of a legal power. Thus the issuing of passports is an example of a prerogative power on both Wade's and Perry's definitions. Notably, Hazell and Foot simply *assume* passports are 'issued under the prerogative', without even arguing the point.[91] A consensus appears to be forming.

There is a further useful aspect of the issue of intentionality in relation to the prerogative of passports. There is an extra problem for Perry's argument which is that Perry takes a somewhat 'snapshot' view of the law in his arguments about non-legal powers. It is indeed true that on the very *first* occasion that the government refused the somewhat opportunistic attempt to renew his passport made by Mr Everett, the court *imposed* a duty to give reasons when refusing to issue passports – and there was no intention to incur that legal obligation. Perry makes a fair point that the *ex post facto* imposition of a duty to give reasons was clearly not foreseen by the minister. Describing it as a legal power on this occasion might

[89] HWR Wade, *Constitutional Fundamentals (Hamlyn Lectures, 32nd series)* (Stevens and Sons, 1980) 51.

[90] PF Scott, *The National Security Constitution* (Hart Publishing, 2018) 185.

[91] R Hazell and T Foot, *Executive Power: The Prerogative, Past, Present and Future* (Hart Publishing, 2022) 171ff.

therefore be somewhat problematic, as Perry claims – although it could be argued that *imputing* an intention to act fairly, which was then breached on this occasion, would not be unreasonable because officials wish to act fairly in their decision-making. On this view, even the first occasion was also arguably an exercise of a legal power.

Nonetheless, on any *subsequent* occasion that a passport renewal was sought, the minister would know fine well that if they wanted to refuse the passport renewal, they would need to give reasons. On a diachronic view, therefore, even the accrual of novel, court-imposed, administrative law obligations on future decision-making processes can thenceforth be understood and explained as the intentional exercise of a legal power with attendant legal duties and obligations intentionally undertaken and met. Voluntarily undertaking the legal duties inherent in going through the relevant processes and giving reasons at the end is a quintessential example of the intentional exercise of a legal power, it is suggested. If the intention is insufficiently direct for purists, then logically such an intention can be imputed to the minister or official because the minister or official intends, and must be presumed to desire, to act fairly. This also arguably addresses a further point made by Raz that the person concerned 'wants to secure those legal consequences'.[92]

Approaching the vexed issue of intentionality in the way suggested in this section would perhaps have the beneficial effect of reconciling the fairly obvious constitutional and political reality that the legal power of the government to issue passports is widely accepted. That legal power carries with it various legal obligations and duties with which the minister must comply to exercise the legal power lawfully. Furthermore, conceptualising prerogative powers in the way suggested here avoids the fairly serious problem of what exactly is being 'quashed' when an official decision is judicially reviewed if the decision being attacked is not a legal decision of some kind. This issue links to the confusion over 'advice' on the exercise of prerogative that was considered in chapter two. It is difficult to improve on the sentiment expressed by Lord Justice Taylor in *Everett* who pragmatically and sensibly held that 'the grant or refusal of a passport is … a matter of administrative decision, affecting the rights of individuals and their freedom of travel'.[93]

Deeper Problem with Intentionality

The insistence on an apparently necessary element of *intention* before the ascription of a legal power to the Crown is reminiscent of the difficulties faced by McLean in grappling with similar issues, which was discussed in chapter six.

[92] Halpin (n 82) 143; J Raz, 'Voluntary Obligations and Normative Powers' (an essay in two parts contributed by MacCormick and Raz (1972) 46 *Proceedings of the Aristotelian Society, Supplementary Volume*, 59–102, 81).

[93] *R v Secretary of State for Foreign and Commonwealth Affairs, ex parte Everett* [1989] QB 811, 820.

It will be recalled that McLean's book is entitled *Searching for the State in British Public Law*. McLean explores the difficulties in locating a single, 'will' at the heart of the state and the inadequacies of the concept of the Crown as a cypher for an individuated will. McLean's search for a controlling mind raises similar issues and problems as imposing the requirement of 'intention' before legal liability can sensibly be imposed on the government for exercising prerogative or other legal powers. As mentioned in chapter six, it might be better to focus on where liability ought properly to be imposed on the government without obsessing over whether an individuated will is present or not. Similarly, excessive focus on intention in the context of judicial review of administration may be something of a red herring.

Perry's focus on intention is problematic because it inappropriately conflates the treatment of the Crown and the treatment of natural persons. The Crown is a legal construct, as Perry admits:[94]

> The Crown in its modern form is a legal entity … The Crown's existence depends on the law. It survives only as long as the law wishes it. Does it not follow that the Crown owes all of its powers to the law? Yes – if the Crown is indeed a creature of the law, then everything it does is only possible because of the law. In that loose sense, the law is the source of all of the Crown's powers.

Perry goes on to argue that natural persons 'have many of the same [non-legal] powers' as the Crown, such as making promises.[95] He later walks back this claim somewhat, rightly citing Lord Sumption in *New London College*,[96] when he admits that ordinary people do not in fact have the power to consult officials, set policies or make promises that are binding on the government. In addition, natural persons have other abilities such as 'baking a cake and running a race' that the Crown does not possess. Furthermore, the Crown has additional obligations not to exercise its powers in ways that breach administrative law norms which are distinct from the obligations imposed on natural persons. Finally, he says that issuing 'guidelines for … a sponsor licence … is the exercise of an administrative power, yet it is too "public" or "governmental" to be sensibly attributed to a natural person'.[97] It might be thought that these differences demonstrate that the overlap between the powers of natural persons and the Crown is of limited utility as an analogy.

It is hard to make sense of the claim made by Perry that the Crown, a purely legal construct, possesses ordinary [non-legal] powers.[98] Perry claims that ordinary actions can be 'attributed' to the Crown based on three factors: agency, authority and funding.[99] The problem for Perry is that all these factors are legal powers exercised by ministers or other Crown servants. The power to appoint someone as a minister, the concomitant power to authorise their actions as accruing liability for

[94] Perry (n 8) 663.
[95] ibid 663.
[96] *New London College* (n 70). Discussed further in ch 10.
[97] Perry (n 8) 665; *Malone* (n 26).
[98] ibid 663.
[99] ibid 666–67.

the Crown, and the power to allocate public funds to pay for whatever the agent is doing are all clearly the exercise of legal powers by the Crown that are legally upstream of the physical actions by ordinary persons on its behalf.

It is important to disaggregate rather than conflate the Crown and the actions of those who act on behalf of the Crown. Perry is therefore wrong to claim that 'the Crown must have had the non-legal power to tap Malone's phone', for example.[100] It makes no sense to claim that 'the Crown' tapped Malone's phone. An individual working for the Post Office physically tapped the phone. The live legal question is whether the Crown authorised that action as a matter of law, which turns on whether a valid exercise of legal power occurred, based on the precedents.[101] Tapping a phone may have had no legal effects at the time, but instructing police officers to seek the cooperation of Post Office officials and allocating the funding to pursue that policy certainly does have consequences which must have been intended or, at a minimum, a constructive or imputed legal intention can be justifiably inferred precisely because it is right to treat actions of officials as intentional. As argued in chapter seven in the context of ministers, it is critical to maintain the distinction between the Crown and servants or agents of the Crown as a matter of law.

Conclusion on Non-legal Powers

Perry's argument is highly complex and technical. Under close examination, however, the claim that the Crown has non-legal powers, and that this generates a rule of law problem, fails. Perry's analogy with the law of tort is unhelpful. The law already imputes intention in certain legal scenarios, and this should be, and arguably already is, extended to actions of the government which have legal effects because it is reasonable to presuppose that governments intend their actions and the legal consequences of those actions, particularly diachronically. Perry's approach would erroneously limit the ambit of the administration prerogative which encompasses many of the issues he raises such as setting policy and making promises, as well as consulting officials and circulating written material.

The administration prerogative itself, which encompasses many of the actions taken by officials about which Perry is concerned, will be considered in the following two chapters, which address the case law on so-called 'third source powers' in detail and explain how it can be re-analysed. Much of that case law, however, concerns instances in which the treatment of so-called third source powers occurs in the context of relevant and significant statutory interventions in the same area. Two distinct streams of authority should be distinguished. Chapter ten considers the first stream – it addresses judicial review of so-called third source powers

[100] ibid 665.
[101] The detail of *Malone* is discussed in ch 10.

simpliciter. Chapter eleven considers the second stream, where prerogative and statute intersect. It addresses the application of the abeyance and frustration principles which apply in those circumstances. The two principles are relevant if, as this monograph claims, third source powers should in fact be understood to be prerogative powers. The third source powers case law therefore needs to be woven into the existing case law on, first, judicial review of prerogative and, second, the relationship between prerogative and statute.

10

Reframing Third Source Case Law I: Judicial Review of Prerogative

Introduction

The previous chapters have defended a conception of the royal prerogative that reconciles Dicey and Blackstone's definitions on a careful reading of their positions. It follows from the definition defended here that all executive government actions in public law are conducted under either statutory or prerogative authority. The first section of this chapter addresses the fact that there are a number of mundane activities undertaken by government (such as writing memos and making ordinary administrative decisions) that do not appear to have, or even need, legal underpinnings. The suggested solution to this mini conundrum is that there is a mostly forgotten prerogative power, although it was mentioned by Chitty's standard treatise, that the Crown has a prerogative power to 'administer government of the … realm' served by 'their officers and ministers'.[1] This book labels it the 'administration prerogative'. If this prerogative is properly understood, it may be thought to cover a wide range of minor administrative matters that would otherwise appear not to be underpinned by any legal authority. This then provides a useful prism through which to consider some of the case law highlighted in this chapter and the next.

This chapter shows how that framework – together with the principles explored in chapter nine – can throw fresh light on the case law in the area of so-called third source powers. If all non-statutory legal powers of the Crown are prerogative powers, then recent case law that analyses alleged 'third source' actions by the government in this area must be reframed and contextualised as concerning prerogative powers. The administration prerogative is the most important and relevant such prerogative power for this chapter. This prerogative can be said to underpin much of the ordinary business of government.

This chapter and the next also seek to demonstrate that when the relevant third source powers case law is reframed as (mostly) centring on the meaning, definition and limits of the administration prerogative, much of it can be explained in a different and more comprehensible way. Rather than conferring on the executive

[1] J Chitty, *A Treatise on the Law of the Prerogatives of the Crown: And the Relative Duties and Rights of the Subject* (Butterworth, 1820) 7.

a slightly alarming presumption that it is free to act as it pleases, subject to any statutory or common law limitations, the meaning of the administration prerogative is defined in the same way that all prerogatives are defined. The definition is grounded on historic precedents. In other words, the administration prerogative is best understood by considering what ordinary governance historically entailed. John Mitchell argues for the 'necessity for preserving effective government' in analysing Blackstone's definition of prerogative:[2]

> These inseparable prerogatives were considered to exist for the 'weal public', and that underlying the idea of the public good was some consideration of the requirements of effective government'.[3]

Such an approach requires the government to demonstrate that its actions are part of the ordinary internal business of government by showing that analogous or similar activities can be identified as a matter of historical record. When put in these rather more constrained terms, then the issue of whether a policy to put some people on a list of those who should not be permitted to work with children because they may pose a risk to them (*ex parte C*[4]) falls within the ordinary business of government, for example, becomes an interesting and novel question for the court to consider.

Government officials have always been able to make lists as a natural function of ordinary governance and in a way that is on close inspection conceptually distinct from a private citizen writing a list of people to invite to a birthday party, for example. The real question is whether this *kind* of list falls outside ordinary precedents of the business of government such that it constitutes, in effect, the conferral of a novel legal power by stealth. This careful historical analysis would be in stark contrast to the actual reasoning of the judges in *ex parte C*, which blithely assumed that the government had to the power to make such a list on the basis that private citizens can make lists.

Finally, we have already seen how the third source powers concept was originally grounded in the famous case of *Malone*, in which the claim that the government has the power to do anything not prohibited by the law was a key part of the reasoning.[5] This chapter suggests that, instead, it would be better to understand the *Malone* case as a modern expression of the long-established prerogative of preventing crime and keeping the peace. This is in part because it is not really plausible to ground the decision to tap Mr Malone's phone in the prerogative of administration. Indeed, there are arguments that *Malone* may best be regarded as simply an anomaly, although the recent *Third Direction*[6] case suggests that the courts feel a continuing obligation to support the police and other elements of the state apparatus where they can. This is explored further below.

[2] J Mitchell, *The Contracts of Public Authorities* (Bell & Sons, 1954) 13.
[3] ibid 10.
[4] *R v Secretary of State for Health, ex parte C* [2000] HRLR 400.
[5] *Malone v Metropolitan Police Commissioner* [1979] Ch 344.
[6] See n 71 below.

The Administration Prerogative

Blackstone explores the meaning of the fact that the Crown heads the administration of the government in this country:

> [T]he king, having the sole administration of the government in his hands, is the best and the only judge, in what capacities, with what qualified to serve, and to act under what distinctions, his people are the best qualified to serve, and to act under him.[7]

Hobbes claims:

> A public minister is he that by the sovereign, whether a monarch or an assembly, is employed in any affairs, with authority to represent [the sovereign], they that be servants to [the sovereign] in their natural capacity are not public ministers; but those only that serve them in the administration of the public business.[8]

When comparing the English and French systems, Dicey reveals his view of the importance and legal basis of executive administration:

> [E]very administrative act, or to use or, to use English terms, … every act alleged to be done in virtue of the prerogative …[9]

There is indeed an underlying legal power that underpins virtually all the apparently disparate minor powers including making policies and writing memos that Perry describes as 'non-legal powers'. It is a prerogative power that is not widely known – indeed it has long been buried in *Chitty on Prerogatives* without anyone appearing to notice it.[10] It is probably best labelled as the 'administration prerogative'. When considered objectively, it cannot be thought controversial that there is a generic legal prerogative power possessed by the Crown to administer the realm independently of statute – after all, the Crown has been doing so for centuries.

It is fair to point out immediately that this power could at one level be said to be the general historical root for a whole host of more consequential powers such as the prerogative of justice, the prerogative power to raise taxes and such like. The important point to recognise, however, is that the other powers have long since been defined and restricted in case law and elsewhere. The residual prerogative of administration is arguably now confined to those more mundane tasks that occupy the time and energy of servants of the Crown in the running of the country in ordinary terms, because to construe it as a plenary power would effectively undermine the legislative supremacy of parliament.

In '*A Treatise on the Law of the Prerogatives of the Crown*', Chitty speaks of the 'regal executive authority' as 'supreme executive magistrate' and states that the

[7] W Blackstone, *Commentaries on the Laws of England* (1753), Book 1, ch 7, 273.
[8] T Hobbes, *Leviathan*, edited by Richard Tuck (Cambridge University Press, 1991).
[9] AV Dicey, *Introduction to the Study of the Law of the Constitution*, 8th edn (Macmillan, 1915) 366.
[10] Chitty (n 1) 7.

'King of England is therefore not only the chief, but the sole magistrate of the nation; all others acting by commission from and in due subordination to him'.[11] Furthermore, the king 'in his political capacity of supreme executive magistrate', 'has the right to administer and execute' the laws of the country. Chitty goes on to say that with

> respect to public offices merely of a ministerial nature [the Crown has] an undoubted prerogative right to appoint officers to fill them … [and] it is highly important that the various duties attached to them should be properly performed.[12]

It must be recalled that 'magistrate' did not have the strict narrow meaning it does now when Chitty was writing – indeed, this can be seen when he uses the phrase 'executive magistrate'. It will also be recalled that even the original circuit judges started as *administrators* and were therefore themselves once part of the executive long ago – as was considered in chapter two quoting Dicey.[13] It is therefore entirely plausible to suggest that Chitty has provided as comprehensive a definition of this particular prerogative as yet exists.

Although Chitty may provide as close to an in-depth definition of what might be termed the 'administration prerogative' as we are likely to find, there is also a brief mention in a 2009 Ministry of Justice Report under the heading of 'Ministerial prerogative powers' where it is stated that there are 'powers concerning the machinery of Government'.[14] This is very general but suggests that the executive themselves believe that there is a prerogative power that relates directly to public administration in the context of the machinery of government.

Finally, there is evidence in case law that judges accept that the government has some general administrative powers that are not statutory. Lord Sumption, for example, says in *New College* that it 'has long been recognised that the Crown possesses some general administrative powers to carry on the ordinary business of government'.[15] He goes on to consider how to classify these powers, and chapter eleven will return to that analysis.

In *GCHQ*, Lord Diplock also held, in passing, that 'those by whom the administration of the realm is carried on do so as personal servants of the monarch who can dismiss them at will'.[16] This is a succinct confirmation that the administration of the realm is done on behalf of the Crown. If the central argument of this book is accepted, then that therefore must be underpinned by royal prerogative. It is only fair to mention that Diplock also speculated that the power to dismiss

[11] ibid 3–4.

[12] ibid 80 and 83.

[13] See further R Craig, 'Black Spiders Weaving Webs: The Constitutional Implications of Executive Veto of Tribunal Determinations' (2016) 79 *Modern Law Review* 166, 172.

[14] Ministry of Justice (2009) Review of the Executive Royal Prerogative Powers: Final Report, data.parliament.uk/DepositedPapers/Files/DEP2009-2493/DEP2009-2493.pdf.

[15] *R (New London College Ltd) v Secretary of State for the Home Department)* [2013] UKSC 51, [2013] 1 WLR 2358, [2013] 4 All ER 195, [28].

[16] *Council for the Civil Service Unions v Minister for the Civil Service* [1985] AC 374, 409.

those servants was a residue of the constitutional rule that 'the king can do no wrong'.[17] It is hard to see how this explains the nature of the legal relationship between the Crown and civil servants. The better view, perhaps, is that the legal relationship between civil servants who can be dismissed at will and the Crown is governed entirely by the administration prerogative by those acting as 'servants' of the Crown. It is worth noting in passing that the civil service was placed on a statutory footing by the Constitutional Reform and Governance Act 2010, s 1.

Chitty does not provide a neat list of what powers fall under the prerogative of administration or indeed a tight definition. It is suggested, however, that implicit in the legal prerogative power of administration is the power to ensure that the 'various duties' of government are 'properly performed'; hence, the full range of basic administrative tasks encompassed in modern civil service bureaucracy may be safely included, such as writing memos, setting policy, reorganising departments and the like.[18] If the exercise of such powers has observable legal effects in particular cases, then litigation may be instigated by the affected party or parties as to whether the particular exercise of that prerogative legal power was *intra vires*. If the exercise of the administration prerogative frustrates the intention of parliament in any Act, that will also be unlawful – an important point that chapter eleven will explore.

It is important to make clear that the administration prerogative is, by definition, narrower than the mooted freedom to do anything not prohibited that is argued for by Harris and supported by Elliott.[19] As a prerogative, it cannot be used in a way that frustrates the intention of any Act and also cannot be used in a way that conflicts with rights possessed by citizens. In this, it shares the characteristics of a freedom to do anything not prohibited that is, slightly concerningly perhaps, defended by others. Its boundaries are explored in the next section but as with all prerogatives it is limited by previous accepted usage. It is suggested that it is confined to the internal mundane activities within government that go to the implementation of policy either in support of statutory schemes and actions or other prerogative executive powers. This then covers the writing of memos, issuing of advice and such like. Its limits are areas where its exercise shades into novel policy, of which the first case in the next section is perhaps a paradigm example.

The Boundaries of the Administration Prerogative

This chapter and the next argue that much of the recent case law on the exercise of allegedly 'common law' or 'third source' powers of the Crown can be reframed as

[17] ibid.

[18] The author is grateful to Martin Loughlin and Julian Rivers for drawing to his attention that any reorganisation of government departments is effected by Order in Council, which would appear to support the claim in this chapter that ordinary administration is a function of prerogative.

[19] See ch 9, pp 177–82.

examples of the exercise of the administration prerogative to administer the realm, including setting and implementing policy. The key examples in recent case law concern making lists of those who should not work with children, reorganising local government, a sponsorship scheme for foreign students, and the decision whether to match benefit payments to widowers with those to widows. These examples shade between administration, *ex gratia* expenditure and sometimes quasi-judicial decision-making that may affect lives, even if not any identifiable rights. As has been argued already, in no case is the understanding of any of these scenarios aided by consideration of the private legal powers of natural persons.

In *ex parte C*, the Department of Health maintained a 'Consultancy Service Index' ('Index') which was effectively a list of those individuals who were thought unsuitable to work with children.[20] The Home Office recorded on the Index those who had any 'convictions or cautions when the individual worked in the childcare field' and also where an individual was moved or resigned 'where the welfare of children' had been put 'at risk'.[21] Although the Index was not published, it was expected that employers in the industry would check it, but only 'once a decision to offer employment has been made'.[22] Whilst there was no 'legal bar to future employment', being on the Index would obviously have a 'powerful effect … upon a person's prospects of employment in the child care field', not least because of the potential risk being taken by the employer if they chose not to rescind the offer of employment.[23]

The appellant was on the Index. He claimed that the Index was unlawful as it effectively prevented him securing employment in the child-care sector. The unanimous judgment was given by Lady Justice Hale (as she then was) and held that the department could maintain the Index. The reasoning of Hale LJ expressly cited Wade in determining that there was no relevant prerogative power that could justify the department having such an Index. Hale LJ did not cite Harris, but her reasoning was uncannily similar, and therefore suffered from some of the same problems.

Hale LJ began by citing Halsbury's Laws of England which state that 'public authorities (including the Crown) may do nothing but what they are authorised to do by some rule of the common law (including the royal prerogative) or statute'.[24] This, the judge held, 'finds a recent echo' in the *Fewings* extract from Laws LJ that was considered in chapter seven:[25]

> For private persons, the rule is that you may do anything you choose which the law does not prohibit … But for public bodies the rule is the opposite … any action to be taken must be justified by positive law.[26]

[20] *Ex parte C* (n 4) 402.
[21] ibid 402.
[22] ibid.
[23] ibid 403.
[24] ibid 405.
[25] ibid and see p 144.
[26] *R v Somerset County Council, ex parte Fewings* [1995] 1 All ER 513, 524.

Recognising that the *Fewings* case concerned a statutory body, the judge then quoted Wade for the proposition that the Crown is in a different position because it has prerogative powers as well as 'powers which the Crown shares equally with its subjects because of its legal personality'.[27] As we saw in chapter four, the assumption that the Crown has legal personality at common law may not be correct and the further claim that the Crown has 'equal' (ie the *same*) legal powers as subjects is not tenable.

The judgment next considered whether the Crown had any basis to maintain the Index. Hale LJ said that the Crown has the same *liberties* as the individual and mentioned that the first instance (unreported) judgment by Mr Justice Richards was decided on this basis.[28] She held that a liberty or freedom is only limited by the inability to interfere with the rights of others, quoting *Entick v Carrington* and the phone tapping case of *Malone*:[29]

> Subject to complying with those rights, it seems to me that private citizens are free to maintain services such as this. I conclude, *therefore*, that maintaining the list is not, in itself, unlawful.[30] (emphasis added)

This extract makes crystal clear that the basis for the claim that the government can make the kind of list at issue flowed *directly* from the fact that private citizens can make lists. This reasoning is flawed. A chasm separates the exercise of public power from the actions of private citizens. Indeed, Hale LJ immediately drew a sharp distinction between private citizens and the government in the next section of her judgment, pointing out that a private citizen would not have 'the power' [sic] to issue guidance that makes the list effective. The simple effect of this is to concede that the comparison with private actions has no purchase or relevance.

Hale LJ further conceded the magnitude of the chasm by quoting from Wade (similarly cited in *Fewings*), to the effect that 'the powers of public authorities are … essentially different from those of private persons'.[31] She also conceded that the European Court of Human Rights held in *Malone* that 'the common law power was not "in accordance with the law" in Convention terms, because it was not sufficiently precise or predictable'.[32] Precise and predictable government legal powers are completely conceptually different from the liberty possessed by ordinary citizens to live their lives freely. Finally, she held that the powers in this case carry with them a duty to act fairly and that they had not been exercised unlawfully or unreasonably. This concedes that public legal powers are subject to myriad public law duties that have no analogue with the freedoms of private citizens to do that which is not prohibited. No one is going to persuade a court to grant an

[27] Sir William Wade, in W Wade and C Forsyth, *Administrative Law*, 7th edn (Clarendon Press, 1994) 248–49.

[28] *Ex parte C* (n 4) 405.

[29] *Entick v Carrington* (1765) 19 St Tr 1030; *Malone* (n 4).

[30] *Ex parte C* (n 4) 406.

[31] ibid 407.

[32] ibid.

order quashing my list of birthday party invitees, which nicely illustrates that viewing this area of law through the 'prism' of remedies is far more illuminating than starting with rights or powers. Choosing which end of the legal telescope to look through is critical.

The error in Hale LJ's reasoning becomes clear once Perry's argument against Harris, discussed in chapter nine, is understood. The judge plainly assumed that if there is no prohibition on the government doing something, then the government has a *power* to do that thing; and not just a power but a *legal* power to do that thing, subject to various public law duties. The shift in the language is plain and the gap in logic insurmountable. It is clear that the fact that the department would not be breaching any rights of the applicant in maintaining the Index does not mean it has the *power* to maintain such an Index. The existence of a particular legal power as a matter of public law is an essential step in the argument that is wholly omitted in this judgment.

As mentioned already, another serious problem for the court was the imposition of significant public law restrictions on a 'power' that is supposed to be 'equal', at least according to Wade, to the power of a natural person to make a list. The judge's reasoning on this point was as follows:

> That of course does not mean that the Department is free to operate the list in whatever way it likes. Its status as a public authority brings consequences which would not apply to a private citizen.[33]

The previous claim of a direct *equivalence* between private freedom and public powers is so unworkable, and the attempt to equate them so obviously unpalatable, that Hale LJ immediately and sharply distinguished the two legal situations. She was right to do so, but the obvious conclusion to be drawn from this is that there is in fact *no* equivalence between the private freedom to make a list as a natural person, and the vastly different circumstances of a formal Index that implements a governmental policy designed to protect children. If the government had failed to protect children by this means, it would be rightly held accountable to parliament in a democracy. What this has in common with making, say, a list of people for a birthday party as a private citizen is very difficult to follow. Thus, underpinning Hale LJ's reasoning is an implicit acceptance that there must be a public legal power that is being constrained by compliance with the public law rules that restrain the exercise of public power. How can a freedom to do what is not prohibited be literally 'outside the legal powers' (*ultra vires*) unless in fact the action is a function of a legal power?

The problem for the court was that if Wade's approach was adopted there was no obvious legal power that could be used as the basis for the policy of issuing guidance requiring those in the industry to check the Index maintained by the department before employing people who might be a risk to children. Indeed, Hale LJ says expressly that there was 'no suggestion of a specific prerogative power

[33] ibid 406.

in this case'.[34] If there had been such a legal power available, the entire argument would have been transformed. The core principle that the government should have legal authority for its actions, found in Halsbury's and echoed in *Fewings*, could have been correctly applied to central as well as local government. There would have been no need to draw inappropriate comparisons with individual citizens in private law, and the imposition of standard judicial review limitations in public law would have been easy to justify and understand.

Solving the Freedom/Power Conundrum

The solution, it is suggested, lies in the recognition of the administration prerogative argued for in the last chapter, which provides a general legal power for servants of the Crown to fulfil their duties and offices in an ordinary sense and based on historical practices.[35] This would reframe the legal question, which would then become whether the particular scheme in question can be understood as a modern example of how the power has been exercised in the past. It might be thought that the hitherto unnoticed existence of the 'administration prerogative' could create some rule of law concerns because if the administration prerogative is indeed found to exist, the use of this power has not been considered by the courts over recent decades. The main counter argument to this objection is that, however difficult it might be to identify the previous historic examples of what 'administration' might include, that possible lack of clarity is as nothing compared to the potential breadth of the notion that the Crown can do anything that is not prohibited, in the manner of a private citizen, which was the basis for the decision in *ex parte C*.

If framed in terms of what *defines* the administration prerogative, it is suggested that the legal dispute in such cases is much easier to understand. It is now clear that the judiciary have the power to review the exercise of some prerogative powers and that same rule can be applied to the administrative prerogative as one such prerogative power. When *ex parte C* is reframed in these terms it can be immediately seen that the Government case was far from strong. The administration prerogative might be understood to underpin the ordinary management of the more mundane and uncontroversial day-to-day activities of civil servants and ministers. There is a real question as to whether this should or should not be taken to include the policy to issue guidance to those working with children to check those who may be employed in the sector, and to maintain an Index to do so.

[34] ibid 405.

[35] The issue of the effect of the Constitutional Reform and Governance Act 2010 on the Civil Service and whether the Act put it onto a statutory footing (and arguably therefore placed many of these ordinary administrative powers onto a sound statutory footing) is beyond the scope of this work. See the Constitutional Reform and Governance Act 2010, s 1 and the long title.

It might be thought that such an important policy, with such significant effects on some individuals seeking to work in the sector, and adverse impacts on their reputations, could cross the line from within the definition of mere administration and into a formal policy scheme of such importance that ministers should seek formal legislative approval from parliament. The boundary between mere administration and the instigation of a novel formal policy is necessarily vague but it is a long established feature of the UK constitution that major policies must be instigated with the approval of the democratic assembly, and it is arguable that the decision in this case is inconsistent with that longstanding approach. This turns on whether the policy is significant or novel enough, which is beyond the scope of this book.

While a *definitive* answer to that question is beyond the scope of this chapter, which is concerned with the *parameters* of the analysis, rather than the determination of particular scenarios, there is at least a strongly arguable case that a court would have held that the ramifications of the policy to maintain a list of people who were *de facto* prohibited from working in a certain area crossed the line from mere administration to something that should have required more formal statutory authorisation. Indeed, the judge specifically mentioned that the Index had been placed on a statutory footing in the Protection of Children Act 1999 which was due to come into force very shortly after the decision. The very fact that this complex scheme had been spelled out in a full statute which had passed through parliament and been exposed to the political winds perhaps serves to strengthen the claim that the government's actions in this went beyond mere administration in implementing the original scheme.

Not only did the maintenance of the Index arguably go beyond mere administration in amounting to matters of important policy, but an issue could also have been raised as to whether the legal rights of those whose details were kept on the Index were affected. The Human Rights Act was not yet in force, but the court concluded anyway that the maintenance of the list did not breach Art 6(1) of the European Convention on Human Rights ('ECHR').[36] Rights under the Data Protection Act 1998 would certainly have been engaged but that Act was not yet in force either.[37] There is, however, some difficulty concerning the potential damage to the reputations of those whose details were kept on the list. Hale LJ referred more than once to this and indeed the headnote states that:

> there was a delicate balance to be struck between the individual's need to safeguard his reputation and interests of children living away from home.[38]

[36] *Ex parte C* (n 4) 407–09. Hale LJ declined to speculate as to whether it might breach another Convention right.

[37] Had it been so, it would have altered the legal and factual matrix considerably since the list clearly amounted to the processing of personal data and hence would have been caught by the Data Protection Act 1998. The information held was obviously personal and had been 'processed' for the purposes of s 1 of the Act. The department was clearly a data 'controller'. Multiple possible defences/exceptions would have been available to the government but the matter would have required full analysis to determine that the list complied with the requirements of the Act.

[38] *Ex parte C* (n 4) 401, summarising remarks by Hale LJ to this effect at 402 and 407.

In light of this recognition it seems odd that there is no discussion of the cause of action – the tort of defamation – that has long protected the right to reputation at common law.[39] This is likely because neither the Index itself, nor even individual's entries on it were actually published to prospective employees, still less to anyone else.[40] Moreover even if the tort could be found to be *prima facie* made out in some particular circumstances the government would likely have had complete defences.[41] Nevertheless the combination of the recognition of the relevance of reputational issues with the failure to explain clearly why the legally protected reputation rights of those included on the list were not even prima facie *engaged* is another example of the partial and cursory legal analysis undertaken in this case.[42] It is suggested that this further illustrates how the failure to couch the issues in terms of prerogative power led to a failure to fully think through the relevant legal issues, including the effects on individuals and, potentially, their legal rights.

It is important to reiterate that – should they accept it – whatever the courts do to work through what is the historically rooted *definition* of the administration prerogative, the starting point will *not* be that the Crown is free to do anything that is not illegal. That kind of wide and undefined starting point would be rejected immediately as a complete abdication of the most basic judicial scrutiny. Instead, a sober assessment of the historic precedents of ordinary administration, where it shades into the setting, implementation and assessment of major policy, would inform the outcome of such an analysis. The administration prerogative is far tighter and narrower than a freedom to do anything not prohibited. It is suggested that this particular example likely crossed the boundary from mere administration to the setting of an important policy. Indeed, the fact that the scheme was shortly thereafter placed onto a formal statutory footing bolsters the claim that this area did raise important policy issues requiring formal statutory regulation. It is the latter point that underpins the claim in this chapter that the approach in this case is inconsistent with restraining the use of the administration prerogative to areas without major policy implications.

A further important limitation would be that, as a prerogative power, such administrative schemes could not infringe the rights of ordinary citizens

[39] Important elements of the tort, principally defences, have been codified in various statutes, including most recently the Defamation Act 2013.

[40] As Hale explains (*ex parte C* (n 4) 402–03) prospective employers send an inquiry and '[i]f no trace of the person is found [on the list] the inquiry will be returned stamped "no observations". If a positive identification is made, a letter will be sent suggesting that a reference be sought from a named local authority or voluntary/private organisation. Unlike the person named in the list, a prospective employer is not told anything about the reasons for the referral, except for any criminal conviction.'

[41] In particular, the defence of justification (now 'truth') and common law qualified privilege would have been available.

[42] More recent ECHR case law now makes clear that reputation itself is a protected right under Art 8: *Radio France v France* App no 53984/00 (30 March 2004) especially at [31]; so under the same facts today there would surely have had to be a proper analysis under the Human Rights Act 1998.

(something true not just of the administration prerogative, but of *all* prerogative powers). Thus, the administration prerogative would simply join the list of other ordinary prerogatives and be legally constrained by the requirements of rationality, procedural fairness and legitimate expectation in the usual way. It would sit alongside other justiciable prerogatives which are not 'high policy' in nature and therefore non-justiciable for that reason.[43]

Of course, the relevant public law rules are not quite the same as those that govern the exercise of *statutory* powers because, unlike them, prerogatives do not have clear statutory wording and obvious verbal limits defining their boundaries along with established linguistic interpretative rules. So, for example, the claims that the exercise of prerogative might be unlawful because they 'fetter the discretion' of the decision-maker or pursue an 'improper purpose' can only rarely make logical sense in the prerogative context because there is no statutory intention to draw upon.[44] It follows therefore that the better approach would be to consider the prerogative in terms of historical precedent and existence. This would be entirely a matter of judicial discretion as they continue their unilateral regulation of prerogative powers over time.

Third Source Powers, *Malone, Third Direction* and the Prerogative of Keeping the Peace

The more recent case law on third source powers, considered earlier in this chapter and in the next one, is important and relevant in any discussion of such alleged powers, not least because some of the points made by Harris are directly considered. It is, however, also crucial to consider the case of *Malone* which started the third source ball rolling.[45] There can be little doubt that the notion of the government having a 'freedom' to act, in the Harris sense, as long as there is nothing prohibiting it from doing so, was originally sourced in that case. *Malone* is also important because, like *ex parte C*, *Shrewsbury* and *New College* it concerns government actions whose legal connection to royal prerogative might be thought to be somewhat opaque.[46] In *Malone*, it is plain that the prerogative of administration played no part. Tapping phones cannot sensibly be included within 'administration' by any reasonable definition. It is suggested, therefore, that the prerogative that was arguably in play was the prerogative of keeping the peace, whose very

[43] *R v Secretary of State for Foreign and Commonwealth Affairs, ex parte Everett* [1989] QB 811, 817. This test was not overruled in the *Miller II* decision in the UK Supreme Court ([2019] UKSC 41, [2020] AC 373).

[44] See, for example, *R (Sandiford) v Secretary of State for Foreign and Commonwealth Affairs* [2014] UKSC 44, [2014] 1 WLR 2697.

[45] *Malone* (n 5).

[46] The latter two cases are considered in the next chapter.

existence Beynon has suggested is 'questionable'.[47] This is mistaken and, as we saw in chapter three, there is powerful evidence that it does in fact have a long and established history.

The prerogative of keeping the peace has received detailed treatment by Sir Carleton Allen and Sir Frederick Pollock.[48] It is furthermore now clear, at the very least since *ex parte Northumbria*, that the Crown has a prerogative duty to keep the peace. This is arguably foundational to an obligation on the monarch to prevent crime and administer justice, both criminal and civil, which stretches back centuries.[49] This is a standard obligation placed on the institutions of state in any system. The curio is that in the United Kingdom, the obligation is historic, well documented, and arguably ongoing. In *Northumbria*, the Home Secretary sought to authorise the distribution of CS gas and batons notwithstanding the necessity for approval of the local police board under statute. The discussion of the prerogative of keeping the peace was strictly *obiter* but the existence of the prerogative of keeping the peace was confirmed beyond doubt.

As argued by the author elsewhere, the circuit judges (along with sheriffs, coroners and others) historically carried out executive and administrative functions.[50] It is important to recall, as McIlwain points out, that the rigid, modern, conceptual separations between different branches would not be recognised in much earlier times.[51] This was long before the role of judges transformed in to one of adjudication.[52] One part of the executive function, now in effect transferred to the police, includes the duty to keep the peace, detect crime and maintain order. In addition, Blackstone made clear that 'the king is considered in domestic affairs … as the fountain of justice and general conservator of the peace of the kingdom'.[53] As Maitland points out, 'if [the king] prosecutes criminals, this is because his peace has been broken'.[54] It is clear therefore that the prerogative duty of keeping the peace, with concomitant powers, exists, as discussed in chapter three. Indeed, it is arguably foundational to the entire legal system, at least until the Judicature Acts 1873–75.

[47] H Beynon, 'Prerogative to Supply Plastic Baton Rounds and CS Gas to the Police' [1987] *Public Law* 146, 149. See also AW Bradley, 'Police Powers and the Prerogative' (1988) *Public Law* 298 and C Gearty, 'The Courts and Recent Exercises of the Prerogative' (1987) 46 *Cambridge Law Journal* 372 for critical comment.

[48] CK Allen, *Hamlyn lectures: 'The King's Peace'* (Stevens & Sons, 1953); F Pollock, 'The King's Peace' (1885) 1 *Law Quarterly Review* 37.

[49] *R v Secretary of State for the Home Department, ex parte Northumbria Police Authority* [1989] QB 26, 44, 51, 58–59. See also *Harrison v Bush* (1855) 5 E & B 344, 353, per Lord Campbell CJ: 'In practice, to the Secretary of State for the Home Department … belongs peculiarly the maintenance of the peace within the Kingdom, with the superintendance of the administration of justice as far as the Royal prerogative is involved in it.'

[50] R Craig (n 13).

[51] CH McIlwain, *The High Court of Parliament and its Supremacy* (Oxford University Press, 1910) 21.

[52] R Craig (n 50) 172.

[53] W Blackstone, *Commentaries on the Laws of England* (1753), Book 1, ch 7, 266. See also ch 3, p 50.

[54] FW Maitland, *The History of English Law before the Time of Edward I*, 2nd edn (Cambridge University Press, 1898–99) 540.

McKechnie traces the King's power to insist that all serious crimes be dealt with in his courts back to Henry II – before even Magna Carta. Dealing with crime is one of the oldest Crown prerogatives and is fundamentally connected to the prerogative of justice.[55] The royal takeover of all justice matters began with serious crime and quickly expanded. As McKechnie observes:

> By his Assizes of Clarendon ... Henry reserved important crimes for the exclusive consideration of his own judges ... heinous crimes were ... admitted on all hands to be ... reserved exclusively for royal jurisdiction.[56]

Kantorowicz entertainingly details how entrenched in the national consciousness was the connection between criminal sanctions and the monarch.

> late descendants of the Englishmen of 1135 or 1272 ... were said to have indulged in robberies and other disturbances because allegedly on the king's death the king's peace ceased to exist ...[57]

In *Coomber v Berkshire Justices* the House of Lords held that the police were 'ultimately a Crown responsibility'.

> the administration of justice, both criminal and civil, and the preservation of order and prevention of crime by means of what is now called police, are among the most important functions of Government [and] these functions ... belong to the Crown.[58]

Malone

The relevance of the prerogative of 'preservation of order' (ie keeping the peace) and preventing crime comes into sharp focus when considering *Malone*.[59] In that case, the Post Office tapped Malone's phone at the behest of the police and pursuant to a warrant signed by the Home Secretary. *Malone* is the rock on which Harris builds his argument for a 'third source' set of freedoms available to the executive because Vice-Chancellor Megarry held in that case that the tapping of Malone's phone was not unlawful because there was no law stopping the authorities from doing so.

It is unfortunate that counsel in *Malone* appears to have conceded without argument that the actions of the police should be considered in terms of freedom to do anything not directly prohibited and not through the prism of prerogative.[60] It would have been better to frame the analysis in terms of a modern

[55] Judicature Acts 1873–75.
[56] WS McKechnie, *Magna Carta*, 2nd edn (Glasgow, 1914) 88.
[57] EH Kantorowicz, *The King's Two Bodies: A Study in Mediaeval Political Theology* (Princeton University Press, 1957) 317; Allen (n 46) 11 fn 8.
[58] *Coomber v Berkshire Justices* (1883) 9 App Cas 61.
[59] *Malone* (n 5).
[60] ibid 366. Discussed in ch 9, pp 179–82.

understanding of the prerogative of investigating and preventing crime. This had been mentioned previously by Lord Parker CJ. He had held that

> it is part of the obligations and duties of a police constable to take all steps which appear to him necessary for keeping the peace, for preventing crime or for protecting property from criminal injury'.[61]

The judge did not attempt to unpack the relationship between the three concepts but if keeping the peace is a prerogative, which it clearly is, it is not too great a stretch to claim that preventing crime and protecting property could be said to fall within prerogative also, not least because actions that fall within the two other categories inevitably result in actions brought against the perpetrators by the Crown for contravening the peace.

Some of the difficulties in *Malone* may have been caused by the issue being framed narrowly, focusing on whether there was a legal power to tap phones. There was obviously no historic prerogative power to tap phones because they are a comparatively recent invention. In addition, the judge's novel idea that the government could do anything that is not prohibited by law made it unnecessary to consider whether phone tapping could be done under residual prerogative powers.

It is tempting to simply write off *Malone* as an aberration and wrongly decided, and certainly, as the source for the idea of third source powers, it has no previous basis in precedent. On closer inspection, however, there are significant parts of Megarry VC's judgment that are often overlooked and may provide useful guidance on the meaning and purpose of the prerogative of preventing crime, administering justice and keeping the peace – which it will be convenient to label holistically as 'preventing crime', at least for the purposes of this chapter.

Megarry VC was clearly troubled by the idea that the police could be hampered in their ability to investigate criminal offences by being unable to tap phones of those engaging in criminal activity. Indeed, he even suggested that 'telephone tapping is a subject which cries out for legislation'.[62] It is suggested, however, that in holding that the police, and therefore the executive in general, have the power to do *anything* not prohibited by law, the courts have unfortunately handed the executive an astonishingly broad power to act in unknowable ways in the future. This is difficult to reconcile with the rule of law.

In those circumstances, it would have been better and more consistent with the history and development of the law, especially the long established requirement that executive actions be grounded in some legal power, if Megarry VC had instead centred his analysis in the prerogative power to prevent crime. Liberal hackles may rise at the potential for a generous reading of this power in favour of the police, but hackles should perhaps rise higher at the prospect that the executive

[61] *Rice v Connolly* [1966] 2 QB, 414, 419.

[62] ibid 380. A great deal of legislation in the area has now been passed, starting with the Interception of Communications Act 1985.

can do anything that is not legally prohibited. It is to be hoped that as the area is heavily regulated by statute and other investigatory authorities, as Phillipson points out, the non-statutory powers of the police in this area will further diminish in importance.[63] Certainly in the context of phone tapping, the area is now entirely regulated by statute, including the Regulation of Investigatory Powers Act 2000, for example. This statutory regulation perhaps reflects the fact that the authorities realised that in the absence of regulation, anyone else could in theory lawfully hack the *government's* telephones.

It is fair to point out that one of the reasons that the judge in *Malone* did not consider the prerogative of preventing crime is that *Northumbria* was decided after *Malone* and was itself one of the first proper attempts to consider the relevant prerogative power in modern times. This should not detract from the fact that the prerogative clearly existed historically and the failure of counsel to argue for it in *Malone* does not prevent us from considering whether it could have formed the basis of the analysis in that case. Recasting our view of *Malone* in this way might help to salvage the case as a useful part of the discussion of prerogative powers and further reduce the potentially damaging influence of the unhelpful doctrine of third source freedoms possessed by the government as if it was a private citizen.

The Prerogative of Keeping the Peace and Preventing Crime

As it happens, there is plenty of material in Megarry VC's judgment that could be interpreted as informing our understanding of the prerogative of keeping the peace and particularly preventing crime. The judge clearly had an instinctive grasp of the reality that it is the responsibility of the executive to investigate crime and enforce the law and that this was something that the judiciary should be slow to obstruct.

> The rights and liberties of a telephone subscriber are indeed important; but so also are the desires of the great bulk of the population not to be the victims of assault, theft or other crimes. The detection and prosecution of criminals, and the discovery of projected crimes, are important weapons in protecting the public. The question is … whether there is *just cause* or excuse for the tapping and for the use made of the material obtained by the tapping.[64] (emphasis added)

The issue of whether the executive had 'just cause' could be read as going beyond whether the government is 'free' to do something because there is no law

[63] G Phillipson, 'Searching for a Chimera? Seeking Common Law Rights of Freedom of Assembly and Association' in M Elliott and K Hughes (eds), *Common Law Constitutional Rights* (Hart Publishing, 2019) 161.

[64] *Malone* (n 5) 377.

prohibiting it. The judge's reasoning on the limits of such a 'just cause' could be interpreted as edging towards including phone tapping as a modern expression of the general power to investigate and prevent crime. The judge also outlines what he sees as the appropriate boundaries of this power under that prerogative, ie investigating crime and protecting the public.

> First … the tapping of the particular telephone will be of material assistance in detecting or preventing crime … Second, no use should be made of any material obtained except for these purposes. Third, [irrelevant information] should be confined to the minimum number of persons reasonably required to carry out the process of tapping.[65]

The judge also appeared somewhat troubled that a higher court or future case could hold that there was a duty of confidentiality owed by the Post Office to the telephone subscriber in relation to the contents of any telephone conversation.[66] If there was a duty of confidentiality then the government would no longer have a 'third source freedom' to tap the phone because that would be in breach of a legal right of the suspect.[67] It could be argued that the same would be the case for any prerogative power because prerogatives cannot be used in a way that breaches rights, but there is a potentially important difference. This difference perhaps illustrates one of the dangers of relying on the idea of the government merely being 'free' to act in contrast with having a positive legal power to investigate and detect crime.

Megarry VC framed the issue of confidence in the context of the fact that someone engaging in criminal activity cannot reasonably expect to insist on a duty of confidence to affect the police who are actively investigating his activities. This would unduly hamper police investigations.

> Even if any duty of confidentiality were, contrary to my judgment, to be held to bind those who overhear a telephone conversation, there remains the question of the limits to that duty.[68]

The limits the judge imposed were if there was a 'just cause or excuse for breaking confidence' and 'whether the disclosure is in the public interest'.[69] It is suggested that if this is framed as a consideration of the interaction between any putative duty of confidence and a prerogative of preventing crime (based on a 'just cause'

[65] ibid.
[66] ibid 376.
[67] See also *Francome v Mirror Group Newspapers Ltd* [1984] 1 WLR 892, 900 where Fox LJ distinguished *Malone* on the grounds that 'Robert Megarry V.-C. was only dealing with a case of authorised tapping by the police' going on to hold that: 'Illegal tapping by private persons is quite another matter since it must be questionable whether the user of a telephone can be regarded as accepting the risk of that in the same way'. It should be noted, however, that the case was an interlocutory matter considering whether there was a 'serious issue to be tried'. See further, H Fenwick and G Phillipson, 'Confidence and Privacy: A Re-examination' (1996) 55 *Cambridge Law Journal* 447, 451 who claim that where 'information was obtained my means of a telephone tap … a duty of confidence may arise'.
[68] ibid.
[69] The just cause quotation was from Lord Denning in another case.

or otherwise), it would not be difficult for a court to hold that the duty of confidence ends where the executive are carrying out an active investigation under the relevant prerogative power. This would be a matter of interpreting the limits of any duty of confidentiality.

By contrast, if a putative duty of confidence were a self-contained non-statutory legal right and the executive were merely 'free' to do anything that does not breach any rights, it is a little more awkward to claim that the duty of confidence ends where any police investigation begins. This is because it is less clear why a duty of confidence should be limited by a mere freedom for the police to do what is not prohibited. This argument of course leaves it open to Harris and his defenders to claim that a robust and positive definition of the prerogative of preventing crime might be more intrusive to civil liberties than a mere freedom, but as Phillipson argues, the judges have long taken an approach that is highly accommodating to police and executive powers aimed at preventing or detecting crime.[70] The advantage of couching this area of law in terms of prerogative powers instead of freedoms remains the concomitant requirement under the rule of law of demonstrating a positive legal power to act, rather than the more nebulous and, frankly, worrying idea that the government is free to do anything not legally prohibited.

Tempting though it is to reframe Megarry VC's judgment as an attempt to modernise the prerogative of preventing crime to encompass technological advances that did not exist historically, such an attempt would be to stretch the limits of that power too far. The matter is moot in any event as the entire area is now heavily regulated by statute. Nonetheless, if the discussion had been framed in terms of prerogative, this would have avoided the slightly embarrassing side effect that ordinary citizens could equally have tapped the government's phones on Megarry VC's approach. This could not have happened if the power was rooted in prerogative. The judge's instinct to support the police in the investigation of crime is understandable, but the facts in *Malone* could have opened the door to further extensions, as perhaps the next subsection illustrates, in the absence of statutory intervention.

The 'Third Direction' Case

An important Court of Appeal decision has thrown some further light on the prerogative of keeping the peace and preventing crime.[71] It concerned agents working for the security services committing crime, ostensibly authorised by state officials. In a unanimous judgment, the court held that 'under the Royal Prerogative, the Secretary of State had authority at all times (not just in times of

[70] Phillipson (n 63) 160ff.

[71] *Privacy International v Secretary of State for Foreign and Commonwealth Affairs ('Third Direction')* [2021] EWCA Civ 330.

war or actual emergency) to maintain the Queen's peace and to keep law and order', agreeing with the case of *Northumbria*.[72] Before the issue was put onto a statutory footing, this prerogative included the power for the security services to authorise agents to 'participate in criminality':[73]

> All this, in our opinion, points strongly to the Security Service having, and always having had, the power, by its officers, to run agents who participate in criminality, whether possible or actual, in order to fulfil its function to protect the public: provided that there is no immunity from criminal sanction.[74]

Malone relied on the lack of any breach of the law to justify the actions of state officials. It is suggested that the *Third Direction* case demonstrates that it seems that the executive, slightly unexpectedly perhaps, has considerable powers under the prerogative of keeping the peace and preventing crime that were not recognised or acknowledged by Megarry VC in the *Malone* decision.

If it is possible for that prerogative to authorise the commission of crime (albeit without immunity) then, *a fortiori*, it is easy to see how a determined judge could have used similar reasoning to deploy prerogative as a basis for tapping Mr Malone's telephone. The latter involved no criminality at all, so it is arguably less controversial to see how phone tapping could have been justified in order to 'maintain the Queen's peace and to keep law and order'.[75] The *Third Direction* case may have sprung from a similar motivation to aid the work of those protecting the public from harm but, as with *Malone*, the area is now regulated by statute.[76] An opportunity to reaffirm the importance of clear legal authority for the actions of the executive was perhaps missed.[77]

Expansion in Police Powers by Stealth

Phillipson provides a useful case study in how the approach of the courts can lead to increased police powers by the back door without rigorous legal scrutiny. He explains how in the case of *Murray*, the courts held that the police were not prohibited from taking photographs of citizens in public because there was no law preventing it.[78] The crucial issue for our purposes is that the third source freedom doctrine led directly to a situation where the executive was able to acquire the legal *power* to photograph suspects and keep their details on a large database. This was achieved without demonstrating a specific historic legal justification in any

[72] *Northumbria* (n 49) per *Third Direction* (n 71) [83]. See also ch 2, p 39.
[73] Security Service Act 1989.
[74] *Third Direction* (n 71) [86].
[75] ibid [83].
[76] Covert Human Intelligence Sources (Criminal Conduct) Act 2021.
[77] See further, R Craig and G Phillipson, 'Protecting National Security by Breaking the Law? Prerogative, Statute and the Powers of MI5' (2022) 85 *Modern Law Review* 1274–88.
[78] *Murray v UK* (1995) 19 EHRR 193.

positive, identifiable law, never mind justifying to democratically elected members of parliament the need for statutory authorisation. Worse still, when the case of *Murray* went to the European Court of Human Rights, the court held that the Court of Appeal decision constituted positive legal authority for taking photographs when of course it did no such thing. The subsequent case of *Wood* then treated the *Murray* judgment as binding authority that there was now a positive legal power to take and store such photographs.[79] Lord Justice Laws in the Court of Appeal said that the 'common law power suffices', which was something of a logical leap.[80]

Thus, by a process of bait and switch, a positive legal power to maintain a large database, that included details of people never convicted of any crime, was inadvertently created by the back door without the government or the police ever having to justify or ground that power in specific previous positive law, for example the prerogative of preventing crime. It is suggested that requiring the government to justify a modern interpretation of the prerogative of preventing crime would at the very least have provided an opportunity for some legal scrutiny of such powers could sensibly be included within the historical precedents of the prerogative of preventing crime at all. It is fair to point out that the generous approach to the police that is generally taken by the courts to matters relating to the investigation of crime would likely mean that they would have been sympathetic to the police point of view as to how the prerogative of preventing crime should be understood. Nevertheless, it is suggested that grounding those powers in the prerogative of preventing crime would be both historically more accurate as well as conceptually neater.

Overall, then, the *Malone* case and subsequent case law in this area have opened the door to worrying expansions in police power without the need to justify those changes as being the modern expression of ancient prerogatives through the pernicious doctrine of third source freedoms. The *Murray/Wood* example is an eye-opening case study in how damaging the third source freedom doctrine can be to the rule of law. Phillipson goes on to critique a further example which is the case of *Catt*.[81] This concerned an application by Mr Catt to be removed from a national database containing data about him following many years of political participation in lawful protests.[82] Lord Sumption held that 'at common law, the police have the power to obtain and store information for policing purposes [including] … the prevention and detection of crime'.[83] The European Court of Human Rights took a more robust view, as Phillipson points out, 'predictably' finding that there had been 'a violation of Article 8' of the ECHR.[84]

[79] *Wood v Commissioner of Police for the Metropolis* [2008] EWHC 1105 (Admin).
[80] *R (Wood) v Commissioner of Police of the Metropolis* [2009] EWCA Civ 414, [2010] 1 WLR 123, [55].
[81] *R (Catt) v Association of Chief Police Officers* [2015] AC 1065.
[82] ibid [1].
[83] ibid [7].
[84] Phillipson (n 63) 160.

The key point is to decide whether to treat this area of law as governed by a positive prerogative legal power that is limited in certain important ways or as a freedom for the government and the police to do that which is not legally prohibited. Phillipson raises a pertinent question about the meaning of the concept of keeping the peace when considering *dicta* in *Rice*[85] about non-statutory powers of the police to detect and prevent crime.

> This might suggest that 'keeping the peace' includes both a broad, general power to prevent and detect crime and a more specific power to prevent an imminent breach of the peace. Alternatively, perhaps the two powers are wholly distinct; no-one seems to know.[86]

In relation to *Catt* itself, the question of whether a national database of protestors falls within a historic framing of police record keeping in order to prevent crime is a matter of degree. The police can obviously keep records. Whether that should include records of people who have not been convicted in the context of powerful and rapidly developing modern technology is another matter. Considered from that point of view, *Catt* may be rather more similar to *Malone* than might first appear. The approval of parliament, and the inevitable drawing up of safeguards and other formalities that would inevitably flow from an Act of Parliament suggests that a statutory framework must be the better course in principle.

As has been argued throughout this book, the prerogative approach has numerous advantages including imposing on the executive an obligation to identify a positive legal power, rooted in previous precedents and historical examples but considered through a modern lens. An approach rooted in prerogative also triggers various legal principles including the frustration principle and the rule that prerogative cannot affect rights, with which the judiciary are very familiar. Finally, an approach based on prerogative is more consonant with the constitutional history of the country, including long standing rule of law principles, which put the burden on the government to justify its actions in law rather than giving the executive a free pass to do anything that is not prohibited.

The next chapter considers third source case law, reframed as actually involving prerogative powers, where statutory provisions are relevant. These cases are conceptually distinct from judicial review of prerogative powers simpliciter.

[85] *Rice* (n 61).
[86] Phillipson (n 63) 161.

11

Reframing Third Source Case Law II: Prerogative and Statute

Introduction

The structure of this chapter and chapter ten illustrates a sharp distinction which must be drawn in the context of judicial review of prerogative powers. This distinction is not always delineated with sufficient care in the case law and academic literature. The previous chapter addressed the situation where the government purports to exercise the executive portion of a prerogative power. This may be labelled 'Category I'. The test in *Everett* makes clear that the jurisdiction of the court to review the decision turns on whether the prerogative relates to a matter of 'high policy'.[1] Chapter ten considered two prerogatives, in particular the administration prerogative and the prevention of crime prerogative, which are justiciable because the prerogatives in question are not 'high policy'. This test remains valid despite the 'one-off' *Miller II* case which fairly unconvincingly purported to turn on a pre-existing liminal issue as to the limits of the power before the 'high policy' test even became applicable.[2] In other words, *Miller II* did not overrule the test.

This chapter, in stark contrast, deals with the wholly different category of prerogative case law, where the executive portion of a prerogative power intersects with a statute. This may be labelled 'Category II'. Here the rules are radically different. No matter how 'high policy' is the prerogative in question, the courts will ensure that the will of parliament prevails. As the author has argued elsewhere, the intersection of prerogative and statute can happen in two distinct ways.[3]

The first scenario may be labelled the 'frustration principle'. Where the prerogative remains in the possession of the government, it cannot be exercised in a way that frustrates the intention of parliament in any Act. This may be labelled 'Category IIA'. The paradigm example of this, and also the authority for the principle, is the *Fire Brigades Union* case where it was held that the *ex gratia* prerogative power could not be used in a way that frustrated the will of parliament expressed

[1] *R v Secretary of State for Foreign and Commonwealth Affairs, ex parte Everett* [1989] QB 811, 820.

[2] *R (Miller) v Prime Minister; Cherry v Advocate General for Scotland* [2019] UKSC 41, [2020] AC 373, [2019] 3 WLR 589 ('*Miller II*').

[3] R Craig, 'A Simple Application of the Frustration Principle: Prerogative, Statute and Miller' (2017) *Public Law (Brexit Special Issue)* 25.

in the Criminal Justice Act 1988, s 171.[4] The second distinct situation is where the statute directly overlaps with the prerogative power, covering the field, so that the prerogative cannot be exercised by the government at all. This may be labelled 'Category IIB'. The paradigm example of this, and the authority for the legal principle, is the *De Keyser Hotel* case.[5] In that case, the court held that where prerogative and statute directly cover the same area, the government must use the statutory powers, and the prerogative power is suspended or goes into abeyance. Hence, this scenario may be labelled the 'abeyance principle'.

One way to understand the more basic distinction between Category I (no statute involved) and Category II (statute involved) is to consider the treaty prerogative. In the *Rees-Mogg* case, Mr Rees-Mogg brought an action claiming that the government's decision to sign the Maastricht treaty was *ultra vires*.[6] The court held that the exercise of the prerogative by the government was non-justiciable because it raised matters of high policy that were unsuitable for judicial consideration. The *ex parte Molyneux* case considered a challenge to the Anglo-Irish agreement.[7] It confirms the fact that the treaty prerogative is not justiciable, pointing out that the agreement in that case between the United Kingdom and another country was 'in the field of international relations' and was 'akin to a treaty'.[8] As such, the court held that 'it is not the function of this court to inquire into the exercise of the prerogative in entering into such an agreement'.[9]

Conversely, in *Miller I*, the same treaty prerogative was treated as wholly justiciable because it intersected with the European Communities Act 1972 and the European Parliamentary Elections Act 2002. Judicial treatment of prerogative is therefore radically different, depending on whether the factual matrix falls within Category I or Category II. If a 'high policy' or 'political' prerogative, such as making treaties, intersects with statute, its exercise becomes immediately justiciable because the will of parliament is paramount. If it does not intersect with any statute, it is not justiciable.

Miller II, the prorogation case, raises an interesting boundary question between the Categories. At first sight, it would appear to be firmly within Category I because there was obviously no existing statute in play in that case. The prorogation did not intersect with any Act of Parliament. Indeed the Divisional Court specifically held that the prorogation was 'political' and therefore 'not justiciable in Her Majesty's courts', which further suggests it should properly be classified within Category I.[10] In a strange way, however, the Supreme Court decision in *Miller II* could perhaps be classified as a Category II case. First, it is interesting to note that despite being so clearly 'political', the exercise of the prorogation prerogative was

[4] *R v Secretary of State for Home Department, ex parte Fire Brigades Union* [1995] 2 AC 513.
[5] *Att Gen v De Keyser's Hotel* [1920] AC 508.
[6] *R v Secretary of State for Foreign and Commonwealth Affairs, ex parte Rees-Mogg* [1994] QB 552.
[7] *Ex parte Molyneux* [1986] 1 WLR 331.
[8] ibid 336.
[9] ibid.
[10] *R (Miller) v Prime Minister* [2019] EWHC 2381 (QB), [51] and [68].

eventually quashed *de facto* even if the *de jure* reasoning was somewhat opaque compared to the admirably clear Divisional Court judgment. Normally, as we saw with the treaty prerogative, quashing a political or high policy exercise of prerogative requires an intersection with statute.

Furthermore, it is notable that the reasoning of the Supreme Court explicitly linked the voiding of the prorogation to the sovereignty of parliament, which is classically expressed solely through legislation. It might be thought, therefore, that *Miller II* could be interpreted as a significant and puzzling extension of the frustration principle.[11] The frustration principle is a Category II principle. The prorogation was arguably struck down because it prevented parliament from legislating in future, so arguably the exercise of the prorogation prerogative was treated as frustrating a potential *future* Act in the specific context of an imminent potential UK exit from the EU. Since any exercise of prerogative power could in theory be inconsistent with some unknown future Act, *Miller II* must indeed be treated as a 'one-off', as their Lordships held, and confined to its facts.[12]

Structurally, then, it should be noted that chapter ten addressed Category I. It attempted to reframe existing case law that ostensibly considers so-called 'third source powers' as in fact addressing the administration prerogative and the prerogative of keeping the peace including preventing crime. This chapter considers Category II. This is the conceptually distinct category where prerogative intersects with a statute. This chapter focuses primarily on the administration prerogative when it intersects with statute. When the legal powers exercised by the government under the administration prerogative are considered in the context of statutory powers in the same area the question for the court is the application of the frustration and the abeyance principles.[13] The first section considers the application of the frustration principle, and the second section considers an interesting borderline case. Finally, the third section considers the abeyance principle.

When the Administration Prerogative Interacts with Statute: Applying the Frustration Principle to 'Third Source' Cases

One of the ways in which the administration prerogative is observably exercised can be seen where it is used in support of statutory regimes that have secured the

[11] As suggested by the author before the case was brought: R Craig, 'Judicial Review of Advice to Prorogue Parliament' (UK Constitutional Law Association, 2019), ukconstitutionallaw.org/2019/07/12/robert-craig-judicial-review-of-advice-to-prorogue-parliament/.

[12] *Miller II* (n 2) [1].

[13] R Craig, 'Casting Aside Clanking Medieval Chains: Prerogative, Statute and Article 50 after the EU Referendum' (2016) 79 *Modern Law Review* 1041, 1045–46; R Craig, 'A Simple Application of the Frustration Principle: Prerogative, Statute and Miller' (2017) *Public Law (Brexit Special Issue)* 25.

imprimatur and approval of parliament. An important example of this is the *New London College* case, which concerned a sponsorship scheme for some foreign students at educational establishments.[14] Much of the judicial discussion in the case is redolent of the analysis in *ex parte C*. The next section will also look at the *Hooper* case, which raised issues concerning the relationship of the administration prerogative and statute.[15]

It is important to reiterate the crucial category distinction between *ex parte C* and these other two cases. *Ex parte C* concerned the exercise of prerogative *simpliciter* because there were no statutory obligations interacting with the administration prerogative. *New London College*, by contrast, was a situation where prerogative and statute intersected, and the issue then immediately became whether the prerogative could be exercised in the way the government wished given the intention of parliament as evidenced in the relevant Act. Once the myth of third source or common law powers of the Crown has been dispelled, it can be clearly seen that, in such circumstances, the relevant principle to apply is found in the clear case law culminating in the case of *Miller I*, where it was confirmed that prerogative powers cannot be used to frustrate the intention of parliament in any Act.[16] As we will see, *Hooper* is a trickier case, and appears to sit on the borderline between the abeyance and frustration principles.

New London College

The *New London College* case concerned an immigration sponsorship scheme run by the Home Office in which the applicants participated.[17] The scheme licensed participants to enrol students from outside the European Economic Area and laid down criteria that had to be satisfied. The lead judgment was delivered by Lord Sumption with whom all the other judges agreed, save Lord Carnwath who agreed on the outcome but not the reasoning.[18] The key question for our purposes is the legal basis for the scheme. Lord Sumption held that the sponsor licensing scheme fell outside the statutory immigration regime because it did not relate directly to the position of the student but instead was 'wholly concerned with the position of the sponsor'.[19] Whilst this saved the scheme from being *ultra vires* for failing to comply with statutory requirements, it left open the question of its legal basis if it was not statutory.

Lord Sumption understandably built on the previous authority provided by Hale LJ in the *ex parte C* case discussed earlier. He also referred to the

[14] *R (New London College Ltd) v Secretary of State for the Home Department)* [2013] 1 WLR 2358.

[15] *R (Hooper) v Secretary of State for Work and Pensions* [2005] UKHL 29, [2005] 1 WLR 1681.

[16] *R (Miller) v Secretary of State for Exiting the European Union* [2017] UKSC 5, [2018] AC 61, [2017] 2 WLR 583 ('*Miller I*'), [51].

[17] *New College* (n 14).

[18] ibid [33]–[45].

[19] ibid [24].

Shrewsbury case, which is discussed in the next section, and the 'third source powers' argument:

> It has long been recognised that the Crown possesses some general administrative powers to carry on the ordinary business of government which are not exercises of the royal prerogative and do not require statutory authority: see Harris, "The 'Third Source' of Authority for Government Action Revisited".[20]

Despite referencing the previous Court of Appeal cases and the Harris article, Lord Sumption was sceptical about that approach, rightly pointing out that the 'extent of these powers and their exact juridical basis are controversial'.[21] Although he mentioned that *ex parte C* had held that 'the basis of the power was the Crown's status as a common law corporation sole, with all the capacities and powers of a natural person', he rightly doubted the efficacy of this approach as well:

> Although in *Hooper* … Lord Hoffmann thought that there was 'a good deal of force' in this analysis, it is open to question whether the analogy with a natural person is really apt in the case of public or governmental action.[22]

Lord Sumption then went on to say that 'the question does not need to be resolved on these appeals', because the legal basis of the scheme rests on a 'statutory power … to administer the system of immigration control'.[23] He held that this system of 'control must necessarily extend to a range of ancillary and incidental administrative powers not expressly spelt out in the Act'.[24] In effect, he held that this amounted to a general *implied statutory power* in this case. On the other hand, and notwithstanding his justified scepticism as to whether the Crown can be treated as a natural person exercising ordinary legal powers, the judgment unfortunately did shade into talking in such terms at one point. Lord Sumption drew a distinction between

> public or governmental action as opposed to purely managerial acts [of the government] of a kind *that any natural person could do*, such as making contracts, acquiring or disposing of property, hiring and firing staff and the like.[25] [emphasis added]

Lord Sumption therefore appears to believe that the government has some 'general administrative powers' that are *not* based on prerogative or statute and that there is a separate category of 'purely managerial acts' that 'any natural person could do' but which are not 'public or governmental' action despite being done by the government. These powers would appear to correspond with 'common law

[20] ibid [28].
[21] ibid.
[22] ibid.
[23] ibid.
[24] ibid.
[25] ibid.

powers' defended by Lord Sales off the bench. These contradictory claims were clearly *obiter dicta* and are somewhat confusing. The better view, as previously argued, is that equating governmental powers with acts that a natural person can do is unhelpful and inappropriate, as was argued at length in part II.

In his dissenting judgment, Lord Carnwath expressly articulated that an *implied* statutory power must be the essence of the legal argument being made by Lord Sumption but argued strongly against the invention of such a *general* implied statutory power. He held that only a *specific*, as opposed to *generalised*, statutory provision could provide the requisite legal authority.[26] In his view, a specific statutory power *was* available in the Act in this case. So, on Lord Carnwath's reading of the statute there was a 'reasonably incidental' statutory power available,[27] but on Lord Sumption's reading there was an implied *general* statutory power available.

Importantly for our purposes, Lord Carnwath disagreed with Lord Sumption on the idea that there is a source of power for the government that is not statutory or prerogative.

> I cannot accept … that there is some alternative, unidentified source of such powers, derived neither from the prerogative nor from any specific provision in the Act.[28]

Lord Carnwath therefore cast very considerable doubt on the existence of 'third source powers', describing Mr Jonathan Swift QC as being 'wise' not 'to seek to rely' on the existence of such powers. He referenced his own judgment in *Shrewsbury* (discussed below) and also prayed in aid the House of Lords Select Committee report that was rightly scathing about the idea of the Ram doctrine being used to justify a generalised power in circumstances such as these.[29]

The Sponsor Scheme and the Administration Prerogative

It is suggested that the administrative prerogative would give a much more logical and straightforward legal grounding for the power that was identified by Lord Sumption to take general administrative steps in support of the statutory scheme and accommodate Lord Carnwath's wise warning about the risks of inventing non-existent legal powers that are not grounded in statute or prerogative. If accepted, this prerogative neatly captures the sense Lord Sumption instinctively articulated when he held that the government has 'general administrative powers' that are not based on any statute. Those powers, contrary to *ex parte C* and Harris, are prerogative powers. Viewed through this prism, the sponsor scheme slots neatly into place.

[26] ibid [33].
[27] ibid. He pointed specifically to the Immigration Act 1971, s 1(4).
[28] ibid [34].
[29] ibid [34] and House of Lords Select Committee on the Constitution,13th Report of Session 2012–13 'The pre-emption of Parliament' (HL Paper 165), 1 May 2013), discussed in ch 9, pp 177–79.

The lack of statutory authorisation for such a scheme is not problematic if there is a pre-existing prerogative power to generate policies, licensing schemes and other administrative procedures that are available to the government to support the meaning, purpose and intention of Acts of Parliament.

Lord Sumption goes on to explain the constraints on the general administrative powers that are available to the government:

> The Secretary of State cannot adopt measures for identifying suitable sponsors which are inconsistent with the Act … Without specific statutory authority, she cannot adopt measures … which infringe the legal rights of others … or which are irrational or unfair or otherwise conflict with the general constraints on administrative action imposed by public law.[30]

This quotation is a neat summary of the frustration principle cited earlier coupled with the rule that the exercise of prerogative 'must be compatible with … the common law'.[31] Case law has established that prerogative power cannot be used in any way that is inconsistent with any statutory power or which contradicts individual rights protected by common law precedent.[32] Understood as an application of the frustration principle which delimits the exercise of royal prerogative, Lord Sumption's summary is unremarkable, even banal, in its orthodoxy. The exercise of the administration prerogative cannot be used in a way that breaches the frustration principle. This area of law becomes much simpler and easier to understand if it is kept firmly in mind that there are only, in the end, two sources for the legal powers available to the government: statute and prerogative.

By contrast, if the power is deemed to be an implied statutory power, the situation is much more difficult. Unlike prerogative, statutory powers – whether express or implied – *can* be used to override common law rights if the intention of parliament is sufficiently clear. If the administrative power postulated by Lord Sumption is in fact an implied statutory power, then it is rather less certain why such a power could not be used in a way that overrides rights at common law. There is also something a little disturbing about the invention of implied statutory powers.

The better view, it is suggested, is that the general administrative power is a prerogative power because it is crystal clear from the case law that prerogatives cannot be used to frustrate the intention of parliament or override or affect common law rights. It would appear that the use of the prerogative power to set up this sponsor scheme would be wholly consistent with the intention of parliament and therefore would not breach the frustration principle at all. Hence under the approach suggested in this chapter, the *outcome* of *New London College* would have been the same but the *reasoning* far clearer, simpler and stronger.

[30] ibid [29].

[31] *Miller I* (n 16) [45].

[32] *Fire Brigades Union* (n 4); *Miller II* (n 2).

The Borderline between the Abeyance and Frustration Principles: *Ex Parte Hooper*

In most situations, it is crystal clear whether the abeyance principle or the frustration principle is in play because normally it is obvious whether or not the relevant statutory power *overlaps* with the relevant prerogative power, covering the field. *Hooper* was a rare example that seems to sit on the borderline between the two, depending on whether the reasoning of the Court of Appeal or House of Lords is to be preferred. The claimants were widowers who were not entitled to benefits that were payable to widows under the relevant legislation, ss 36–38 Social Security Contributions and Benefits Act 1992 ('the 1992 Act').[33] The 1992 Act was amended by legislation coming into force on 9 April 2001, which granted the same benefits to widowers from that point onwards. Hooper claimed, under the Human Rights Act 1998, that he was discriminated against in breach of Art 14, read in conjunction with Art 8. This was because, as a man, he was not entitled to the benefit that a woman in his position would have been because his wife died in 1997, before the new legislation came into effect. He claimed that the government had a duty to remedy the situation by introducing a remedial scheme to make *ex gratia* prerogative payments to the widowers to bridge the gap in the historic coverage.

This case is an important and useful example of where there may be identifiable effects in the real world of the analysis suggested in this book. This can be illustrated by considering an argument made by Philip Sales, now Lord Sales, then acting as counsel for the Government in the House of Lords. He claimed, perhaps on instructions, that the power to make administrative payments such as this was to be distinguished from the exercise of a 'power which the Crown enjoys as executive' because paying money was a 'commonplace' power that the Crown can exercise 'simply by virtue of being a legal person like any other' and 'statute would have to be a good deal more explicit before it could be interpreted as extinguishing such a commonplace power'.[34] The effect of this argument, if it were accepted, would have been to preserve flexibility for the government in the disbursement of *ex gratia* funds. Whilst understandable in context, this framing led to significant complications in the appellate judgments and speeches.

The framing of the status of these payments by Mr Sales is important precisely because, as argued in chapter three, it is wholly wrong to liken gifts or other disbursements in private law, made by private (or indeed corporate) persons, to the payment of taxpayers' money for the benefit of those seeking either compensation or aid from the public purse under some kind of administrative scheme set up by the government. Such an approach would blur the very real legal and political boundaries and accountability which are rightly imposed on official decision-makers who distribute taxpayers' money. Such funds do not 'belong' to

[33] *Hooper (HL)* (n 15).
[34] ibid [46].

the government in the way that the resources of private individuals 'belong' to them to spend, or waste, as they so desire. Rather, the money is democratically conferred through politically infused and contested decisions about supply that include decisions about what funding to allocate to exercises of prerogative that draw on the public purse.

Furthermore, Mr Sales also argued that a decision in this case could have wider impacts, for example on the Criminal Injuries Compensation Scheme.[35] This again could be seen to be a function of treating the power to disburse taxpayers' money not as an exercise of prerogative but as an ordinary 'commonplace' common law power. Counsel was implicitly claiming that if the statute in this case ruled out the 'commonplace' legal power to spend public money *in a general sense* then this could cause damage to a wide range of government schemes including criminal injuries compensation. If the court were to rule out *all* payments that look analogous to private gifts as a result of their reading of the statute in this case, then that could indeed have had wider implications. The absurdity of such a broad reading of the effect of such a decision in this particular case, however, reveals the weakness of the argument. It is suggested that if the issue is considered through the prism of a scheme set up under the administration prerogative as an executive power of the Crown, which could only be exercised in accordance with the intention of parliament, such errors would be more easily avoided. Any apparent resultant loss of flexibility is inherent in the fact that the government must act at all times in line with the intention of parliament.

If the payments are treated as exercises of prerogative power, then it is well understood that while the prerogative *as a whole* is an extremely broad set of powers, it has many branches. It would therefore not be sensible to treat *all* prerogative powers that result in financial disbursements as being excluded in any wider sense by such a decision. Rather, a decision that an *ex gratia* payment could not be used in these specific circumstances would only restrict the exercise of the administrative prerogative in this particular area. In other words, restricting financial disbursements under prerogative in this small area is much less likely to be interpreted as having wider effects than if the power to disburse money in a general sense had been struck down. The concern expressed by counsel that *all* disbursements could be threatened would therefore be less likely, if not impossible, if the issue is framed in terms of prerogative.

Finally, it is arguable that the prerogative model is more consistent with constitutional history. Throughout the case, the legal power to administer an *ex gratia* payment scheme is referred to as a common law power. When payments such as this are treated in this more mundane way, the risk increases that the genuine wider constitutional implications are missed precisely because the payments may look like banal and commonplace dispensations of money. If, by contrast, the payments are seen properly as exercises of prerogative power, the egregiousness

[35] ibid.

of them being made in any way that conflicts with the intention of parliament, which won a Civil War that in large part began on questions of supply, must be immediately and unavoidably confronted. It is damaging and unhelpful to reframe the issues as being in some sense less controversial because they are akin to private gifts rather than the exercise of public legal powers that must be lawfully deployed and at all times consistent with the intention of parliament. This issue is explored further below.

It is true that the different outcomes in the Court of Appeal and the House of Lords did not turn on the public or quasi-private nature of the legal powers underpinning the payments. However, counsel certainly attempted to *press* these kinds of arguments as reasons for the court to take a generous view of their exercise. It is submitted that the proper approach is to treat such payments as clearly exercises of prerogative power with all the constitutional implications that flow from that fact.[36] It is notable that Lord Nicholls, and the first instance judge incidentally, refused to decide the legal point as to the status of the power to make these payments at all.[37]

Hooper in the Court of Appeal – The Core Reasoning

The legal reasoning in this case is somewhat complex, not least because it was a very early example of the courts working through the correct way to deploy the new powers conferred on them by the Human Rights Act 1998 which had come into force a bare year earlier. The Court of Appeal determined that the government had a legal obligation to pay benefits to the widowers using the prerogative of *ex gratia* payments so as to bring their position in line with widows who received statutory payments. Lord Phillips MR, with Lord Justice Rix and Lord Justice Mantell in the Court of Appeal reached that destination after a series of legal steps.

The first step was to hold that on the original true construction of the relevant Acts, 'Parliament intended the express statutory provisions for payment of benefits to widows to occupy the entire field of entitlement to payment of benefits as a result of the death of a spouse'.[38] In essence, the original statute would have put *ex gratia* power into abeyance in this area. It followed that, prior to the Human Rights Act 1998 coming into force, 'it would have been an abuse of power for the minister to introduce a scheme of making matching extra-statutory [*ex gratia*] payments to widowers'.[39] The legislative intention of Parliament was clear: widowers should *not* be paid equivalent benefits to widows.

[36] Nothing can be drawn from the fact that counsel pressed these arguments which may have been made as a result of direct instructions from government officials. See also n 46 below.

[37] *Hooper (HL)* (n 15) [3]; *R (Hooper) v Secretary of State for Work and Pensions* (CA) [2003] EWCA Civ 813, [2003] 1 WLR 2623, [111].

[38] *Hooper (CA)* [135].

[39] ibid.

The next step was that the court then found that failing to pay the benefit in question to widowers was in breach of Art 14 of the European Convention on Human Rights, read in conjunction with Art 8. Under the Human Rights Act 1998, s 3(1), the court is required to construe legislation 'as far as possible' so as to comply with human rights norms.[40] The court held that the intention of parliament was so clear that it could *not* be construed so as to require the statutory payments to be made to widowers as well – this would flatly contradict what the statute said. However, the Court found that, even though this was so, s 3(1) could still be used in a much more limited way so as to make the statute no longer prevent the exercise of the *ex gratia* prerogative power in favour of the widowers:

> Acts of Parliament should be read, in so far as possible, as not precluding common law or prerogative powers of the Crown to take any action that may be necessary to prevent infringement of Convention rights.[41]

It is immediately apparent that this was a very odd use of s 3(1), since the abeyance principle is not itself a statutory provision that could justify the use of s 3 to 'construe' it. However, the reason for this convoluted reasoning becomes clear when one considers the terms of the Human Rights Act 1998, s 6, which is the power the Court of Appeal *wanted* to use. Section 6(1) states: 'It is unlawful for a public authority to act in a way which is incompatible with a Convention right.' The Court reasoned that this duty meant that the government came under an obligation to use its 'common law' powers to make *ex gratia* payments to the widowers equivalent to those received by widows under the legislative scheme. How the outcome reached by the Court is distinguishable in effect from interpreting the statute in effect to include widowers is not immediately obvious.

This ingenious way to secure the goal of providing a remedy that the court clearly sought to achieve met with a further problem. Section 6(2) provides that the s 6(1) duty 'does not apply' to an act if either primary legislation requires an incompatible act or incompatible primary legislation clearly authorised it.[42] Since it had just found the relevant legislation *was* clearly incompatible with the Convention rights, it seemed the court could not leverage the s 6(1) duty to achieve the Convention-compliant outcome it wanted. Hence the court's strange use of s 3(1) to re-read the original statute so that – as the Court saw it – it no longer blocked (via the abeyance principle) such payments being under the *ex gratia* power.[43]

[40] Section 3(1): 'So far as it is possible to do so, primary legislation and subordinate legislation must be read and given effect in a way which is compatible with the Convention rights.'

[41] ibid.

[42] Section 6(2): 'Subsection (1) does not apply to an act if – (a) as the result of one or more provisions of primary legislation, the authority could not have acted differently; or (b) in the case of one or more provisions of, or made under, primary legislation which cannot be read or given effect in a way which is compatible with the Convention rights, the authority was acting so as to give effect to or enforce those provisions.'

[43] Suffice to say that this somewhat novel approach to the use of the Human Rights Act 1998 has not been replicated in later case law.

Hooper – The Relationship between Statute and Prerogative

What is fascinating about *Hooper* for our purposes is that the case can be understood as falling under either the abeyance principle or the frustration principle, depending on how the statute is understood to affect widowers. The case was not *fought* in these terms because the two principles had not been clearly distinguished at that point in the case law. Nevertheless, there were serious disagreements about whether the legal power used by the government had been completely put beyond use, or whether it could be used, but not in ways that were inconsistent with the intention of parliament. In other words, this case is clear evidence that the two principles were unconsciously present in the case law long before they were formally distinguished in the academic literature and this case is strong evidence to that effect.

The Court of Appeal and the House of Lords split on which approach to apply. As we saw in the last subsection, the Court of Appeal thought that, before applying s 3(1), the statute occupied the entire field and so excluded the *ex gratia* payments prerogative. This was, in effect, an application of the abeyance principle. It is interesting that the court used the phrase 'occupy the entire field' about a power to make payments that was argued in the case to be a '*common law*' power rather than a prerogative. The 'occupy the field' language is normally to be found in the context of prerogative powers, and in particular the abeyance principle. This anomaly was not explored in the judgments, but it arguably further bolsters the claim that this area of law is in fact underpinned by prerogative not 'common law' powers exercised by the government.

However, as we also just saw, the Court of Appeal went on to hold that the obligation in s 3 to read all legislation compatibly with the Convention 'so far as is possible to do so' required the Court, in effect, to disregard the abeyance principle and that s 6(1) 'placed upon the Secretary of State an obligation to make extra-statutory payments'.[44] The problem for this argument is that if the statute 'occupies the field' then the prerogative power cannot be used by the executive at all because it is in abeyance in this area. Furthermore, the Court of Appeal had already held that the statute could not itself be construed to comply with the Human Rights Act 1998.

It is simply inconsistent to hold that the field was entirely covered by the statute and at the same time that the Crown could make *ex gratia* prerogative payments even though the intention of parliament could not be construed in any way that justified making the treatment of men and women interchangeable. In particular, the finding that clear intention of parliament was to treat men and women differently should immediately have precluded any use of the prerogative in a way that would contradict that intention. The Court of Appeal was therefore wrong

[44] ibid [136].

to hold that compensation was payable: its purported use of the Human Rights Act 1998, s 3(1) to get round this inconsistency was erroneous precisely because it was not using that power to actually re-read the statute in question but to displace the abeyance principle, which of course does not appear in that (or any) statute.

It is suggested that part of the reason why the important and well-established rule regarding the subordinate relationship of prerogative in relation to statute was missed is precisely as a result of the confusion over the legal status of *ex gratia* payments. Under the Harris doctrine, the making of such payments is a mere *freedom* to make gifts, possessed not just by the Crown but by everyone, to dispose of their property, and money, as they wish. It is easy to see how the making of such payments could be inappropriately differentiated from the intention of parliament if it is viewed as a mere freedom unrelated to royal prerogative. Indeed, statutory exclusion of such a 'freedom' might seem difficult if not impossible.[45]

If, by contrast, the scheme to make such payments is properly understood to flow from an exercise of the administration prerogative as a legal *power*, this immediately triggers all the constitutional concerns about the use of prerogative in ways that contradict the intention of parliament that go all the way back to the Glorious Revolution. It is suggested that this provides further ballast to the argument that it is *defining* prerogative powers in the very narrow sense suggested by Harris – which makes such powers *distinct* from 'third source' freedoms – that is confusing and unhelpful.

The confusion between whether making *ex gratia* payments is done under prerogative or is a mere freedom was not helped by counsel for the government conceding that the legislation did not preclude the making of *ex gratia* payments.[46] Further, and as Lord Phillips pointed out, it is somewhat paradoxical that counsel for the claimants conceded in his turn that the legislation *did* preclude payments where they would be paid to *all* widowers; his argument was that only the claimants and those in a similar position should receive *ex gratia* compensation. The Court of Appeal summarised the problem succinctly before rejecting the government's concession that the power to make *ex gratia* payments survived the passing of the legislation:

> It is unfortunate that we approach this important issue of the powers of the Secretary of State in circumstances where the two parties have made conflicting concessions against interest. The result is that the issue has not been fully explored in argument.[47]

[45] Indeed, Lord Hoffmann alludes to the fact that counsel for the government made an argument along these kinds of lines in the House of Lords judgment at [46]. See discussion at [46]–[47].

[46] As it happens, the government legal team included Philip Sales, now Lord Sales. It would not be reasonable to treat any of the arguments or concessions made in this case by counsel as representing the views of Lord Sales. Some of the arguments, and particularly the refusal to admit that statute placed any restriction on the exercise of the prerogative, may have been made on direct instructions. There is some limited evidence that there may indeed have been some instructions along these lines in the Court of Appeal judgment at [112].

[47] *Hooper (CA)* (n 37) [123].

Part of the difficulty in analysing the distinction between the abeyance and frustration principles in the context of *Hooper* is that at the time no distinction was drawn between the two principles. This is not unreasonable as the distinction was only properly identified during the *Miller I* litigation a decade later.[48] This made the concession by counsel for the government that much more significant because if the power to make *ex gratia* payments was *not* excluded by legislation, it is difficult to see what would stop it being used to mitigate the effects of the Act on widowers in circumstances where the frustration principle and abeyance principle were never distinguished.

If the frustration and abeyance principles *are* clearly distinguished, then the concession that legislation does *not* fully overlap with the prerogative power is less troublesome because the frustration principle would independently prevent the prerogative being exercised in a way that frustrates the intention of parliament, *even if* the legislation does not fully cover the field. The frustration principle in a sense 'sweeps up' situations where statute does not directly overlap.

A further example of the problems created by a lack of clarity over prerogative powers occurred in the House of Lords. Counsel argued that if the principle from *De Keyser* did apply to the *ex gratia* prerogative, then that would have a deleterious effect on other schemes such as the Criminal Injuries Compensation scheme (before it was put on a statutory footing).[49] This also misunderstands the nature of prerogative powers. Prerogatives are not like statutory powers which are usually quite narrow and 'all or nothing', so if a statutory power to do something conflicts with a later statutory provision it would indeed be wholly extinguished. Prerogatives are not as narrow as most statutory provisions. They are like the 'ground' under the statutory 'buildings'.[50] To the extent that a building sits on top of them, they go into abeyance – but if they are not overlapped, they can continue to be exercised as long as this is not in conflict with any statute. Hence counsel's argument that if legislation overlaps with the *ex gratia* power in *Hooper* that could imperil other *ex gratia* schemes was not tenable.

Hooper in the House of Lords

The House of Lords overruled the Court of Appeal, arguably applying the frustration principle rather than the abeyance principle. The majority of the judges held that the government *retained* the power to make *ex gratia* payments in theory. Lord Scott held that 'it is the provisions in … the 1992 Act that make it inappropriate

[48] R Craig (2016) (n 13) 1045–46; *R (Miller) v Secretary of State for Exiting the European Union* [2017] UKSC 5, [2018] AC 61, [2017] 2 WLR 583, [51].

[49] *Hooper (HL)* (n 15) [46].

[50] This analogy is explored by the author in more detail elsewhere: see R Craig, 'Restoring Confidence: Replacing the Fixed-term Parliaments Act 2011' (2018) 81 *Modern Law Review* 480, 495–97. See also O Jones (ed), *Bennion on Statutory Interpretation*, 6th edn (Butterworths, 2013) 168.

for the Secretary of State to create, via his common law power, a scheme entitling widowers to the same benefits'.[51] Lord Brown of Eaton-under-Heywood gave clearest expression of, in effect, the frustration principle:

> Given Parliament's unambiguous intention in the matter it would seem to me an obvious abuse of power for the Secretary of State to have introduced a scheme to make matching extra-statutory payments to widowers. Whatever his general common law power to make such payments, he could not lawfully exercise it inconsistently with Parliament's clearly expressed will.[52]

Since it was clear that parliament deliberately intended to discriminate against widowers, their Lordships applied the frustration principle, in effect, which meant that the government could not *exercise* the prerogative of *ex gratia* payments since this would undermine the effect and intention of the Act. Indeed, to do so would be an unlawful abuse of the *ex gratia* power because it would conflict with the obligations in the original statute and frustrate the intention of parliament. Considered in the round, this case is a fairly straightforward application of the *ratio* of *Fire Brigades Union*.[53]

The House of Lords then confronted the Court of Appeal argument that, despite the above, the new Human Rights Act 1998, s 6(1) obligation nevertheless obliged the Government to use the *ex gratia* power so as to satisfy the demands of the Convention. Lord Hoffmann's response to this was the correct one: as we saw above, the s 6(1) duty does not apply where the terms of an incompatible statute rule out the proposed action (s 6(2)), which was the case here. Lord Hoffmann put the point starkly in terms of the intention of parliament:

> If legislation cannot be read compatibly with Convention rights, a public authority is not obliged to subvert the intention of Parliament by treating itself as under a duty to neutralise the effect of the legislation.[54]

In other words, the s 6(1) duty was negatived by the presence of the incompatible legislation, *requiring* that payments only be made to widows. In short, Lord Hoffmann found that s 6(2) applied, and afforded the government a complete defence to the argument that it must use the *ex gratia* power to make payments also to widowers. He further held that there was 'no point in making' a declaration of incompatibility because 'both sections have been repealed'.[55]

This case incidentally also provides further evidence that the frustration principle applies regardless of whether the government proposes to use the prerogative either to take away *or to confer* rights or benefits. If the government

[51] *Hooper (HL)* (n 15) [95].

[52] ibid [123].

[53] *Fire Brigades Union* (n 4).

[54] *Hooper (HL)* (n 15) [51]. It is interesting to contrast this result with the obligations placed on the Crown following the *Factortame* litigation where the courts held that it could neutralise an Act by preventing the Crown from enforcing it.

[55] *Hooper (HL)* (n 15) [52].

had proposed to use the prerogative to pay widowers, it would still have been unlawful even though this would have been to *confer* not remove a benefit. The relevance of this particular point will be seen in the next section.

Overall, then, *Hooper* is a fascinating case study and a vivid application of the frustration principle. Notwithstanding attempts by counsel to muddy the basis of the legal power, the judges in effect applied rules indistinguishable from the frustration principle as if the legal power in issue was in fact a prerogative power. This is useful since making *ex gratia* payments is indeed a prerogative power and should be treated as such.

The Administration Prerogative and the Abeyance Principle

This section considers the application of the abeyance principle in this area in the context of the *Shrewsbury* case,[56] which concerned a decision by the government to reorganise local government administration. This might appear at first sight to be a quintessential example of the exercise of the administration prerogative, but for the fact that parliament had stepped in to regulate the area in 1992 through the Local Government Act 1992. The administration prerogative thus went into abeyance to the extent that it overlapped with the Local Government Act 1992. The Act mandated that changes to the structure of local government could only take place after a review and recommendation by the Electoral Commission, but such a review had not happened in this case.

Lord Justice Carnwath's Views on the Nature of the Legal Powers in *Shrewsbury*

The applicants claimed that the refusal of the government to follow the statutory procedures and instead attempt to use a non-statutory power was unlawful. The Court of Appeal held that they were bound by *ex parte C*. This meant the court was bound to hold that the powers exercised by the Crown included 'anything that could be done by a natural person'.[57] It is not entirely clear how reorganising local government is something a natural person can do.[58] Carnwath LJ made clear that he was bound by this authority, but his language made tolerably clear that he did not agree with Harris and Hale LJ on this point.

[56] *Shrewsbury & Atcham Borough Council, Congleton Borough Council v Secretary of State for Communities and Local Government* [2008] EWCA Civ 148; *Hooper (HL)* (n 15).

[57] ibid [44].

[58] The author is grateful to Gavin Phillipson for this point.

Carnwath LJ began by citing a number of heavyweight cases prior to *ex parte C* and said that it is 'not easy to reconcile such statements of high authority with the existence of a residual category of substantive "third source" powers, apart from the prerogative'.[59] The clearest example he gave is *Northumbria* where he pointed out that in that case, 'there was no suggestion that the Secretary of State could rely on some "third source" power' – in circumstances where such an argument might well have been expected.[60] The judge also mentioned that counsel for the applicants had 'sought to rewind the clock to a time when the accepted wisdom was that Ministers had, in the end, only two sources of power: statute or prerogative'. Importantly, Carnwath LJ then stated that he had 'some sympathy with that approach'.[61]

In the circumstances, this is a fairly clear steer as to the judge's actual views on alleged third source powers, which were of course made considerably clearer in the case of *New College* discussed earlier in this chapter. Carnwath LJ's position in this and other cases is entirely consistent with the view defended throughout this monograph and provides, it is suggested, material support for the arguments made here. Carnwath LJ also appeared to agree that the government possesses a general legal power to carry on its normal business. His language provides support for the claim that an administrative prerogative exists, particularly if the words 'general administrative' are substituted for 'ancillary' in the following quotation, which would do little damage to the sense of the excerpt:

> However, the examples given … ('the power to make contracts, employ servants and convey land') do seem to me, with respect, of limited assistance. They are in the nature of ancillary powers, necessary for the carrying out of any substantive governmental (or indeed non-governmental) function, whether statutory, corporate or common law.[62]

He held that the 'ordinary business' powers possessed by the government can be used alongside any 'statutory, corporate or common law' powers:

> I do not see that it is necessary to invoke a 'third source' category for that purpose. I see it as simply a necessary and incidental part of the ordinary business of central government, part of which is the promotion of new policies through legislation.[63]

He went on to distinguish, fairly sharply, the position of the government and that of natural persons whilst he also took careful aim at the contested claim that analogies with corporations are helpful in understanding the role of ministers and the Crown:

> Reference to the status of a Minister as 'corporation sole', or to analogies with the powers of natural persons, seem to me unhelpful … Unlike a local authority, the Crown is not

[59] ibid [47].
[60] *R v Secretary of State for the Home Department, ex parte Northumbria Police Authority* [1989] QB 26.
[61] *Shrewsbury* (n 56) [45].
[62] ibid.
[63] ibid [49].

> a creature of statute. As a matter of capacity, no doubt, it has power to do whatever a private person can do. But as an organ of government, it can only exercise those powers for the public benefit, and for identifiably 'governmental' purposes within limits set by the law.[64]

It is respectfully suggested that Carnwath LJ's view is, correctly, that there are no 'third source' powers of the Crown. Furthermore, his Lordship cautiously indicated that his views expressed in this case were still his views later in the case of *New College*, which must carry extra weight as that case was decided in the Supreme Court.[65] It is also worth mentioning that Carnwath LJ attracted the express, albeit cautious, agreement of Lord Justice Waller on whether the powers should be treated as untrammelled and akin to a natural person, or more limited and exercised 'for the public benefit' as governmental powers.[66] Lord Justice Richards expressly disagreed and endorsed the reasoning of Hale LJ, pointing out that he was the first instance judge in *ex parte C*.[67]

Carnwath LJ characterised the rule in *De Keyser's Hotel* as the 'inconsistency principle'. He defined it with some care:

> [W]whatever the scope of the Secretary of State's 'common law' powers, they may be expressly or implicitly excluded by a statutory scheme covering the same subject-matter.[68]

Crucially, he then expressly endorsed as 'correct' the key argument of counsel that the statute in this case had put any legal powers of the minister into abeyance such that they were unavailable as long as the statute was in force. In other words, the minister had no legal power to undertake the reorganisation of local government outside the existing statutory regime, pending the new legislation. It is important also to point out that Carnwath LJ's reasoning on this point was expressly endorsed by Waller LJ, forming a majority in the case in terms of reasoning:[69]

> So long as the existing system remained in place, it was wrong for [the minister] to pre-empt Parliament's decision by initiating and pursuing proposals under a wholly different 'common law' process[70]

Carnwath LJ even went so far as to hold that the government could have undertaken an informal process before approaching the Electoral Commission as the Local Government Act 1992 demanded, but he pointed out that the government had 'made quite clear' that 'the 1992 machinery was not to be used', holding that the question was whether the existing legislation covered the whole of the relevant 'field'. If it did, there were no residual common law powers.[71]

[64] ibid [48].
[65] *New College* (n 14) [34].
[66] *Shrewsbury* (n 56) [81].
[67] ibid [72]–[73].
[68] ibid [50].
[69] ibid [82].
[70] ibid [52]–[53]. This was counsel's submission that Carnwath LJ expressly endorsed as 'correct'.
[71] ibid [54]–[55].

On the face of it, then, it would appear that Carnwath LJ unequivocally held that the government had acted outside its powers and therefore unlawfully. It is suggested that this can only properly be understood, given the judge's clear views on the two available sources of law, as a finding that the administration prerogative that underpinned the government's decisions in this area had gone into abeyance to this extent.

Do the Frustration and Abeyance Principles Only Apply where Rights are Taken Away?

An important but ancillary issue is what the judge did next. Crucially, Carnwath LJ refused to treat the government's actions as constituting a nullity. In so doing, he drew a distinction between the *Shrewsbury* case and other case law that has consistently held that whenever the government acted outside its legal powers, the act itself is void *ab initio*. In one sense this was understandable because by the time the litigation reached the Court of Appeal, a subsequent statute had retrospectively validated all the prior steps.[72] Carnwath LJ was therefore recognising the new legal reality in a quite pragmatic way. However, his reasoning here raises an important separate issue that must be addressed.

Carnwath LJ drew a sharp distinction between the *Shrewsbury* case and previous case law. This difference turns on his characterisation of the previous cases as involving examples of the government exercising legal powers in a way that sought to override statute or *take away legal rights*. This is important because no rights were affected in *Shrewsbury* and that is how the judge sought to *distinguish* this case from previous case law. It will be recalled that in *Shrewsbury*, the court refused to quash the government's decision as a nullity. It is suggested that the 'inconsistency principle' set out by Carnwath LJ is a useful generic label for the frustration and abeyance principles although it relates possibly more to the former:

> The inconsistency principle was developed by the courts in response to attempts by the executive to override statutory controls, in a way which materially affected private or public rights: compensation for expropriation of property (*De Keyser*), compensation for criminal injuries (*Fire Brigades Union*), a police authority's right to determine policing policy (*Northumbria*).[73]

By contrast, Carnwath LJ held in the *Shrewsbury* case that the actions of the government did not have any legal effects on rights and in any event were retrospectively validated by parliament. This led the judge to *refuse* to hold that the decisions made during the process were a nullity. This was a pragmatic finding without wider implications – indeed Carnwath LJ went on to say that matters

[72] ibid [70].
[73] ibid [57].

might have been rather different if the claim had been brought earlier and there was no Act retrospectively remedying the situation.

As mentioned above Carnwath LJ purported to distinguish this case from *Fire Brigades Union*, *Northumbria* and *De Keyser* on the grounds that those three cases involved attempts to 'override statutory controls' and 'materially affected private or public rights', unlike *Shrewsbury*.[74] The rest of this section argues that the attempt to distinguish the facts of this case from the previous case law does not in fact withstand serious scrutiny. Or to put the point more bluntly, the judge was wrong to differentiate this case from previous case law in this area (regardless of whether the abeyance or frustration principle was applied).

In *De Keyser*, it is certainly true that statutory rights to compensation were at stake. No such statutory or other rights were at stake in *Shrewsbury*. This is much less important than it might first appear, however, because as the rest of this section will argue, the issue of rights is not actually relevant to the frustration and abeyance principles. In other words, and put simply, Carnwath LJ was wrong to *limit* the rule that prerogative may not be used to frustrate the intention of parliament where that would *remove* rights. On the contrary, both rules hold true even if the executive actions have no effect on rights or even *confer* rights. The key is the intention of parliament not the effect or otherwise on rights.

In *Fire Brigades Union* there were no private rights or public rights at stake, contrary to Carnwath LJ's claim. *Fire Brigades Union* is therefore vivid proof that the frustration principle relates to the intention of parliament not to rights. The case did not concern rights at all (as Phillipson and Alison Young argue in an article that takes the frustration principle as its starting point).[75] Compensation for criminal injuries was originally *ex gratia* and the statutory scheme in the *Fire Brigades Union* case was not yet in force. Furthermore, and in any event, the putative statutory scheme built in discretion for the Compensation Board to refuse awards if not satisfied by the conduct of the claimant. This means that there was no actual statutory, public or private *right* to compensation that was affected. Most importantly, the only provision of the statute actually frustrated was the implementation section, which, the House of Lords found, laid on the Home Secretary a continuing duty to consider *when* to bring it into force. Plainly, breaching this duty did not directly affect anyone's rights, but the frustration principle still applied and prevented the executive from acting.

A similar argument can be made about the *Northumbria* case, which concerned the prerogative of keeping the Queen's peace. A statute mandated that new equipment could not be used by the police unless sanctioned by the local police authority. The Home Secretary sought to make available tear gas and other riot gear outside the statutory scheme using prerogative. The police did not have any 'right' to that gear, nor did the police authority have any 'rights', in any meaningful sense, that

[74] ibid; *Att Gen v De Keyser's Hotel* [1920] AC 508; *Northumbria* (n 60); *Fire Brigades Union* (n 4).

[75] G Phillipson and AL Young, 'Would use of the prerogative to denounce the ECHR "frustrate" the Human Rights Act? Lessons from Miller' (2017) *Public Law (Brexit Special Extra Issue)* 150–75.

were overridden. Instead, the case was considered through the prism of 'duties'. In particular, the court held that the Home Secretary had a duty to keep the Queen's peace that underpinned his ability to make the equipment available.

In neither case does it make sense to argue that the prerogative was being used to override any 'rights', be they private or public. Yet in *Fire Brigades Union*, the government was still prevented from exercising the prerogative power because it would frustrate the intention of parliament in the relevant Act. Rights had nothing to do with it. If a prerogative cannot be used if it would frustrate the intention of parliament, then it follows, *a fortiori*, that the government cannot use a prerogative that is entirely unavailable because a statutory regime covers the field and has put the prerogative into abeyance, as Carnwath LJ effectively held in *Shrewsbury*. The latter case is therefore indistinguishable from *Fire Brigades Union* on this point and Carnwath LJ should have so held.

In *Northumbria*, the court held that there was no attempt to override any rights. On the contrary, the court held that since the provision of such equipment was for the 'benefit' of citizens, the government was entitled to pick and choose whether to make the equipment available through prerogative or through the statutory scheme.[76] It would be a considerable stretch to argue that this was an attempt to 'override statutory controls' given that the court in that case specifically held that the two sets of powers were not in conflict. As it happens, the author believes this case was wrongly decided precisely because the two sets of powers overlapped, and the abeyance principle should have applied, but the key issue for our purposes here is that no *rights* were at stake. The same was true in *Shrewsbury*.

Additionally, the case of *Hooper* illustrates why rights are not relevant to the frustration principle. As we saw earlier, any attempt to confer additional benefits on widowers would have had no effect on any rights possessed under the statute by widows. Nor, in fact, would it have conferred any rights to compensation on widowers, being *ex gratia* and discretionary. Yet the House of Lords held that exercising the prerogative in that way would be contrary to the intention of parliament and therefore an abuse of power that was *ultra vires*. This is a paradigm example of the frustration principle and applies even more obviously where the power is not even available to the government because it is in abeyance. Indeed, if the reasoning of the Court of Appeal in *Hooper* had prevailed, the statute would have been construed as putting the prerogative into abeyance and would been a very close analogue of the facts in *Shrewsbury*.

A final example that may be thought to illustrate the point in this section happened during the Brexit negotiations in 2017, when the possibility of the UK revoking its Treaty on European Union, Art 50 notification using the royal prerogative was seriously mooted. As the author argued in a blog at the time, such a use of the prerogative would clearly have frustrated the intention of the

[76] *Northumbria* (n 60) 53 per Purchas LJ. The author discusses this in more depth in R Craig, 'A Simple Application of the Frustration Principle: Prerogative, Statute and *Miller*' (2017) *Public Law (Brexit Special Extra Issue)* 25, 30–31.

European Union (Notification of Withdrawal) Act 2017 ('EUNoWA 2017').[77] This is because the intention of parliament in EUNoWA 2017 was for the UK to leave European Union, as can be seen in the preamble and s 1 of the Act:

> An Act to confer power on the Prime Minister to notify, under Article 50(2) of the Treaty on European Union, the United Kingdom's *intention to withdraw* from the EU. [Emphasis added]
>
> 1 Power to notify withdrawal from the EU
>
> (1) The Prime Minister may notify, under Article 50(2) of the Treaty on European Union, the United Kingdom's *intention to withdraw* from the EU. [Emphasis added]

What is most useful about this example is that EUNoWA 2017 demonstrates the intention of parliament that the public should *lose* some rights because it mandated that the UK should leave the EU in due course. If the prerogative had been used to revoke the Art 50 notification, that would have had the effect of *increasing* the rights of citizens rather than taking away any rights. This demonstrates that the frustration principle has nothing to do with taking away rights but instead is wholly determined by the intention of parliament. Prerogative cannot be used in any way that is inconsistent with the intention of parliament, regardless of whether that takes away rights, confers rights or has no effect on rights.

Application to the *Shrewsbury* Case

When these clear principles are applied to the case of *Shrewsbury*, the reasoning of Carnwath LJ may be partially challenged. His Lordship was right to say that the later Act retrospectively rendered the point somewhat moot, but it is important to emphasise that the issue of 'affecting private or public rights' is strictly irrelevant to the application of the frustration or abeyance principles (or the 'inconsistency principle' as the judge put it, which appears to encompass both principles). The abeyance principle means that the prerogative was unavailable because statute had covered the field – any attempt to undertake actions normally grounded in the administration prerogative must by definition be *ultra vires* because the government had no such legal powers after the Act passed. It does not matter that the government's actions did not 'affect' legal rights or had no legal consequences.[78]

[77] ukconstitutionallaw.org/2017/10/16/robert-craig-why-an-act-of-parliament-would-be-required-to-revoke-notification-under-article-50.

[78] It is also worth mentioning for the sake of clarity that this does not mean that the administration prerogative is in abeyance in relation to all policy matters. The prerogative is only in abeyance in the context of the reorganisation of local government, not generally. A similar scenario in the case of *XH*, in the context of passports, is discussed, along with an analysis of the frustration and abeyance principles, in R Craig (n 76) 32–33. See *R (XH) v Secretary of State for the Home Department* [2017] EWCA Civ 41, [2017] 2 WLR 1437.

This example again helps to show why it is positively unhelpful to characterise the relevant actions as being done via a 'third source freedom' rather than under a specific legal power. It is much less clear, under the third source power approach, that the government is limited in its legal power to actions that Waller LJ described as 'simply preliminary' in his concurring judgment.[79] This would include activities such as publishing a White Paper, which is a necessary preliminary to any Act of Parliament and cannot sensibly be argued to have been put into abeyance by the statutory regime.[80]

If the government's options are wrongly characterised as being anything a natural person has the freedom to do, the limitations necessarily concomitant on an Act of Parliament that prescribes what the government can do are much more likely to be disregarded, as indeed happened in this case. It is suggested that if, by contrast, the legal options had been couched in terms of the administration prerogative, the statutory requirements in the Local Government Act 1992 (which required the procedure be conducted in accordance with its strict limitations) would have been much less likely to have been disregarded.

The government cannot act using prerogative where statute has covered the field and it is submitted that in this case, the Act required the government to follow the statutory procedure involving the Electoral Commission before it could reorganise local government. Even though the problem was fixed retrospectively by subsequent legislation, it would have been better if Carnwath LJ had made clear that the 'inconsistency' between the Act and the legal powers purportedly exercised rendered those actions *ultra vires* prior to the retrospective validation. This would have sent a clear signal in the event of any future attempts by the government to rely on the administration prerogative when it was unavailable because a statutory regime had put it in abeyance to that extent.

Part III: Conclusion

Part III began by challenging the claim made by Harris and others that there exists a third source of power available to ministers. In claiming that such a power is in fact mythical, it was also suggested that Perry's claim that the Crown also possesses certain non-legal powers did not withstand serious scrutiny. Ministers and courts rightly operate on the basis that the actions undertaken by government are done intentionally and in the acknowledgment that legal effects flow inevitably from those actions. Chapter ten sought to identify a narrower basis for ministerial action in the slightly forgotten prerogative perhaps best known as the 'administration prerogative'.

[79] *Shrewsbury* (n 56) [82].

[80] There are examples of Acts which were not preceded by White Papers but such exceptional examples need not concern us here.

Part III also considered the third source freedom case law and sought to demonstrate that the cases are better understood as orthodox examples of the use and perhaps misuse of prerogative powers by the government. It has further been suggested that the notion of third source or common law powers is incoherent when applied to the government. The better approach would be to treat exercises of government power using prerogative as a separate and important legal category that is subject to significant, familiar public law constraints.

If this is accepted, then it will be seen that this area of law provides a fertile source of new examples in the case law considering familiar public law questions such as the extent to which a prerogative power can be used to implement an important new policy in the absence of recent examples of its use. This can be seen in the vexed question discussed in the previous chapter of whether the administration prerogative can be understood to provide sufficient and clear legal grounding for maintaining a list of people who should not be permitted to work with children. This kind of legal scrutiny can be favourably compared to the non-existent scrutiny that the legality of the policy actually received in that case, where it was simply assumed that keeping such a list was lawful because of the banal and irrelevant fact that ordinary people can make lists.

The previous chapter also considered a wholly separate prerogative which was labelled the prerogative of preventing crime but is perhaps more familiarly known under the rubric of the prerogative of keeping the peace. It was argued that Megarry VC in *Malone* demonstrated an instinctive grasp of the importance of this legal power and, in a sense, applied it in parts of his judgment, notwithstanding that he had previously held that Malone's phone could be tapped because no law prevented it. Properly understood, it is suggested that *Malone* is in fact an example of the exercise of the prerogative of preventing crime and it is a matter for the courts how that prerogative is interpreted and understood in future case law based on historical examples and precedents evidencing the prerogative of keeping the peace.

Equally, this chapter has examined the conceptually distinct area of law where prerogative intersects with statute. This triggers the consideration of familiar principles known as the frustration principle and the abeyance principle, as has happened on a number of occasions in the area of so-called third source powers. As we saw in *New College*, where the exercise of the administration prerogative would frustrate the intention of parliament, the courts will quash it as an abuse of power. Similarly in *Hooper*, it was clear that the courts would not countenance the prerogative being used in a way that contradicted the intention of parliament, although it is also possible to consider this case alternatively as one where the statute overlapped with the prerogative and put it into abeyance. Finally, *Shrewsbury* showed that where prerogative is put into abeyance by a statutory regime, the courts will step in to prevent the misuse of prerogative power – although in that case a later Act of Parliament retrospectively validated the actions taken by the government.

Conclusion

12

Summary and Outlook

English law once started with the Crown. Indeed, ministers of the Crown still bring forward Bills they hope to be clothed with the authority of the representatives of the people in parliament. *Modern* English law, however, starts with parliament. The Crown-in-Parliament is now the fountain of justice. This is not just because parliament is where ordinary people can seek redress, through their representatives, from ministers of the Crown. It is also because the many intervening centuries since the Crown was supreme have seen the radical restructuring of the constitution, not least as a function of the Glorious Revolution. As we saw in chapter five, the authority, jurisdiction and power to grant remedies was conferred on the modern, wholly statutory courts by parliament and the original prerogative courts were abolished in 1873. The prerogative jurisdiction of the ancient courts, rooted in the prerogative of justice, was thereby put into abeyance. We have come a long way from the claim in the opening line of this book that English law starts with the Crown. But then the United Kingdom constitution has also come a long way. The Glorious Revolution, Act of Settlement 1701 and the Judicature Acts 1873–75 saw to that. One purpose of this book has been to tell the story of the constitutional shift from Crown to Parliament.

Core Arguments of the Book

Despite these enormous changes, there remains an important set of legacy prerogative legal powers whose monarchical origin predates parliament. They are held by the Crown in the modern era. Those powers are exclusive to the Crown, and they are residual in nature. There are thus only two ultimate sources of original legal and jurisdictional authority in England and Wales: the Crown and the Crown-in-Parliament. Parliament confers statutory powers on the executive. Further, as we saw in chapter five, it deliberately left the remaining legislative prerogative powers at the time of the Glorious Revolution in the hands of the Crown, which in turn conferred the executive aspect of those powers onto ministers. All Crown non-statutory legal powers, broadly defined, are prerogative powers. Indeed, as chapter six argued, the Crown may usefully be defined as the bearer of all non-statutory legal prerogative powers, including immunities, liabilities and duties.

All legal power was originally rooted in the Crown. This included the most important domestic prerogative which is the prerogative of justice. This prerogative, as outlined in chapter five, was the originator of common law through the king's judges. The set of common law judicial decisions is a discrete set of binding legal norms, just as prerogative executive powers comprise a discrete set of binding legal norms. The existence of these different sets of legal norms is of course not denied and is distinct from the claim made in this book that the source of the legitimacy, validity and authority of judicial decisions at common law was once grounded in prerogative and is now grounded in statute.

After the Revolution, the remaining prerogative powers effectively received the implicit approval and imprimatur of parliament as a set of distinct legal powers.[1] Tempting though it is to follow through the logic of Kershaw's ingenious claim that parliament effectively adopted and then delegated the remaining prerogative powers to the Crown at the time of the Glorious Revolution, the better view is probably that the prerogative remains a distinct and original source of legal powers. Nonetheless, Hart's 'itch to uniformity' is strong,[2] and there would be a certain constitutional neatness in the claim that *all* current legal norms can ultimately be traced back to the supreme legal authority of a democratically underpinned Crown-in-Parliament – particularly now that the Crown, through its ministers, now resides within parliament. Too neat, perhaps, in a famously flexible, uncodified and organic constitution with a thousand years of relevant history.

Reconciling Dicey and Blackstone

This book has sought to reconcile as far as possible the two leading definitions of royal prerogative given by Blackstone and Dicey (chapters two and three). Much of the substance of the book has involved working through the logic of the simple premise that all the non-statutory powers of the Crown are prerogative legal powers and that they are exclusive to the Crown. In addressing Blackstone, the claim that all legal powers of the Crown are prerogative powers has inevitably required the rejection of any interpretation of his work, particularly by Wade (chapters four and seven), that ascribes *other* types of legal powers, such as common law powers, to the Crown. Equally, it has been claimed (chapter seven) that all actions of the executive not based on statute are either the exercise of executive prerogative powers or the separate legal actions of ministers distinct from their appointment as such via prerogative. Making good this claim involved extending Dicey's definition to mean that *all* remaining legal powers, duties and immunities of the Crown were rooted in prerogative power without distinction.

[1] D Kershaw, 'Revolutionary Amnesia and the Nature of Prerogative Power' (2022) 20(3) *International Journal of Constitutional Law* 1071.

[2] HLA Hart, *The Concept of Law* (Oxford University Press, 1961) 32.

If the only non-statutory powers that the Crown possesses are prerogative powers, then, as chapter seven argued, it necessarily follows that the Crown does not possess any powers at common law. Common law is properly defined as the complete set of judicial precedents, although we have also noted that it can sometimes be defined more narrowly as the judicial precedents flowing from the court of King's Bench. Common law was originally royal law. Given that the prerogative of justice, which was the source of validity and authority for the common law until that point, went into abeyance, there is no residual element of the prerogative of justice that remains available to the courts. It is suggested that not only is this *descriptively* accurate, it benefits from also reflecting the slow democratisation of the system over the last century or so including placing the judicial system on to a statutory, footing as the changes in the late nineteenth century have been confirmed and extended over time.[3] Defined as a putative non-statutory, non-prerogative third *source* of judicial legitimacy, authority or jurisdiction, 'common law' does not exist.

The importance of consistently framing the legal powers of the Crown in terms of prerogative is that it helps to illustrate the chasm between prerogative and common law powers. Crown powers are older, separate and independent of the common law powers possessed by citizens. Prerogative powers are exclusive to the Crown, as Blackstone said, and underpin all the non-statutory legal actions of the Crown, as Dicey pointed out. The common law legal powers of citizens may be vindicated by seeking a remedy from the formerly royal courts. The functioning of the common law may seem somewhat 'backwards' to modern eyes, as chapter seven argued. Originally, the courts granted *remedies* and sought to correct wrongs. From that starting point, legal rights were in a sense reverse engineered, at least originally. The modern view appears increasingly to be that courts vindicate *rights* and protect the exercise of powers and then fashion a remedy to suit. This approach can also be seen in ancient civil systems where the maxim *ubi ius ibi remedium* was an important ideal.[4] In England and Wales, as argued in chapter two, it was probably more accurate to say *ubi remedium ibi ius*.[5]

The reason these conceptual framings are so important is because it is mistaken to describe *the Crown* as possessing 'rights' and 'powers' at common law: when properly viewed through the historical prism of seeking remedies for wrongs from the courts, the idea of the Crown seeking a remedy for itself via courts it established makes little or no sense. Nor does this model describe what actually happens. Instead, as chapter four argued, the Crown has always had prerogative powers and rights that operate in their own 'domain' and are merely *recognised* by the (formerly) royal courts. The Crown could not, and cannot, sue or be sued

[3] See, for example, the Senior Courts Act 1981 and Constitutional Reform Act 2005.

[4] 'Where there is a right, there is a remedy', or perhaps more colloquially, 'where justice requires, a remedy will be found'.

[5] 'Where there is a remedy, there is a right', or perhaps 'where a remedy can be secured, a right will be generated'. See also discussion in ch 1.

in court. Citizens, by contrast, sought *remedies* for their wrongs from the Crown's judges, and only by a process of evolution, as set out in chapter two, were powers and rights reverse engineered from these remedies. This slow and organic process developed and changed further over time.

Issues with Wade's Analysis

If the prerogative rights, powers and immunities of the Crown are correctly disaggregated, parsed and (via the concept of *remedies*, compared properly to common law powers possessed by citizens), it is much easier to recognise just how mistaken it is to equate common law powers with anything done by the Crown. As chapters four and seven showed, Wade is the primary offender here. He made the startling assumption that there is some equivalence between Crown prerogative powers in public law and powers possessed by private citizens in private law. His primary aim appears to have been to prevent a separate stream of public law actions developing, with the potential concomitant effects on the volume of purely procedural litigation – but his fears were misplaced. Further, and more concerningly, Wade's purported taxonomy led to a number of legal absurdities.

His two central claims were, first, that a true prerogative must have legal effects and, secondly, a true prerogative must be unique to the Crown such that any legal powers of the Crown that are said to be analogous to those exercised by ordinary people are in some sense 'common law' powers. Both these claims are mistaken. The first, discussed in chapter four, is probably more serious because it is long established that prerogative cannot be used in a way that is inconsistent with statute or common law. Taken seriously, therefore, Wade's definition would reduce the class of true prerogatives to a null set.

The quickest way to understand the error in Wade's second claim, discussed in chapter seven, that the Crown has common law powers, is to consider the prerogative of making *ex gratia* payments. A moment of reflection reveals that the allocation of public money for, say, criminal injuries compensation has no private law correlate, not least because the funds are public moneys for the disbursement of which the government is accountable to both parliament and, ultimately, the people. Wade extrapolated further from his mistaken assertion that some powers that are similar to common law powers of citizens are not, for that reason, prerogative powers. He put forward, as an example, the claim that the prime minister is effectively 'employed' by the Crown. This argument is untenable.

The Crown

In considering the claim that the Crown has common law powers, it is an unavoidable necessity to consider the Crown itself and its legal status. The concept of the Crown is a challenging one and there are legitimate disagreements about its meaning and definition. Some have argued that it is a corporation, either sole or aggregate, at common law. It has also been suggested that the Crown retains a residual capacity as a natural person as a matter of law. Chapter six challenged each of these claims. It suggested an alternative way to understand the legal status, role and importance of the Crown. Rather than attempting to pigeonhole the Crown into one or other common law straitjacket, it has been suggested that the Crown is *sui generis* and defined as the bearer of the remaining prerogative powers. It remains to this day outside the jurisdiction of the common law courts.

The claim that the Crown is outside the jurisdiction of the common law required careful consideration, in chapter eight, of the effect of the Crown Proceedings Act 1947, which appears to make the Crown liable at common law in tort and contract. This assumption was challenged and an alternative reading of the effect of the Act – in light of *M v Home Office* – was put forward.[6] The Act in no way constituted the Crown as a legal person at common law and attempting to read the Act as doing so was argued to be a red herring. It was further argued that the legal relationship between the Crown and ministers remained entirely one of prerogative. This means that where a minister undertakes what looks like a private law transaction on behalf of the government, it is assumed that the *vires* of the underlying prerogative relationship between the minister and the Crown is sound. In other words, if there are no liminal public law grounds to challenge the transaction, then it can be treated as in effect a private law action between the minister or department and the counter party. If, however, there is a flaw in the exercise of the prerogative in public law terms, that will affect the apparently private law aspect between the minister and the other party.

The Case Law

Chapter nine then considered a further corollary of the claim that the Crown exercises only prerogative powers: that the Crown cannot logically possess or exercise so-called 'third source' powers or freedoms. Such powers are sometimes described as actions that the Crown can undertake that are not prohibited by common law or statute. This book has argued that the better view is that the Crown only exercises prerogative legal powers. The idea that the Crown can operate without specific legal authority is not reconcilable with even the thinnest conception of the rule of law. It is further not tenable to claim that the Crown has a series of non-legal powers. The book has argued for the revival and recognition of the prerogative of administration and for the reframing of *Malone* as in effect exploring the boundaries of the prerogative of keeping the peace.[7] Chapter ten argued that what it

[6] *M v Home Office* [1994] 1 AC 377.
[7] *Malone v Metropolitan Police Commissioner* [1979] Ch 344.

termed the 'administration prerogative' underpins much of the day-to-day work done by the government (such as setting policies, entering contracts and writing internal memos) that have been mistakenly thought to need some 'third source' of legal or non-legal powers or freedoms to explain them.

Chapter eleven argued that much of the case law concerning so-called third source powers are disguised reviews of the exercise of prerogative powers, in particular the administration prerogative, when the exercise of such powers intersects with statute. In order to understand that relationship it is necessary to distinguish two types of interaction between statute and prerogative, labelled the abeyance and the frustration principles. Where statute overlaps with prerogative, it is not possible for the government to use prerogative power because the statute supersedes the prerogative power and puts it into abeyance. The second type of interaction is where a statute does *not* overlap with an existing prerogative. It then remains available to the government. This is, however, subject to the principle that the exercise of any prerogative may not be done in a way that frustrates the intention of parliament in any Act.[8]

Chapter eleven also argued that the third source power case law must be reframed if the arguments put forward in this book are accepted. Far from being examples of the government's alleged ability to do anything not prohibited by law (itself an alarming proposition), third source case law should be understood as framed through the prism of the exercise of prerogative powers, usually the administrative prerogative but perhaps also the *ex gratia* prerogative or even the prerogative of keeping the peace. This would allow the judicial deployment of long-standing principles governing the exercise of prerogative powers without needing to reinvent the wheel. Crucially, the mistaken presumption that a government is free to do anything unless it breaches statute or common law would then be rejected. Instead, precedents for any given action, even in a modernised context, would need to be identified in the usual way in the prerogative domain. As Lord Reid put it in *Burmah Oil*, 'the proper approach is a historical one: how was it used in former times and how has it been used in modern times'.[9] Usefully, the case law in this area throws extra light on the relationship between prerogative and statute and how the courts instinctively deal with situations where prerogative powers are either in conflict with, or are overlapped by, statutory provisions.

Potential Consequences of the Claims in this Book

The more ambitious claim of this book has been its attempt to reframe the entire legal architecture of the United Kingdom constitution, and in particular the status

[8] R Craig, 'A Simple Application of the Frustration Principle: Prerogative, Statute and Miller' (2017) *Public Law (Brexit Special Issue)* 25.

[9] *Burmah Oil Company (Burma Trading) Ltd v Lord Advocate* [1965] AC 75, 101.

and source of authority of the courts. The remainder of this chapter considers what might be the practical consequences of such a claim.

More pragmatically, the book has also attempted to reframe consideration of the third source case law and reanalysed judicial review of keeping the peace and the administration prerogative. Potential future ripple effects might usefully be considered using the concept of the separation of powers. One potential consequence is that in future it is hoped it will be necessary for the executive to think carefully about whether a desired outcome or exercise of prerogative power can be identifiably brought within the historic fixed previous usage of that power, or whether fresh statutory authorisation is needed. This follows inevitably if the claim that 'the government can do anything that is not prohibited' is abandoned. This issue involves careful consideration of the boundary between executive prerogative power and the need to seek legislative authority when the limits of that power are reached. This issue therefore operates on the executive and legislative boundary.

A second potential consequence relates to the boundary between the judiciary and the executive exercise of prerogative powers, another separation of powers boundary. The arguments in this book could frame a novel analysis of the development of judicial review of prerogative powers. Notably, the novel extension of jurisdiction to include some prerogative powers did not occur until the jurisdiction of the courts became wholly statutory. This fact may be of considerably greater significance than hitherto realised. It would be valuable to explore how the courts' review of prerogative and the standards imposed by the courts on its use has developed over time. Those standards are unsurprisingly grounded in analogous judicial review approaches to statutory powers, to which judges obviously defaulted, but there are some important differences. Furthermore, the longstanding debate over whether common law or *ultra vires* is the proper basis of judicial review was predicated on a universal but mistaken assumption that the jurisdiction of the courts is non-statutory.[10]

The final section of this Conclusion briefly addresses the third classical separation of powers boundary: the relationship between the judiciary and parliament. It suggests that wider recognition of the modern statutory source of the jurisdictional authority of the courts could inhibit any moves towards judicial challenge to the validity of controversial statutory provisions, which has been mooted in recent years. This issue is not core to the book, but instead is perhaps an intriguing codicil that logically flows from the core arguments made here.

Cavaliers and Roundheads

A useful starting point is to attempt to place some of its themes into the context of the most ancient constitutional dispute in this country: the divide between

[10] C Forsyth (ed), *Judicial Review and the Constitution* (Hart Publishing, 2000).

the Cavaliers and Roundheads. The Cavaliers were royalists; the Roundheads were parliamentarians. The ripples of the civil war between the Cavaliers and Roundheads continue to lap at our constitutional shores. Of course, the substantive dispute is long over. In a sense, we are all Roundheads now. It might be interesting, however, to briefly consider whether there are any modern echoes of that ancient dispute. It is worth mentioning immediately that in strict constitutional terms, and as Tomkins has pointed out, the making of an Act of Parliament represents the historic settlement between the two camps.[11] The Crown now operates, through ministers, *inside* parliament and when an agreement is reached between the Crown and Members of Parliament, and an Act is passed, the highest form of law is thereby created.

Despite this, there have been some recent suggestions that the judiciary may one day hold that in certain circumstances a provision of a statute may not be given effect by the courts. To be clear, any such move would be to cross the Rubicon from judicial review of executive powers to judicial review of legislation itself, which is quite another matter. Although there are other well known *dicta* which would need to be considered in a fuller treatment of the issues canvassed in this subsection,[12] Lord Carnwath's intervention in *Privacy* is sufficient to set the stage for now.

> [A]lthough it is not necessary to decide the point, I see a strong case for holding that, consistently with the rule of law, binding effect cannot be given to a clause which purports wholly to exclude the supervisory jurisdiction of the High Court.[13]

It is on this issue, extreme and seemingly unlikely as it may be that this outcome ever actually occurs, that the ghosts of Cavaliers and Roundheads past may again rear their heads. If the courts were ever to refuse to give effect to a statute, it is not tenable to suggest that this would be an *intra vires* exercise of their existing legal powers rooted, as they are, in their wholly statutory jurisdiction. On no sensible view could it be argued that the statutory jurisdiction conferred by parliament on the courts could be interpreted that way or that parliament could ever have intended to confer such a legal power. Refusing to implement a provision would be to act *outside* that statutory jurisdiction, by definition. It would be, literally, *ultra vires* and would incidentally spell the end of the *ultra vires* doctrine as the basis of judicial review.[14]

It follows, therefore, that the only possible *legal* basis for such a radical decision must be non-statutory. Within the parameters and conceptual architecture defended in this book, there is only one other source of legal authority beyond statute. That is royal prerogative. In other words, if the courts were ever to disobey parliament and act outside their jurisdiction by refusing to give legal effect to an

[11] A Tomkins, *Public Law* (Oxford University Press, 2003) ch 3.

[12] See, for example, Lady Hale's infamous *dictum* in *Jackson*.

[13] *R (Privacy International) v Investigatory Powers Tribunal* [2019] UKSC 22, [2020] AC 491, [144].

[14] C Forsyth, 'Of Fig Leaves and Fairy Tales: The Ultra Vires Doctrine, the Sovereignty of Parliament and Judicial Review' (1996) 55 *Cambridge Law Journal* 122.

Act, they would inescapably be seeking to suspend or dispense with an Act of Parliament *by regal authority*, in direct breach of Article I, Bill of Rights 1689. This is because there is no third source of judicial legitimacy, authority or legal power outside the prerogative of justice or statute. An appeal today to a putative alternative ultimate legal authority would, on the logic defended in this book, inescapably be an appeal to royal law and its prerogative foundations. To refuse to give effect to a provision of an Act of Parliament would be to revive the ancient battle between Crown and parliament that was thought to have been decently interred centuries ago. It almost goes without saying that this would precipitate a serious constitutional clash between parliament and any judges who had refused to implement the Act.

It is hoped that the arguments in this book may form an extra obstacle to the, with luck, vanishingly remote possibility of any direct judicial challenge to statutory authority. The book aims to demonstrate how, in the modern era, the authority and legitimacy of the courts and of common law is now entirely and solely rooted in parliament. Modern Cavalier Ministers and modern Roundhead Members of Parliament inhabit parliament now, and its authority is final and should be unquestionable. Any judicial decision that refuses to give effect to the provisions of a statute allegedly grounded on the authority of the 'common law' would necessarily involve reviving an older, regal view of the source of judicial authority. In terms of the positive constitution, this really ought to be legally impossible after the Glorious Revolution, the Act of Settlement 1701 and the Judicature Acts 1873–75 but it is hoped that this book may help nail another board across that particular door to a constitutional blind alley.

BIBLIOGRAPHY

Allen, CK, *Hamlyn Lectures: 'The King's Peace'* (Stevens & Sons, 1953).

Allen, J, *Inquiry into the Rise and Growth of the Royal Prerogative in England* (1849).

Allen, JG, 'The Office of the Crown' (2018) 77 *Cambridge Law Journal* 298.

Allen, JG, *Non-Statutory Executive Powers and Judicial Review* (Cambridge University Press, 2022).

Allan, T, *Constitutional Justice: A Liberal Theory of the Rule of Law* (Oxford University Press, 2001).

Anderson, S, 'Public Law' in W Cornish and others (eds), *The Oxford History of the Laws of England* (Oxford University Press, 2010).

Anson, WR, *The Law and Custom of the Constitution*, 2nd edn (Clarendon Press, 1896).

Arendt, H, *The Human Condition* (University of Chicago Press, 1958).

Aristotle, *Politics*.

Austin, J, *Province of Jurisprudence Determined* (John Murray, 1832).

Aylmer, GE, 'From Office-Holding to Civil Service: The Genesis of Modern Bureaucracy: The Prothero Lecture', *Transactions of the Royal Historical Society*, 1980, Vol 30 (1980).

Bacon, M, *A New Abridgement of the Law* (1768).

Bagehot, W, *The English Constitution* (1867).

Baker, J, *An Introduction to English Legal History*, 5th edn (Oxford University Press, 2019).

Baker, JH, 'Coke's Note-Books and the Sources of His Reports' (1972) 30 *Cambridge Law Journal* 59.

Banfield, A and Flynn, G, 'Activism or Democracy? Judicial Review of Prerogative Powers and Executive Action' (2015) 68(1) *Parliamentary Affairs* 135.

Barber, NW, *The United Kingdom Constitution: An Introduction* (Oxford University Press, 2021).

Barendt, E, *An Introduction to Constitutional Law* (Oxford University Press, 1998).

Bartlett, G and Everett, M, 'The Royal Prerogative' (Briefing Paper No 03861, House of Commons Library, 17 August 2017).

Bentham J, *A Fragment on Government*, W Harrison (ed) (Basil Blackwell, 1948).

Beynon, H, 'Prerogative to Supply Plastic Baton Rounds and CS Gas to the Police' [1987] *Public Law* 146.

Billings, P and Pontin, B, 'Prerogative Powers and the Human Rights Act: Elevating the Status of Orders in Council' [2001] *Public Law* 21.

Bingham, T, *The Rule of Law* (Penguin, 2011).

Blackburn, R, 'The Summoning and Meeting of New Parliaments in the United Kingdom' (1989) 9(2) *Legal Studies* 165.

Blackburn, R, 'Monarchy and the Personal Prerogatives' [2004] *Public Law* 546.

Blackburn, R, 'The Prerogative Power of Dissolution of Parliament: Law, Practice, and Reform' [2009] *Public Law* 766.

Blackburn, R, 'The 2010 General Election Outcome and Formation of the Conservative-Liberal Democrat Coalition Government' [2011] *Public Law* 30.

Blackstone, W, *Commentaries on the Laws of England* (1753).

Blackstone, W, *Commentaries on the Laws of England* (1765–69), edited by Hardcastle Browne (St Paul West Publishing, 1897).

Blackstone, W, *Commentaries on the Laws of England* (1765–69), reprinted in in G Jones, *The Sovereignty of the Law* (Macmillan Press, 1973).

Blick, A, 'Emergency Powers and the Withering of the Royal Prerogative' (2014) 18 *International Journal of Human Rights* 195.

Blick, A and Gordon, R, 'Using the Prerogative for Major Constitutional Change: The United Kingdom Constitution and Article 50 of the Treaty on European Union' (The Constitution Society, 2016).

Bogdanor, V (ed), *The British Constitution in the Twentieth Century* (Oxford University Press, 2003).

Bradley, AW, 'Police Powers and the Prerogative' [1988] *Public Law* 298.

Bradley, AW, Ewing, KD and Knight, CJS, *Constitutional and Administrative Law*, 17th edn (Pearson, 2018).

Bracton, H de, *Bracton on the Laws and Customs of England* (1268).

Brazier, R, '"Monarchy and the Personal Prerogatives": A Personal Response to Professor Blackburn' [2005] *Public Law* 45.

Brazier, R, 'Legislating About the Monarchy' (2007) 66 *Cambridge Law Journal* 86.

Brazier, R, 'A Small Piece of Constitutional History' (2012) 128 *Law Quarterly Review* 315.

Brazier, R, 'Royal Assent to Legislation' (2013) 129 *Law Quarterly Review* 184.

Brooke, H, 'The History of Judicial Independence in England and Wales' (2015) *European Human Rights Law Review* 446.

Burgess, G, *The Politics of the Ancient Constitution* (Palgrave, 1992).

Burke, E, 'Reflections on the Revolution in France, November 1790' in I Kramnick (ed), *The Portable Edmund Burke* (Penguin, 1999) 416.

Burnett, I, 'What's in a Name? The High Court and its Divisions' *(Pilgrim Fathers Lecture 2019, Plymouth)* (14 November 2019).

Campbell-Smith, D, *Follow the Money* (Penguin, 2008).

Cane, P, 'Prerogative Acts, Acts of State and Justiciability' (1980) *International & Comparative Law Quarterly* 680.

Chitty, J, *A Treatise on the Law of the Prerogatives of the Crown: And the Relative Duties and Rights of the Subject* (Butterworth, 1820).

Cohen, E, *The Growth of the British Civil Service 1780–1939* (Frank Cass & Co, 1965).

Cohn, M, 'Medieval Chains, Invisible Inks: On Non-Statutory Powers of the Executive' (2005) 25(1) *Oxford Journal of Legal Studies* 97.

Cohn, M, 'Judicial review of Non-Statutory Executive Powers after Bancoult: A Unified Anxious Model' [2009] *Public Law* 260.

Cohn, M, 'Non-Statutory Executive Powers: Assessing Global Constitutionalism in a Structural Institutional Context' (2015) 64 *International and Comparative Law Quarterly* 65.

Cohn, M, 'Tension and Legality: Towards a Theory of the Executive Branch' (2016) *Canadian Journal of Law & Jurisprudence* 321.

Cornford, T, 'Legal Remedies against the Crown and its Officers' in M Sunkin and S Payne, *The Nature of the Crown: A Legal and Political Analysis* (Oxford University Press, 1999) 233.

Cox, N, 'The Gradual Curtailment of the Royal Prerogative,' (2012) 25 *Denning Law Journal* 65.

Cox, N, *The Royal Prerogative and Constitutional Law: A Search for the Quintessence of Executive Power* (Routledge, 2021).

Craig, P, 'Prerogative, Precedent and Power' in C Forsyth and I Hare (eds), *The Golden Metwand and the Crooked Cord: Essays in Honour of William Wade QC* (Oxford University Press, 1998) 65.

Craig, P, 'Competing Models of Judicial Review' [1999] *Public Law* 428.

Craig, P, 'Constitutional Foundations, the Rule of Law and Supremacy' [2003] *Public Law* 92.

Craig, P, *UK, EU and global administrative law, foundations and challenges (The Hamlyn lectures)* (Cambridge University Press, 2015).

Craig, P, 'Brexit: A Drama In Six Acts' (2016) *European Law Review* 447.

Craig, P, 'Miller, Structural Constitutional Review and the Limits of Prerogative Power' [2017] *Public Law* 48.

Craig, P, 'Constitutional Principle, the Rule of Law and Political Reality: The European Union (Withdrawal) Act 2018' (2019) 82 *Modern Law Review* 319.

Craig, P, 'The Supreme Court, Prorogation, and Constitutional Principle' [2020] *Public Law* 248.

Craig, P, *English Administrative Law since 1550* (Oxford University Press, 2024).

Craig, P, and Tomkins A (eds), *The Executive and Public Law: Power and Accountability in Comparative Perspective* (Oxford University Press, 2005).
Craig, R, 'Black Spiders Weaving Webs: The Constitutional Implications of Executive Veto of Tribunal Determinations' (2016) 79 *Modern Law Review* 166.
Craig, R, 'Casting Aside Clanking Medieval Chains: Prerogative, Statute and Article 50 after the EU Referendum' (2016) 79 *Modern Law Review* 1041.
Craig, R, 'A Simple Application of the Frustration Principle: Prerogative, Statute and Miller' [2017] *Public Law (Brexit Special Issue)* 25.
Craig, R, 'Restoring Confidence: Replacing the Fixed-term Parliaments Act 2011' (2018) 81 *Modern Law Review* 480.
Craig, R, 'Judicial Review of Advice to Prorogue Parliament' (UK Constitutional Law Association, 2019).
Craig, R, 'Of Virus and Vires: Lockdowns, Vaccine Mandates and Role of the Courts' [2023] 6 *European Human Rights Law Review* 579.
Craig, R, and Phillipson, G, 'Protecting National Security by Breaking the Law? Prerogative, Statute and the Powers of MI5' (2022) 85 *Modern Law Review* 1274.
Craig, R, 'The Fixed-term Parliaments Act: Out, Out Brief Candle' in R Johnson and Y Yi Zhu (eds), *Sceptical Perspectives on the Changing Constitution of the United Kingdom* (Hart Publishing, 2023).
Cromartie, A, *The Constitutionalist Revolution* (Cambridge University Press, 2006).
Daintith, T, and Page, A, *The Executive in the Constitution* (Oxford University Press, 1999).
De Smith, S, and Brazier, R, *Constitutional and Administrative Law*, 6th edn (Penguin, 1990).
Dicey, AV, *Introduction to the Study of the Law of the Constitution*, 8th edn (Macmillan, 1915, reprinted 1927).
Dicey, AV, *Introduction to the Study of the Law of the Constitution*, 10th edn (Macmillan, 1959).
Dickson, J, 'Methodology in Jurisprudence: A Critical Survey' (2004) 10 *Legal Theory* 117.
Digby, K, *An Introduction to the History of the Law of Real Property* (Clarendon, 1875).
Dixon, D, 'Godden v Hales Revisited – James II and the Dispensing Power' (2006) 27 *Journal of Legal History* 129.
Donoughmore Committee, *Report of the Committee on Ministers' Powers*, Cmd 4060/1932.
Ekins, R, 'Constitutional Practice and Principle in the Article 50 Litigation' (2017) *Law Quarterly Review* 347.
Ekins, R, 'Parliamentary Sovereignty and the Politics of Prorogation' (Judicial Power Project/Policy Exchange, 2019).
Ekins, R, and Gee, G, 'Miller, Constitutional Realism and the Politics of Brexit' in M Elliott, J Williams and AL Young, *The UK Constitution after Miller* (Hart Publishing, 2018).
Elliott, M, *The Constitutional Foundations of Judicial Review* (Hart Publishing, 2001).
Elliott, M, 'The Supreme Court's Judgment in Miller: In Search of Constitutional Principle' [2017] 76 *Cambridge Law Journal* 257.
Elliott, M, 'Constitutional Adjudication and Constitutional Politics in the United Kingdom: The Miller II Case in Legal and Political Context' (2020) 16 *European Constitutional Law Review* 625.
Elliott, M and Thomas, R, *Public Law*, 4th edn (Oxford University Press, 2020).
Elliott, M and Thomas, R, *Public Law*, 5th edn (Oxford University Press, 2024).
Elliott, M, and Perreau-Saussine, A, 'Pyrrhic Public Law: Bancoult and the Sources, Status, and Content of Common Law Limitations on Prerogative Power' [2009] *Public Law* 697.
Elliott, M, Williams, J, and Young, AL, *The UK Constitution After Miller* (Hart Publishing, 2018).
Ely, JH, *Democracy and Distrust, A Theory of Judicial Review* (Harvard, 1980).
Endicott, T, 'Was *Entick v Carrington* a Landmark?' in A Tomkins and P Scott (eds), *Entick v Carrington: 250 Years of the Rule of Law* (Hart Publishing, 2015).
Endicott, T, 'Parliament and the Prerogative: From the Case of Proclamations to Miller' (Judicial Power Project/Policy Exchange, 2016).
Endicott, T, 'The Stubborn Stain Theory of Executive Power: From Magna Carta to Miller' (Judicial Power Project/Policy Exchange, 2017).

Evatt, HV, *The Royal Prerogative* (Law Book Co, 1987).
Ewing, KD and Gearty, C, *Freedom under Thatcher: Civil Liberties in Modern Britain* (Oxford University Press, 1990).
Ewing, KD, 'Brexit and Parliamentary Sovereignty' (2017) 80 *Modern Law Review* 685.
Feldman, D, 'The Human Rights Act 1998 and Constitutional Principles' (1999) 19 *Legal Studies* 165.
Feldman, D, 'Brexit, the Royal Prerogative, and Parliamentary Sovereignty' (UK Constitutional Law Association, 2016).
Fenwick, H and Phillipson, G, 'Confidence and Privacy: A Re-examination' (1996) 55(3) *Cambridge Law Journal* 447.
Fenwick, H, Phillipson, G and Williams, A, *Text, Cases and Materials on Public Law and Human Rights*, 4th edn (Routledge, 2017).
Filmer, R, *Patriarcha* (Walter Davis, 1680).
Finch, H, *Nomotexnia* (1613).
Finnis, J, 'Brexit and the Balance of Our Constitution' (Judicial Power Project/Policy Exchange, 2016).
Finnis, J, 'The Unconstitutionality of the Supreme Court Prorogation Judgment' (Judicial Power Project/Policy Exchange, 2019).
Fisher, L, *The Law of the Executive Branch: Presidential Power* (Oxford University Press, 2014).
Foley, M, *The Silence of Constitutions* (Routledge, 2011).
Forsyth, C, 'Of Fig Leaves and Fairy Tales: The Ultra Vires Doctrine, The Sovereignty of Parliament and Judicial Review' (1996) 55 *Cambridge Law Journal* 122.
Forsyth, C (ed), *Judicial Review and the Constitution* (Hart Publishing, 2000).
Fortescue, J, *De Laudibus Legum Angliae* (1476).
Fortin, M-F, *The King Can Do No Wrong: Constitutional Fundamentals, Common Law History, and Crown Liability* (Oxford University Press, 2024).
Fuller, L, *The Morality of Law* (Yale University Press, 1964).
Gearty, C, 'The Courts and Recent Exercises of the Prerogative' (1987) 46 *Cambridge Law Journal* 372.
Goldsworthy, J, *The Sovereignty of Parliament: History and Philosophy* (Clarendon Press, 1999).
Goldsworthy, J, *Parliamentary Sovereignty: Contemporary Debates* (Cambridge University Press, 2010).
Gordon, JW, 'The Crown as Litigant' (1929) 45 *Law Quarterly Review* 186.
Graber, M, '*Ship Money*: The Case that Time and Whittington Forgot', University of Maryland Francis King Carey School of Law Legal Studies Research Paper, No 2020–06.
Grant, J, 'Prerogative, Parliament and Creative Constitutional Adjudication: Reflections on Miller' (2017) 28(1) *King's Law Journal* 35.
Griffith, JAG, 'The Political Constitution' (1979) 42 *Modern Law Review* 1.
Griffith, JAG, *The Politics of the Judiciary*, 5th edn (Fontana, 1997).
Griffith, JAG, 'The Brave New World of Sir John Laws' (2000) 63 *Modern Law Review* 159.
Hale, M, *The Prerogatives of the King* (1676).
Halliday, PD, *Habeas Corpus: From England to Empire* (Harvard University Press, 2010).
Halpin, A, 'The Concept of a Legal Power' (1996) *Oxford Journal of Legal Studies* 129.
Harris, BV, 'The "Third Source" of Authority for Government Action' (1992) 108 *Law Quarterly Review* 626.
Harris, BV, 'Judicial Review, Justiciability and the Prerogative of Mercy' (2003) 62 *Cambridge Law Journal* 631.
Harris, BV, 'The "Third Source" of Authority for Government Action Revisited' (2007) 123 *Law Quarterly Review* 225.
Harris, BV, 'Replacement of the Royal Prerogative in New Zealand' (2009) 23 *New Zealand Universities Law Review* 285.
Harris, BV, 'Government "Third Source" Action and Common Law Constitutionalism' (2010) 126 *Law Quarterly Review* 373.
Hart, HLA, *The Concept of Law* (Oxford University Press, 1961).
Hart, HLA, 'Definition and Theory in Jurisprudence' in *Essays in Jurisprudence and Philosophy* (Oxford University Press, 1983).

Hazell, R, and Foot, T, *The Prerogative, Past, Present and Future* (Hart Publishing, 2022).
Hearn, WE, *The Government of England* (Longmans, Green, Reader, and Dyer, 1867).
Hobbes, T, *Leviathan* [1660], edited by R Tuck (Cambridge University Press, 1991).
Hobbes, T, *Discourses* [1681], collected and edited by W Molesworth, vol VI (John Bohn, 1840).
Holdsworth, WS, 'The Power of the Crown to Requisition British Ships in a National Emergency' (1919) 35 *Law Quarterly Review* 12.
Holdsworth, WS, *A History of English Law* (Methuen, 1924).
Holdsworth, WS, *A History of English Law*, 2nd edn (Methuen, 1938).
Bartlett, G and Everett, M, 'The Royal Prerogative' Briefing Paper Number 03861, House of Commons Library (17 August 2017).
Harpum, C, Bridge, S and Dixon, M, *Megarry and Wade: The Law of Real Property*, 8th edn (Sweet & Maxwell, 2019).
Haves, E, 'Coronavirus Bill: What emergency powers does the Government already have?' (House of Lords Library, 23 March 2020).
House of Commons Public Administration Select Committee, 'Taming the Prerogative: Strengthening Ministerial Accountability to Parliament' (16 March 2004).
House of Commons Public Administration and Constitutional Affairs Committee, 'The Fixed-term Parliaments Act 2011', Sixth Report of Session 2019–21 (15 September 2020).
House of Lords Select Committee on the Constitution, 'The Pre-Emption of Parliament' (2013) House of Lords Select Committee on the Constitution, 12th Report of Session 2019–21.
House of Lords Paper 121 'A Question of Confidence? The Fixed-term Parliaments Act 2011' (4 September 2020).
Howell, J, 'What the Crown May Do' (2010) 15 *Judicial Review* 36.
Jacob, J, 'The Debate Behind an Act: Crown Proceedings Reform, 1920–1947' [1992] *Public Law* 452.
Jacob, J, *The Republican Crown: Lawyers and the Making of the State in Twentieth-Century Britain* (Dartmouth, 1996).
Jennings, WI, *Cabinet Government* (Cambridge University Press, 1937).
Jennings, WI, *Parliament* (Cambridge University Press, 1948).
Jennings, WI, *The Law and the Constitution* [1933] 5th edn (University of London Press, 1960).
Johnson, R and Zhu, YY (eds) *Sceptical Perspectives on the Changing Constitution of the United Kingdom* (Hart Publishing, 2023).
Johnston, W, 'First Adventure of the Common Law' (1920) 36 *Law Quarterly Review* 9.
Jones, O (ed), *Bennion on Statutory Interpretation*, 6th edn (Butterworths, 2013).
Jowell, J, 'Of Vires and Vacuums: The Constitutional Context of Judicial Review' [1999] *Public Law* 448.
Jowell, J and O'Cinneide, C (eds), *The Changing Constitution*, 9th edn (Oxford University Press, 2019).
Kantorowicz, E, *The King's Two Bodies A Study in Mediaeval Political Theology* (Princeton University Press, 1957).
Keir, DL, 'The Case of Ship-Money' (1936) 52 *Law Quarterly Review* 546.
Kelsen, H, *General Theory of Law and State*, translated by Anders Wedberg (Harvard University Press, 1949).
Kershaw, D, 'Revolutionary Amnesia and the Nature of Prerogative Power' (2022) 20(3) *International Journal of Constitutional Law* 1071.
Kenyon, J, *The Stuart Constitution, 1603–1688: Documents and Commentary*, 2nd edn (Cambridge University Press, 1986).
Laski, H, 'The Responsibility of the State in England' (1918–19) *Harvard Law Review* 32.
Laws, J, 'Illegality: The Problem of Jurisdiction' in M Supperstone and J Goudie, *Judicial Review*, 1st edn (Butterworths, 1992).
Laws, J, 'Law and Democracy' [1995] *Public Law* 72.
Le Sueur, A, Sunkin, M and Murkens, J, *Public Law: Text, Cases, and Materials* (Oxford University Press, 2010).

Le Sueur, A, Sunkin, M and Murkens, J, *Public Law: Text, Cases, and Materials*, 4th edn (Oxford University Press, 2019).
Lemmings, D and Prest, W (ed), *The Oxford Edition of Blackstone: Commentaries on the Laws of England, Vol 1: Of the Rights of Persons* (Oxford University Press, 2016).
Lester, A and Weait, M, 'The Use of Ministerial Powers without Parliamentary Authority: The Ram doctrine' [2003] *Public Law* 415.
Lienen, C, 'Common Law Constitutional Rights: Public Law at a Crossroads?' [2018] *Public Law* 649.
Locke, J, *Two Treatises of Government* [1689], edited by P Laslett (Cambridge University Press, 1988).
Loughlin, M, *Public Law and Political Theory* (Clarendon Press, 1992).
Loughlin, M, 'The State, the Crown and the Law' in M Sunkin and S Payne (eds), *The Nature of the Crown: A Legal and Political Analysis* (Oxford University Press, 1999).
Loughlin, M, *The Idea of Public Law* (Oxford University Press, 2004).
Loughlin, M, *Foundations of Public Law* (Oxford University Press, 2010).
Loughlin, M, 'The Constitutional Imagination' (2015) 78 *Modern Law Review* 1.
Loughlin, M, 'Evolution and Gestalt of the State in the United Kingdom' (2017).
Loughlin, M, *Political Jurisprudence* (Oxford University Press, 2017).
Loughlin, M, 'In Search of the Constitution', LSE Working Paper 19/2019.
Loughlin, M, Review of Heller, Hermann and Dyzenhaus, David, *Sovereignty: A Contribution to the Theory of Public and International Law*, Belinda Cooper (trans), (Oxford University Press, 2019).
Loughlin, M, 'The Case of Prorogation' (Policy Exchange, 2019).
Loughlin, M, 'A Note on Craig on Miller; Cherry' [2020] *Public Law* 278.
Loughlin, M, *Against Constitutionalism* ((Harvard University Press, 2022).
Loughlin, M and Tierney, S, 'The Shibboleth of Sovereignty' (2018) 81 *Modern Law Review* 989.
Loveland, I, *Constitutional Law, Administrative Law and Human Rights – A Critical Introduction*, 5th edn (Oxford University Press, 2009).
Maitland, FW, 'The History of English Law' in HM Cam (ed), *Selected Historical Essays of F. W. Maitland* (Beacon Press, 1957).
Maitland, FW and Pollock, F, *The History of English Law before the Time of Edward I*, 2nd edn (Cambridge University Press, 1898–1899).
Maitland, FW, 'The Crown as Corporation' (1901) 17 *Law Quarterly Review* 131.
Maitland, FW, *Equity: A Course of Lectures* (Cambridge University Press, 1936).
Maitland, FW, *The Constitutional History of England: A Course of Lectures* (Cambridge University Press, 1908).
Markesinis, BS, *The Theory and Practice of Dissolution of Parliament* (Cambridge University Press, 1972).
Markesinis, BS, 'The Royal Prerogative Re-visited' (1973) 32 *Cambridge Law Journal* 287.
MacCormick, N, *H L A Hart* (Stanford University Press, 1981).
MacCormick, N, *Questioning Sovereignty – Law, State, and Nation in the European Commonwealth* (Oxford University Press, 1999).
McHarg, A and Mullen, T (eds), *Public Law in Scotland* (Avizandum Publishing, 2006).
McIlwain, CH, *The High Court of Parliament and its Supremacy* (Oxford University Press, 1910).
McKechnie, WS, *Magna Carta* (James Maclehose and Sons, 1914).
McLean J, *Searching for the State in British Legal Thought* (Cambridge University Press, 2012).
Mill, JS, *On Liberty* (1859).
Millett, P, 'Prerogative Power and Article 50 of the Lisbon Treaty' (2016) *The UK Supreme Court Yearbook* 190
Milsom, SFC, *Historical Foundations of the Common Law* (Butterworths, 1969).
Ministry of Justice, *The Governance of Britain – Constitutional Renewal* (March 2008).
Ministry of Justice, *Review of the Executive Royal Prerogative Powers: Final Report* (2009).
Mitchell, J, *The Contracts of Public Authorities* (Bell & Sons, 1954).
Moore, HM, 'Crown as Corporation' (1904) 20 *Law Quarterly Review* 351.
Moore, HM, 'Liability for Acts of Public Servants' (1907) 23 *Law Quarterly Review* 12.

Munro, C, *Studies in Constitutional Law*, 2nd edn (Oxford University Press, 1999).
Murkens, JEM, 'Mixed Messages in Bottles: The European Union, Devolution, and the Future of the Constitution' (2017) 80 *Modern Law Review* 685.
Neuberger, D, 'Who Are the Masters Now?' *Second Lord Alexander of Weedon Lecture* (6 April 2011).
Oakeshott, M, *Rationalism in Politics and Other Essays* (Liberty Fund, 1991).
Payne, S, 'The Royal Prerogative' in M Sunkin and S Payne (eds), *The Nature of the Crown: A Legal and Political Analysis* (Oxford University Press 1999).
Perry, A, 'The Crown's Administrative Powers' (2015) 131 *Law Quarterly Review* 652.
Pettit, P, *Republicanism: A Theory of Freedom and Government* (Clarendon Press, 1997).
Phillipson, G, 'A Dive into Deep Constitutional Waters: Article 50, the Prerogative and Parliament' (2016) 79 *Modern Law Review* 1064.
Phillipson, G, 'The Miller Case, Part 1: A Response to Some Criticisms' (UK Constitutional Law Association, 2016).
Phillipson, G, 'Brexit, Prerogative and the Courts: Why Did Political Constitutionalists Support the Government Side in Miller?' (2017) 36(2) *University of Queensland Law Journal* 311.
Phillipson, G, and Young, AL, 'Would use of the Prerogative to Denounce the ECHR "Frustrate" the Human Rights Act? Lessons from Miller' [2017] *Public Law (Brexit Special Extra Issue).*
Phillipson, G, 'EU Law as an Agent of National Constitutional Change: Miller v Secretary of State for Exiting the European Union (2017) 36(1) *Yearbook of European Law* 46.
Phillipson, G, 'Searching for a Chimera? Seeking Common Law Rights of Freedom of Assembly and Association' in M Elliott and K Hughes (eds), *Common Law Constitutional Rights* (Hart Publishing, 2019).
Plucknett, TFT, 'Genesis of Coke's Reports' (1941–1942) 27(2) *Cornell Law Quarterly* 190.
Pollock, F, 'The King's Peace' (1885) 1 *Law Quarterly Review* 37.
Pollock, F, 'The King's Peace in the Middle Ages' (1900) XIII *Harvard Law Review* 177.
Poole, T, 'Dogmatic Liberalism? TRS Allan and the Common Law Constitution' (2002) 65 *Modern Law Review* 463.
Poole, T, 'Back to the Future? Unearthing the Theory of Common Law Constitutionalism' (2003) 23 *Oxford Journal of Legal Studies* 435.
Poole, T, 'Constitutional Exceptionalism and the Common Law' (2009) 7(2) *International Journal of Constitutional Law* 247.
Poole, T, 'Judicial Review at the Margins: Law, Power and Prerogative' (2010) 60 *University of Toronto Law Journal* 81.
Poole, T, 'United Kingdom: The Royal Prerogative' (2010) 8(1) *International Journal of Constitutional Law* 146.
Poole, T, *Reason of State: Law, Prerogative, and Empire* (Cambridge University Press, 2015).
Poole, T, 'Devotion to Legalism: On the Brexit Case' (2017) 80 *Modern Law Review* 685.
Poole, T, 'The Strange Death of Prerogative in England' (2018) 43(2) *University of Western Australia Law Review* 42.
Potter, H, *Law, Liberty and the Constitution: A Brief History of the Common Law* (Boydell Press, 2015).
Raz, J, 'Voluntary Obligations and Normative Powers' (an essay in two parts contributed by MacCormick and Raz) (1972) 46 *Proceedings of the Aristotelian Society, Supplementary Volume.*
Raz, J, 'Legal Principles and the Limits of Law' (1972) 81 *Yale Law Journal* 823.
Raz, J, *Practical Reason and Norms* (Oxford University Press, 1975).
Raz, J, *The Authority of Law: Essays on Law and Morality* (Oxford University Press, 1979).
Raz, J, *Concept of a Legal System*, 2nd edn (Clarendon Press, 1980).
Reeves, J, *Reeves' History of the English Law, from the Time of the Romans, to the End of the Reign of Elizabeth* [1603] (Murphy, 1880).
Reid, J, 'The Judge as Lawmaker', *Society of Public Teachers of Law (New Series)*, Vol 12, Issue 1 (January 1972).
Report on the Organisation of the Permanent Civil Service, Together with a Letter from the Rev. B. Jowett (Parliamentary Papers 27, 1854).

Sales, P, 'Crown Powers, the Royal Prerogative and Fundamental Rights' in H Wilberg and M Elliott (eds), *The Scope and Intensity of Substantive Review: Traversing Taggart's Rainbow* (Hart Publishing, 2015).
Scott, PF, *The National Security Constitution* (Hart Publishing, 2018).
Secretary of State for Justice and Lord Chancellor (Jack Straw MP), 'The Governance of Britain' (July 2007).
Sedley, S, Book Review, Supperstone & Goudie, *Judicial Review* [1993] *Public Law* 543.
Sedley, S, 'The Sound of Silence: Constitutional Law without a Constitution' [1994] *Public Law* 270.
Sedley, S, 'The Common Law and the Constitution' (1997) 19(9) *London Review of Books.*
Sedley, S, 'The Crown in its own Courts' in C Forsyth and I Hare (eds), *The Golden Metwand and the Crooked Cord* (Clarendon Press, 1998).
Sedley, S, *Lions under the Throne: Essays on the History of English Public Law* (Cambridge University Press, 2015).
Sieghart, P, *The Lawful Rights of Mankind* (Oxford University Press, 1986).
Simpson, AWB, *A History of Land Law*, 2nd edn (Clarendon Press, 1986).
Simpson, J, 'The Third Source of Authority for Government Action Misconceived' (2012) 18 *Auckland University Law Review* 86.
Stewart, J, *The Rights of Persons, According to the text of Blackstone* (Edmund Spettigue, 1839).
Stubbs, W, *The Constitutional History of England in its Origin and Development*, 3rd edn (Clarendon Press, 1887).
Stubbs, W, *Select Charters* (Clarendon Press, 1888).
Sunkin, M and Payne, S (eds), *The Nature of the Crown: A Legal and Political Analysis* (Oxford University Press 1999).
Sunstein, C, 'Incompletely Theorized Agreements' (1995) 108 *Harvard Law Review* 1733.
Thompson, EP, *Whigs and Hunters: The Origin of the Black Act* (Penguin, 1977).
Tierney, S, 'Turning Political Principles into Legal Rules: The Unconvincing Alchemy of the Miller/Cherry decision' (Judicial Power Project/Policy Exchange, 2019).
Tomkins, A, 'Crown Privileges' in M Sunkin and S Payne (eds), *The Nature of the Crown: A Legal and Political Analysis* (Oxford University Press 1999).
Tomkins, A, 'In Defence of the Political Constitution' (2002) 22 *Oxford Journal of Legal Studies* 157.
Tomkins, A, *Public Law* (Oxford University Press 2003).
Tomkins, A, *Our Republican Constitution* (Hart Publishing, 2005).
Tomkins, A, 'Crown Proceedings, Remedies and Liability of the Crown' in A McHarg and T Mullen (eds), *Public Law in Scotland* (Avizandum Publishing, 2006).
Tomkins, A, 'The Crown in Scots Law' in A McHarg and T Mullen (eds), *Public Law in Scotland* (Avizandum Publishing, 2006).
Tomkins, A, 'The Authority of *Entick v Carrington*' in A Tomkins and P Scott (eds), *Entick v Carrington: 250 Years of the Rule of Law* (Hart Publishing, 2017).
Tomkins, A and Scott, P (eds), *Entick v Carrington: 250 Years of the Rule of Law* (Hart Publishing, 2015).
Torrance, D, 'The royal prerogative and ministerial advice', Briefing Paper CBP9877, 8 July 2024.
Twomey, A, 'Legal Advice by Judges on the Exercise of Reserve Powers' [2016] *Public Law* 285.
Twomey A, *The Veiled Sceptre: Reserve Powers of Heads of State in Westminster Systems* (Cambridge University Press, 2018).
UK Government, 'Government Response to the Public Administration Select Committee's Fourth Report of the 2003–4 Session: Taming the Prerogative: Strengthening Ministerial Accountability to Parliament (HC422)' (July 2004).
UK Government, 'The Cabinet Manual: A Guide to Laws, Conventions and Rules on the Operation of Government' (2011).
Wade, HWR, *Constitutional Fundamentals (Hamlyn Lectures, 32nd series)* (Stevens and Sons, 1980).
Wade, HWR, 'Procedure and Prerogative in Public Law' (1985) 101 *Law Quarterly Review* 180.
Wade, HWR, 'Sovereignty – Revolution or Evolution?' (1996) 112 *Law Quarterly Review* 568.

Wade, W, 'The Crown, Ministers and Officials: Legal Status and Liability' in M Sunkin and S Payne, *The Nature of the Crown: A Legal and Political Analysis* (Oxford University Press, 1999).
Wade, W and Forsyth, C, *Administrative Law*, 11th edn (Oxford University Press, 2014).
Wade, W, Forsyth, C and Ghosh, J, *Wade & Forsyth's Administrative Law*, 12th edn (Oxford University Press, 2022).
Ward, H, 'Baton Rounds and Circulars' (1988) 47 *Cambridge Law Journal* 155.
Warren, WL, *Henry II* (Eyre Methuen, 1973).
Westminster and Foreign Quarterly Review (1876) Vol 105.
White, H, 'Parliamentary Scrutiny of Government' (Institute for Government, 2015).
Winterton, G, 'The Limits and Use of Executive Power by Government' (2003) 31 *Federal Law Review* 421.
Wolff, M, 'On the Nature of Legal Persons' (1938) 54 *Law Quarterly Review* 494.
Young, A, *R (Miller) v Secretary of State* for Exiting the European Union: Thriller or Vanilla?' (2017) 42 *European Law Review* 280.
Young, A, 'The Constitutional Role of the Monarch' in the Constitution Unit and UK in a Changing Europe, *The British Monarchy* (25 April 2023).

INDEX

www.ingramcontent.com/pod-product-compliance
Ingram Content Group UK Ltd.
Pitfield, Milton Keynes, MK11 3LW, UK
UKHW020247290926